The Dark Landscape of Modern Fiction

For Kevin, Patrick, Joanne, Kathleen, Sean,
Martin, Claudia and Mark

The Dark Landscape of Modern Fiction

PATRICK REILLY

So, if you can escape these lands of darkness
and see the lovely stars on your return,
when you repeat with pleasure, 'I was there',
be sure that you remember us to men.
Dante, *Inferno*, XVI, 82–5

Routledge
Taylor & Francis Group
LONDON AND NEW YORK

First published 2003 by Ashgate Publishing

Reissued 2018 by Routledge
2 Park Square, Milton Park, Abingdon, Oxon OX14 4RN
711 Third Avenue, New York, NY 10017, USA

Routledge is an imprint of the Taylor & Francis Group, an informa business

A Library of Congress record exists under LC control number: 2002027784

ISBN 13: 978-1-138-71531-8 (hbk)
ISBN 13: 978-1-138-71530-1 (pbk)
ISBN 13: 978-1-315-19762-3 (ebk)

Contents

Acknowledgements *vi*

Introduction: Lands of Darkness 1

1 Dostoyevsy 13

2 Hardy 33

3 Conrad 51

4 Wharton 69

5 Kafka 91

6 West 113

7 Camus 133

8 Waugh 153

9 O'Connor 171

Notes *191*

Bibliography *215*

Index *229*

Acknowledgements

My preeminent obligation is to my daughter, Patricia, for her patience and skill in typing the manuscript. My wife, Rose, also helped greatly with the typing.

I would also like to thank my colleague and friend, Professor Philip Hobsbaum, for his generous advice and encouragement.

Introduction

Lands of Darkness

I want to identify a moment and to isolate a theme in the *Inferno* in the belief that together they will supply a context for the exposition of a major impulse in modern literature. The moment occurs at the close of Canto XXIV in the encounter between the Pilgrim and Vanni Fucci, damned to the eighth circle in the bolgia of the thieves. The theme is 'the strife with the pity' that pervades the whole canticle from beginning to end. A close attention to both will illuminate much that is dark or repugnant in some of the major fictions of our time.

On the bridge over the seventh bolgia, Dante hears strange sounds rising from the impenetrable darkness below and he asks Virgil for permission to descend to investigate what's happening. Virgil consents and they climb down to confront

> a terrible confusion
> of serpents, all of such a monstrous kind
> the thought of them still makes my blood run cold.[1]

The hell of the poetic imagination far surpasses anything existing in reality. Libya, with its swarms of serpents so graphically described in Lucan's *Pharsalia*, cannot even begin to rival Dante's dream. Keats claims that the melodies of the mind are sweeter than any music we may actually hear.[2] Dante's is the negative version of this claim for the superior creativity of the imagination. Libya, Ethiopia and all the lands along the Red Sea 'never bred so great a plague of venom' as the poet now surveys in hell. The seventh bolgia is a venomous place, and, within it, running amok in blind panic, are its naked victims, hands tied behind with vipers, serpents knotted through their loins, 'with no hope of a hole or heliotrope' – that is, with no place to hide or rest invisible. Hell is the forfeiture of privacy; suffering is a spectacle, and Dante sees Vanni Fucci before recognizing him. At first, he is simply 'a sinner running by our bank' who is suddenly struck by a snake just at the junction of neck and shoulder. The stricken man is instantaneously incinerated upon the spot, and then, to Dante's amazement, from the pile of ash, in parodic imitation of Christ, comes a dreadful, undesired resurrection. Like (but so unlike) the phoenix, the bewildered sinner is restored to the flesh and looks around, in agony at his suffering:

> how harsh the power of the Lord can be,
> raining in its vengeance blows like these![3]

Vanni Fucci is resurrected only for perpetually recurring incineration, to be stung, consumed and made whole again throughout eternity.

Dante, as shocked as the victim, still does not recognize him, but Virgil demands his identity and Vanni Fucci is compelled to comply, acknowledging as he does so the justice of his damnation:

> I loved the bestial life more than the human,
> like the bastard that I was; I'm Vanni Fucci,
> the beast! Pistoia was my fitting den.[4]

Having chosen bestiality on earth, he now has his choice forever among the serpents, punished not *for* but by his sins, in yet another striking instance of the device of *contrapasso* employed so brilliantly by Dante throughout the poem. Dante, surprised and puzzled at this revelation, asks Virgil to detain the sinner for further questioning. Dante knew Vanni Fucci in the world above, but as a man of blood and anger whom he would have expected to find immersed in Phlegethon, the river of blood, with the shades of the violent in Canto XII. Why is he so apparently mislocated? How has Minos come to send him to the wrong part of hell?

Vanni Fucci responds directly to the Pilgrim, though 'colouring with a look of ugly shame'. That he has no choice but to reply is made clear when he says that he is suffering more from this moment of compulsory disclosure than when he parted from his first life. Yet he can neither lie nor evade: 'Now I am forced to answer what you ask.'[5] He is in his proper place, condemned to this lower circle, not for his violence, but for the baser sin of robbing the sacristy and letting someone else take the blame. In hell the sinner appears absolutely naked, exhibited in all his shame. Vanni Fucci is at humiliation's nadir and Dante is responsible for it.

But at this point in the interchange there is a startling reversal as the tormented, defensive spirit suddenly launches a counter-attack, in stunning retaliation against his interrogator. One of the pleasures of paradise, says Tertullian, will be the privilege of looking down unscathed upon the torments of the damned.[6] It is a satisfaction that Vanni Fucci is resolved to deny his inquisitor. Dante is not to be permitted to enjoy the spectacle free of charge – a price must be paid for the confession wrung from the thief. Vanni Fucci does not share the error, later exhibited by Guido da Montrefelto, of believing that to be in hell is to be damned forever.[7] Perhaps, he concedes, Dante may succeed in finding a path out of hell, but, even if he does, what awaits him in the world above? In revenge for his own discomfiture, the robber forces Dante to listen in turn to a dark foretelling of his own approaching misfortunes. Vanni Fucci's motive is openly, unashamedly malicious; he wants to hurt the person who has hurt him:

> I don't want you to rejoice at having seen me,
> if ever you escape from these dark pits,
> so open your ears and hear my prophecy.[8]

There follows a summary of the calamities soon to befall Dante in the world above (they have, of course, already happened *before* Dante writes his poem), the calamities that will lead to exile from Florence, with enforced residence and possible death far from home among strangers.

Luoghi bui – dark pits, unlit regions, lands of darkness. It is a phrase we have already heard in the circle of the sodomites, when Dante's three fellow citizens ask him to remember them in the world above if and when he escapes from hell:

> therefore, if you survive these unlit regions
> and return to gaze upon the lovely stars,
> when it pleases you to say 'I was down there',
> do not fail to speak of us to living men.[9]

But, if the words are identical, the context is completely different. The Florentines wish their countryman well. Far from showing malice, they courteously request him to preserve their memory on his return to the world of light. Vanni Fucci, by contrast, like the snakes afflicting him, spits malice in his wounding words: in the venomous place is the venomous man. Himself in hell, he would make Earth a hell for Dante, and he seeks relief for his suffering by communicating it to another.

Dante's party in Florence, the Whites, are about to be overthrown – 'every White be struck', just as Vanni Fucci himself has just been struck by the serpent. Retaliation could not be more naked. The real quarrel is, of course, with God, but Dante is a much easier target. Vanni Fucci's final obscene insult to God at the opening of Canto XXV, his last appearance in the poem, simply recoils upon himself as the avenging snakes once again commence the work of retribution. Insofar as he gains any compensation for his agonies, it can only be through the damage done to Dante. In a similarly malignant spirit, Milton's Satan proposes and himself undertakes the voyage through Chaos to Eden, where he will seek to revenge himself upon God by ruining Adam and Eve. The obscene gesture to God makes the parallel with Satan clear – for Dante and Milton alike (it is where they differ so strikingly from Shelley), the enemy of God is *ipso facto* the enemy of man. For the pilgrim, Vanni Fucci represents an especially detestable low point in hell:

> Throughout the circles of this dark inferno
> I saw no shade so haughty towards his God[10]

but perhaps the pure, concentrated malice, so palpably displayed toward Dante himself, plays some part in forming this estimate. Vanni Fucci tries to hurt Dante as Satan tries to hurt Adam. His spite and lust for revenge are made brutally explicit in his parting word of malediction, designed to sting Dante as the serpents stung him: 'And I have told you this so you will suffer.'[11]

It is to his credit that he eschews any hypocritical attempt to justify the pain he inflicts. In this respect he is a pioneer of that same ferocious honesty displayed by

Orwell's O'Brien in *Nineteen Eighty-Four* when he derides the lies and hypocrisies of former totalitarians.[12] They had pretended that pain was a regrettably necessary means to an end. They were compelled, so they claimed, to punish and kill those who stood in the way of the just society – that so longed-for society in which pain and exploitation would be no more. For, this once achieved, the need to inflict pain upon others will become redundant and the world a pain-free zone. In the meantime, with the utmost reluctance and against all their instincts, they have to torture and kill. O'Brien contemptuously dismisses this as claptrap. Torture is not just a transit camp on the road to paradise – torture *is* paradise. The future is a boot in the face forever and sadism is for its own sweet, delectable sake, not a means to an end, but the end itself. The world of Oceania will forever be a sadist's elysium.

Vanni Fucci anticipates O'Brien's candour by disdaining to dress up what he says as somehow tending to his hearer's good; his sole, malicious concern is to make him grieve. The allegedly educative value of pain, so integral to the Western tragic heritage from Aeschylus to Shakespeare, makes no sense in hell – hell is pain for its own sake, anguish without object or term, and, in this sense, Orwell's dystopia is clearly patterned upon it. Vanni Fucci is no covert ill-wisher like Iago or Claggart – it is the purity, the frankness of his malice that is so remarkable. Not so much the words themselves as the spirit in which they are spoken commands attention. After all, back in Canto X Farinata has already informed Dante concerning the setbacks that await his return to Earth.[13] It follows Dante's taunt that Farinata's allies in Florence, Dante's enemies, have not mastered the art of regaining lost power. In a kind of tit for tat, Farinata warns Dante that he himself will learn just how difficult an art it is when he, too, soon becomes a loser. But there is no malice in this; Farinata wishes Dante well and hopes for his safe return to the sweet world. The vehemence of the robber's malediction is an altogether different matter.

It is crucial to remark that he does not lie. What he predicts is true; has, in fact, already happened to Dante the Poet as distinct from Dante the Pilgrim – the poem was written after Vanni Fucci's words have been verified. These disasters will befall. It is exactly what Dante's own ancestor, Cacciaguida, will later tell him in Canto XXII of the *Paradiso*.[14] Yet Dante is grateful to Cacciaguida, while signally omitting to thank Vanni Fucci. Why treat the messengers so differently when the message is exactly the same?

The essential distinction is, of course, that between the prophecy spoken in love and concern (Cacciaguida) or simply as information (Farinata) and the prophecy spoken in malice (Vanni Fucci), between the desire to forewarn and fortify and the desire to dismay and wound. We need only change T.S. Eliot's verb: the greatest treason is to *say* the right thing for the wrong reason.[15] The prophet's intent is never irrelevant. Bonhoeffer warns us that 'truth' may have the appearance of truth while lacking its essential character, that every individual utterance is always part of a total reality that seeks expression in this utterance, that the man who stands behind the word makes his word a lie or a truth.[16] The truth, used murderously like a stiletto, is worse than a lie. Fielding's Blifil in *Tom Jones* is such a truth-teller, and so, too, is Vanni Fucci. *Unum solamen doloris socios habuisse miseriae* (misery loves company). Like a spiteful leper, like a vindictive AIDS victim bent on spreading the contagion, Vanni Fucci tries to detain Dante in hell, to pull him down into his own circle of torment. We shall meet his like again in the pages of modern fiction, from Dostoyevsky's Underground Man to the sneering monologist of Camus's *The Fall,* sufferers themselves who are determined to make others suffer. How to engage the spiteful truth-tellers, Bellow's 'reality instructors'[17] – it is a key problem in modern literature.

In this longing to hurt, to broadcast unhappiness, Vanni Fucci is a progenitor of modern fiction. This fiction is distinguished from previous writings (with the significant exceptions of the work of the Old Testament prophets and the seventeenth-century Calvinist divines) by its peculiarly punitive character. No previous body of secular writing has been so intent upon discomfiting the reader, of depriving him or her of what is plainly taken to be an offensive and unwarrantable happiness, a deplorable sense of feeling securely and comfortably at home in the world. The pages of our most representative modern fictions bristle with an unmistakable hostility towards the reader, resonating with an animus that demands explanation. From Thomas Hardy to Flannery O'Connor, a challenge to a spurious sense of well-being rings inescapably through these texts. By what right are you happy? Could your self-satisfaction reflect either folly or pharisaism? Might your assurance of the essential rightness of things proceed simply from an inability to see true? Some such questions lurk disturbingly in the depths of these intimidating fictions, with their succession of grimly harrowing finales unmatched in any previous literature and so completely at odds with the placatory, reassuring conclusions of nineteenth-century English fiction.

In trying to account for this transformation, we refer almost automatically and justifiably to the spirit of the age, but the bald expression by itself, however correct, will not much advance our understanding. Popper is surely right when he insists that 'the spirit of the age must be demoted from an explanation to a social phenomenon that we have to explain'.[18] It is not enough to detect the spirit of Vanni Fucci in the literature of our time; the real task is to explain why this spirit is so virulently at home in the pages of modern texts.

There is, doubtless, an element of retaliation, of exasperated backlash against what is now generally seen as the facile optimism of nineteenth-century society, with its consoling doctrine of sins too easily forgiven and paradise too cheaply regained. The dominant theme of nineteenth-century fiction from *The Ancient Mariner* onward is of sin expiated and a sinner rescued:

> The selfsame moment I could pray;
> And from my neck so free
> The Albatross fell off, and sank
> Like lead into the sea.[19]

It is a literature informed and sustained by a mythology of redemption, of delinquents plucked from the brink of moral catastrophe, of second chances and *felix culpas*, exhibiting a gallery of escapees, of castaways reclaimed and lives recovered from crime, waste and despair. In Dickens and George Eliot, in Hugo, Tolstoy and Dostoyevsky, we see the same infallible triumph of love over hatred, the same recurring pattern of sin, expiation and redemption. For almost the whole of *The Devils*, Stepan Verkhovensky is a foolish and foppish man, but, dying, he is allowed to pronounce Dostoyevsky's highest *credo* concerning life: 'Love is higher than existence. Love is the crown of existence. And how is it possible that existence should not be subjected to it?'[20] *Amor vincit omnia*. Verkhovensky's exalted profession of faith is a secularized version of Christ's claim to have overcome the world. There is a similar reassurance in the buoyant promises of Schiller's *Ode to Joy*:

> *Alle Sündern soll vergeben und die Hölle nicht mehr sein,*
> *Alle Menchen werden Brüder* ...
> (All sinners shall be forgiven and hell shall be no more,
> All people shall be brothers ...)

There are no problems either in life or literature beyond the power of love to solve. When the Beatles sang that all you need is love, the idiom may have been modern, but the sentiment was almost embarrassingly traditional, not to say *passé*. Orwell's O'Brien dismisses with withering contempt Winston's indignant protest that a world based on fear and cruelty could never endure: 'Nonsense. You are under the impression that hatred is more exhausting than love. Why should it be?'[21] Winston anticipates the Beatles in assuming that all *he* needs is love. O'Brien disagrees, and uses Room 101 to show just how mistaken Stepan Verkhovensky, Winston Smith and John Lennon all are. It is Orwell who is modern, the Beatles who are Victorian. Not until Hardy, near the close of the Victorian age – in particular *Tess* (1891) and *Jude* (1896) – does a major nineteenth-century English novel end on a note of defeat or desolation. Misfortunes abound in Dickens and George Eliot, but the end is always a reconciliation, and the tragedies (Little Em'ly, Hetty Sorrel) are always subordinate to and contained within a matrix of comedy. 'Sin is behovely, but all shall be well, and all shall be well, and all manner of things shall be well.'[22] It is a guarantee vindicated again and again in the pages of our great nineteenth-century fictions.

The contrast with modern fiction and its very different set of savage finales could not be more striking. Rehearsing some of these may be helpful as a reminder of how peculiarly malevolent they tend to be. At the close of *Tess of the d'Urbervilles*, the heroine, victimized all her short life by the men about her – her drunken, work-shy father, her selfish seducer, her priggish husband, her unfeeling priest – is finally destroyed by the primal, archetypal male tyrant, the President of the Immortals, who summarily ends his sport with her on the gallows. All those hitherto apparently guilty ones (feckless father, rapist-lover, self-righteous husband) are, if not in the clear, certainly less censurable, since they are merely pawns in the hands of the real enemy, the God who rules his universe so cruelly and unjustly. It is a chilling conclusion, because, if true, there is no preventive or evasive action that Tess could have taken against it. Her mother's fatalistic capitulation to events turns out, depressingly, to be the right course after all; the animal that struggles in the trap merely augments its pain while doing nothing to effect its escape. What is true for Tess applies equally to ourselves, for we are all in the same position as she, all the helpless playthings of sadistic, suprapersonal jokers beyond control or conciliation. Alcohol, a Wordsworthian trust in Nature's holy plan, conventional religious belief: in *Tess* Hardy exposes these traditional escapes from the pain of existence as no more than self-administered stupefactions.

At the end of *Ethan Frome* is the most chilling introduction in all literature, when the owner of the whining, complaining voice is finally identified: 'And this is Miss Mattie Silver'.[23] Only then do we sickeningly apprehend just how hideously awry the aborted suicide pact has been. 'I guess things'll straighten out', says Ethan, just before the disaster that leaves *him* maimed and twisted, and Mattie paralyzed, for the rest of their protracted lives.[24] Edith Wharton is being deliberately cruel, both in putting these seemingly banal words into Ethan's unsuspecting mouth and in denying the lovers the blessing of suicide. One imagines her racking her brain to devise the worst possible resolution to her story, and one has to congratulate her, however reluctantly, on the brilliance of her invention. But it is a brilliance of the sort that appalled the Giant King when Gulliver offered him the secret of gunpowder.[25] There seemed only three ways of ending the story: Ethan leaves Zeena for Mattie, Ethan sacrifices Mattie for Zeena, or the baffled lovers commit suicide. Only the malicious genius of the author produced a fourth, truly hideous resolution in which all three – husband, wife, lover – are locked together for life in a deathly relationship of poverty, sickness and paralysis. Abandon hope all you who enter here. The inscription placed by Dante over the gates of hell has been removed by modern writers and re-situated over the world we live in. An early reviewer speaks of how difficult it is to forgive Edith Wharton for the bitter remorselessness of the book – 'nowhere has she done anything more hopelessly, endlessly grey with blank despair'.[26] Edith Wharton must have read this with a sense of immense satisfaction, since this is precisely what she set out to do. I have told you this to make you grieve. What is the point of protesting to Vanni Fucci that he has hurt you when that is exactly what he is trying to do?

In *The Secret Agent*, the narrator (is there any reason for not regarding him as Conrad?) has a highly amusing time showing how a family, living together without knowing each other, succeeds in killing themselves without even trying to do it. The whole tone of the book is one of Olympian derision – 'Lord, what fools these mortals be!' – but with none of Puck's forgiving affection. Conrad's fools deserve all they get for being so stupid and the last thing he wants us to do is to feel sorry for them.

Similar pitilessly pessimistic finales round off Waugh's *A Handful of Dust* and Kafka's *The Trial*. At the end of the latter, Joseph K., baffled to the last, charged with an unnamed crime by an unknown court, which he is never allowed to enter, is found guilty and is stabbed in the heart by his executioner, dying 'a dog's death', insultingly inexplicable, while a window opens meaninglessly upon the execution. In Waugh's book, the hapless hero begins yet again his lifelong sentence of reading Dickens, spokesman of Victorian humanism, to the illiterate madman in his jungle prison. There is no injustice in this – his woefully incorrect reading of life entitles Tony Last to no better fate. In Orwell's *Nineteen Eighty-Four*, a gin-sodden Winston, despicable and defeated, turns adoring eyes toward the telescreen image of his beloved emasculator. In *Miss Lonelyhearts*, the would-be Christ, self-appointed saviour of his world, is accidentally shot to death by the cripple whom he is desperate to redeem. In Camus's *Le Malentendu*, a frantic woman, on her knees supplicating heaven for help, hears the brutal refusal of the old, supposedly deaf–mute servant in the only words spoken by him in the play. It is *Tess* all over again – Camus's God hears Maria's prayer, but sadistically rejects it. In *Lord of the Flies*, the ambiguously rescued Ralph, simultaneously saved and lost, weeps for his dead, underprized friend and for the incurable darkness of man's heart. In Flannery O'Connor's short story, *The Lame Shall Enter First*, the belatedly contrite and finally enlightened father, the ironically misnamed Sheppard, rushes at last in love to his long-neglected child, only to find him swinging from the rafters. Many other examples could be cited, but by now it is surely not necessary. The inescapable conclusion is that these texts, with their harrowing endings, have no other purpose than to force upon us a sense of the irremediable bleakness of life. In these chill closures, so opposed to those of nineteenth-century fictions, so deliberately designed to demoralize and dismay, there is no hint of purgation or cleansing pain, no harvest of moral good from the suffering inflicted. No more than Tess, Ethan Frome, Winnie Verloc, Winston Smith, Tony Last, Miss Lonelyhearts, Ralph, Maria or Sheppard does the reader find moral sustenance in these texts. Characters and readers alike simply discover how dreadful a world this is. This is pain for its own sake, and pain for its own sake is hell. The key texts of twentieth-century fiction – whether the master be Conrad, Orwell, Camus, Golding, whether the setting be the heart of darkness or Airstrip One, the Dantean circles of Jean-Baptiste Clamence's Amsterdam or Beelzebub's island in *Lord of the Flies* – begin from the assumption that this is hell, nor are we out of it. Their authors are the heirs of Vanni Fucci, and, as he spoke to Dante, so they speak to us, with the same remorseless intention to make us grieve.

This is what gives modern fiction its distinctively characteristic note, distinguishing it from the literature of the previous age. It would be foolish to imply that the nineteenth century was somehow unacquainted with the suffering of life. Even before the great Victorian poets, Wordsworth had written 'Michael' and 'The Ruined Cottage', while Keats had warned against the destructive power of beautiful dreams in 'Lamia' and 'La Belle Dame sans Merci'. Yet, sad though the stories of Wordsworth's Margaret and Michael are, they remain essentially tributes to the unconquerable power of love, as the stories of Ethan Frome and Winston Smith so manifestly are not; and Keats never derides the dreamers (how could he, being one himself?) that he so bravely brings himself to reject. Tony Last and Miss Lonelyhearts, those twentieth-century dreamers, receive an altogether different treatment at the hands of *their* creators.

Tennyson, described by T.S. Eliot as the saddest of all English poets, supplies the clearest contrast with modern literature and with the new, vindictive temper whose convenient chronological marker is the work of Hardy. We shall look long in modern fiction to find anything to rival, far less surpass, the monotonous diurnal agony of Tennyson's Mariana. Even the bleakest of modern texts will not present a deeper loathing for life than that portrayed in the catatonic despair of the listless heroine. Carlyle, forever proposing action as the remedy for all our ills, was predictably unsympathetic to this long wail of passive suffering. Tennyson, he argued, should either have allowed Mariana to commit suicide or supplied her with another man, otherwise he 'had much better have left her alone'.[27] Anyone conversant with Tennyson's early (and best) poetry is unlikely to indict him for too rosy a view of existence. The contrast with his source in Shakespeare confirms this. In *Measure for Measure* everything turns out well for the jilted woman waiting alone in the moated grange. Angelo, admittedly duped, does at last come, and Mariana's torment is over, thanks to the Duke's providential management of affairs. But Tennyson's doleful cast-off has no Duke working on her behalf. There is no benevolent overseer in the world of the poem, which is why it ends so pessimistically. He cometh not – and never will. Tennyson abandons Shakespeare's providential scheme; in Tennyson's world (the real world as he conceives it), Mariana is left in clear-eyed, immitigable despair, like any other resident of hell.

But she is not mocked or ironized. Distinctively new in the fiction of our time is a curt withdrawal of sympathy for the victim and the emergence of a new, punitive, even cruel element, undetectable before the advent of Hardy. Tennyson solicits our sympathy for his hapless heroine; Arnold exhorts us in 'Dover Beach' to find in private love our sole haven from the darkling plain on which we live. Sustaining almost every great Victorian poem (Browning is the exception) is a pity that is really self-pity – much of Tennyson himself is invested in Mariana and the Lady of Shalott. We are not to condemn, far less mock, them, for they are the poet at second remove and it is his own sublimated woes we contemplate.

Consider the very different treatment of the sufferer in modern fiction. The anguish is as real, but it is distanced. A new judgemental and even jeering note can be heard; pity gives way to derision. No one could read these modern texts and dream that we are to sympathize with the incompetents who crowd their pages. Sympathy would be an incrimination, a damaging admission that one shared the errors and was in line for a like chastisement. Not just the blundering character or, sustaining him in his error, the foolish teacher, but also the reader naive enough to share the folly – these are the targets in modern fiction. Not just Wordsworth and his prattle about 'Nature's holy plan', not just the Christian doctrine of a superintending Providence, but any reader still deluded enough to believe these absurdities in a post-Darwinian age, invites Hardy's scorn in *Tess of the d'Urbervilles*. Those who accept this nonsense, whether as characters in the text or readers of it, deserve what they get. The author is resolved to punish such fools and to destroy whatever bogus consolations they continue to cherish.

This is why the *Inferno* is our best guide to much that is going on in the fiction of our time, explaining both the desire to hurt and the veto on pity. Someone who knows that he is damned confronts someone who hopes to be saved: Vanni Fucci is to Dante as the modern author is to his reader. The information Vanni Fucci supplies is true. His superior knowledge is inseparable from his greater suffering – he knows because he is in hell. He resents, and is angered by, the ignorance that sustains Dante's optimism, and he is determined to be, in Bellow's phrase, a reality instructor. But the motive is punitive rather than educative, and in this respect Vanni Fucci anticipates characters like Dostoyevsky's Underground Man, and Jean-Baptiste Clamence in Camus's *The Fall*. All three know because they suffer; all three are in hell, wide-eyed to the realities of the human situation.

But they suffer, too, from the fact that there are fools who do not know this and they resent this ignorance. The fury provoked by the spectacle of a stupid happiness inspires their mission of malevolent instruction. The sustaining pipe dreams of O'Neill's *Iceman*, the saving lie endorsed by Ibsen in *The Wild Duck*, are not to be tolerated. There is to be no salvation through lies, which, in effect, means no salvation at all. Nothing will do but truth – an ominous stipulation in the age of the reality instructors who tell us that, if we are not already disillusioned, it's simply because we are uninformed. How, after Freud, dare we believe in a truth that comforts? In *Tess*, Angel Clare abandons Christianity precisely *because* of the doctrine of the Resurrection – how can such good news be true?[28] Truth *is* disenchantment; whatever consoles is *ipso facto* a lie.

This mentality helps to explain why modern fiction is so ruthless and unforgiving. Since this is hell, the false guides who, teaching us otherwise, have led us astray (in particular, the great Victorian novelists) must be exposed and their optimistic delusions demolished – the bad educators must be rejected before the true lesson can be communicated. Conrad arraigns the fatuous folly of Europe in believing that it has a commission to bring light to the heart of darkness. Orwell in *Nineteen Eighty-Four* lambasts the self-flattering complacencies of the liberal outlook, which, uncorrected, will lead us straight to disastrous defeat in Room 101. Golding's castaways, heads stuffed with ruinous nonsense about English grit and coral islands – what chance do they have of survival when they come so ill-prepared to the testing? The individual targets are as many as the individual writers: pharisaical humanism in the short stories of Flannery O'Connor, New England Polyannas in *Ethan Frome*, debilitating dreams in *Miss Lonelyhearts* and *The Day of the Locust* (originally called *The Cheated*), liberal delusions in *Nineteen Eighty-Four*, and so on – but all exhibit what Hazlitt called the spirit of the age; and in our time the spirit of the age derives from Vanni Fucci's desire to demoralize and dismay, to reveal to the reader that the world he mistook for home is a place of insecurity and terror. How else is one to read *The Secret Agent* than as a vendetta against the self-satisfied egoism that leads to destruction? In works like these it is impossible to miss the element of retaliation.

Hence the pitiless character of modern fiction, its stark denial of mercy to its sufferers. Again, Dante is our best guide. To pity those damned in hell is to come dangerously close to criticizing the God who condemned them. As he proceeds through hell, the Pilgrim has to be taught the inappropriateness of pity. Standing on the banks of the Acheron, surveying, appalled, the army of souls waiting to be ferried across, Dante has to be reminded by Virgil that 'a good soul never comes to make this crossing'.[29] From here on, the strife with the pity is a major theme in the poem. The first serious test comes in the encounter with Paolo and Francesca, and the Pilgrim flunks it. Listening to Francesca's siren words, glancing at the silent, weeping Paolo, Dante loses consciousness.[30] It is no way to negotiate the pitfalls of hell. Virgil is indulgent toward this first failure, but, as the journey proceeds, his patience wears thin until his explosion of anger in Canto XX. The travellers have come upon the shades of the soothsayers, those who had blasphemously presumed to predict the future. In a striking *contrapasso*, their heads have been grotesquely twisted on their bodies, so that now they can only look backwards, forced to walk to the rear since they cannot see even one step ahead. At the sight of this distortion, the Pilgrim gives way to tears of pity in which he seeks to involve the reader:

> just ask yourself
> how I could keep my eyes dry when, close by
> I saw the image of our human form
> so twisted.[31]

You would have wept too. But if so, you too would have called down upon yourself the savagely corrective response of Dante's guide:

> So you are still like all the other fools?
> In this place piety lives when pity is dead,
> for who could be more wicked than that man
> who tries to bend divine will to his own![32]

Pieta means both piety and pity. The pun is untranslatable, but it is plain that the Pilgrim has dangerously confused the two meanings, failing to see that in hell they are mutually exclusive. The choice is piety or pity – Dante can have one or the other, but not both. The choice for the reader is equally troublesome. Either Virgil has suddenly become a false guide in rebuking Dante for his tears or he is right to denounce a misguided pity that would leave Dante adrift in hell. The episode with the deformed soothsayers brings to an end the theme of 'the strife with the pity'; no more will Virgil need to rebuke the Pilgrim for misplaced compassion. The Pilgrim has come to appreciate the logic and the justice of hell – that things are as they are because they cannot be otherwise, that to weep for those who have damned themselves is both foolish and futile. The inhabitants of the *Inferno* are there because they chose, and go on choosing, to be there. It is what puzzled Walter Landor when he read the poem: 'Not a single one of the condemned', he remarked, 'wishes to escape'.[33] Exactly. These sinners are getting what they both want and deserve, so why should we feel sorry for them?

The revelations of modern fiction, so harshly educative, so inflexibly uncompassionate, make better sense when seen in the dark light of the *Inferno*. Combine the spirit of Vanni Fucci, the retaliatory impulse, with the refusal of pity and it becomes easier to understand what's going on in twentieth-century fiction. Why do modern writers wish to make us grieve? Why are they so unforgiving toward characters and readers alike? The *Inferno* supplies the answers. There are no innocents in hell, says Virgil. It is the exact reply given by the anarchist Emile Henry when asked why he had placed a bomb in a Paris restaurant filled with innocent people. '*Il n'y a pas d'innocents* (There is no one who is innocent)', he said, with chillingly, undebatable certitude.[34] If you are not with him, you are against, hence a legitimate target for his bombs. As Henry sees late nineteenth-century France, so Dante sees hell – and so, at certain crucial moments, does Flannery O'Connor see twentieth-century Georgia.

From Dostoyevsky's Underground Man to the bad-news evangelist of Camus's *The Fall*, there is the same stark representation of our condition as one without cure or remission. These characters suffer and they clearly intend that the reader should share their torment. Sometimes it might be argued that the reader's suffering is meant to be purgative, salvific. But there are also moments, perhaps the most significant ones in these texts, when it seems that the suffering is for its own sake, with no other object than to impress upon us that life is damnation. This is the diabolic condition, the mindset of Vanni Fucci, the outlook of hell. Modern fiction is a re-enactment of Dante, but with *Purgatorio* and *Paradiso* omitted. Where there's life, there's hope. It is the key, the sustaining, tenet of Christian salvation and humanist optimism alike. In the dark pages of twentieth-century fiction, in the texts of the heirs of Vanni Fucci, we have the opportunity to ask characters like Tess, Ethan Frome, Winnie Verloc, Miss Lonelyhearts, Tony Last, Winston Smith, Jean-Baptiste Clamence *et al.* if they agree.

Chapter 1

Dostoyevsky

No apology is needed for including *Notes from Underground* in a book about twentieth-century literature, especially one concerned with the present theme – the real difficulty would be justifying its exclusion. Published in 1864, it is an extraordinarily prescient work, with many of its later sequels no more than pale simulacra of this great original. It is not a question of our condescendingly accepting Dostoyevsky as a contemporary; it is we who lag behind as we strive to keep pace with the dizzying twists of this intimidating text. No modern work will so severely test our powers of discrimination, in particular, our ability to recognize that moment when we can properly part company with its unnervingly truthful narrator who tells us what we would rather not hear but cannot reject. Scholars may continue to insist that it can only properly be understood as a satire of its own times, that we distort it by detaching it from its matrix in the Russia of the 1860s, but they caution in vain:[1] as well insist on restricting *Gulliver's Travels* to a study of English politics in the early eighteenth century or Burke's *Reflections* to a discussion of the outbreak of the French Revolution. The greatness of such texts is that they transcend their occasion, demanding the attention of all who come after as works perennially pertinent to the human condition, not about Englishmen, Frenchmen or Russians, but about Man. So despite the scholars' disapproval and notwithstanding our gratitude to them for their illuminating investigations, people will go on reading the *Notes* as a contemporary work speaking directly to their present condition. To take a single instance, Camus's last novel, *The Fall*, is inconceivable without Dostoyevsky's first truly great work; although it is perhaps a sign of Dostoyevsky's superiority that where his career begins, that of Camus ends – Dostoyevsky went on to write masterpieces, but *The Fall* (and not simply because of its author's premature death) was Camus's last word. To put it more concisely, Dostoyevsky contains Camus; no one would dream of saying the converse. Giant though he undeniably is, perhaps Dostoyevsky's true greatness is yet to be fully discovered.

This greatness first announces itself with *Notes from Underground*. True, he had already established a reputation, especially among the progressives, with works like *Poor Folk*, before being sent to Siberia for his part in the Petrashevsky affair; but it is the Dostoyevsky of the return who becomes a giant of literature, thereby posing a problem for those who would argue that the Siberian experience had an entirely negative effect upon him. He was sentenced for being a liberal and a westernizer; he returned ten years later (so runs the accusation) as a reactionary and a slavophile of the worst kind. Freud, predictably, lent his authority to this view. Dostoyevsky had (so Freud said) perverted his great gifts, throwing away the chance of becoming a teacher and liberator of human beings in order to join up with their jailers.[2] At the same time, he also happened to write some of the greatest masterpieces in Western literature. To present the post-exile Dostoyevsky as a broken and brainwashed man, victim of procedures that Pavlov would soon describe and elaborate, seems outrageously paradoxical. Are we seriously to believe that arguably the greatest novelist of all is what he is because he was psychologically broken, that it would somehow have been better for everyone had he never been sent to Siberia? We do not know what Dostoyevsky would have accomplished had he been left in peace in St Petersburg; we do know what he achieved after and because of his Siberian ordeal and it is surely perverse to construe this experience as in any sense injurious to his art. By their fruits you shall know them: Winston Smith, released at the end from the Ministry of Love, is not about to embark upon a series of unrivalled masterpieces, because he *has* been psychologically broken. We need only point to the great works from *Notes from Underground* onward to prove beyond dispute that their creator was no psychological cripple. To go on clinging to such a view, as the Soviets did to the end, is to discredit oneself, not Dostoyevsky. The real challenge is not to establish the greatness of this first fruits of the exile – that is now settled beyond recall – but to determine the precise nature of this greatness and, in particular, to assay exactly the relationship between Dostoyevsky and his underground narrator, a task of discrimination which has not always been properly undertaken by critics in the past. The encounter between the Pilgrim and Vanni Fucci can be of service here in helping us to negotiate the pitfalls of contending yet erroneous interpretations.

There are two wrong extremes: one, to regard the Underground Man as the unqualified hero of his tale, Dostoyevsky's spokesman from start to finish; two, to dismiss all he has to say because we disapprove of what he is. Despite his frequent echoing of Dostoyevsky's own views, the Underground Man is not simply a mask for his creator, nor is he the indisputable hero, despite his superiority to the self-deceivers he exposes. His critics rightly cite his atrocious behaviour toward the helpless prostitute and protest that such a man can never be regarded as a hero. But they go astray when they conclude that because he's a rogue, then he's also a liar. It is a sentimentalist error to hold that virtue comes all of a piece or not at all – bad men can speak true, as Vanni Fucci has already shown.

But neither should it be carelessly assumed that Dostoyevsky and his character are one, with everything the latter says and does carrying the seal of his creator's approval. As early as 1883, only two years after Dostoyevsky's death, in an article that was to have a considerable influence on future readers, Nikolai Mikhailovsky attributed sadistic passages in Dostoyevsky's text to the author himself, the narrator functioning simply as a ventriloquist's dummy.[3] Dostoyevsky was the true possessor of the 'cruel talent' and Mikhailovsky cited with ease the evidence from Dostoyevsky's own writings: man is a despot by nature and likes to be a tormentor (*The Gambler*); tyranny is a habit that turns into a need (*Uncle's Dream*); love really consists in the right, freely given by the beloved object, to tyrannize over it

(*Notes from Underground*). Mikhailovsky had no difficulty in convicting Dostoyevsky of these sentiments. If the Underground Man is a specialist in spite and a connoisseur of cruelty, it is because he has been made in his creator's image. The sheer gratuitousness of his cruelty toward Liza, this sadism for its own sake such as O'Brien will insanely preach to Winston deep in the Ministry of Truth, as motiveless as the malignity of Iago toward Othello or Claggart toward Budd: this is the distinctive trait of the 'cruel talent' being examined and, standing behind the Underground Man, prompting and inciting, is Dostoyevsky himself.

Yet Dobrolyubov had previously hailed Dostoyevsky as a great humanitarian, the bard of the insulted and injured, instinctively siding with the sheep against the wolf. Mikhailovsky places him with the wolves, lusting to cause the sheep even more suffering than they already endure. There is a simple explanation. Dobrolyubov's view is based upon the writings prior to *Notes from Underground*, whereas Mikhailovsky's portrait of the sadist derives from *Notes* and the works that follow. *Notes* is the pivot upon which the whole career turns: sympathy for the downtrodden turns into contempt, as Dostoyevsky joins the jailers. The writer becomes a sadist, delectably aware for the first time of the hideous power he possesses and unwilling to discipline himself in its exercise. The writing itself is now the equivalent of some kind of Spanish bullfight or Roman games, the writer the soul-mate of Nero or Ivan the Terrible, tormenting characters and readers alike simply because he has the power to do so.

Underlying this attack is the assumption that the beliefs and behaviour of Dostoyevsky's characters are Dostoyevsky's own; even a critic of the stature of Lev Shestov falls into this error.[4] He rightly points out that his Siberian experience led Dostoyevsky to repudiate the sentimental idealism of the earlier fiction and to recognize instead the grim reality of human egoism. Reluctantly but courageously, Dostoyevsky came to accept, with all its demoralizing implications, a philosophy of amoralism: 'let the world perish, if I can always drink my tea'.[5] Nothing must stand in the way of the Underground Man's self-gratification. This *is* his view, but Shestov errs in attributing it to his creator. Far from endorsing the Underground Man, Dostoyevsky is showing, in a *reductio ad absurdum*, the extreme to which innocents like Chernyshevsky, without in the least intending it, were leading Russia through an altogether reprehensible importation of the ideas of the English Utilitarians into the country. The breathtaking egoism is meant to discredit Dostoyevsky's radical enemies, not embody his own beliefs. The larger point can be more simply expressed: because the Underground Man sometimes speaks for Dostoyevsky does not mean that he always does. We are sensibly cautioned today against identifying the polyphonic Dostoyevsky with any of his characters, even Father Zossima or Alyosha Karamazov who might plausibly be accepted as spokesmen for his values.[6] If true of them, it is *a fortiori* so of the Underground Man. Failure to observe this results in the aberrations of Mikhailovsky, Shestov and others. Knowing when and when not to side with the Underground Man – here precisely is the key critical problem of the book.

Undoubtedly, Dostoyevsky has a large personal investment in the character and it is difficult, intentionally so, to disentangle the author and, more important, ourselves from this troublesome narrator. It is the problem that confronts the Pilgrim with Vanni Fucci and it has a relevance for the whole of this present study. How to handle the malevolent truth-teller is the reader's problem in *Notes from Underground* and it can only be solved by paying the closest attention to the subtle shifts of Dostoyevsky's dialectic. 'There is truth in you, but no virtue.'[7] It is the Underground Man who puts this charge against himself into the mouth of his imagined adversary. How to deal with poisoned truth: this is what the *Notes* is about.

Dostoyevsky himself has to disengage from his character's potentially paralyzing embrace – to this extent, Mikhailovsky and Shestov are right: in a sense, Dostoyevsky *is* his character. It is a highly personal, almost autobiographical, work, and if the Underground Man is so memorably powerful a character, it is at least partly because of the wealth of personal feeling and belief invested by Dostoyevsky in him. Dostoyevsky's own self-disgust, his egoism and guilt, his unhappy days at the Academy of Engineers are all deeply, authentically present within the text. Even in the tiniest detail, the raw nerve of personal experience is exposed. When the fatuous Zverkov speaks of exercising his *droit de seigneur* with all the young peasant women on his estate while flogging the menfolk who dare to protest, all to the applause of the admiring company, it is surely not amiss to remember that Dostoyevsky's father was murdered by his serfs for, among other things, keeping a regular harem of peasant girls – or to believe that Dostoyevsky is remembering it too.[8] When, at the close, the narrator refers to his story of the falling snow as a mode of penal correction, it is inconceivable that Dostoyevsky, using this expression, did not have in mind the literal punishment he had recently suffered. It is all too easy to see how character and author have become confused, and yet we must tell them apart or else misunderstand the text.

Not an easy task, because from the outset and with Dostoyevsky's apparent endorsement, the Underground Man presents himself as a truth-teller. With the first sentence we realize that the spirit of Vanni Fucci is alive and well and living in mid-nineteenth-century St Petersburg – the malice is unmistakable, but so, too, is the communication of unwelcome truth. We must wait for Part Two and the story of the falling snow before the parallel with Dante's damned robber is complete, but in Part One he pours fully deserved scorn upon two sets of Dostoyevsky's enemies – high-flown Schillerian idealists and clinical utilitarian rationalists. However otherwise different, both are linked in their crystal palace mentalities, their equally misguided, doomed attempts to lift themselves above the human condition with no other equipment than the human imagination and the human will. The Schillerians, dismissing matter in favour of an impossible etherealism, ignore the animal man. The rationalists, attempting to contain human nature in a blueprint and to make reason and logic sovereign, slight life. Matter against spirit, life against logic: these are what the Underground Man champions and throughout Part One the assured vehemence of his ridicule sweeps all before it, mainly because he enjoys his creator's support. For much of the road, Dostoyevsky and the Underground Man are travelling companions. *Notes* is a passionate rejection by Dostoyevsky of his own once-cherished beliefs, repudiated with all the violence of one now completely disgusted by what had once entranced him, the most spectacular falling out of love in all literature. It was as if he was trying to pay back the spiritual leaders of his youth for the terrible ordeal of his years as convict.[9] As he now sees it, this is where his foolish trust in those blind guides had led him – straight to Siberia. Not the Czar, but those false teachers and his former foolish self: these are the ones to blame.

The follies of Schillerism are the Underground Man's first target (fifteen times he refers to 'the sublime and the beautiful', contempt incrementally accumulating with each repetition); and we know, from an early letter to his brother, that Schiller was the idol of Dostoyevsky's youth.[10] Orwell described his own turning against H.G. Wells as almost an act of parricide, but Orwell's revolt against his master is almost complimentary compared with the ecstasy of spiteful repudiation in Dostoyevsky's abjuration of Schiller.[11] Wells, however, merely misled Orwell, he had not caused him to be sent to Siberia.

That the *Notes* is the decisive watershed in Dostoyevsky's career can be seen by comparing it, not only with the masterpieces that followed, but also with the work immediately preceding it. Prince Valkovsky in *The Insulted and Injured* can be seen as a rehearsal for the much greater figure of the Underground Man just two years later. 'I have no ideals and I don't want to have them'.[12] Idealism exasperates him; the sentimental narrator's efforts to help a beloved woman who loves another man elicits a withering scorn: 'you, like some Schiller, are ready to go to the stake for them' in 'a sickening show of noble feeling'.[13] It is all too much for the Prince who is 'so sick of all this innocence, all these pastoral idyllics ... all this Schillerism'.[14] He is consumed with 'hatred for all these vulgar and worthless naivetés and idyllic nonsense' and burns to expose it for the egregious folly it is. The narrator senses the malice and relish in Valkovsky's exhibitionism, 'the cynicism with which at last he threw off his mask before me'.[15] It sounds very similar to the Underground Man: 'He was obviously longing to wound, to sting, to bite, to jeer.'[16] Valkovsky is another disillusioned idealist who has swung over to cynicism. Addressing 'my poet', he claims to be no worse than other men, that if only people were uninhibitedly honest, 'the world would be filled with such a stench that we should all be suffocated'.[17]

'If you want to keep a secret you must also hide it from yourself'[18] – it is Winston Smith's discovery in *Nineteen Eighty-Four*. There is a hierarchy of untruth: what we shrink from telling other people, from telling our best friends, from telling ourselves. The Underground Man repeats Valkovsky almost verbatim and with the same motive: to move from individual confession to universal indictment. We are all Valkovsky save for his honesty: he reveals, we conceal. What he preaches is delicious surrender to the temptation to walk naked – it is the exhibitionist, the naked man beneath the cloak, thrilling to the thought of throwing it aside and revealing all to the scandalized bystanders. We would all do it if we dared. To call this beastliness is simply a sign of cowardly submission to the conventional world, but 'the whole world is created for me ... Love yourself, that's the only rule I recognise.'[19] In a similar spirit the Underground Man resolves to let the world perish provided he gets his tea.

Yet, despite the similarities, there is not the same pressure to identify Dostoyevsky with the Prince as there is with the Underground Man. The latter is a greater, more complex creation, the *Notes* far superior as a novel of ideas, an intellectual achievement, a sustained polemic, Dostoyevsky creatively arguing with himself at a far deeper level than in *The Insulted and Injured*. Valkovsky is plainly a villain, his sometimes salutary rebukes to extravagant idealism notwithstanding, and the reader is never at risk of defecting to his side. The altogether new sense of intense personal involvement in *Notes* makes it more tempting to conclude that author and character are one.

Those who disagree invoke a supposed opposition between Parts One and Two, with the Underground Man, the author's spokesman in the first, philosophical section, finding himself exposed and undercut in the second part.[20] Dostoyevsky is as clearly against him in Part Two as he was for him in Part One – which explains why the latter is so often anthologized as an overture for existentialism while the former is almost always overlooked. But, however tempting, the problem cannot be solved in this way. If the Underground Man, as seems plausible, speaks for Dostoyevsky in key sections of Part One, he just as plausibly continues to do so throughout Part Two. Conversely, the characteristics that understandably alienate readers in Part Two – spite, meanness, aggression, truculence, servility and general bad manners – are all in plain view from the opening sentence of Part One. The idea of two Underground Men – a good one whom Dostoyevsky supports in Part One, a bad one whom he reprehends in Part Two – will not stand up to examination. However laudable the attempt to separate Dostoyevsky from his character, this is not the way to do it.

Even the most persuasive part of the argument – that the character speaks for the author in Part One – needs careful qualification, for it is a more complicated business than this. The Underground Man *is* Dostoyevsky's spokesman, but sometimes obliquely, indirectly, unintentionally or in ways that the speaker does not comprehend. Consider the notorious tea allusion that links the Underground Man, in his unbridled egoism, to Prince Valkovsky. Much of Part One is an attack upon the doctrine of psychological egoism, of rational self-interest, appropriated from the English radicals and imported into Russia by progressives like Chernyshevsky: 'if it is demonstrated that half an ounce of your own fat ought essentially to be dearer to you than a hundred thousand of your fellow-creatures ... simply accept it; there's nothing to be done about it, because twice two is mathematics'.[21] We shall hear the odious Luzhin in *Crime and Punishment* advance a less florid but equally uncompromising version of the same dogma: 'But science tells us, "Love yourself before everyone else, for everything in the world is based on self-interest. If you love only yourself, you'll transact your business as it ought to be transacted, and your coat will remain whole."'[22] (This ridicules the hopelessly impractical advice in the Gospel to halve your coat with your destitute neighbour – you simply end up both shivering.) Leave aside for the moment the question as to how fairly this represents the views of Bentham, Mill or Chernyshevsky himself – although it must surely be conceded that it doesn't sound too distant from Hume's assertion that it is 'not contrary to reason to prefer the destruction of the whole world to the scratching of my finger'.[23] It clearly fits in with the ongoing polemic against so-called natural or scientific or mathematical or logical laws. Don't capitulate to mere power, don't surrender to the reality instructors and sit down in blank despair when they lead you until your face is touching the stone wall. It is in passages like these that the Underground Man has been hailed as the existentialist hero, champion of humanity against the irresistible laws of an uncaring universe.

But when he declares that the whole world can go to ruin so long as he gets his tea, he is manifestly carrying the doctrine of psychological egoism to a *reductio ad absurdum*, prizing his own half-ounce of fat as more precious than anything else in the universe. It is not, of course, that such selfishness was unknown to the world before the coming of the English Utilitarians. Ben Jonson condemns Volpone's wantonly irresponsible hedonism:

> and, could we get the phoenix,
> Though nature lost her kind, she were our dish.[24]

But Jonson condemns what the Utilitarians seem to be recommending – so at least thought Dickens when, in the person of Bitzer in *Hard Times*, he attacked the same rationalist enemy as Dostoyevsky in the *Notes*. Bitzer has learned, in Gradgrind's school and with his complete approval, to prize himself above all else and to follow unswervingly his own self-interest. This he does to his teacher's consternation. Have you no heart? begs Gradgrind from the depths of his misery, only to receive the uncomforting reply that a human being cannot live without this pump for circulating the blood – but it wasn't to a pump that Gradgrind appealed.[25] Bitzer is Gradgrind's creation and Gradgrind lives to be horrified by the monster he has made. Dostoyevsky intends Chernyshevsky to be equally dismayed when the egoism he advocates is incarnated in the Underground Man. It is a question of responsibility. Father Zossima's insight is that we are all responsible for each other, but this does not preclude special, additional responsibilities, such as Gradgrind's for Bitzer or Ivan's for Smerdyakov – the impossibility of denying this finally drives Ivan to breakdown. Chernyshevsky is equally responsible for the Underground Man; that he neither foresaw nor wished for him in no way diminishes the responsibility. Dostoyevsky is presenting the radicals with the logical embodiment of their theory and asking them how they like it. They don't, of course, but honesty should compel them to repeat the words of Prospero confronting Caliban: 'This thing of darkness I acknowledge mine.'[26]

The attack upon Chernyshevsky and the radicals is a much more complex business than is usually assumed. Dostoyevsky denounces ideas and philosophies he doesn't like through a character whom he doesn't like either. Far from being Dostoyevsky's spokesman, the Underground Man has temporarily become Chernyshevsky's spokesman, even if Chernyshevsky would vehemently repudiate him. No matter, as far as Dostoyevsky is concerned: this is where Chernyshevsky ends, had he but the sense to see it. Only paradox will serve: the Underground Man is Dostoyevsky's spokesman by not being his spokesman.

But things are not always so complicated. 'Oh, what a baby!' exclaims the Underground Man, shaking his head in stunned incredulity at the follies of the rationalists in building their grandiose schemes of social regeneration upon a wildly mistaken view of human nature. 'Poor innocent child,' he remarks of his opponent – for innocent read stupid.[27] St John tells us that Christ needed no lessons in human nature because he could look into the heart; the radicals, for Dostoyevsky, can barely see the epidermis and no one has the right to be so abysmally misinformed. They are ignorant of the nature of the creature for whom their crystal palaces are so elaborately, pointlessly constructed. Nothing alive can be calculated, says Kafka.[28] Many years before Kafka the Underground Man had already said this and added that we had better not try.

The Grand Inquisitor, rejecting St John, makes a similar accusation of well-intentioned ignorance against Christ: Christ is woefully adrift in his exalted view of human nature; man simply cannot live up to his exorbitant demands, for man is not fit to be free. Yet, despite the gulf between the Grand Inquisitor and the radicals, they concur in their shared aim of creating an organized, anthill-type society. For the radicals, the price of utopia is the sacrifice of freedom; the Grand Inquisitor will similarly guarantee bread in exchange for servitude. But he is not, for Dostoyevsky, the fool that Chernyshevsky is. He knows human nature and the difficulty of subduing it – which is why he will use terror, miracle and authority to discipline these otherwise ungovernable men. He makes a powerful case and many, D.H. Lawrence included, believe an unanswerable one: Christ kisses the old man because he cannot refute him.[29]

Chernyshevsky's view of things is altogether more facile and uninformed: 'They'll come to love the good as soon as it's possible to do so without harming themselves.'[30] It is all so easy that the wonder is that no one ever thought of it before, preventing at source all the misery from which mankind has so long suffered. All the addict has to do is stop being addicted and this can be easily done through reason and logic. *Calculemus*, advises Condorcet – let us calculate and everything else will logically follow: self-interest alone will teach us to avoid disadvantageous evil and pursue the beneficial good. Freedom will be the first casualty, but no one will weep for that, since an irrational freedom is what is ruining us. Ruinous freedom in exchange for clockwork order: to refuse such a trade is to reveal oneself as one of the irrational malcontents whom the crystal palace is designed to eliminate.

Dostoyevsky stands foursquare behind the Underground Man when he says it would be pointless to agree such a deal since we couldn't keep it. Even if by some miracle we arrived in the crystal palace, we would almost at once start vandalizing the place, because that's how we are. It's perverse and contradictory, but it's true – and we must always prefer reality to the pipe-dreams of the rational imagination. We must begin from what man is, not what we would have him be. The Underground Man speaks unequivocally for his creator in affirming this and in condemning the rationalists for so flagrantly flouting it.

Socrates, father of rationalism, may say that no man does evil knowingly, but Socrates is wrong. *Video meliora proboque deteriora sequor*: Ovid's Medea does wrong with eyes wide open.[31] St Paul talks of doing the evil that he would not do, while omitting the good that he ought to do. The Underground Man completes the trio. He knows, better than any of his advisers, that he is harming himself by staying on in St Petersburg – but that's precisely why he stays. Medea and St Paul are both describing an experience of being somehow overcome, of being driven where they do not wish to go. The Underground Man's mentality is more akin to the perverse voluntarism of Milton's Satan: Evil, be thou my good. He *will* go to the dinner party, spending money he cannot afford on an evening he won't enjoy with people he cannot abide, simply *because* it is the wrong thing to do. There are clearly differences between, on the one hand, Medea and St Paul, and, on the other, the Underground Man; but they join forces in routing the simplistic notions of the rationalists. The rationalists inhabit a superficial heaven of their own devising; but the Underground Man lives in hellish reality and, as with Vanni Fucci, this is the source of his insight.

It is equally impossible to separate author from character in the latter's ridicule of the English historian, T.H. Buckle. Like all historians, Buckle has a story to tell, in his case the standard nineteenth-century recital of the inevitable march of civilization. As this occurs, men become milder and less bloodthirsty. It is not only plausible, it is also how we want things to be. It underwrites, among other things, our wholly commendable commitment to education, especially to our study of the humanities. The humanities humanize: of course they do or what good are they? The more civilized, the more humane. It justifies our campaign to extend our own enlightenment to the still savage places on earth. This is Buckle's story and, again, 'logically, it appears that that ought to be the result'.[32] But the Underground Man has his own story to counter Buckle's. Forget logic and look at what is actually happening in our civilized, nineteenth-century world. Blood is flowing as merrily as champagne and precisely in the heartland of Western culture. The most wanton shedders of blood are to be found among the most refined members of humanity. The Underground Man's story is one that will be taken up by Conrad in the next century and embodied in Kurtz, the knight-errant of Western civilization, no one better qualified to serve as our emissary; yet we see what befalls him in the heart of darkness. Conrad, in turn, is now seen as prophesying the death-camps of mid-century Europe and the last thing we can say about many who served the ovens is that they were deficient in culture or learning. Culture proved no barrier to bestiality, no more than it hindered Cleopatra from sticking golden pins into her slaves' breasts or stopped Browning's fastidiously elegant Duke of Ferrara from murdering his wife.[33]

Ideologues like Buckle, besotted with their theories, will go on clinging to them, but the Underground Man is right and clearly has Dostoyevsky's backing. In the end, man is not the automaton of reason or rational history, logarithms or logic. He simply likes to do what he likes to do, even when this means throwing away either Eden or the crystal palace. He wants his own way even when it is the primrose path to the everlasting bonfire, for he cares nothing about destinations, only about routes. He loves his own will above all else and he is right to do so, since this alone redeems him from being the 'falling stones' of Spinoza's description.[34] Unless men are free to defy their best interests, they are not free – without the freedom to eat the apple (that all-inclusive symbol of the acts of the unfettered will), we would simply be God's piano keys and Dostoyevsky wants us to be nobody's piano keys, neither God's nor nature's, neither science's nor logic's. Piano keys, if conscious, might dream they are playing themselves, but the pianist knows better. Nobody, however, is playing us and we should resist anyone who tries to do so. Men are, finally, not to be dragooned. For Winston Smith, it is a promise: if there is hope, it is in the proles. For the Professor in *The Secret Agent* it is a sickening reminder, as he ponders the imbecile mass life of London, of human intractability: 'numerous like locusts, industrious like ants, thoughtless like a natural force ... impervious to sentiment, to logic, to terror, too, perhaps'.[35] It is the nightmare of the social engineer with his meticulous blueprint for reorganizing human kind. Human life is simply too disorderly for regimentation: as well summon waves or clouds to parade-ground order – it cannot be done and should not be attempted. The blueprints come from the drawing-boards only to be trashed. An authorial voice reinforces the Underground Man's at this stage in the text.

Modern readers will readily join Dostoyevsky in cursing the Russian censor for mangling the penultimate section of Part One. 'The censors are a bunch of pigs – those passages where I mocked everything and occasionally blasphemed for the sake of form they allowed to stand; but when, from all that I deduced the need for Christ, they took it out.'[36] Something of the utmost importance is going on in the mangled remnants of Section X, but as to what we can only guess at. The Underground Man repeats his opposition to the crystal palace because its establishment would revoke his right to stick out his tongue at it – yet what institution so richly deserves it? But a new note is startlingly heard in the entirely genuine appeal, uncontaminated by the habitual cynicism, for something truly worthwhile to believe in. You wish him to be serious? Then 'give me a different ideal'.[37] The crystal palace won't do, but there is an unmistakable yearning, a wistful seriousness unheard until now, in his remark that perhaps his rage stems from the fact that he has never yet found an edifice, a home for man, that doesn't impel him to stick out his tongue at it. If only he could, then he would gladly let his mocking tongue be cut out in sheer gratitude. He ceases momentarily to be a mocker and the monologue becomes a threnody, a complaint against the tragic incongruity of man's destiny. 'Why was I made with such desires? Can I have been made for only one thing, to come at last to the conclusion that my whole make-up is nothing but a cheat? Is that the whole aim? I don't believe it.'[38] St Augustine, similarly frustrated, turns to God as the remedy: 'Our hearts are restless, O Lord, until they rest in thee.'[39] Camus (there are anticipations in Hardy) designates this mismatch between supply and demand as the Absurd: man has unassuagable longings and he must learn to live with, and, incredibly, like Sisyphus, love this. For a moment the Underground Man stands on the brink of some salvific revelation but it passes and he resumes his habitual cynical self. Although 'green with envy of the normal man' (he means the stupid man of action who gets things done simply because he lacks the intelligence to see the pointlessness of doing them), he concludes that 'it is best to do nothing'.[40] If action is stupidity, inertia is wisdom. The underground is at least preferable to the idiot world of pensions and promotions. Yet this is no sooner stated than it is revoked: 'Devil take the underground!'[41] However idly uttered, it is a prayer we shall see fully answered at the close of Part Two in some of the cruellest, darkest pages in all Dostoyevsky.

'What was the matter with the master-at-arms?'[42] Melville poses this question in *Billy Budd*, fully aware that the answer he is about to give will drive many of his readers to indignant incomprehension. Claggart is depraved from the womb, a destroyer whose 'love' can only find vent as hatred. The Underground Man has something wrong with him, too, and, like Ivan Karamazov with the devil, his thoughts are confusingly interwined with those of his putative adversary. 'There is truth in you but no virtue ... your heart is clouded with depravity, and without a pure heart there can be no full, correct understanding.'[43] It is what the Pilgrim might have retorted to Vanni Fucci and we know this is the Underground Man's own reflection, for how otherwise could these words have found their way into his adversary's mouth, since the latter can only say what the Underground Man allows. He doesn't need Father Zossima to tell him that he suffers from a lack of love, not of intelligence. Buckle's nineteenth century is morally, not culturally, benighted – its bloodlust is completely civilized and there's the problem. The parallel between the Underground Man and Vanni Fucci is complete: both suffer, both speak true, both are consumed with malice, both lack charity and therefore, as St Paul says, they have nothing.

The Underground Man also permits the adversary to make a further accusation: 'you keep your last word hidden'.[44] The Underground Man accepts the implicit challenge (it is really his own) and the last two pages of Part One are a preparation for the story of the falling snow in Part Two. His last word will be a confession, an attempt 'to test whether it is possible to be completely open with oneself and not be afraid of the whole truth'.[45] His threefold classification of shameful truth is borrowed straight from Prince Valkovsky: the things a man will reveal only to his friends, the things he will reveal only to himself, and the things, most despicable of all, that he will not even reveal to himself.[46] It is to this last loathsome level that the Underground Man wants to see if he can descend: 'a fancy has come into my head, and cost what it may I want to translate it into reality'.[47] Is there any truth too hideous to be confronted, even within the privacy of one's own mind?

This may help to explain his strange, contradictory attitude toward his own literary creation. He denies that it is a literary creation: 'But you can't really and truly be so credulous as to imagine that I'm going to print all this and give it to you to read, can you?'[48] Well, someone did. He proposes that this is merely a mind game he's playing, the words inviolably locked within the skull, but admits to being puzzled by the fact that he addresses the 'gentlemen' as though they are indeed 'readers'. Nevertheless, he insists, 'confessions of the kind I intend setting forth do not get printed or offered to others to read'.[49] The vindictive story he wrote, with such enjoyment, about the overbearing officer never did get printed and is lost for ever, but this one is here before us for us to read. The contradictions multiply as he tries to extricate himself from these authorial difficulties. Why is he telling all this? Dante has an easier task explaining the indiscretions of the damned: they speak without restraint to Dante because he, too, is in hell and cannot carry their shameful admissions back to the world above. Dante does nothing to disabuse them and they blab away indiscriminately, exposing all. The Underground Man has no such excuse for his shameless self-exhibition other than illogically insisting that, unlike the exhibitionist Rousseau, he is writing for himself alone: 'I shall never have any readers. I have already made that clear.'[50] How many thousands of people have read *Notes from Underground* since its narrator made this categorical pronouncement?

Contradictions aside, he is assigning his story to the second level of shameful truth where a man tells himself what he would not tell his friends. The only question to be decided is: does it qualify as truth at the deepest, most shameful level of all, when a man summons up the courage to dredge up the filth he resolutely conceals from himself? The Underground Man imposes upon himself an experiment in the possibility of total, full-frontal disclosure. It is to make the experiment a complete success that he writes at all, for in writing, he says, 'one sits more severely in judgement on oneself'.[51] We talk of committing our thoughts to paper – words on the page have a kind of finality, they *commit* us, in a way that the spoken word – fleeting, easily forgotten – cannot possess. He believes, too, or at least hopes that the act of writing will in itself be therapeutic: 'I shall get relief from writing it down.'[52] He is nagged by a memory evoked by the snow falling and 'for some reason I believe that if I write it down I shall get rid of it'.[53] This is the bridge by which he makes his passage from the philosophizing of Part One to the storytelling of Part Two.

Some critics would persuade us that the existentialist hero of Part One is suddenly replaced by the blackguard of Part Two, with the earlier rhetoric exposed as mere talk. But there is no such division. He tells us he's spiteful in the first sentence and confirms it on the last page. Part One is a theoretical discourse on the theme of man's perversity; Part Two is a practical demonstration of the thesis in his own person. Nor is Part One just empty talk; what the Underground Man says about Buckle and the crystal palace has the full support of Dostoyevsky and whatever he later does cannot retrospectively invalidate what he said earlier – at most, it damages his personal integrity. There is no immediate divorce between author and character in the transition from Part One to Part Two.

Consider the Underground Man's attack at the beginning of Part Two upon the nullity of middle-class Russian life ('playing whist, drinking vodka, talking about promotion'[54]) and compare it with Dostoyevsky's own onslaught upon the Parisian middle class in *Winter Notes on Summer Impressions*.[55] It might be the same voice condemning the same vacuity, with the unease of the French bourgeoisie made symptomatic of the *Angst* of modern man. In *Winter Notes* the lie of bourgeois civilization is exposed in the discomfort of those who are its alleged happiest exemplars. No one knows better than the bourgeois himself what an absolute fraud he is. Others may hail him as the end of history, the consummation of the entire evolutionary process, and he may even bask in this envious admiration and pretend that it's fully deserved, but in his heart he knows the truth. Hence his abiding unease. Painfully aware of the gulf between perception and reality, he cringes inwardly when the world looks at him in befooled reverence. Yet in a trapped sort of way he still somehow regards himself as the end of history, because he cannot conceive anything that might surpass or transcend him. He cannot go back, for that would be retrograde; he cannot go forward, because he has reached the human limit. Hence the despair beneath the self-deception. It is to this pathetic fraud that Belinsky and his followers had bowed down in the 1840s, urging their fellow-countrymen to make him their model.

'What is the tiers état? Nothing. What ought it to be? Everything.'[56] What the Abbé Siéyès so ardently desired is now reality. The bourgeois has triumphed and the Western world is his trophy, no serious competitor in sight. Francis Fukuyama, surveying the world today after the collapse of communism, tells us the same thing: the market is supreme and Western liberal man, choosing among his commodities, is the entirely satisfactory terminus of history.[57] There is nowhere higher to go; we are the end. The Underground Man would have stuck his tongue out at this new crystal palace and Dostoyevsky would have been as scathing today as he was in 1863. Not that he advocates socialism, for he ridicules the foolish dream of conjuring the spirit of brotherhood out of thin air: 'to make rabbit stew, you first of all need a rabbit.'[58] We cannot manufacture fraternity to order; either it is a sentiment born with us or it is a habit carefully nurtured and assimilated over the centuries. It simply cannot be created by fiat, above all not in the highly individualist culture of western Europe where each person stands aloof and isolated, sword in hand, demanding his rights. In *Culture and Anarchy* Arnold identified this as the English disease, but Dostoyevsky finds it most perfectly exemplified in the Parisian bourgeois. In this individualist culture people still prefer freedom with hunger, even death, to slavery with bread and security. The socialist may deplore such folly and contrast men, to their complete discredit, with ants, but there it is – till the rabbit shows up, there can be no rabbit stew, and his experience of Paris convinced Dostoyevsky that it would be a long wait. The bourgeois victor is left in sole possession of the field: 'all the others have made fools of themselves; all the others have proven destitute before him.'[59] So why isn't he happy? Dostoyevsky won't even argue this point – just look at the bourgeois for yourself – but he will suggest an answer: 'he who prospers most fears most.'[60] To live at the end of history is to experience its meaninglessness; to believe that you are its end is to question the whole purpose of the evolutionary process. Yet, simultaneously, there is the pressing obligation to keep up the lie: here we are in the crystal palace, the land of heart's desire; isn't it wonderful and aren't we blessed?

The Underground Man, like his creator, sees through the lie and, despite spasmodic, half-hearted attempts to play the bourgeois game, cannot succeed in doing so. He despises his colleagues, won't even speak to them, is sickened by the empty routines of office life – Camus had not far to go to find the model for Meursault and Sisyphus. But, in his characteristically zigzag way, he periodically swings to the other extreme: 'Once I went so far as to become really intimate with them; I began visiting their homes, playing whist, drinking vodka, talking about promotion.'[61] Occasionally, in moments of feverish benevolence, 'when my dreams were so happy that I absolutely must embrace somebody', he even pays social calls to his head of department.[62] But invariably 'the talk was about excise duties, arguments in the Senate, salaries, promotions, His Excellency the Minister and how to get on the right side of him, and so on'.[63] These visits take on the character of a half-therapeutic, half-penitential rite. The Underground Man sits stunned by the sheer imbecility of it all: 'I would sit there dumb, almost paralysed, and sometimes breaking into a sweat; but it did me good. Returning home, I was able to lay aside for a time my desire to embrace all mankind.'[64] Ivan Karamazov declares that a man can be loved only if he stays hidden.[65] The Underground Man, looking at the unlovely face of his bourgeois colleagues, is immediately cured of his infatuation.

'Upon my word, the French are a nauseating people.'[66] In *Notes* the nausea is induced, not by a single nation, but by modern man in general. Dostoyevsky is still supporting his hero well into Part Two and there is no possibility of driving a wedge between them here. Dostoyevsky shares the Underground Man's justified contempt for the banal inanities of his companions' conversation at the scandalous dinner party to which he so shamelessly invites himself. 'And finally they came to the conclusion that Shakespeare is immortal.'[67] This follows jumbled drivel about the Caucasus, true passion, baccarat, prestigious postings, the incomes of men they don't know and the beauty of women they have never seen. The Underground Man has every right to demand the reader's acknowledgement of his superiority to such fools – and we are now deep into Part Two. The argument that Dostoyevsky breaks with his character at the end of Part One is simply untenable; the Underground Man is still talking sense and, above all, still telling the truth.

The change comes through his contact with Liza. From his first sight of her, a process of disengagement begins, culminating in that decisive moment when Dostoyevsky and reader alike can finally disburden themselves of this troublesome companion. 'Something foul seemed to sting me; I went straight to her.'[68] It is after being stung by the serpent that Vanni Fucci directs his own venom at Dante. 'I'm glad to seem repulsive to her; I like that.'[69] Vanni Fucci, similarly, has no wish to endear himself to Dante; he wants to wound, not woo, and his Russian reincarnation has the same desire, the major difference being that *his* victim is female and so the vendetta assumes a sexual character. He has not suddenly become spiteful or vicious, for he has always been so, but for the first time in the text he has found someone even weaker, more vulnerable, than himself and he seizes upon her as a surrogate scapegoat for all those previous humiliators he dared not challenge. It looks forward to that moment in Joyce's 'Counterparts' when the brutal father beats his small, defenceless son in revenge for all the setbacks of his long, unhappy day.[70] Behind the Underground Man and Joyce's Farrington stands Vanni Fucci, progenitor of this whole tribe of tortured torturers and humiliated humiliators. What links them is a sensation of failure suddenly giving way to a delectable experience of new-found power, an ability to dispense pain rather than endure it, a consciousness of being the victimizer rather than the victim.

Even yet, however, he continues to speak true; a perverse motive does not, of itself, turn a statement into a lie. No one will deny his ill will toward Liza, but he just as surely predicts her future as Vanni Fucci does the Pilgrim's. Exploitation, sickness, degradation, death, a drunken funeral and a pauper's grave: this, miracle excluded, is her future – that he relates it with relish discredits him but not what he says. Even when he makes up stories – his ghoulish description of the water-logged grave, for example – it is not a lie. Every artist knows that stories, fictions, imaginative creations, can convey truths unattainable by fact, and, however repulsive the Underground Man's invention, it carries its own irrefutable authenticity. Hideous stories can also be true. Forget for the moment his entirely reprehensible emotions (vindictiveness, resentment, envy); forget, too, that he is an actor skilled in fabricating feeling ('I turned away, sickened'[71]) – it is he himself who openly admits that 'knavery so easily goes with sentiment'[72]; he 'pities' the fictitious prostitute within his head, not the woman of flesh and blood lying beside him in the bed. All true and it makes him a detestable human being, but not, except in Bonhoeffer's singular sense, a liar.

'It sounds just like a book,' says Liza when he begins to admonish her and the remark, with its hint of mockery, provokes him to new heights of eloquent denunciation: 'At twenty-two you'll look like thirty-five, and you'll be lucky if you are not a sick woman – pray God you won't be!'[73] Can a bad man give good advice, even, further paradox, without really meaning it? Chaucer's Pardoner is a swindler, but his warning is no less powerful for all that. 'In the end you'll come to the Haymarket' (that is, the depths of degradation[74]): it is all too probable and the fraudster is actually overcome with his own fake rhetoric: 'I had let myself be carried away to such an extent that a lump was rising in my own throat.'[75] No wonder Liza is devastated. No longer does she think it bookish as she lies crushed in the bed: 'No, never, never had I witnessed such despair!'[76]

To censure him, as some critics do, for unsettling her with dreams of reform and idyllic family life, for defiling the simple, innocent life of the young prostitute, is to confuse what he says with his motive for saying it. Is it seriously being proposed that it would be better for her to stay a prostitute than take his advice and forsake the profession? The still innocent young prostitute is on an unavoidable course for the vilest degradation; this is true, regardless of what we think of the man who tells her so. Of course, he is disgusting. Having so completely established his power over her (something he can only do by convincing her that he speaks true), he is now eager to escape: the game is over and he wants away. Yet, still overacting the role of saviour, the secular redeemer of Nekrasov's poem in the flesh, he commits the sentimental blunder of giving her his address, flattered beyond circumspection by her treatment of him as 'some higher kind of creature who knew everything without being told'.[77] He has no sooner escaped than he curses himself for this piece of folly and for the whole sentimental rigmarole in which he has got himself entangled. He dreads her visit, but as time passes and she doesn't come, he begins again to indulge his fantasies of redeeming the fallen woman. The less probable the visit, the more expansive the dream. In Nekrasov the self-satisfied hero invites the prostitute to become 'mistress of my house and me', while simultaneously issuing an even more important invitation to the reader to admire his breathtakingly magnanimous offer.[78] The hero of Chernyshevsky's novel *What Is To Be Done?* goes further still, marrying the prostitute before later committing suicide so that she can marry her new lover. These sentimental scenarios were, for Dostoyevsky, the stuff of which French melodrama is made ('melodrama will not die as long as the bourgeois lives'[79]) and Chernyshevsky and his like have imported the nonsense into Russia. Chernyshevsky, however, fatuously thinks that it's real, whereas the Underground Man keeps it confined to fantasy – Liza is dream-fodder, that's all.

It is a dream that consoles him in the demeaning stand-off with his stupidly obstinate servant, Apollon. But when Liza refuses to stay inside his dream and instead visits his house, she inadvertently compels his return to sordid reality. It bodes ill for her that her visit should coincide with his inevitable defeat by his servant. Just as he first struck at her following his humiliation at the dinner party, so it is predictable that he should do so again after being bested by the servant, the more so since she has witnessed his disgrace. It is the Vanni Fucci law of behaviour. The Underground Man stands before her 'crushed, discredited, foully covered with confusion', but 'aware that I should make her pay dearly for all this'.[80] Someone must pay. That the Pilgrim has looked on while Vanni Fucci suffered qualifies him as a target for the robber's venom. The Underground Man is the more incensed because, having revered him as a hero, Liza now sees him as he really is: how can we forgive those who truly know us? '"She is the cause of it all", I thought.'[81] She isn't, but she's a convenient victim and can be hurt without fear of retaliation. It almost exactly replicates the situation between Vanni Fucci and the Pilgrim.

Knowing his own baseness, the Underground Man nevertheless cannot restrain himself. The foul thing that stung him in the brothel does so again and so ferocious is his malice that it stuns the appalled girl. 'Why did you come here?' he demands and then proceeds to tell her: for another serving of the pity that she got from him in the brothel bedroom.[82] But he now tells her 'the filthy truth' – that he never pitied her, that he was secretly laughing at her in revenge for those who had laughed at him, that the law of life is to find someone whom you, kicked yourself, can kick in turn: 'I had been humiliated, so I wanted to humiliate somebody else; I had been treated like dirt, so I wanted to show my power.'[83] It is the voice of Vanni Fucci. The impact of his words is devastating; in the brothel he had made her feel despair, now it is terror. She drops back 'as though she had been felled with an axe'[84] it anticipates that moment in *Crime and Punishment* when the old pawnbroker's simple-minded sister cowers terror-stricken as her murderer closes upon her. The Underground Man's analysis of his behaviour in the brothel is searingly honest, but it's the honesty of hell: 'let the world perish, if I can always drink my tea'.[85] What does he care whether she lives or dies, recovers innocence or falls to the Haymarket? He cares only for himself.

Even yet we cannot completely shake off the companionship of this unwelcome confidant. The claim to a superior sensitivity, made even as he confesses his baseness, is not easy to dismiss. He is, he admits, 'the nastiest, most ridiculous, pettiest, stupidest, most envious of all the worms on this earth' but he knows it, unlike all the other worms, no better than he, who 'are never put out of countenance'.[86] To know you are in hell: it puts you above all those fellow residents too stupid to realize that they are damned. It is Gulliver's claim to superiority over the other Yahoos; it is the *tu quoque* strategy of the self-accusing accuser of *The Fall* that he employs to intimidate his auditor. Gulliver, the Underground Man and Jean-Baptiste Clamence visit the confessional, not to seek absolution, but to incriminate the priest.

The Underground Man is a soul in torment – tormented by Apollon ('He stretches me on the rack!'[87]) and now tormented by Liza. It is to this anguish that Liza responds in a manner for which he is totally unprepared, returning compassion for his abuse. In an inversion of Nekrasov, the prostitute comes to the rescue of the fallen man. Living in his world of victims and torturers, her conduct strikes him as 'exceedingly strange'.[88] With luck you may switch from being victim to torturer and when the opportunity comes, you must grab it with both hands. The axe allusion reveals the Underground Man to be, at heart, as much a murderer as Raskolnikov. Now that she has the advantage, he naturally expects her to retaliate; instead, to his astonishment, she offers pity and love and she does so because she sees the link between his unhappiness and his malice. Her own unhappiness, by contrast, makes her compassionate, not because she has some abstract theory about the solidarity of suffering, but simply because she is instinctively, uncalculatingly merciful.

For a moment salvation becomes a possibility: 'she held out her arms to me ... Now my heart too turned over. Then she rushed towards me.'[89] Vanni Fucci is about to be plucked out of hell: *amor vincit omnia*. But it is not to be. Stepan Verkhovensky in *The Devils* is wrong and O'Brien in *Nineteen Eighty-Four* is right – love is not all-conquering. Vanni Fucci is in hell because he wants to be there. It seems an incredible claim in the light of the eternity he's choosing: stung, incinerated, resurrected, in a process that goes on forever. How could anybody choose that? How indeed. Vanni Fucci could and does. What has logic got to do with life? It is the argument of Part One fearfully, concretely dramatized.

The Underground Man prefers his hellish round of humiliation and revenge to the heaven offered by Liza. He prefers rape to love: 'Without power and tyranny over somebody I can't live.'[90] Somebody. Anybody. Only afterwards does Liza realize that she has been violated, for it can be rape even when the woman is willing. This is not the straightforward buying and selling of the brothel; this is betrayal and, to savour it in full, the betrayer must make the victim know it, which is why he presses the money into her hand as she leaves the house. He is a client; what she mistook for love is simply commerce. The superiority, which he came so perilously close to losing, is restored and he can resume his 'normal' existence. What an escape he has had! He knows that people will object to his story as incredible, for no one could be 'as ill-natured and stupid as I am'.[91] But he simply confirms what Landor found so perplexing in the *Inferno*: hell is a choice, not a doom. None of the damned wants to escape, because that would mean ceasing to be oneself. 'What I was once, alive, I still am, dead!'[92] Capaneus is boasting that he is still the same condemned soul; that hell has not changed and will not change him. Even were change possible for the Underground Man, it is not what he wants to do.

He seems to have passed the test he imposed upon himself at the close of Part One; the experiment in total self-revelation has proved a success – one can, after all, be unreservedly truthful. In his last moments with Liza, the Underground Man reveals himself as the worthy heir of Vanni Fucci, malice incarnate, yet still truthful: 'I wish I could lie now and write that I had done it without premeditation, without thinking, absentmindedly, out of stupidity. But I won't lie.'[93] Not even to himself. He gives the money with cold deliberation in order to hurt her, make her grieve. The disasters lying in wait for Liza are not enough; she must be made to suffer now. Truth and sadism have become indistinguishable.

The Underground Man is a lost soul; Liza is, at worst, a lost body. When he discovers that she has trumped him after all by dropping the money unnoticed on the floor – she is a prostitute but not *his* prostitute, she will not take money for what *she* gave as love – his first impulse is to run after her and beg her forgiveness, fall to the ground and kiss her feet. But that would be salvation, which he neither wants nor is capable of. He is, in any case, too honest not to see what would follow: 'Could I avoid torturing her?'[94] Next day he would hate her precisely for having kissed her feet and the same old futile round of hell would begin all over. In like manner, the hero of *The Fall* rejects the very idea of a second chance on the Seine bridge, for he knows he would behave in exactly the same way.[95] And so, like Winston Smith wearily 'deciding' (but that's far too positive a word for what actually happens) not to follow the disappearing Julia at the close of *Nineteen Eighty-Four*, the Underground Man lets Liza go, never to see her again. In each of these texts, love might have been salvation, but in each it is equally plain that even to dream of this is the cruellest of delusions.

We leave the Underground Man in the hell he has chosen with a sense of relief at parting finally from such a disturbing companion (for it has not been a pleasant road we have travelled with him), and yet, paradoxically, with a compulsion to keep going back to this fascinating book. Is it partly because he continues to have the last word and we return to confront him yet again in an attempt to reverse this verdict? For he tells us that hell is our home, too, but that we are too crass and complacent to see it. He moves from first person singular to first person plural with an ease that underwrites the validity of the transition. It is 'a long story about how *I* missed life', but soon we are reading about how '*we* are all in a greater or less degree crippled'[96] (my italics). It is, and is meant to be, an incriminating shift to a general inculpation: 'And what is it we sometimes scratch about for, what do we cry for, what do we beg for? We don't know ourselves.'[97] It is to teach us about ourselves that the story is told – it is as much about us as it is about him: 'You don't think, do you, that I am ashamed of all this, or that this was sillier than anything in your lives, gentlemen?'[98] The tone is truculent, insulting, jeering: who are we to look down on him? The Underground Man's 'gentlemen' has the same ironic animus as Gulliver's 'gentle reader' – under a guise of politeness the insult could not be more pointed in this, the greatest *tu quoque* in literature.

The narrator has, of course, anticipated the indignant reflex protest that this story has nothing to do with us, is 'only about yourself and your underground miseries, don't dare speak of "all of us!"'[99] He denies any attempt to excuse himself in this *allness*. It is a story of self-condemnation; the only condition is that the rest of us should confess our complicity. Dostoyevsky's narrator is in the underground simply because he is our precursor, the baptist of our new dispensation. When we are equally honest and clear-sighted, we shall admit the justice of his claims and the pertinence of his story. The outrage of the 'gentlemen' in 1864 seems less sustainable in our own day.

Dostoyevsky declared his character to be 'the real man of the Russian majority ... a representative figure from a generation still surviving', not just someone who exists but who *must* exist.[100] We have been listening with revulsion to what we thought was an individual story, totally unaware of its universal relevance. The faults depicted, like those in Browning's poem, 'The Statue and the Bust', are, dismayingly, our own: *De te, fabula*!; so, at least, the Underground Man insists: 'I have only carried to a logical conclusion what you yourselves didn't dare take more than half-way; and you supposed your cowardice was common sense, and comforted yourself with the self-deception.'[101] It is unnerving to be told, after the vile story we have heard, that only our cowardice and self-deception distinguish us from its chief actor; that, if anything, the superiority is with him: 'So perhaps I turn out to be more alive than you. Look harder!'[102]

It is his final, unnerving bid for kinship with us *(mon semblable, mon frère!)* and it would be facile to believe that we can deny the claim simply by calling him mad or mistaken. Thackeray's blunder with Gulliver–Swift will serve no better with the Underground Man. There is no verbal defence against the charge of being Yahoo. And there is a similar challenge at the end of *Notes from Underground*. If it is 'one of the most difficult of all Dostoyevsky's works',[103] this is because it makes throughout such exceptional demands upon the reader's nimbleness of discrimination and powers of readjustment, the literary equivalent of being on a surf-board. How we take leave of the narrator is the last of the tests it poses.

Some readers believe that the Underground Man exits his story as its hero, or, at least, that this is what Dostoyevsky intends. It is not in the end a convincing thesis. The narrator has certainly succeeded in his aim of telling the whole truth, but has just as surely failed in his second, therapeutic aim of finding relief by writing it down – it ends as 'no longer literature, but penal correction'.[104] Literature as Siberia, as the knout: can this really be the end toward which Dostoyevsky the writer was aspiring? Not, finally, Dostoyevsky, but the Underground Man is scourging himself, and, not just himself, but the reader, too. He is a lost soul and he tells his story to make us grieve, because he insists that we are lost souls too. Perhaps we are. But if we are not and he is, finally, a liar, then we can only prove this by not being like him; and to do that, we must begin by acknowledging, like the Pilgrim with Vanni Fucci, the partial truth of what he says.

Chapter 2

Hardy

Every critic knows how Hardy's novels could have been better written. When Virginia Woolf described him as a sleepwalker of a novelist, carrying his books to completion as unconsciously as Angel Clare carried Tess to the empty coffin, she effectively fired the pistol for a kind of Oklahoma land-grab in Hardy studies, inviting the critics to rush in and stake their claim.[1] The critics happily did so and the result is a number of different Tesses, each proposed as the genuine article even if the author did not himself comprehend his true achievement. This interpretative licence was encouraged by Hardy's own occasionally misleading comments about his novel, for example, that it was just a simple tale, neither didactic nor aggressive, and that he was at a loss to understand why its readers had become so perturbed. Hardy is not always to be trusted as his own explicator and sometimes the disingenuousness is deliberate. In his 1912 preface he tells us that the subtitle, which provoked such furious controversy, was a virtual afterthought and, in retrospect, would have been better not to have been written: 'But there it stands.'[2] His complaint to his publisher about the early reviews is completely at odds with this: 'they alter my preface and omit the second title, which is absolutely necessary to show its meaning'.[3] Some afterthought. True, Hardy seems to have been genuinely incapable of anticipating the effect of his work on readers less 'advanced' than himself, but even he must have known and intended that his subtitle would have the impact of a grenade lobbed into a smug Victorian garden party. You simply don't write the first novel in English presenting a seduced woman as the unqualified heroine without knowing what you're doing. In addition, there is sufficient internal evidence to make the later wide-eyed disclaimers seem thoroughly unconvincing.

Between his own evasiveness and the allegations of others that he was an artist despite himself, creating in a kind of stupor like the God of his poem 'New Year's Eve', the way has been left open for the critics to tell us what Hardy was really doing, albeit unawares, in *Tess of the D'Urbervilles*. In general, the critics deplore those frequent intrusions into the text by the philosophic narrator (Hardy himself?) who insists on directing us toward conclusions we could either easily reach without him or don't want to reach at all. The art is at odds with the didacticism and the artist has gratuitously encumbered himself with a teacher whom he would be much better without. Like Balaam's ass, Hardy speaks other than he intends and his novels are the greater for this unconscious artistic usurpation. Conversely, it is the meddlesome didact, ineptly gatecrashing his own fictions, who damages their integrity.

True, Hardy describes himself as 'a mere tale-teller, who writes down how the things of the world strike him, without any ulterior intentions whatever', but it's doubtful whether he or anyone else ever believed this.[4] Like Lawrence and Orwell after him, he believed that all serious art is moral, a criticism of life, not aesthetic or decorative – style in itself, art for art's sake is a vanity and a trifling. The artist (it is Hardy's own image) is an Ancient Mariner, he stops and detains us with the mysterious beauty, but even more with the moral significance, of his tale.[5] Orwell openly declared his willingness to injure, perhaps ruin, the aesthetic integrity of what some regard as his most important book, *Homage to Catalonia*, for the sake of inserting a chapter of newspaper quotations exposing the lies spread by the communists about their anarchist rivals, Orwell's friends, within Barcelona.[6] In any conflict between truth and beauty, Orwell prefers truth, and the same is true of Hardy. The authorial interventions deplored today as resistant to aesthetic cohesion are, for him, integral to the work. The modern reader is free to disagree, provided he acknowledges that he is challenging Hardy himself on what the latter regards as a matter of paramount importance. Whatever we may think, Hardy did not deliberately set out to damage his work, far less lead us astray. He thought he was aiding us, like the chorus in Greek drama, toward a deeper understanding of his novel, teaching us things about the world and ourselves that we need to know.

Even his admirers find fault with his fatally relaxing impulse to theorize, classify and schematize, and warn us against reading his books as he instructs us to do.[7] Hardy, it seems, forever sells himself short. *Tess*, for example, is not 'what Hardy appears to have intended, a philosophic comment on Life in general and the fate of Woman in particular'; it's really (though only the subconscious artist in Hardy knew this) a parable about the destruction of the English peasantry.[8] But another admirer tells us that it is precisely the story of an individual, particularized woman, Tess Durbeyfield, a modern rendition of the ruined maiden of the ballad tradition who kills her seducer and dies on the scaffold.[9] A woman, not a social class, has been violated and destroyed. Everyone knows what Hardy means even when this contradicts what he actually says.

The question of what Hardy himself intended is crucial in a text that has spawned so many diverse interpretations, each claiming to be either what he really meant to write or, more presumptuous still, what he would have written had he been more intelligently self-aware. Consider, for example, the famous blighted star allusion, 'Tess's most uncharacteristic reflection'.[10] All agree that it sits uneasily in the mouth of a sixteen-year-old peasant girl just out of the sixth standard, that its real begetter is Hardy himself. It is not only, we are told, inappropriate but philosophically unacceptable to us, 'an image too facile to satisfy'; yet the same critic assures us that 'the whole organisation of the book makes us give it the weight of the author's full sympathy'.[11] Someone is confused and it isn't Hardy.

Hardy, let me repeat, cannot compel us to agree with him and if we find the blighted star unconvincing, that is our privilege. What we may not say is that Hardy didn't mean it or that, even if he did, we can safely disregard it. We have caught him in possession of this image – it belongs, surely, to him and not to the character who seems to own it. By what right do we say today that Hardy would have discarded it in 1891 if only he had had the benefit of our advice? We may continue to say that it harms the book's artistry, but we must not assume that Hardy agrees. When critics talk of Hardy's unconscious artistry triumphing over his all-too-conscious philosophizing, this triumph invariably coincides with the particular view of the text being promoted by the critic (destruction of the peasantry, ballad heroine, etc.). Whatever fails to fit this thesis is either omitted or marginalized, dismissed as either superfluous to the true meaning or injurious to it. The present argument also has a view of *Tess* to propound, but it involves taking the authorial intrusions seriously, the more so because Hardy is speaking in his own voice. What was it he so urgently wanted to communicate that he could not forbear intervening in his fiction to do so? We should try reading the book Hardy wrote rather than the one we wish he had written.

Tess is a text about truth-telling, about the obligation to reject error even when error is bliss and truth torture. Alcohol, optimism and religion are linked throughout because of their shared propensity for deluding us into believing that the world is a better place than it is and for inhibiting us from thinking clearly and seeing true. They are all forms of intoxication and religion and alcohol differ, not in kind, but in degree. Hence Hardy's use of the language of religion to describe the shiftless topers in the village pub: if alcohol is like religion, then religion is like alcohol – it is a kind of commutative law, a two-way street. When we read that after a few drinks 'a sort of halo ... came over life', that 'troubles ... took on themselves a metaphysical impalpability, sinking to mere phenomena for serene contemplation', we see that the pub customers have reached that state of quiescent detachment recommended by Christ that causes Angel Clare such perplexity: 'Let not your heart be troubled, neither let it be afraid.'[12] Angel regards this as easier said than done, at least by an intelligent, thinking man. But it can be done with ease by village drunkards or by their religious equivalents tippling on inebriating doctrine. Housman ironically praises alcohol as the superior rival of religion – 'malt does more than Milton can to justify God's ways to man' – but Hardy presents them as allies, parallel routes to the same delectable goal, keeping us, while under their influence, pleasantly stupefied. Believing in salvation and alcoholic indulgence alike help you to view the world in the same fallacious rosy glow. 'The ensnaring inn', where Tess's parents lose themselves, is, like the Church, a trap for the wilfully blind.[13] Tess comes upon a dozen people, 'all seeking beatitude', and finding it, too, as the sordid reality of their surroundings is alcoholically transformed into the glory of Solomon's temple.[14] It is precisely the place for Mrs Durbeyfield to dream her destructively foolish dreams of her daughter's wonderful future. In the pub all things are possible, for if the ale is for us, who can be against? Tess can be sent off by her befuddled parents in the imbecilic assurance that in no time at all she will be Alec's wife, the lady of the manor.

A corrupt dream, certainly, but is it any more senseless than believing in Christian providence or 'Nature's holy plan'?[15] Wordsworth is a purveyor of the same fatuous optimism, the same mindless happiness, as the pub landlord. When Tess learns in anguish that the serpent hisses where the sweet birds sing, it is a lesson, in Hardy's view, beyond the power of Wordsworth's comprehension.[16] Nothing is gained if we replace the myth of Christian salvation with a secularized but equally deluded myth of salvific nature. Wordsworth's nature poetry – the nonsensical 'holy plan', the newborn infant trailing clouds of glory – is, as much as Christianity or alcohol, a drug that rots the brain and saps the will. The song may be 'breezy and pure', but the thinking behind it is folly.[17] If nature has any plan at all, we can be sure it is far from holy and devised with no thought of pleasing human beings. We know that Hardy read and was influenced by T.H. Huxley – when Tess inadvertently reverses Alec's hothouse conversion it is by arguments drawn from Huxley's *Essays* relayed to her by her husband[18] – and Huxley had declared that 'the world is not subordinated to man's use'.[19] He states this with about the same level of anxiety as he would tell you that there are seven days in a week, but Hardy is not nearly so equable in the face of this discovery. Huxley's dispassionately factual view of an indifferent universe is transformed at certain characteristic moments of Hardy's art into a poetic vision of the universe as torture chamber, not simply uncaring but actively malign.

The lines from the 'Immortality Ode' describing our entry into existence trailing clouds of glory are introduced at a point in the story when Tess's brothers and sisters, about to be evicted following their father's sudden death, have just finished singing a Sunday-school hymn about meeting in heaven when our earthly travail is done.[20] Wordsworth's folly about how life begins is matched with the Christian folly as to how it ends. The partly enlightened Tess knows from personal experience the cruelty of life; knows, too, that no Providence watches over these children – if she does not save them, no one will. The crucial and fatal decision to go back to Alec is taken by an atheist *because* she is an atheist. A believing Tess (so Hardy tells us) might have trusted in Providence, rejected Alec, and still been with her family when Angel belatedly returns. There would have been no murder, no hunt, no execution. The final tragedy of the hanging is a direct consequence of the heroine's loss of faith. Yet faith is delusion. The contradictions simply highlight the ironic cruelty of life.

Even before her personal disaster, Tess senses, with an intuitive wisdom owing nothing to formal education, that Wordsworth is wrong. Whatever else we think about the blighted star allusion, it is surely testimony of her unillusioned view of things even before her own experiences so cruelly confirm her intuition. Any body of teaching, religious, poetic or whatever, that tells us what we want to hear is, for that very reason, suspect, not to be credited – Hardy is already anticipating Freud. The Durbeyfield parents, dreaming among the alcoholic fumes of their daughter's imminent elevation, are simply vulgar exemplars of a pervasive mentality that prevails in many superior people who would be indignant to be linked in any way with such wretches. Whatever consoles – alcohol, Christianity, Wordsworth – must be rejected. There is no consolation, because truth is bleak: that's what makes it truth. These witless parents are, at bottom, no more culpable than the believers in eternal happiness: both exhibit the same imbecile conviction that what we desire will be provided. We may condemn Tess's parents only on condition that we do not share the same fault.

They blithely despatch their daughter to be ruined, her father wishing that 'my young friend (Alec) will like such a comely sample of his own blood'.[21] Alec is not his friend, it is not Alec's blood, but he will certainly like it and Tess will pay for his liking with her life. Her mother is saddened at parting from her daughter, but 'she always managed to find consolation somewhere', and she finds it in the fantasy of the Cinderella marriage.[22] This facility for finding consolation is, for Hardy, her unforgivable sin. She knows that her own former beauty, her best attribute, had not brought success in life to her – why should it be any different for her daughter? Everything will, because everything must, turn out for the best: Orwell was to denounce this as the key delusion of the English imagination and warned that it brings about the very disasters that it insists cannot happen.[23] Hardy likewise advises us to live in the real world and not in some Cloud-cuckoo-land of the imagination.

It is significant that Angel Clare abandons Christianity for being too hopeful, too pleasing. Throughout the text various aspects of Christianity are exposed that might well justify its rejection: the clergyman's refusal to bury the illegitimate child in consecrated ground, the whispering congregation who drive Tess from the church, the harsh doctrine of the sins of the fathers being visited upon the children (Hardy scornfully dismisses the argument that Alec simply does to Tess what Tess's long-distant ancestors did to countless peasant women in the past and that accordingly it is a kind of justice),[24] the still harsher teaching of everlasting fire for the unrepentant sinner – there is much that might so easily have been used to explain why Angel can in conscience no longer remain a believer. So it is the more remarkable that he should break with Christianity, not because of its bad, but because of its good news. He explains to his unhappy father why he cannot follow him and become a minister of the Gospel – it is precisely because it *is* the Gospel, the good news. The insuperable difficulty is that article of the Church's teaching that refers to Christ's resurrection and to the assurance that, in thus overcoming the tomb, He has brought salvation to all mankind. Much as Angel admires the Church as an historical institution, he cannot remain in her while she 'refuses to liberate her mind from an untenable redemptive theolatry'.[25] He renounces Christianity not for threatening hell but for promising heaven – it is too good to be true. Nobody rises from the dead – Angel is as convinced of this as Orwell's O'Brien – here is the impassable obstacle to belief. Brainless happiness or informed disenchantment: the choice of Swift's 'Digression on Madness' is the one that confronts Angel. Nevertheless (it is Hardy who finds this remarkable) Angel has somehow made this choice without paying the full price: 'Considering his position he became wonderfully free from the chronic melancholy which is taking hold of the civilized races with the decline of belief in a beneficent Power.'[26] Not for the first nor the last time in this chapter we have occasion to note a connection between Hardy and Orwell in the latter's remark that the loss of belief in personal immortality is the greatest single problem confronting modern man.[27] The connection is further emphasized by the manner in which they both diverge from the customary attitudes of the Anglo-Saxon atheist tradition. T.H. Huxley, who may be taken as representative of this tradition, seems untroubled by the fact that there is no God and that we shall die forever. His equability here is poles apart from the anxiety of the very different continental tradition of Nietzsche, Dostoyevsky, Sartre and Camus. Hardy and Orwell seem almost 'continental' in the seriousness with which they react to the death of God and its momentous consequences – it signals a break with their own native tradition.

Angel's heroism in rejecting the optimism of Christianity separates him from the topers in the pub, the singers of Sunday-school hymns, and the devotees of Wordsworth, all avidly swallowing whatever cheers them up – the optimism is the offence, not the manner of its procurement. Tess learns by experience, testing theories against facts in the best empirical tradition and allowing the evidence, rather than her own wishes, to determine the outcome. That is why Hardy can declare, with a certain crass insensitivity, that, were it not for the gratuitous moral condemnation attending it, her experience with Alec might have been regarded as a liberal education; not many readers today would be prepared to take so indulgent a view of rape.[28] It is, however, true that whatever fantasies she may have still entertained concerning a benevolent, superintending Providence are routed by what happens to her in the wood. As always, the narrator stands obligingly at hand to interpret for us: 'But, some might say, where was Tess's guardian angel? Where was the providence of her simple faith? Perhaps, like that other god of whom the ironical Tishbite spoke, he was talking, or he was pursuing, or he was in a journey, or he was sleeping and not to be awakened.'[29]

This is one of a number of audacious inversions made by Hardy throughout the novel where he appropriates quotations and devastatingly employs them to subvert their original meaning. Elijah (the ironical Tishbite) mocked the priests of Baal when their god failed to respond to their appeals and proclaimed instead the greatness of the one true God, the God of Israel, who is always there when we need Him – which is why He's real, while Baal is a fraud. But when Tess is violated by Alec, it is Elijah's God, the God of the Judaeo-Christian tradition, who is posted missing and hence becomes deservedly in turn the target of the same derision once directed at Baal. Elijah's God is also a fraud and the prophet's sarcastic words are employed for a purpose that would have shocked and enraged him. God is another Baal, missing when needed, and the real folly is to believe otherwise.

Tess simultaneously learns to see through Christianity and Wordsworthian nature. The proximity of the hissing serpent to the sweet-singing birds is a fact that Wordsworth, if we are to believe Aldous Huxley, either could not or would not acknowledge.[30] The narrator tells us that the lesson entirely changes her view of life; the landscape, once beautiful, is now 'terribly beautiful', and 'Nature's holy plan' makes way for 'the plight of being alive'.[31] The massacre of the small field animals, driven into the centre of the field by the mechanical reaper to be killed by the sticks and stones of the harvesters ('unaware of the ephemeral nature of their refuge, and of the doom that awaited them later in the day') is an aspect of nature never touched upon by Wordsworth, but impossible to ignore after Darwin.[32] Tess's own fate is foretold in that of the animals, for she, too, will be hunted down, caught and killed. We *can* learn from nature, as Wordsworth insisted, but her lessons are very different from those he so piously found.

Christianity is equally misleading and the death of her child shows Tess still in thrall to its false notions, brokenhearted at the thought of the unbaptized child burning in hell. When the narrator speaks of 'the hour of emancipation for that little prisoner of the flesh', he means something very different from conventional Christian ideas of the soul escaping the body's bondage to enter into a higher spiritual life.[33] Hardy (why bother to separate him from the narrator here?) means a liberation from life into extinction, a sentiment closer to Schopenhauer than to Christianity.

Even after Sorrow's death, Tess has much to learn about life's cruelty. She resolves sensibly that there shall be no more D'Urberville castles in the air (they were her mother's, in any case): 'she should be the dairymaid Tess, and nothing more'.[34] Later, uneasy with the names of the classical goddesses showered upon her by Angel, she asks him to call her Tess.[35] No character in fiction is less guilty of hubris or extravagant ambition. All she wants is to be herself and happy – a modest request. She might as well have demanded to be Empress of India; to wish to be happy is the exorbitant dream that calls down retribution:

> Meanwhile, the best way to escape His ire
> Is, not to seem too happy.[36]

But the caution of Browning's Caliban will not help Tess; being the dairymaid Tess will not save her any more than being Tess of the D'Urbervilles. The maternal legacy of beauty is even more fatal than the father's gift of blood – an ugly Tess, her lineage notwithstanding, would have been spared both Alec's seduction and Angel's wooing.

Her recovery from her initial misfortune is no more than a cruelly deceptive remission in the course of an inexorably terminal disease. We read how the energy of youth fortified by the irresistible pleasures of nature combine to produce in her 'an invincible instinct towards self-delight'.[37] The pleasure principle is strong in her and the narrator seems to approve. He is scathing against those narrow-minded moralists who vindictively predict nothing but gloom for a fallen woman – everyone, fallen women included, has strong recuperative powers and there is a way back to happiness even for such as Tess. 'While there's life there's hope is a conviction not so entirely unknown to the "betrayed" as some amiable theorists would have us believe.'[38] The irony is obvious: far from being amiable, these theorists are spitefully determined to kick a woman when she's down – Tess has fallen and that's how she'll stay if they have anything to do with it.

The deeper irony is one that Hardy didn't intend and, in his eagerness to tick off his moralistic enemies, has surprisingly overlooked. To hear him approving hope is like hearing a Rechabite praise brandy. What could the most vindictive moralist have wished upon the fallen woman that could be worse than what happens to her in Hardy's novel? Why, if he really wanted to refute their gloomy thesis of an irreversible fall, didn't he dish the moralists by writing a story in which Tess surmounts all her difficulties and ends up the happy wife of Angel Clare? The truth is that Hardy had no wish to write such a story. As much as the amiable theorists, though for a very different reason, Hardy wants to show that the fallen woman is fallen forever, that, fleeting gleams of delusive hope notwithstanding, there is no way back for her. Tess has her recovery as Vanni Fucci his resurrection: so that they may suffer the same torments all over again. It would have been kinder had Tess capitulated to despair after the death of her child. When, 'in good heart, and full of zest for life',[39] she puts her sad experience behind her and bravely goes out to confront life once more, the reader and Hardy both know that she is really going out to take another brutal, pointless beating. Where there's life there's hope: did ever a text more devastatingly expose the falsity of this axiom of optimism? The command to abandon hope situated over the portals of hell is more appropriate to *Tess of the D'Urbervilles*.

This is the more merciless because Hardy insists that this life is the only one we have – 'the single opportunity of existence ever vouchsafed to Tess by an unsympathetic First Cause – her all; her every and only chance'.[40] We think of Hemingway's sadistic umpires, so eager, at your first slip, to dismiss you from the game;[41] of Kafka's dark parable when the dying man, after a lifetime before the door, asks the doorkeeper why no one has ever passed through, only to be told that it was meant for him to enter and that it can now be closed forever.[42] Tess's one door to happiness is as insultingly barred to her by Hardy as the entrance to the Law is for the man from the country: peasants both, both deluded, both destroyed.

Yet Hardy continues to refer to Tess's suffering as educative. Her 'passing corporeal blight had been her mental harvest'.[43] This idea, that suffering teaches and enlightens, is at the heart of Western religion and art from Aeschylus to Shakespeare: 'man must suffer to be wise'; 'only misery sees miracle'.[44] Hardy does not really fit into this tradition. One wants to ask the narrator to explain more precisely what it is that Tess is being taught and what the purpose of the lesson is. She learns that she is ineluctably doomed, learns what the field animals learn: that finally you reach a space where you can run no more and that it's there that they kill you. It is a fearfully expensive education, the results of which are achieved whether you study hard or are a dullard – a strange syllabus where it makes little difference if you are a bright or a poor student.

Tess has still to learn that her own sufferings, however extreme, are those of all mankind. She is puzzled as to why Angel (good family, well educated, comfortable income) 'should look upon it as a mishap to be alive'.[45] *She* has plenty to complain about (rape, a dead infant, extreme poverty), but what's wrong with him? Angel, however, has his sufferings, too, and the fact that they are not so pressingly material as her own does not, for Hardy, minimize the pain. The irony is that, ignorant of how she truly feels, he is attracted to something in this daughter of nature that 'carried him back into a joyous and unforeseeing past, before the necessity of taking thought had made the heavens gray'.[46] Where Swinburne blames the pale Galilean for turning the world grey, Hardy identifies modern thought as the destroyer of religious belief. It is ironical that each of the lovers mistakenly believes the other to be happy and looks in the other for a cure that is not there nor anywhere else. She wants to know why the sun shines on just and unjust alike, 'but that's what the books will not tell me'; he, with all his education, can only tell her that that's the way things are.[47]

'God's not in his heaven: all's wrong with the world!' Hardy inverts Browning as he inverts Wordsworth, Elijah, Tennyson, Augustine and Christ himself throughout the text.[48] Not the particular circumstances of any individual life but life itself is the curse – the Fall is into existence: there is 'a penal sentence in the fiat, "You shall be born."'[49] It is as Hamm says: 'use your head, you're on earth, there's no cure for that!'[50] It is not simply that Angel and Tess blunder in believing the other to be happy; it is the possibility of happiness at all that is the delusion. Ecclesiastes is rebuked for being too optimistic – if only all *were* vanity; but what happens to Tess is abominable and to call it vanity is woefully inadequate.

Angel educates Tess. As she tells Alec, she has abandoned prayer, since it is childish to believe that the powers above rearrange things to suit people's petitions. She never goes so far as to say that the power that rules the universe is not simply unhelpful but malign, but neither does her teacher, Angel – it is the narrator who claims for himself this disclosure at the story's end. She is an exemplary student of her husband and can repeat, almost verbatim and without fully understanding them, arguments culled by him from Voltaire and Huxley to discredit Christian belief – by doing this, she easily reconverts Alec back to his creed of psychological hedonism, much to her own dismay. A few words from Tess and Alec's febrile faith expires: 'you've knocked it out of me; so the evil be upon your own sweet head!'[51] Alec relapses into his old libertinism, thanks to a combination of Tess's irresistible beauty and Angel's unanswerable atheism.

Tess (her husband's influence again evident) condemns the restored libertine for confusing in his 'dull brain' two entirely separate matters, theology and morality.[52] Angel insists that his own loss of religious faith has in no way undermined his absolute belief in the moral law. Hence his compulsion on his wedding night to confess his sexual misconduct in London: God is dead, but the ban on loose living is even more binding than when He reigned in heaven. Religion is nonsense, but the Ten Commandments stand strong as ever. Alec is an atheist of a very different type.

If human actions entail no consequences of reward or retribution in a future life, he genuinely sees no reason for not pleasing himself in this one. Why, Svidrigaylov asks Raskolnikov in *Crime and Punishment*, should he restrain himself?[53] The question is perfectly sincere and it puts Svidrigaylov in the same camp as Alec. Angel may say that people like Alec are confused, but this argument can boomerang. Nietzsche (who was far from being a 'dull brain') also linked the death of God with the revaluation of all values and mocked atheists like Angel for irrationally clinging to the Ten Commandments; in a world of strictly human horizons there can be no moral absolutes. Angel is only timidly halfway down a road that Alec has travelled in full.

Nor does the novel make it clear that Angel is a better upholder than Alec of the Commandments which the former ostensibly reveres and the latter explicitly repudiates. Angel, with his fine talk of forsaking God for the service of humanity, deserts his wife and leaves her in indigence. The libertine, intent on his own gratification, is kinder than the hero of agnosticism: 'I, at any rate, try to help you out of trouble, but he does not, bless his invisible face!'[54] Alec is no altruist, for sex is his motive, but what he says about Angel is undeniable.

Angel is as invisible as the Providence that failed Tess in her hour of need – and *he* doesn't have the excuse of not existing. The ironical Tishbite might have been as justifiably scornful of the new religion of humanism as he was about the old religion of Baal, since neither is to hand when wanted. Tess does not attack God for her tribulations, she just stops believing in Him. But she does, vehemently and with justice, condemn her husband, that substitute deity whom she obeys in everything and for whom she would die, for ignoring her prayers as pitilessly as any Christian God could ever do. 'Come to me, and save me from what threatens me!'[55] Did ever Christian pray with such desperate futility as Tess? The Christian can, at least, fall back upon the consolation that God works in mysterious ways and that, when most apparently unreachable, he may suddenly respond. The Christian can go on hoping against hope. Tess has no similar recourse: her god is an abject failure and there is nothing mysterious in the petulant withdrawal of his favour from Tess. When he finally does relent and return, it's too late and a disaster, for he comes to cause her to become a murderess and to ensure that she's hanged. Tess kills Alec for two reasons: he insults her husband-god; and only his death can expiate the sin she has committed against this divinity. 'Will you forgive me my sin against you, now I have killed him?'[56] If pagan Tess, on the altar of Stonehenge, is a sacrificial victim to the ruthless God of the Christians, then to what deity has Alec been sacrificed in the bed of the Sandbourne hotel? Or are we to think that he, unlike Tess, fully deserves what he gets?

Alcohol, Wordsworth, Christianity – none will suffice; add humanism to the list of failed creeds. Hardy, in effect, advises us to disbelieve in salvation from any source. Angel's high humanist sentiments are as empty as Christian promises or Wordsworthian flourishes. 'It is my fault', he finally admits, but only when the fault is past repair.[57] The two men between them send Tess to the gallows, but Angel is the greater culprit – she recovers from the rape but not from the desertion.

Even then, when she has come to terms, however bleakly, with his absence, he returns to make sure she is hanged.

'Once victim, always victim – that's the law!'[58] The text verifies Tess's pessimistic conclusion – her execution simply confirms what she already knows. But what law and what law-giver? Getting rid of vengeful Jehovah isn't much help if it only means succumbing to a savage Darwinism or a hypocritical humanism. Hardy (it is the recurring paradox of his work) rejects Christianity as untrue and often cruel before imprisoning his readers in a world at once inescapably true and far crueller. He attacks narrow-minded moralists for refusing to give fallen women a second chance and then writes a story in which his fallen woman is not even given a first chance.

As much as *Nineteen Eighty-Four*, *Tess of the D'Urbervilles* is a novel about atheism, its implications and its consequences. Both texts have as their main characters two men and a woman, all atheists, though of highly contrasting types. Angel and Winston are alike in their ineffectual idealism and failed humanism. O'Brien shares Alec's scorn for any moral curb upon the human will, although he has chosen to become a devotee of power rather than a pleasure-seeker. In each case, despite the other differences, a 'good' atheist confronts a 'bad' one, a division related to the divergence between the English and continental traditions of disbelief. Angel is scrupulous in his behaviour toward the beautiful milkmaid and this self-discipline results from his sense of the finality of life – here, at least, in a text where he is otherwise criticized, Wordsworth got it right:

> But in the very world which is the world
> Of all of us, – the place where in the end
> We find our happiness, or not at all![59]

How, believing this, could Angel even dream of taking advantage of another fellow creature under the same sentence of everlasting death? Since we live only once, we must love and respect each other, because it is the only opportunity we shall have. Angel is a disciple of the religion of humanity as preached by Feuerbach and adopted so eagerly by disbelievers of the English tradition.

Alec, using identical data, reaches a very different conclusion. The certainty of annihilation fuels a resolve to gratify his desires to the full, regardless of the consequences to others, before the opportunity to do so is taken away forever. It seems to him plain common sense that he should please himself while he can and not sacrifice his one chance of happiness to a list of prohibitions as fictitious as the God who allegedly gave them. The action of the novel is played out among these three characters: a young woman whose sad experiences have caused her to lose her faith, a priggish young man who has left the service of God to serve humanity, and another young man who has forsaken belief for debauchery. The novel is not, finally, about the village maid who is seduced, kills her betrayer and is hanged, still less about the rape of the English peasantry or the hypocrisy of a society that labels

Tess a fallen woman. It is a text about the loss of belief in God and a study of the consequences in its three major characters.

The old religious answer to the problem of innocent suffering is totally repudiated. It is not for eventual sanctification – Tess is 'educated' only for the gallows and when she is hanged, she dies forever. Becoming an unbeliever does not help her in any practical sense; it simply reveals how inconsolably bleak life is: 'Why am I on the wrong side of this door?' – although, significantly, she is rebuked by her priggish husband for even hinting at the possibility of suicide.[60] 'Both seemed to implore something to shelter them from reality.'[61] In a book exposing the falsity of the various shelters constructed by men (religion, alcohol, nature), it is a mark of their heroism that the harried lovers will not bow down to a creed they no longer believe in to hide from the harshness of life. But it clearly shows, too, the gulf between the bleak atheism of Hardy and the consolatory, melioristic atheism of the habitual English tradition.

Nowhere is this heroism better displayed than in the last, most audacious of Hardy's 'misquotations', when Angel, begged by Tess to tell her that they shall meet again in a world to come, remains as silent as Christ confronting his accusers.[62] In a parallel predicament at the close of *Heart of Darkness*, Marlow, despite his instinctive aversion to untruth, gives Kurtz's intended the lie she so desperately craves; but Angel is made of sterner stuff and will not lie even for the one he loves. There is one world, one life, one chance of happiness, and Tess has irreprievably, eternally lost them all. Only truth will do, however brutal.

It is a break from his earlier, less rigorous position when, with the narrator quoting Tennyson in justification, Angel seemed prepared to leave Tess untroubled in the comfort of her religious delusions:

> Leave thou thy sister, when she prays,
> Her early Heaven, her happy views;
> Nor thou with shadow'd hint confuse
> A life that leads melodious days[63]

although it's notable that Angel (and Hardy) regard the advice as less honest than musical. But now the need to be truthful takes precedence over every other consideration: Tess must go unconsoled to the gallows because any consolation would be a lie. Yet the two refusals to speak, Christ's and Angel's, have nothing in common; the provocative linking of the atheist hero with the Son of God is Hardy's real motivation in a comparison that is both strained and factitious. But in a book ruthless in renouncing every attempt to hide from reality, this last refusal is entirely consistent. The very existence of the book is sufficient proof that Hardy disagrees with Tennyson's instruction to leave believers in peace with their bogus consolations. Above all, Hardy is a truth-teller and he must speak out, however dismaying his news. There are no atheists in foxholes. It is a gibe that Hardy is resolved to repudiate; in his foxhole, expect no prayers.

'The sun's rays smiled on pitilessly' as Tess is hanged.[64] Neither religion nor nature, this world or the next, will avail in the end. Angel and Liza Lu bend down to the earth 'as if in prayer', but in a text that makes plain the futility of prayer we know that they are not praying. Hardy simply needs a gesture, a human reflex, no matter how rationally absurd, for the final emotional impact of his heart-rending tale. To kneel down: it is what human beings have immemorially done at such tragic moments, and they go on doing it even in the pages of Hardy's most contentious, post-religious novel. But the reader would be foolish to seek solace here. No more than Angel with Tess will Hardy grant the reader the consolation he requires; he tells the stark truth and he does so with the clear intent to make us grieve.

This is why his retort to Andrew Lang's criticism concerning the President of the Immortals is disingenuous and unconvincing. 'To exclaim illogically against the gods, singular or plural, is not such an original sin of mine as he seems to imagine.'[65] But Hardy must have known that citing the famous quotation by Gloster in *King Lear* was no defence against those angered by the concluding statement in *Tess*. Gloster's indictment of the gods is a dramatic statement in a play where many different and opposing voices are heard. We cannot disregard these other voices to promote Gloster's alone as the authoritative Shakespearian view. The play is polyphonic; all the voices are Shakespeare's, which is to say that Shakespeare himself is mute. By contrast, the statement at the close of *Tess* is not dramatic, is not spoken by a character but by the narrator and there seems no good reason to distinguish here between the narrator and Hardy himself. Hardy is inexcusably confusing a dramatic utterance in a play with a narratological intervention in a novel – an intervention that is provocative and even gratuitous. Tess is hanged and for most readers that's bad enough without this extra twist of the knife. We have no right to link Gloster with Shakespeare, but every right to link Hardy with the narrator, the more so since we find similar sentiments being openly advanced in Hardy's poetry. The puzzle is why Hardy should be so coy about acknowledging beliefs in his prose that he is very ready to claim as his own in his poetry. He said he preferred poetry to prose for, among other things, conferring a greater freedom to speak your mind without incurring the public anger that the same confession in prose fiction inevitably unleashed – Galileo would have been safe from the Inquisition if he had said it in verse.[66]

Why, in any case, is it 'illogical' of Gloster to attack the gods for inflicting his torments upon him? There is no immediate contradiction between believing that God exists and that He's a sadistic joker. What *is* illogical is to believe that there is *no* God and that He's a sadistic joker. *Le salaud, il n'existe pas*, says Hamm in Beckett's *Endgame* and a non-existent bastard is a strange being indeed. Hardy is just as illogical when at the end of *Tess* he attacks a God in whom he doesn't believe. God is called into existence so that he can be denounced – it is He who 'lets the nettles grow' in the unconsecrated part of the graveyard where Tess's child lies buried.[67] Vanni Fucci obscenely insults the God whom he knows, only too well, but Hardy, by contrast, ascribes sadism to a God who isn't there, inventing Him for the purpose of vilifying Him. It is an empty blasphemy that recurs in the pages of twentieth-century texts: in West's *Miss Lonelyhearts*, in Camus's play *Le Malentendu*, when God is given being simply to reject brutally the prayers of a suffering woman, in those Beckettian references to a Godot who is not coming but for whom the tramps continue vainly to wait. Not Shakespeare's *King Lear*, not what comes before, but Camus and Beckett, what comes after: this is the real context for understanding what is going on in Hardy's novel. This is an angry atheism, not the untroubled disbelief of George Eliot, Huxley and J.S. Mill; there is a sense of hurt and betrayal, an orphaned resentment at the loss of the Father, a refusal to forgive Him for having abandoned us by not existing – West's original title for *The Day of the Locust* was *The Cheated* and the application extends beyond the disappointment of California. As much as Tess, Newman believed that we live on a blighted star, but he believed, too, in a God of love who would finally put all to rights.[68] Hardy's God, by contrast, when permitted to exist, is the sadistic creator of the blighted star, the tormentor of Tess and, by extension, of all suffering humanity. Listening to the wind, Tess hears 'the sigh of some immense sad soul, coterminous with the universe in space, and with history in time'; or, rather, the narrator hears this for her, since Hardy makes no attempt to palm this speculation onto his sixth-standard heroine – it's plainly his own.[69] Alvarez calls Hardy 'a precursor of modernism' and declares that 'the blankness and emotional dislocation he delineated so sharply in *Tess* in 1891 were to become the characteristic note and preoccupation of twentieth-century literature'.[70] Anyone still unconvinced of this after reading *Tess* need only turn to that startling anticipation of modern themes, 'Barbara of the House of Grebe'.

In poems such as 'The Ruined Cottage', 'Michael' and 'Resolution and Independence', Wordsworth presents us with uplifting examples of the human spirit triumphing over adversity. The worst thing in the world, Orwell's Room 101, happens, but the insuperable greatness of the human being shines through the calamity. Hardy's story is, by contrast, about humiliation and the triumph of Room 101. First published in 1890, it is strikingly prescient of our own contemporary nightmare. Hardy's declared wish to be fifty years ahead of his time is almost weirdly realized with clockwork accuracy if we reflect that Koestler's *Darkness at Noon* appeared in 1940, while, more appositely still, *Nineteen Eighty-Four* was published in 1948. Aversion therapy, operant conditioning, behaviourist psychology – all these lay in the future when Hardy wrote his tale. Pavlov's work on the conditioned reflex took place in 1906. Watson's behaviourist techniques applied to the training of children were introduced in 1913. Fetishism (Barbara's obsession with the statue might easily be included under this) was an aberration as yet undiscussed by the general public. Lord Uplandtowers is a pioneer of aversion therapy half a century before it was practised. The blocking of gratification so that the patient will forsake his inappropriate sexual behaviour – this is how Uplandtowers views his wife's passion for the statue – and seek a new, 'legitimate' way of gratifying his sexual needs: modern sex therapists would only discover this many years after Uplandtowers used it to rehabilitate his wife. The practice of attempting to 'cure' male homosexuals by showing them pictures of naked men accompanied by electric shocks or nausea-inducing drugs had to wait for the 1930s, but the technique is already implicit in Hardy's story. Only at a later stage was it discovered that subjects respond better to rewards than to punishments, to positive rather than to negative reinforcements, but even then aversion strategies were not completely discarded. In Huxley's *Brave New World* (1932), pain is an instrument of operant conditioning alongside pleasure and his vision of the future came forty-two years after Hardy's tale. Even as late as *A Clockwork Orange* (1962), Anthony Burgess describes a future society in which violent criminals are turned into docile, cheek-turning citizens by being literally sickened by pain – made virtuous, obedient citizens in exactly the same way as Barbara is made a virtuous, obedient wife. The fantasy of 1890 became the horrifying reality of our own day; in his insight into the manipulative control of human beings, Hardy shows himself a prophet of the totalitarian age.

The reviewers of the 1890s were predictably hostile and perhaps we do them too much credit in attributing to them some intuition of the threat to the human being implicit in the tale. 'Fool, do not boast, thou canst not touch the freedom of my mind.'[71] The Lady's scornful dismissal of the attempt to enslave her responds to some longstanding conviction of Western man that in the spirit he is finally free. The enchanter has subjugated her body, but this is the limit of his control. Within the few cubic centimetres of her skull (it is the as yet unconquered Winston Smith's formulation), the Lady is and will remain inviolable. Such was the commonly held belief of the West up to and for years after Hardy wrote his tale. Hardy brings the bad news that it is just one more delusion.

The reviewer in the *Pall Mall Gazette* of July 1891 took Hardy to task for the gratuitous horror of the story, describing it as 'a hideous and fateful fantasy'.[72] Hardy's defence is characterized by the evasiveness and plain wrongheadedness that recur in his comments on his own work. His first recourse was the story's structure, the tale within a tale, designed (so he said) to protect the reader's sensitivities by throwing back the action into a middle distance, related by a character to other characters, not point-blank by author to reader. This, in itself, is revealing, indicating as it does that such direct narration would have been blameworthy. The reviewer, replying, had no difficulty in dismissing this defence of technical construction: a hateful picture to the imagination is no less hateful because of the technique used to present it.[73]

Hardy's second defence is equally ineffective; worse, it seeks to exonerate by trivializing. 'A good horror has its place in art. Shall we, for instance, condemn *Alonzo the Brave*? For my part I would not give up a single worm of his skull.'[74] It's as though Orwell had defended *Nineteen Eighty-Four* as a piece of *grand guignol* extravagance and recalls Charles Lamb's attempt to rescue Restoration Comedy from its moralistic enemies by arguing that they had mistaken frivolity for serious social commentary, but not many readers are convinced. Hardy's reviewer made short work of this attempt at justification. *Alonzo the Brave* is hokum, a harmless piece of sensationalist folderol, with nothing to say to us as serious readers. 'Barbara' is altogether different and what is acceptable in fantasy or in the fiction of a faraway past is less so within the context of realistic fiction. When Hardy asks in injured innocence why anyone should be 'shocked at the mere tale of a mutilated piece of marble', he tries to save himself by devaluing his story.[75] It contains elements of fairy-tale, but not in the mode of *Alonzo the Brave*. It is a wicked reprise of Beauty and the Beast combined with Pygmalion, a fairy-tale as *Great Expectations* and *The Great Gatsby* are fairy-tales, modern renditions of Poor Hans finding and losing his fortune, or as *Nineteen Eighty-Four* is a dispiriting account of how the Giant destroys Jack. The fairy-tale element in these works, far from transporting us to a fantasy realm immune from the pain of life, serves rather to reinforce and intensify a sense of loss and anguish. As has been remarked, 'nor does the invocation of *Alonzo the Brave* entirely remove one's sense of discomfort at the peculiar perversity, not to say perversion, of Hardy's tale'.[76] The reading of 'Barbara' that follows will pay Hardy the compliment of taking his story more seriously than his own words do.

Hardy's tale can be read as a rehearsal for *Nineteen Eighty-Four*, with Uplandtowers as determined to master Barbara as O'Brien is to dominate Winston and just as assured that in the end he will succeed. It is a matter not of hot blood but of cold will. 'We shall squeeze you empty, and then we shall fill you with ourselves.'[77] The sexual imagery links the violator of Winston with the violator of Barbara: old loves are evacuated to make room for new. Barbara's elopement is merely a temporary setback; her flight from Uplandtowers is as futile as that of Oedipus from his home. Just as surely as the *Titanic* for the iceberg, so Barbara is destined for Uplandtowers – the Immanent Will is his ally too. The catastrophe of the fire that transforms her Adonis of a husband into a monster, an *écorché*, is too much for her to bear. She can no more control her revulsion than Winston can resist Room 101. 'Sometimes they threaten you with something – something you can't stand up to, can't even think about.'[78] More than fifty years before Julia confessed this humiliation of the spirit, Barbara experienced it: Orwell was to learn from Hardy. Barbara's guilt is a barren remorse, the guilt of being human, and it links her with the Underground Man before, Winston Smith and Jean-Baptiste Clamence after, her. None of them can help what they do, yet all endure the additional pointless penalty of feeling ashamed.

And so she falls ineluctably into the sadistic embrace of Uplandtowers. It is a Room 101 of a marriage, a diabolically successful experiment, looking backward to Hawthorne's chill projectors (Chillingworth, Aylmer, Rappacini), forward to our own grim world of brainwashing and terror. No more than Big Brother will Uplandtowers tolerate a rival love. Discovering his wife's infatuation with the nude statue of her once beautiful husband – 'Are you going to stay here all the morning worshipping him?'[79] – he resolves to turn this passion into abhorrence. Four decades more and he would have made a splendid commandant of a death camp. No more than for Orwell's O'Brien is it the crude business of punishing a culprit, rather the much more taxing problem of reclaiming a lost soul. Conversion is the goal. In forcing Barbara to look upon the ghastly, deformed statue, Uplandtowers has the same demoralizing aim as O'Brien as he drives Winston to confront his hideous reflection in the mirror – the only difference is fifty years on and a new ideology acquired. In each case the aversion therapy only ends when the cure is complete. Compare the two conclusions. 'Firm in enforcing his ferocious correctives, he continued the treatment till the nerves of the poor lady were quivering in agony under the virtuous tortures inflicted by her lord, to bring her truant heart back to faithfulness.'[80] 'O cruel, needless misunderstanding! O stubborn, self-willed exile from the loving breast! ... But it was all right, everything was all right, the struggle was finished. He had won the victory over himself. He loved Big Brother.'[81]

The theme in both texts is defeat, humiliation, self-loathing. Hardy intuited what Orwell experienced, achieving these insights without the ambiguous privilege of being contemporary with death camps and gulags. Barbara will be minutely faithful to her wedding vows as long as she lives; she, too, loves her violator. Were Hardy's nobleman to apply for a post in the Ministry of Love, he would be welcomed with open arms.

T.S. Eliot was criticized for describing 'Barbara' as a masterly work in the diabolic mode, but it is his critics who are wrong.[82] There *is* a diabolic power in this tale. Hardy's defenders argue that he sympathizes with Barbara and disapproves of Uplandtowers, that his dislike of operant conditioning is unmistakable throughout – the story is about sadism, not in favour of it. None of this changes the fact that it is about the triumph of sadism, that evil prevails because it is stronger. This is a new thing in literature. Even at his most pessimistic (*Lear*, *Othello*) Shakespeare never concedes so sweeping a victory to evil. 'Barbara' is a new departure, anticipating the bleak works of our time, particularly *Nineteen Eighty-Four*. It is not self-evidently a law of nature that the brainwashers, the sadists, must win. If Hardy and Orwell seem to think so, we have a right to ask why. There are only two answers: either they wish it so or they have resignedly accepted that it must be so. It is easy enough to explain why Orwell, all the grim evidence of twentieth-century history to hand, might have reached so dire a conclusion. But why Hardy, in the relatively peaceful garden of late nineteenth-century English society, should have anticipated Orwell's worst findings, is a much more problematic affair that no serious reader will dismiss or downplay.

Hardy's defenders insist that his story does not condone cruelty, that goodness *is* present, if only implicitly in the narrator's voice. But what is narrated is the triumph of the diabolic spirit; if we sympathize with Barbara, so much the worse. The object is not to stay alive but to stay human. So says Winston Smith before providing in his own person a signally depressing instance of the failure to do so. Barbara is another such failure. To die like Leonidas or Bonhoeffer is a triumph, to live like

Wordsworth's Margaret or Michael a tribute, but to exist like Barbara or Winston is the worst, most humiliating fate of all. Why their creators chose such fates for them, why in writing such stories they so clearly set out to make us grieve: these are questions that go straight to the general predicament of our time.

Chapter 3

Conrad

Not the least intriguing thing about *The Secret Agent* is the mystifying Author's Note, written thirteen years after the first publication, remarkable for what it fails to say and producing more obscurity after reading it than there was before. Its purpose, wrote Conrad, was not to defend his book against its detractors, but to justify himself against the reproof of having written it at all.[1] As a distinction this seems tenuous, but Conrad plainly felt a need to repudiate the charge of elaborating mere ugliness simply in order to shock. He vehemently denies any trace of sadistic indulgence. Despite the sordid surroundings and moral squalor of the tale, he insists that 'there was no perverse intention, no secret scorn for the natural sensibilities of mankind at the bottom of my impulses'.[2] He is not taking us down to the sewer for the pleasure of watching us retch; such devilment is not part of his objective. The story came to him when he was 'certainly not thinking of going out of my way to look for anything ugly',[3] but the very disclaimer is an admission that the ugliness is there and needs justifying – searching for it or not, ugliness is what he found.

His unease as to the harrowing content is clear from his reiterated denial (four times in six pages) that, in pursuing Winnie Verloc's story to its anarchistic end of desolation, madness and despair, he had not intended to commit a gratuitous outrage on the feelings of mankind.[4] It is a striking disavowal when set against the content of the story, particularly the outrage demanded by Vladimir that sets the whole confused train of events in motion; but even more than the noun it is the adjectives – anarchistic, gratuitous – that claim our attention. Conrad sensed that he himself is the perpetrator of the real outrage, that the true anarchist in this tale of *fainéant* incendiaries is the author himself. Not the bungled affair at Greenwich, but the madness that takes possession of Winnie from the moment she learns of her brother's death to our last sight of her on the cross-Channel ferry: this is the real atrocity, and it is the work of the terrorist author, not of any of the speechifying poseurs who crowd the text. It is Winnie's story, as Conrad himself said, and the author is her destroyer. 'There have been moments during the writing of the book when I was an extreme revolutionist.'[5] Conrad perhaps spoke truer than he knew. For it is not simply a matter, as he cryptically put it, of attending to his business[6] – he means presumably surrendering to that negative capability that allowed Shakespeare to delight as much in an Iachimo as an Imogen: to delight in his Professor, Conrad had to know and become him.[7] The narrator of *The Secret Agent* is far more dangerously subversive, more radically anarchist, than any of the characters. They *talk* of committing outrages; he commits them – *The Secret Agent* is the deed itself. *Their* words betoken helplessness; *his* resonate with a terrifying power. That he knew of this power, sensed this kinship with the terrorist, is shown by his care in qualifying the noun with the adjective 'gratuitous'. It reveals a concern to justify his action, a need, such as the revolutionary experiences, to reject the charge of carnage for its own sake, of wanton and indiscriminate slaughter. Clearly, the subject-matter left him vulnerable to this accusation – dismemberment, murder and suicide might well qualify as outrage – but he decided to make his stand on the ground that this was not gratuitous destruction. Unpleasant things have to be said and done to bring about the overall good – not the least important link between politics and fiction in our century is the readiness of each to resort to violence in order to achieve its ends.

We are told why the book was *not* written, but not why it was. Conrad first says that the book was begun impulsively, but disappointingly fails to specify the nature of the impulse. He then declares that 'I need not have written that book. I was under no necessity to deal with the subject. This I fully admit.'[8] It was, apparently, an impulse he chose not to resist. He insists, too, that it was purely a work of the imagination, presumably to vindicate its originality against those who emphasized its borrowings from contemporary events.[9] Exactly what kind of imagination is at work in the text? This is the question that confronts us.

The Author's Note provokes more questions than it solves. Conrad speaks of 'simply attending to my business', but what was this business, apart from the artistic completion of the task undertaken? Was it really necessary to write an Author's Note to tell us that he was creating a work of art? The really important question is: what particular vision of life is embodied in this art, for the sake of what view of reality did Conrad take such strenuous artistic pains?

What stimulated his imagination was the 'criminal futility of the whole thing'. The man who had blown himself up was the idiot victim of 'a brazen cheat exploiting the poignant miseries of a mankind always so tragically eager for self-destruction'.[10] But Conrad's treatment of the story was not at all tragic, as Thomas Mann pointed out when he identified *The Secret Agent* as characteristic of modern art in its rejection of the ancient categories of tragic and comic in favour of a new fusion of both.[11] Even the inspiring revelation of Winnie's all-consuming love for her backward brother – the story, as Conrad himself tells us, is *her* story and its title, placing her husband at its centre, is misleading – did not lead to a more tender or exalted treatment of the material. Conrad refers to her tragic suspicion that 'life doesn't stand much looking into', but he presents the confirmation of this, not as tragedy, but as the blackest comedy.[12] Her story shows the disastrous consequences of *not* looking into life, of simply attending to immediate practical necessities and ignoring everything else. Looking or not looking: it makes no difference to the final outcome and the night that awaits us all.

Conrad defended his chosen ironic mode by claiming that this alone would enable him 'to say all I felt I would have to say in scorn as well as in pity'.[13] The pity is well disguised, the scorn all too evident. The explanations of the Author's Note do not explain. Conrad offers his 'whole treatment of the tale, its inspiring indignation and underlying pity and contempt' as proof of his 'detachment from the squalor and sordidness which lie simply in the outward circumstances of the setting'.[14] Far from clarifying his intentions, this only makes them more obscure. Indignation against what? Pity for whom? Contempt, certainly – the most cursory scanning of the text easily discovers this. But what can he mean in making a virtue of detachment when a standard complaint against the work is that the narrator is too callously detached from the agonies he depicts, that no political fanatic was so heartless in pursuing his goal than was the author of this text in pursuing his? Conrad must surely have realized that the most troubling aspect of his dark book was the jeering unconcern with which it handled the destruction of its chief characters.

The Secret Agent is a terrorist text as well as a text about terrorism, and outrage is a term as appropriate to it as penal correction is to *Notes from Underground*; as much as Kafka's 'In the Penal Colony', it is a literary enactment of its own content, replicating in words the deeds of terrorism that are its action, with the chief plotter the author himself. Like violation in *Tess*, like the knout in *Notes*, terrorism in *The Secret Agent* is a metaphor for what the author does to the reader. Nowhere is this terrorist desire to inflict the maximum possible damage more devastatingly demonstrated than in the tale's peculiar chronological structure. It is a major irony that what, at first sight, seems to confer a god-like privilege upon the reader – the power to see the future – should turn out to be a chief source of disturbance and pain. Vanni Fucci invites Dante to look into the future, too, but not so that he may feel superior and secure.

Flannery O'Connor tells us that the novelist selects every word, detail and incident for a reason, 'and arranges them in a certain time-sequence for a reason'.[15] 'There may never be anything new to say, but there is always a new way to say it, and since, in art, the way of saying a thing becomes a part of what is said, every work of art is unique and requires fresh attention.'[16] The first thing any reader notices about *The Secret Agent* is its highly unusual time-sequence. Taking our cue from O'Connor, we may put the following questions: what statement is Conrad's peculiar selection of words, details and incidents designed to make? What was his reason for devising such an unusual time-sequence? How in *The Secret Agent* does the way of saying the thing become a part of what is said?

The basic statement is that expressed in the parable of the Fool, who spent a lifetime storing up wealth only to discover that he had no life left to enjoy: the world is a perilous place and we should not let destruction take us unawares. To drive home this lesson, Conrad constructs his chronology much as a terrorist primes his bomb to explode at the peak traffic hour in the busiest part of town – to inflict the maximum damage upon his opponents. The time-sequence is shaped to reveal the inexcusable folly of those who dream of dictating the future. These are the terrestrial equivalents of the grotesquely misshapen soothsayers in the eighth circle of the *Inferno*: they move through the world backwards, but, unlike the damned in Dante, they do so oblivious to their predicament and blindly falling into the pit.

When the Pilgrim weeps over these distorted souls whose heads have been turned to face the rear, he is roughly rebuked by Virgil for his culpable pity – he, too, is, emotionally speaking, facing in the wrong direction. Conrad, as severe as Virgil, tells his story in a mockingly ironic way designed to exclude pity for its victims: scorn overwhelms compassion. The jeering disdain of the olympian narrator, looking down like a vengeful Brobdingnagian upon the follies of these pygmies, or like the God of Swift's 'Day of Judgement' derisively dismissing the whole offending race of humankind – this is irony, not just as technique, but as meaning: the way of saying becomes the thing said.

The unforgivable folly is to think oneself safe. Browning's Caliban recommends a secret happiness to avoid the ire of God. The narrator-god who presides over *The Secret Agent* is amused that anyone could dream of being even secretly happy. It is a book about folly – 'there are more kinds of fools than one can guard against', laments the Professor, pining for a foolproof detonator – and we see what the world does to them.[17] But it is a particular kind of folly that Conrad sets out to punish. A fool like Toodles is of no consequence. He believes that this earth is 'a nice place to live on', is aghast to learn that the Explorers' Club has a rogue member.[18] The idiocy is so inanely inoffensive that the reader can safely smile without wondering what the cost might be. Toodles is the absurd extreme of a general imbecility, for the world is a ship of fools on a voyage to oblivion and we are all, Toodles and sages alike, its condemned passengers. The night that falls so suddenly upon Mr Verloc is the inevitable reward of men's labours on this earth, with no one exempt from its descent. Life itself is the joke and we are all its dupes. It is substantially the same dark vision as that conveyed by Arnold's darkling plain or by the cruelly indifferent gods of 'The Lotus Eaters'. But where Arnold and Tennyson protest against the tragic injustice of it all, Conrad, in characteristically modern mode, sees it as ironically comic and prefers to highlight the folly of the victims. The porno shop in Soho is a particularly squalid corner of the darkling plain, and the bleak abandonment depicted – all those bogus saviours from science, politics and religion – is in the style of a satire by Swift rather than a Tennysonian plea for hard-done-by man.

For Conrad, we can confront our predicament, not change or control it. Those who look upon life as a bomb, always liable to explode, are equipped for the world: they will not survive, but neither will they be confounded. Those, by contrast, who believe they can elude disaster, either by their own astute provisions or the grace of some superintending Providence, will not only be destroyed but demoralized. No one has the right to feel safe, and those who do will pay dearly. 'Nothing on earth can stop me now,' says Verloc to the woman who is about to kill him, but it is Conrad, even more than Winnie, whom he so rashly, provocatively challenges.[19]

Within a few pages of the story's opening we encounter the first of what will be a series of examples of this culpable mentality, a hubris democratized and made common. If the text has an admirable character at all, it is Winnie's mother – self-sacrificing, altruistic, heroic. She plans the best and, by the law of the novel, promotes the worst. A more selfish woman would not have done such harm. The unforeseen consequences of our actions are often appallingly at odds with what we intend, yet act we must, since inaction, too, is a choice and may just as easily lead to disaster. 'Her act of abandonment was really an arrangement for settling her son permanently in life.'[20] Instead, it blows him to bits. A selfless mother destroys her son where a selfish one might have saved him. Yet, were Stevie's mother to appeal to us and ask where she had chosen wrong, how could we answer? She is not accountable because, in trying to do good, she in fact served evil; if life is a cruel hoax, how is she to blame?

Precisely for not recognizing from the outset that life is a cruel hoax. She is guilty of believing that the world will be a safe place, especially for her retarded son, once her daughter marries and the family passes to the protection of her indolently good-natured son-in-law. The move from Belgravia to Soho may have affected her legs adversely, but this is amply compensated by the euphoric assurance that she need worry about Stevie no more. Her son-in-law fills her with 'a sense of absolute safety. Her daughter's future was obviously assured and even as to her son Stevie she need have no anxiety.'[21] The major family problem is resolved. Winnie loves her brother; Verloc, as well as loving Winnie, is kind and generous, and so the worried mother can feel reasonably certain that 'the poor boy was pretty safe in this rough world'.[22] This is how she feels, how she *wants* to feel, when she learns to her surprise that Winnie has agreed to marry the late-sleeping lodger. 'If you had not found such a good husband ... I don't know what would have become of that poor boy.'[23] She makes it sound accidental, a stroke of good fortune, but the reader knows that Winnie only found what she sought – not a husband for her bed, but a guardian for her brother. Verloc's sole superiority as a suitor to the butcher-boy was that he was willing to take Stevie, while the butcher-boy was not.[24] There was nothing fortuitous about Stevie's finding a protector in his sister's husband, since the husband was selected for that very reason. In marrying Verloc, Winnie made a bargain, albeit of a peculiar kind, since the other partner knows nothing about it. No more does her mother. Ignorance, deliberately contrived, leads to all-round destruction. What would have become of the poor boy if Winnie had not 'found' Verloc? He would not have been blown to bits outside the Greenwich Observatory. Nobody in this family group of mother, daughter and son-in-law knows the others because nobody wants to know. The less we know, the safer we will be; it is enough that the everyday needs of ordinary life are conveniently served – why should we wish to pry deeper? Like Queen Elizabeth I, these people care only for outward conformity, are not in the business of making windows into souls, so it is not surprising that they are strangers to each other, acquainted with the shapes they see but not the selves within. Compounding this, they see only what they want to see. Verloc seems kind and caring to the mother because she needs such a man to look after her son. It would be crazy to look a gift horse in the mouth when the troublesome Stevie will be safe for life. Verloc sees a wife who loves him for his own precious sake. Winnie sees a father for the fatherless boy. 'Might be father and son', she reflects with satisfaction as she watches the dark, heavy man and the fair, slight youth – they could scarcely be more different – walk off together for the last time.[25]

Why Winnie agreed to marry Verloc is a question her surprised mother declines to ask. Uttered, it might have saved a whole family from destruction – the two women would, at least, have understood each other and might have been able to plan together for what each, unknown to the other, considers paramount, namely, Stevie's welfare – but it is precisely the kind of dangerously destabilizing question that could have had an unsettling effect on the marriage itself and so must not be asked. *Quieta non movere.* As the Author's Note tells us, man is not an investigating animal; he prefers safety to knowledge, security to curiosity.[26] Stevie is safe for life and nothing else matters, so say nothing and be mutely grateful that things have turned out so well. Alas, *The Secret Agent* shows that there is no more salvation in incuriosity than there is in investigation.

Conrad is far more severe to his subjects than is Setebos or Queen Elizabeth toward theirs. Keep your joy or your Catholicism hidden and you can escape punishment on Caliban's island or in Tudor England. In *The Secret Agent* to feel secure, however discreetly, is to call down retribution. That Winnie's mother, with disciplined fortitude, keeps her assurance of Stevie's safety to herself, does not serve. Thought crime is as reprehensible in Conrad's London as it will be in Orwell's Oceania. Bravely, privately deciding to go to the almshouse to save her son, she does the calamitously wrong thing for the most praiseworthy of reasons. Winnie is baffled by the apparently wilful act, but no more enquires into the mother's reason to leave than the latter had done into her own decision to marry. Believing that silence is safety, the two women delude each other into disaster. Acting to save her son, the mother destroys them all. A demon could not have planned a more ruinous course of action than the old woman initiates in the goodness of her heart. There is no safety anywhere. Those who live above the San Andreas fault must expect the earth to open at any moment.

We learn that Inspector Heat is not truly wise, because 'true wisdom, which is not certain of anything in this world of contradictions, would have prevented him from attaining his present position'.[27] This very position and the speed of his promotion are proofs of his unwisdom, because, in the human world, self-confidence and certitude are prized and rewarded. But woe unto those who are sure of themselves, says *The Secret Agent*, and it invariably shows this state of mind as a prelude to punishing it. The chief characters are not chastised for being bad but for being blunderers, for misconceiving the world, mistaking a jungle for a haven, a wild and savage place for a cosy and comfortable home. 'One can't think of everything.'[28] So Verloc, in the last minutes of his life, consoling himself for the mishap over the label on Stevie's overcoat. He knows at last what his wife meant in assuring him that the boy would not get lost, but it is no help to him now, seconds away, without knowing it, from his own extinction. To be secure in this world, one would have to think of everything, including the carving knife so innocuously on the kitchen table. Verloc is not to blame for not being able to think of everything (who can?), but for feeling secure, despite this, in a world where this is so.

The brutal ultimatum to bomb Greenwich or lose his salary fills Verloc with all the indignation of a man over 40 'menaced in what is dearest to him – his repose and security'.[29] Why the world should be a place of repose and security for him is a question he never asks. It is axiomatic that the world exists for Verloc to be comfortable in and when his tranquillity is disturbed, it is as though the laws of nature had been violated. This is not wickedness, but it is folly and he shares it with the rest of mankind. Even the thoroughly dislikeable Vladimir can, without fully knowing it, speak true and his remarks about 'the imbecile bourgeoisie' of England have an unintended wider application: 'They have no imagination. They are blinded by an idiotic vanity. What they want just now is a jolly good scare.'[30] He says this to the most conspicuous example of unimaginative, blind, idiotic vanity in the book, but it would be a mistake to believe that *The Secret Agent* is simply about the deserved destruction of one exceptionally egregious fool. We are not to preen ourselves on being superior to Verloc – the book does not condemn his vanity to flatter ours. Verloc is a fool for believing that his wife loves him and it is easy for us to see this because the narrator has obligingly let us into the secret of Winnie's decision to marry him: she loves her brother, not her husband. But it would be foolish and impertinent to conclude that we know and he doesn't because we are clever and he isn't. Unlike us, Verloc is kept in the dark. If believing that your wife loves you is clear proof of idiocy, then the world is crowded with imbeciles.

Verloc dies for believing that his wife loves him, but, more culpably, he believes that the world loves him, that it exists for his comfort and convenience, that he has been given life that he may live in unalloyed contentment. Hence his outrage when the hyperborean brute orders him either to earn or forfeit his pay. He is, however, not uniquely foolish in this regard. Inspector Heat (scarcely a fool) exhibits the same astonished indignation when *his* chief begins to question him a little too closely about the bombing. It is a link between the two men that they should both be plagued by their gentleman superiors. Heat is as incensed as Verloc at this unwarrantable interference from above – although the narrator's image is of sabotage from below: 'He felt at the moment like a tight-rope artist might feel if suddenly, in the middle of the performance, the manager of the Music Hall were to rush out of the proper managerial seclusion and begin to shake the rope. Indignation, the sense of moral insecurity engendered by such a treacherous proceeding joined to the immediate apprehension of a broken neck, would, in the colloquial phrase, put him in a state.'[31] It is a revealing image. Life, for Conrad, is a tight-rope walk over an abyss and we should realize this before we take a step. Never believe yourself safe, for that's when you'll surely fall.[32] Verloc and his fellow fools think they are strolling along the broadest of highways – they need and will get 'a jolly good scare', and their angry reaction to this simply confirms their fatuity. To the very end Verloc holds himself blameless – 'like slipping on a bit of orange peel in the dark and breaking your leg'.[33] Heat, as conscious tight-rope artist, is only marginally superior to Verloc (who dreams that he's treading solid earth), for Conrad's warning is that there will always be somebody, especially the theatre manager, to shake the rope. Expect to fall.

It will not, of course, stop you from doing so; sensing life's insecurity will not make life secure. Winnie's mother, conscious of something amiss with Verloc but misconstruing it, decides 'in the astuteness of her uneasy heart' to deflect impending disaster by going to the workhouse and precipitates it instead.[34] But to be uneasy at all is to win Conrad's approval, for it is to part company with the likes of Winnie and Verloc. Even had he known he was walking a tight-rope, Verloc would never have expected Winnie to be the one to shake it. To the end he is confident that he can elude the vengeance of his revolutionist associates and *he* is right – all that hot air will not make the rope vibrate. On the point of death he is planning his release from prison two years ahead. 'He was excusable.'[35] This is not, as it seems, third-person narrative – this is Verloc thinking. It is this impertinent sense of invulnerable innocence that Winnie indignantly recalls when she tells Ossipon what finally drove her over the edge: 'he had been telling me that nothing could touch him'.[36] It is a dead man who is talking and he talks himself beyond our pity as well as his wife's.

Not that his executioner is any better. Winnie is as innocently unsuspecting of danger as the unsuspecting man she kills. Her marriage is a business contract, 'seven years' security for Stevie loyally paid for on her part; of security growing into confidence'.[37] This, despite the fact that her partner knows nothing of the contract and so can scarcely be accused of breaking it. 'Oh yes, I can trust you,' she tells him, with both contract and Stevie in fragments.[38] When she learns the truth, she reacts 'with the rage and dismay of a betrayed woman'[39] – it is the fury of the tight-rope walker looking down to see the manager shaking the rope. 'She was no longer ignorant,' the narrator tells us earlier, but in reference only to her sexual enlightenment.[40] She knows her husband in the biblical but in no other sense, has been sleeping with a stranger for seven years for her brother's sake. Like Verloc she, too, thought she was on solid ground and discovers she is on the rope only after killing her husband, by which time it is too late for rescue, especially when her chosen saviour is the craven Ossipon who deserts her once he realizes the risk to himself. The text has by now come to resemble an idiot relay race with a succession of cretins passing the baton to each other. It is now Ossipon's turn to feel himself 'losing his footing in the depths of this tenebrous affair'.[41] By the close he, too, knows he is on the rope, destined to walk the last section with the leather yoke of the sandwich board strapped to his shoulders. Enlightenment means knowing how endangered one is.

And yet in this world of dark mischance, man is ambitious to command events and has devised certain communal enterprises (politics, science, religion) to help him to do so. Conrad dismisses these as fetishes, as empty of resource as the sticks and stones of savage men. The book rejects politics as a cure for human ills; it is no more than a backcloth to the real action. *The Secret Agent* is, as the Assistant

Commissioner self-mockingly declares (his own marital difficulties in mind), 'a domestic drama' in much the same way as *Othello*, with the war between Venice and the Turks supplying a background similar to the establishment–revolutionary conflict.[42] Certainly, the narrator has *Othello* in mind as certain echoing allusions to putting out the light surely indicate.[43] The tragic outcomes hinge upon humdrum details: Desdemona destroyed by a handkerchief, Verloc by a label, Desdemona in the bedroom with a pillow, Verloc in the parlour with a carving knife, in each case by a trusted spouse. The Verlocs are destroyed, not by politics, but for failing to see that there's no place like home so far as danger is concerned. Verloc worries about every knife except the one on the kitchen table. Winnie impatiently scouts the idea of danger: 'We aren't German slaves here, thank God. It's not our business – is it?'[44]

She is right: it is not Prussian brutality that threatens her household. But she blunders in concluding that if there's no political threat, there's no threat at all: since England is not Prussia, life is secure. But we are secure nowhere. 'You ain't a slave,' she tells her husband. 'No one need be a slave in this country – and don't you make yourself one.'[45] But 'this country' in the sense intended by Winnie – a haven of invincible security – does not exist anywhere: at any moment a label or a kitchen knife may destroy you. They live as imperilled as Gulliver in the land of the giants – but whereas Gulliver knew it, they don't. 'I call it silly ... We ain't downtrodden slaves here.'[46] Her scornful reply to Heat's question shows how fearfully unaware she is. In Conrad's world we are all puppets, all slaves. Winnie is not worried: England is not Prussia. Verloc *is* worried, but about the wrong things – the brutal Vladimir, the revenge of betrayed comrades. His real, unapprehended problem is domestic: the assassin comes from the kitchen.

Science fares no better than politics. Vladimir speaks for Conrad when he calls it the new idol, the wooden-faced panjandrum, of the bourgeoisie; Thomas Mann praises Conrad's discernment in showing how the middle-class contempt for art is complemented by its awe for applied utilitarian science.[47] Ossipon is a superstitious fool who has simply blind faith in physiognomy. He reacts to Yundt's attack on Lombroso with all the outrage of an Italian peasant hearing his patron saint traduced. Conrad describes him as 'exhibiting that glance of insufferable, hopeless dense sufficiency which nothing but the frequentation of science can give to the dullness of common mortals'.[48] Far from being the solution to human ills, science simply deludes fools into thinking themselves wise men.

The supreme folly, however, the wellspring of all others, is Christianity, scornfully dismissed by Conrad as 'that absurd oriental tale'.[49] The key Christian dogma of God's illimitable love for man spawns the idiotic belief that the individual self is the supreme value in all creation; God so loved humankind that he sent his son to die for it. Nietzsche lashed this as vanity masquerading as piety, the most monstrous piece of presumption ever to enter the head of conceited, inconsequential man. This inane self-importance is Conrad's chief target and Christianity is its promoter. Science and revolutionary politics are born of the same delusion. It is fitting that the murderous Professor, raging at a world that does not share his wild exaggeration of his own worth, should be the son of a fanatically religious father, a preacher 'supremely confident in the privileges of his righteousness'.[50] Like father, like son. The Professor's is the same zealotry in secular dress. There is no great difference in claiming to be God's prophet or History's spokesman, since History is the name given to God by an irreligious age.

Michaelis, so ostensibly different from the Professor, is substantially the same, 'one of those saintly men whose personality is lost in the contemplations of their faith ... inaccessible to reasoning ... confident of the future'.[51] His socialism is secularized religion and he has merely exchanged Christ for Marx as Ossipon has traded St Francis for Lombroso. Only the identity of the saviour and the location of the paradise have changed: every other article of the faith remains intact. Behind socialism lies Judaeo-Christianity: it is a Nietzschean insight. The peasant bows down before technology, Ossipon before Lombroso, the socialist before dialectical materialism; Conrad makes it plain that at the root of all these devotions is the salvific dream sponsored by Christianity. Vladimir is unfair in limiting idiotic vanity to the blinded bourgeoisie, for it is a universal human characteristic most flagrantly encouraged by a creed that tells every paltry little mortal that the Lord of the universe died for *him*. It was precisely this democratic indiscriminateness, this promiscuous egalitarianism, that provoked Nietzsche's elitist disdain; and Swift is equally scathing in holding up for ridicule the foolish notion that God Almighty is at all concerned with the drivelling little dolt in the pulpit whose words have no more significance than his belchings.[52]

A similar mindset underlies the sarcastic description of Verloc's turmoil after the interview with Vladimir as his 'mortal envelope' carries 'that part of him to which it would be unwarrantably rude to refuse immortality' back to the Soho shop.[53] Rude or not, a very large question mark has been placed over Verloc's eventual entry into eternity. He is indignant at having been treated as someone of no account – the hurt to his self-esteem is even more painful than the threat to his income; he is still complaining about it to his wife just before she kills him. But if he thinks Vladimir has treated him badly, what would he say about his treatment at the hands of Conrad? He pays dearly for his inflated view of his place in the scheme of things. The question is: what, as Conrad sees it, is his true place? Not, most certainly, what Christianity says it is – no wonder people are so idiotically vain when they are told that they are the children of God and the heirs to heaven. Either Christianity reports true or it panders disgracefully to human vanity: no reader of *The Secret Agent* can doubt what Conrad believes. Admittedly, Verloc is not himself religious, nor is his vanity explicitly linked to Christianity, but where else, finally, could it have come from? In the Professor, Michaelis and Ossipon, Conrad shows the religious roots of revolutionary politics and modern science. So, too, Verloc's ludicrously high opinion of himself can be traced back to the impertinent mentality of Eden.

Religion is discredited without even being mentioned. The language of faith is employed to sabotage all faith: religious, political, scientific, legal, familial, matrimonial, or just simply a sense of trust in the routine stability of the workaday world – *The Secret Agent* subverts belief in everything. Winnie's mother blesses Providence for sending Verloc to the boarding house; she is really thanking it for the cannibal feast of Stevie's mangled remains and for Winnie's wedding ring lying on the deck while its erstwhile wearer finds her only salvation in the dark waters of the Channel. Blessing turns into disaster. And yet in the mother's position, might not we have prayed the same cruel benediction? Perhaps at this very moment we, too, are going similarly astray. *We witan nat wat thyng we preyen here.* Conrad remorselessly undermines any confidence we might have in our own judgements, decisions, anticipations: is it so clear that we are wiser than Winnie's mother? How could she have foreseen the son blown to bits at Greenwich, the daughter dead by her own hand in the Channel?

We are not to look down upon this doomed family, however sordid their circumstances, baseless their beliefs, mistaken their expectations – the narrator claims this privilege for himself while denying it to us. The serpentine chronology is designed to intimidate, to destabilize our own certainties, to humiliate us through association with those who have gone so badly astray. This is prophecy in the mode of Vanni Fucci, revealing the future not to empower but to dismay. The narrator takes us on high with him to share his olympian view but not his disdainful amusement. Our lot is to look down in impotent dismay, present like a spectator at a disaster, knowing the dreadful future but helpless to prevent or amend it. It's as though we were carried back in time to watch the *Titanic* begin her voyage. The prevision of God is joined to the helplessness of man in an unhappy fusion: foreknowledge simply intensifies anguish.

Contemplating the Verlocs, how can any of us feel secure? A religious person will recommend us to trust in God, but in a text designed to expose the absurd oriental tale, this is simply a further folly. Conrad's world is one in which a group of blind people are set down amid cliffs and crevasses and invited to make their way home; we should not be surprised at the high casualty rate. The truly frightening thing is that it may well be our world. We are given eyes so that we can see the Verlocs go disastrously astray, but the fear is that, outside the fiction, we are as blind as they.

We can clearer see the anti-providential nature of *The Secret Agent* by contrasting it with that other great work in our language which it resembles in structure but not at all in spirit or meaning. *Paradise Lost* is as chronologically dislocated as Conrad's tale, but with a completely opposite intention. Milton shows us the future in the spirit of Dante's Cacciaguida: the Pilgrim is exhorted not to lose heart or give up but to battle on toward the promised salvation. Paradise is lost only to be regained. Conrad reveals the future to the reader as Vanni Fucci reveals it to Dante – to induce despair. Here, even before it happens, is a ruined family and there is no salvation. Milton begins in hell, Conrad ends in it.

If the future is a place of damnation, what are we as readers meant to do about it? We cannot command events, but we can alter our outlook. There is a similarity between what Conrad is doing in his novel and what Swift claimed to be doing in his satire.[54] He protested that he never attacked people for being what they are (for how can they help it?), but for failing to see what they are. An ugly man who thinks he's handsome, a fool who thinks he's clever: these are legitimate targets for satire. Neither will Conrad condemn you for stumbling blind amid the precipices, but for pretending that you are eagle-eyed and goat-footed. What must be acknowledged is that the window-pane is 'a night without end', and, although this will not dispel the darkness, it will prepare you for it.[55]

Chief among the deniers of darkness is Mr Verloc. Conrad punctiliously employs the title in incrementally derisive fashion. Mr Verloc – it is a fatal delusion – 'imagined himself loved by that woman'.[56] To be undeceived he would have to cease being Mr Verloc. He simply cannot conceive that his wife might prize the idiot above himself and this is entirely 'excusable since it was impossible for him to understand it without ceasing to be himself'.[57] How can we be what we are not? Winnie, trying to imagine herself Mrs Neale, thinks she would be just as fond of gin as the cleaning woman: 'We can never cease to be ourselves.'[58] It is fatal if you are Mr Verloc. We are told that 'the mind of Mr Verloc lacked profundity';[59] he is as much a moral idiot as Stevie is a mental one. He blames everyone but himself for the catastrophe: Vladimir for his bullying, Stevie for his clumsiness, Winnie (good intentions notwithstanding) for sewing on the label without telling him – he's the injured party, even if Stevie had to be gathered up with a shovel. Stevie's death is merely a minor distraction in the far greater affair of his own misfortunes. He is a moral Ptolemaic, regarding himself as the centre of existence; in his idiotic vanity, he thinks that Winnie sewed on the label for his convenience rather than her brother's safety, which is why he magnanimously refrains from reproaching her for bringing the police down upon him. Conrad enjoys parading this numbskull as he large-mindedly forgives his wife, devours roast beef and anticipates sex with his assassin the moment before she kills him.

Who is responsible for Verloc's lack of profundity and moral cretinism? 'He was excusable ... he was generous and indulgent.'[60] This seeming third-person narrative is, of course, Verloc's own deluded, self-flattering view of himself, but, although Conrad is plainly having fun at the fatuity of his victim, the text nowhere suggests how Verloc could have been different – if ought implies can, then ought is totally inapplicable to Verloc's situation; as well say that water ought to run uphill. He cannot help being Verloc, cannot help being killed. He dies, deserves to die, for being himself, for seeing only the blank wall but not the writing on it, for telling his stricken wife, devastated by the news and manner of her cherished brother's death, to have a good cry and be done with it. It is the criminal ignorance of the man that cries out for vengeance; stupidity cannot be the excuse when it is the offence.

Yet he is not the sole culprit. Stevie dies because the two women who love him have inculcated in him 'the doctrine of [Verloc's] supreme wisdom and goodness'.[61] These are the attributes of God and the God Stevie unreservedly trusts destroys him. He is, admittedly, an idiot and as such peculiarly at risk, but the text makes it plain that his is a fate not restricted to idiots. Winnie's consternation when she learns how her brother died is likened to the despair that people might feel were the summer sun suddenly to be extinguished by 'the perfidy of a trusted providence'.[62] The real imbecility is to place one's trust in an idiot universe – Conrad is here making the first tentative advances into a territory to be more fully explored by Camus. *Le Malentendu* is a title that would be just as applicable to the murderous misunderstandings and cross-purposes within the Soho household; and, at bottom, *The Secret Agent*, in its black ironic way, displays the same hurt and resentment at the missing God as do works more lyrically associated with the Absurd such as *The Outsider* and *The Fall*. To believe, to trust, to feel secure: these are the cardinal sins in the world of *The Secret Agent* and they all evince an anachronistic reliance on Providence that Conrad is provocatively prepared to link with idiocy. Men cannot help it if they live on the cusp of a volcano, but they ought not to feel secure.

Verloc's death is presented within a context of comedy, with the polite title sardonically affixed to the name lest we forget what a fool he is. 'Night, the inevitable reward of men's faithful labours on this earth, night had fallen on Mr Verloc.'[63] But the irony of this end cannot be restricted to this particular corpse: death is a folly in which we all participate, an impertinence inflicted on us all – Verloc and the Fool in the parable are simply especially egregious examples of a universal *sottise*. Tennyson in 'The Lotus Eaters', Camus in *The Outsider*, adopt a sombre approach to the topos, citing death's inescapability as the ultimate injustice done to men, siding with the victims, expressing pity for their torments and indignation at their injuries. Conrad in *The Secret Agent* prefers an ironic stance, joining those jeering gods who find diversion in the suffering and death of men. There is pain aplenty in the book and he speaks of pity in the preface, but the *leitmotif* is scorn rather than compassion and the narrator's amusement at the murderous misunderstandings of the characters is impossible to miss. Lord, what fools these mortals be: the words of Puck are conveyed in the spirit of Swift.

It demands no special discernment to see the religious basis for the dead man's 'belief that he lacked no fascination for being loved for his own sake'.[64] St Paul invites us to contemplate the mystery of God's incredible love when he tells us that Christ died, not for the deserving, but for the worthless.[65] As certain of his wife's total devotion as St Paul is of Christ's, Verloc dies for this blunder. He believed that he was 'loved for himself. Upon this matter, his ethical notions being in agreement with his vanity, he was incorrigible.'[66] It is what Conrad, following Nietzsche, finds so insufferable in the whole deluded, smug assurance of salvation.

With Verloc dead, the idiot baton passes to Winnie, and the allusions to religion become more explicit as the focus shifts to the equally deluded wife. Stevie, betrayed by his brother-in-law, reduced to a pile of blood-soaked rubbish, identified by his label, is a grimmer version of the biblical Joseph. The end of the seven-year marriage (with Winnie, who has faithfully observed the terms of her unilateral contract, feeling even more cheated than Jacob) is rendered in a context of discredited religion – the foolish, pharisaical husband, the terrified, salvation-seeking wife. The imagery of Eden is employed to describe the panic-stricken woman and the bogus saviour she relies on. Winnie clings desperately to Ossipon's legs, while he, appalled at what he now knows she has done, 'saw the woman twined round him like a snake, not to be shaken off. She was not deadly. She was death itself – the companion of life.'[67] In however jumbled a form, with whatever reassignment of roles, the components of Eden (man, woman, snake, death) are all present. Ossipon sees the woman as the death-dealing serpent; she sees the shivering poltroon as the messenger of life, the redeemer come to her rescue as the *messo da ciel* comes to help Virgil and Dante, as the messiah promised to fallen Adam and Eve.[68] When she leans on the coward, grateful for his protecting strength, the folly is so great as to overwhelm any consideration of pity. Her words of entreaty are an ironic reverberation of Genesis. '"You can't throw me off now," she murmured from the floor. "Not unless you crush my head under your heel."'[69] It echoes God's promise that the serpent's head will be crushed under the heel of the second Eve, the Virgin Mary. Winnie is no second Eve and in this image she presents herself, albeit unconsciously, as the serpent cursed to crawl upon the earth – she is, literally, crawling, coiled around Ossipon's legs, as she speaks the words. Eve, Mary, Winnie – it is a linking as cruelly ironic as when Vanni Fucci, resurrected from his own ashes, is associated with the risen Christ. But where Genesis and Dante promise salvation, *The Secret Agent* denies the very possibility.

If Verloc exists to prove that there is no security, Winnie exists to show that there is no salvation. There is no messenger from heaven, no messiah, in Conrad's text, and this revelation extends beyond the craven Ossipon to include Lombroso, Bakunin, Marx, Christ and any other claimant to the title. We survey a series of fraudulent saviours and a gallery of gulls naive enough to believe in them. No security, no salvation, is the bleak report on life that *The Secret Agent* presents for our consideration.

Everyone is found wanting: left and right, government and revolutionaries, the indolent and the meddlers, those who pry and those who cultivate ignorance. 'I haven't the slightest wish to spare this man Verloc,' says the Assistant Commissioner, but his is a selective ruthlessness, for he does wish, for his own selfish motives, to spare Michaelis.[70] Conrad spares no one. Virgil would have no cause to complain about an inappropriate pity in this text – it seems, if anything, too uncomfortably close to the malice of Vanni Fucci. Inspector Heat's merciless contempt for the anarchists is extended by the narrator to everyone, Heat included; and while Verloc's 'scorn was equally distributed over the whole field of his operations', Conrad's field of operations is more extensive still and he scorns, in addition, the scorner.[71]

Closest to the spirit that informs *The Secret Agent* is the ironic view of life discernible in Swift's poem, 'The Day of Judgement'. 'I damn such Fools – Go, go, you're bit.' No one is exempt from the grim practical joke that Jove plays upon the whole offending race of humankind when he finally annihilates all parties to the pointless disputes of earth, Catholic and Protestant alike, each arrogantly convinced that God is their God and that their enemies are His enemies. He spares no one, neither the sinners who fell nor those who stayed erect – through pride. In the end, as in *The Secret Agent*, nothing really matters except the night that befalls us all. In the embassy Verloc hears against the window-pane the faint buzzing of a fly and 'the useless fussing of that tiny, energetic organism', so futilely busy, symbolizes the pointlessness of all human endeavour in 'this world of vain effort and illusory appearances'.[72] The activity of the fly is as significant, finally, as the idiotic act toward which Verloc will be driven by Vladimir – between man and insect there is nothing to choose. Indolence or activity, what does it finally matter given the doom that is as inescapable in Conrad as in Swift?

Linking Conrad's novel and Swift's poem is a shared resolve to block every possible escape route from condemnation. There is no pleasing Swift: if the physically dainty Lilliputians are corrupt, the morally decent Brobdingnagians are repulsive – evading one accusation merely means running into another. *The Secret Agent* enacts a similar entrapment. If settling for a surface contentment is blameworthy, burrowing to the unpleasant truth is equally self-destructive. The Assistant Commissioner is not a jolly fool like Toodles, but neither is his acuteness an unqualified blessing. The daily whist party at the club is his drug against the secret ills of existence, but Conrad is not recommending us to avoid Toodles' folly by taking up cards.

Just what he *is* recommending is the key problem of the book. Consider the discussion between Winnie and Stevie on the problem of human suffering and what we should do about it. The idiot's compassion is stirred at the spectacle of pain and his immediate instinct is to relieve it – the instinct, admirable in itself, that Conrad accuses the revolutionary fanatics of exploiting. Winnie's advice is to do nothing since nothing can be done: 'You can't help that.'[73] Leave it alone, otherwise you will only succeed in making yourself ill. It anticipates the advice given to the hero by his fiancée in *Miss Lonelyhearts*. The two women advise their respective idiots to cultivate an indifference toward life's evils, but neither of the idiots can comply. No more than Miss Lonelyhearts after reading the letters can Stevie forget the exhausted horse and the one-armed driver: 'Unlike his sister, who put her trust in face values, he wished to go to the bottom of the matter.'[74] But it is no more clear to the reader here than in the 'Digression on Madness' as to which, if any, of these contrary positions is being endorsed. Stevie's compassion makes him Verloc's dupe and causes him to be blown to pieces; Winnie's policy of willed ignorance toward all but the practical needs of the moment contributes to her own and her brother's destruction. 'By their fruits' is of no help here – because the fruits are the same whatever you do.

Winnie's defence against life is a willed incuriosity as Conrad repeatedly makes clear throughout the text: 'obviously it may be good for one not to know too much'.[75] But, equally, it may be bad for one not to know enough. It is tempting, given the catastrophe that occurs, to conclude that Conrad is passing judgement upon such willed myopia. Yet, given the vision of life implicit in the text, the 'moral nihilism' at its core, 'the secret ills of existence' against which the Assistant Commissioner fortifies himself with his daily fix of whist, it is not immediately obvious that Winnie's choice of nescience is mistaken.[76] There is nothing frivolous about it; it is as though, having pondered the alternatives of the 'Digression on Madness', she has settled for the tranquil surface rather than the troubled depths. Mistaken, perhaps, but not foolish. 'I don't trouble my head much about it . . . she felt profoundly that things do not stand much looking into.'[77] It is not evident that Conrad disagrees. 'Human kind cannot bear very much reality.'[78] If Eliot is right, then perhaps Winnie is in the right in deciding to bear as little as possible. The Assistant Commissioner has his whist, Winnie has her brother: these preoccupations keep them from the abyss. What might happen to him deprived of his whist we do not know; what befalls her deprived of her brother is made appallingly clear. She advises her anguished brother to ignore the suffering world, thereby avoiding the madness and alienation predicted by Swift for those who go down into the depths. How are we to live in a world of evil? This is Stevie's question and Winnie's advice is not to trouble your head about it. But when evil irrupts into her own life the hollowness of this advice becomes manifest. She cannot calmly accept her brother's destruction, but, becoming his avenger, descends into madness and despair. Is it better to be Winnie before or after, indifferent to the world's evil or possessed by retributive frenzy? This is unanswered. Yet to fault Conrad for not giving a clear answer would be as sensible as blaming Swift for leaving us equally bewildered in the 'Digression on Madness': that's what each means to do. To try to corner Conrad to extort from him a straight, unequivocal reply is to overlook the deliberate nihilism at the heart of this dark text.

The characteristic modern strategy, confronting insoluble evil, is to turn despair into a joke – at all costs, pity and self-pity must be avoided. This is what distinguishes writers like Kafka, West, Beckett and Ionesco from their predecessors who look at life with a tragic, pitying eye. *The Secret Agent* is a major pioneering work in establishing the ground rules of this new tradition. The narrator's relish is unmistakable as he tells this tale of dismemberment, murder and suicide – the delight in manipulating his puppets is almost palpable. Even before these tight-rope walkers step onto the rope, he has zestfully shown us their broken bodies on the ground.

This relish is manifest in his employment of a macabre zeugma to describe 'the late faithful Stevie blown to fragments in a state of innocence and in the conviction of being engaged in a humanitarian enterprise'; or when he refers to Winnie straight from her husband's murder as Mr Verloc's widow, much as one might describe Lizzie Borden as an orphan.[79] The one single word in the text that irrefutably proves the jeering mentality of the narrator is the arresting term, 'villegiature', from the passage conveying Winnie's complacent, completely mistaken reflections on her brother's supposedly pleasant holiday in the country.[80] Recalling Flannery O'Connor's counsel that not a word is chosen by the artist without some precise purpose in mind, we have every right to ask why Conrad employs so strikingly unusual a word. What is still recoverable of the fragmented Stevie – as the reader, but not Winnie, knows – has already been collected on a shovel, and this is surely irony enough when juxtaposed with his ignorant sister's happy meditations on her brother's excursion. But not, apparently, for the narrator, as his choice of word testifies. For it is clearly not her word and would never have found its thoroughly implausible way into her reflections. It is, unarguably, the narrator's word, chosen to reveal his amusement at the contrast between the fancy term and the frightful fate. The joke is on Winnie and here, preeminently, the reader is impelled to protest against an excessive cruelty, a sadistic indulgence, in the telling of the tale. Not Winnie, not any human being, deserves to be mocked in this way. The narrator's desire to punish these fools transgresses all permissible limits: comedy and cruelty are indistinguishable.

Admittedly, the materials of folly are abundantly to hand, the provocations to satire irresistibly present. 'Never had a sage a more attentive and admiring disciple': this is Verloc taking Stevie off to blow him to bits.[81] As the Assistant Commissioner remarks, it's all 'a ferocious joke', and the dramatic ironies, the *double entendres*, proliferate as the tale proceeds.[82] Vladimir taunts Verloc at the outset that he 'wouldn't deceive an idiot', but here, at least, Verloc proves him wrong.[83] But, finally, the story is about Winnie's maternal passion and it is Winnie who is the chief target of the irony. She never speaks save to prepare her own damnation, and, without the usual rights being read, every word is taken down and used in evidence against her. 'He would go through fire for you,' she tells her husband, predicting what he will literally do.[84] She pesters Verloc to take the boy out with him, so much so that he can later say, with some justification, that, in so thrusting Stevie upon him, she is as much to blame for his death as Verloc himself. 'Don't dirty your clothes,' she warns Stevie as he goes off to be turned into blood and dirt.[85] She assures her husband that the boy won't stay lost for long as he leaves to be lost forever. 'Oh, yes. I can trust you,' she says to the husband who has so unforgivably betrayed her.[86] 'I'll have you laid up on my hands,' she chides, in wifely fashion, when she thinks, mistakenly, that he's coming down with a cold; but the reader remembers this when Verloc lies, the carving knife at right angles to his waistcoat, on the sofa in the parlour.[87]

Blood and dirt. Blood and dirt. She dreamily recites the words near the end of this book to which Conrad so unblushingly, impertinently, inadmissibly gave the subtitle 'A Simple Tale'.[88] Not even Conrad's prophetic genius could have anticipated just how chillingly apposite Winnie's incantation would be within three decades to the hideous operation of the death camps of Central Europe. But it is difficult to believe that the creator of so dark a text would have been greatly surprised.

Chapter 4

Wharton

'The world is too vile.'[1] The verdict is Lily Bart's, the hunted heroine of *The House of Mirth*, but it would be even more appropriate in the mouth of her successor, Ethan Frome. Just before her suicide, Lily surveys her wasted life and finds that 'the future stretched out before her grey, interminable and desolate'.[2] This is why, with no hint of Edith Wharton's disapproval, Lily decides to have done with it. Before she overdoses on chloral, she has an uplifting meeting with the working-class girl she once saved, now a happily married mother. Holding the baby (significantly a girl), Lily realizes, too late to save herself, that here is reality and that the society-world to which she had sacrificed her life is a sham. The meeting with the working-class mother tells Lily what she has lost, but it is a positive encounter for all that. She dies dreaming that the baby is sheltered in her arms. From childhood on, her blunder, inculcated by her bitter, dispossessed mother, had been to confuse world and society. She now understands, in her last hour of life, that not the world but society is vile. Lily is the victim, albeit complicitly, of a bad society, not a bad world. When, finally, she decides to kill herself, fearful that society may corrupt her completely, that to go on living will simply multiply her shame – 'how could she trust herself to keep her footing?'[3] – society can do nothing to prevent it.

One need only contrast Lily's fate with Ethan Frome's to see how much more pessimistic the later novel is. Ethan's world truly is vile; he is the victim of life itself. Nature is almost entirely absent from the artificial world of *The House of Mirth*, figuring mainly as a backcloth for country mansions and luxury yachts. Nature *is* in *Ethan Frome* present, oppressively and malignantly so, almost as actor, certainly as agent, in the catastrophe recounted. Starkfield is a Dantean landscape, cursed and forsaken, a wasteland of snow and ice as forbidding as anything in the *Inferno*. Lily's suicide is, paradoxically, a sign of hope, a stand against further debasement, almost a case of death before dishonour: there is a hint of victory in this death. There is, by contrast, nothing but degradation in the over-prolonged life of Ethan Frome. The worst thing about the book – in this it anticipates *Nineteen Eighty-Four* – is that the lovers survive. Ethan and Mattie, like Winston and Julia, are denied the option of death so liberatingly exercised by Lily Bart in modern New York as it was by Antony and Cleopatra in ancient Egypt.

'Life is the saddest thing there is, next to death.'[4] Edith Wharton reverses her own valuation in *Ethan Frome*: the life exhibited here is worse than the worst imaginable death. The lovers fail to die; the escape of suicide is disallowed – like Swift's Struldbruggs, Tennyson's Tithonus, Eliot's Sybil, they are condemned to life. The gift granted to Lily Bart is denied to Ethan Frome. Deciding that Lily shall die, Wharton provides the infallible chloral; deciding that Ethan and Mattie must live, she has them attempt suicide by the most improbable, unrealistic method. The odds are that, rather than be killed, they will be smashed and crippled – which is what Wharton wants. When we ask why, there is only one answer and we can find it in the mouth of Stevie Smith's sadistic emperor: death is too easy, too lenient, too obliging.[5] Begged by his tortured captives to put them out of their misery, he refuses on the ground that they are not yet friends enough for him to confer such a favour: more torment must be dealt out and endured before they will be allowed to die. Ethan, too, is kept alive against his will for a similar reason – Wharton's plans for him do not include a liberating death.

It is important to be clear that these plans are the author's; it is not the engineer-narrator who is responsible for Ethan's survival. The characters do not want to end up crippled: that is the author's preferred denouement. This is a crucially significant point. It is not surprising that a book so highly contrived in its construction – there is nothing natural or spontaneous about the manner of its telling – should be praised for its intricate artistic skill.[6] But it has all the prefabricated perfection of the lathe rather than the instinctive vitality of the organism. It is too planned – its purpose, its essence, precede its existence and this pre-existent purpose, clearer than in most twentieth-century fictions, is that of Vanni Fucci: here is a text unarguably designed, in every sense of the word, to make us grieve.

We have the author's own word as evidence. The chiselled art of *Ethan Frome* stands dutifully at the service of a deeply pessimistic view of life: the world is vile and the book exists to prove it. In *The House of Mirth* Lawrence Selden muses upon 'the subjection of husbands to their wives and ... the cruelty of women to their kind'.[7] *Ethan Frome* is a far more harrowing confirmation of the truth of these perceptions. If Lily Bart is a champion sufferer, Ethan Frome is the gold medallist. Lily is made aware of 'an inner destitution compared to which outward conditions dwindled into insignificance' and it would be unjust to ascribe her misery to a lack of means rather than a lack of meaning.[8] But Ethan's predicament is worse still: a world with a clear, unmistakable purpose, existing to make him suffer and wonderfully adapted to its purpose. Writing on *The House of Mirth*, Edith Wharton tells us that 'the problem was how to extract from such a subject the typical human significance which is the story-teller's reason for telling one story rather than another'.[9] This legitimizes our question: what was the typical human significance that caused Edith Wharton to choose the story she told in *Ethan Frome*? A number of possible resolutions contended for her approval. She could have had Ethan leave Zeena for Mattie in a tale of love triumphing over convention. Or Ethan could have stayed with his wife, duty prevailing over passion, as in *The Age of Innocence*. Or the lovers could have escaped the trap through romantically exalted suicide, their own preferred option. Why, these various solutions available to her, did she select the worst of all possible outcomes? What was the story-teller's motive for telling this, rather than any other story? To answer these questions will be the task of this chapter.

Ethan Frome (again we have the author's word for it) aims to reveal the world of New England as a vile place and to expose the folly of those who think otherwise. Its success in achieving these ends situates it as *Tendenzstück*, highly effective propaganda, rather than the flawlessly executed piece of art for art's sake that even those lukewarm about it so often concede it to be. An early reviewer describes it as 'a structure whose purpose is the infinite refinement of torture ... (its) victims lie stretched upon the rack for twenty years', yet caps this by calling it 'Mrs Wharton's most conspicuous achievement ... an impressive tragedy'.[10] It is surely a revealing insight into the spirit of our age that, in almost the same breath, sadism should be identified and its artistic presentation praised. *Ethan Frome* is, indeed, a highly elaborate work of art, but, far from being art for its own sake, this art is submissively at the command of a particular view of life. As we read, we become increasingly aware, like the master of the field sown with tares, that some enemy has done this. Everything is so clearly a consequence of deliberate authorial intervention. The text is so indisputably a planned thing, its cruelty intentionally crafted, all for the sake of that shocking introduction ('And this is Miss Mattie Silver') towards which it so implacably moves. It is as though the readers were challenged to match their own catastrophic imaginations against that of the author's. The grim finale lies in wait for the reader as the spiteful tree waits for the lovers and the impact is equally shattering. Just try to imagine the worst fate that might befall Ethan Frome and see how it compares with what actually happens: some such challenge lurks within the pages of Wharton's text.

This challenge explains the author's tipping of the scales toward the pessimistic side; and the straining to achieve this effect is most clearly discernible in the strange, not to say baffling, narrative structure – how can a story be told before it is known? – as well as in the inconsistent behaviour and motivation of its chief character at crucial points in the action. But even when these are remarked, they are misconstrued. We are told that *Ethan Frome* is an outstanding example of art for art's sake and that a proper appreciation means neglecting its harrowing content for its intricate technique.[11] The true centre of interest is not, despite appearances, the crippled farmer but the young engineer – it is *his* story and it is not primarily about what happened to three people many years ago, but about what is going on inside the narrator here and now. Strangely moved by his first sight of the maimed giant in the village square, the narrator probes his own hidden fears rather than Ethan's distant disaster. It is to control, to exorcize, these fears of the ruin he himself may become that the narrator, in an impossible telegnosis, invents a story from the long-gone past that he cannot possibly know – the events narrated are important only insofar as they throw light upon the narrator's own peculiar psychology.

The oddity of the book's construction makes the provenance of such theories easy to understand. It is tempting to solve the puzzle by declaring *Ethan Frome* to be a text, not about New England or its eponymous hero, but the narrator himself;

and this is especially seductive in an age when all stories have become suspect and when truth has surrendered to perspective. But it is a false solution. The problems, inconsistencies, contradictions, all undeniably present in the text, have in reality nothing to do with any supposed anxieties or apprehensions in the narrator; they are the unavoidable byproduct of Edith Wharton's resolve to present the story in a way calculated not just to devastate the New England optimists, but to show just how terrible a place the world really is. The difficulties are entirely of her own making and they reveal the price she is willing to pay to maximize the unsparing bleakness of her tale. Ethan Frome *is* the proper centre of attention and Edith Wharton, not the engineer, is the true narrator of the tale.

She tells the story as she does simply to make it more appalling than it would otherwise be. The content was always grim enough; how she tells it makes it more harrowing still. If the intention was to debunk the folksy apple-pie renderings of the roseate regionalists, then this all-important objective would have been undermined by diverting our attention to the alleged psychological anxieties of the young narrator. Either Swift wrote *Gulliver's Travels* to lash the world or he wrote it to expose the follies of its hero-gull. Either *The Turn of the Screw* is a genuine ghost story of voracious demons and imperilled children or it is a case study of a neurotic young woman, but not both. Similarly, either *Ethan Frome* is an exposé of the hitherto concealed evils of New England life or it is a private nightmare, the sinister fabrication of a troubled narrator who manipulates what he sees and hears into a dire warning of the hell that awaits him unless he avoids the fate of that other would-be engineer, his ruined double, his Winterman, Ethan Frome. If the New England presented is an objective vision, it is Edith Wharton's, and the story of Ethan is a true account, with the narrator simply a technical device for intensifying the horror. But if this New England is the narrator's invention, born of a need to protect himself against internal fears, then the vision is subjective, a completely conjectural version of what *might* have happened all those years ago. Far from being obliged to accept it as true, the reader has good reason to reject it as a mere product of the narrator's insecurities. There is no question of the Pilgrim's *inventing* hell; Dante has in Virgil a guide who not only confirms but explains what they both see. The engineer has no such assistance: he has to piece together what he sees all by himself, because his village informants, so he tells us, lack the capacity to enlighten him. Far from playing Virgil to his Dante, they cannot even match him, a newly arrived stranger, in perception and insight: he sees the hell that they miss. He must discover the truth for himself or live in the same state of incurious half-knowledge as Mrs Hale and Harmon Gow. The book records this discovery, but it follows that there can be, by the very nature of the case, no corroborating testimony, no external proof that what he says is true. Either it authenticates itself or it does not: either we accept the narrator's version as true or we undermine it by tracking it to its roots in his own psychological difficulties. Myself am hell: gifted with Satan's insight, the engineer would see that he has not discovered but created Ethan's story, that Starkfield is what it is because he has made it so.

But the book is about Ethan, not the narrator, and the account it renders of those long-distant events is a true one – it is what Edith Wharton wants us to believe, not simply the narrator's version, with all the insinuations of uncertainty and unreliability implicit in that word. The problem stems from the contrived narrative structure – how can the narrator possibly know what he relates? – but this structure was adopted, not to cast doubt upon the narrator's reliability, but to intensify the grimness of the tale. The first-time reader of *Ethan Frome* will readily acknowledge Edith Wharton's success in achieving this; only in retrospect will he recognize the price she had to pay.

It is the penalty for writing what Lionel Trilling described as a factitious and contrived book.[12] It *is* factitious, in a sense that Trilling perhaps never realized nor intended. Its fictive premise is that the story is told by a young engineer newly arrived in New England on business. Shortly after his arrival, he is intrigued by the sight of a twisted giant tortuously dragging himself from his buggy across the village square to the post office. From this initial stab of curiosity the story unfolds. Only once does Edith Wharton's control momentarily falter when she seems to forget who is telling the story. When we read that Ethan's 'dread was so strong that, man-like, he sought to postpone certainty', we feel that this is the female author rather than the male narrator speaking.[13] It is a unique lapse and, in any case, our worries about the oddity of the narrative have nothing to do with gender confusion. But it is revealing because it provokes the all-important question as to who is the real narrator, Edith Wharton or the engineer; and, inseparable from this, what is the real subject: what happened to Ethan Frome twenty-four years ago or what is happening to the engineer–narrator now?

The book surely bears its appropriate title. It might be objected that *The Secret Agent* is a misnomer, since Winnie, not her husband, is the central character, but no one could fault the accuracy of Wharton's title. It is, indisputably, Ethan's story. 'You've had a mean time, Ethan Frome,' remarks one of the characters and the book, in confirming this judgement, situates Ethan at its centre.[14] Toward the close another member of the chorus comments: 'then Ethan's face'd break your heart ... When I see that, I think it's *him* that suffers most.'[15] Ethan is the chief sufferer because it is his story. Hence the basic fallacy of those theses, focusing upon female tribulations and injustices, that place Mattie or Zeena at the centre. Mattie suffers even greater physical injuries than Ethan, but, as the narrator says, the story is less about physical than spiritual anguish and here Ethan's claim to preeminence is incontestable. Were it not that he so irresistibly captures the narrator's interest, there would be no story at all – like Wordsworth's Michael, he is at the heart of his story, and both begin in the same conditional mood. The poem is an invitation to future discovery:

If from the public way you turn your steps
Up the tumultuous brook of Green-head Ghyll[16]

you will come upon a heap of stones and you will learn not just that this is the unfinished sheepfold but how it comes to be in its present dilapidated condition. *Ethan Frome* begins on a day three years past when the narrator first sets eyes upon 'the most striking figure in Starkfield'. We enter upon a series of incremental conditionals. If you know Starkfield, you know the post office. If you know the post office, you will have seen a crippled giant drag himself across the square to its doors. If you have seen him, you *must* have asked who he was.

Struggle in Wordsworth becomes compulsion in Wharton. To learn Michael's story you have to labour up the steep ascent ('your feet must struggle'),[17] but the reward is great: a sad yet uplifting tale of love as the indomitable force in the universe, surviving loss, betrayal and disappointment. No such effort is required with Ethan: simply to see him is to be compelled to learn his story, but the 'reward' in this case is a wintry tale of love distorted, of life-long servitude and malice triumphant. 'Michael' presents a ruined sheepfold, *Ethan Frome* a ruined man. The poem looks back to 'Comus' ('thou canst not touch the freedom of my mind'), the triumph of the heart over adversity, the self over the world: life may destroy but cannot denature us. *Ethan Frome*, by contrast, looks forward to Room 101 and the deformation of man, the self overcome by the world. Starkfield, emerging from its winter siege like 'a starved garrison capitulating without quarter', is not just a place but a state of mind:[18] human life, too, is beaten down – neither the religious grace vouchsafed by St Paul nor the secular resources commanded by Wordsworth's Michael are available to Ethan Frome.

To begin with, the narrator is struck by the careless, powerful look of the man, despite the lameness checking each step like the jerk of a chain, and later he describes Ethan's profile against the background of snow as 'the bronze image of a hero'.[19] But this impression of heroic power is contradicted by the story about to unfold in which Ethan figures as a weakling (the name in Hebrew means, ironically, firmness and strength), helplessly swept along by the course of events, forever bested in his feeble attempts to stand up to his sickly, implacable wife. When he blusteringly countermands Zeena's instructions, Jotham Powell's contemptuous response shows all too plainly who the real decision-maker in the family is.[20] Ethan is a man forever subservient to others: father, mother, wife, lover. The faint opening hints of Milton's ruined archangel are misleading: Ethan is weak, a victim of circumstances, of the landscape and the winter (but for the season he might not have married Zeena at all) – the reverse of a man of action. His is that species of passive suffering so deplored by Matthew Arnold as subversive of real tragedy, suffering that 'finds no vent in action; in which a continuous state of mental distress is prolonged, unrelieved by incident, hope, or resistance; in which there is everything to be endured, nothing to be done'.[21] Arnold, who condemned this as morbid rather than tragic, would surely have identified *Ethan Frome* as a salient instance of what he was attacking.

It is the look of suffering on Ethan's face that first catches the narrator's attention. The narrator is surprised to learn that he is only 52. It is no exaggeration to say that

Ethan Frome is a story about a look on a man's face. It is the face of a soul in hell; Ethan is one of the damned. When Harmon Gow casually remarks that Ethan will probably live to 100 – the Fromes being so hardy a breed – the aghast narrator exclaims: 'Good God!', for he simultaneously sees Ethan's face 'as it probably looked when he thought himself alone', and the idea that the possessor of such a look should survive so long strikes him as appalling.[22] Kent's rebuke to Edgar for trying to keep the tortured Lear alive comes to mind. Where there's life there's hope: it is the abiding axiom of Western optimism. *Ethan Frome* repudiates it completely.

The book exists to explain the look on Ethan's face – a look truly there, not merely the fanciful construct of a troubled narrator in search of a convenient surrogate. Within the last four pages, Mrs Hale twice calls attention to what first attracted the narrator's interest; it is not just his fantasy. 'It's bad enough to see the two women sitting there – but his face, when he looks round that bare place, just kills me.'[23] Medusa has had a sex change and moved to New England. 'But sometimes the two of them get going at each other, and then Ethan's face'd break your heart.'[24] The mystery of this look – the unimaginative Mrs Hale ascribes it simply to a life of hardship and physical pain – enthrals the narrator from the start: '*That* man touch a hundred? He looks as if he was dead and in hell now!'[25]

Death and life, Starkfield and hell – what is the relationship between them in the text? The narrator's idiomatic expression about hell is as close to being literally true as a disbelieving age will allow. Why this is hell nor am I out of it: Ethan could as justly speak the words as Marlowe's devil.[26] Not for the first time in modern literature Dante is our best guide:

> That's why I shudder
> And always will when I see a frozen pond.[27]

The most chilling revelation in all of the *Inferno* is reserved for the penultimate canto, set in the frozen lake of Cocytus. A sinner trapped in the ice, identifying himself as Friar Alberigo, asks Dante for help before startlingly announcing that he does not know if he is alive or dead. His soul is in hell, but as to what has happened to his body on earth, he has no way of knowing.[28] He is in a part of hell unique in the sense that the soul can be sent there, leaving the body on earth, tenanted by a demon and to all appearances still alive. It is Ethan's situation, bodily alive and set to live to 100, while his soul, as the look on his face testifies, suffers the pangs of hell. The black joke with which the book ends – the only difference between the Fromes in the farm and the Fromes in the cemetery is that the women are quieter – is grimly pertinent to Ethan's case.[29] He would be better off dead, if only to escape the quarrelsome, querulous women.

> Here the weeping puts an end to weeping,
> and the grief that finds no outlet from the eyes
> turns inward to intensify the anguish.[30]

No more than the sinners of the frozen lake, unable to weep as the tears freeze on their eyes, can Ethan find relief in his iced-over anguish. 'But now it's all snowed under,' he tells the narrator, alluding to his deep-buried memories of Florida long since interred under too many Starkfield winters, but the words have an unmistakably deeper significance.[31] Ethan is as spiritually frozen in the ice as the souls met by Dante on his road through Cocytus.

Friar Alberigo identifies the shade behind him as Branca D'Oria, who arrived in Cocytus many years ago. It seems that Dante has not believed what he has been told about the separation of the damned soul from the living body, because he at once rejects this news as a lie. Branca D'Oria cannot be in hell

> for Branca D'Oria is not dead at all;
> he eats and drinks, he sleeps and wears out clothes.[32]

He was doing all of these things less than three days ago when Dante himself was still on earth. Alberigo is either deceived or a liar. It is, of course, Dante himself who is deceived in assuming that if you are doing these things you cannot be in hell – Ethan Frome could serve as yet another instance of Dante's mistake. The now enlightened Dante tells the people of Genoa that their fellow citizen, seen daily in the city, is really already in hell suffering the torments of the damned. The narrator of *Ethan Frome* communicates the same message: Ethan's body is in Starkfield but his soul is in hell – the look on his face is explained.

That attention has been diverted from this, the book's whole purpose, to the narrator's psychology is an understandable but misleading consequence of the book's peculiar construction. The problem is that the story is told before it is known. Some critics conclude, wrongly, that the story is therefore not what actually occurred, but is the narrator's fiction, his vision or revision of an undiscoverable past concocted to serve his own present needs. He does not know that Mattie Silver exists, has never even heard her name, yet he relates in minute detail a story in which she plays a crucial role. All he knows at the moment he crosses the Frome threshold is that Ethan had a bad accident twenty-four years ago, before which he had spent his life successively caring for his father, mother and wife. He knows that Ethan's wife is still alive because Ethan continues to pick up medicines for Mrs Zenobia Frome at the post office. He knows nothing, because he has been told nothing, about another woman. This is the position when the snowstorm forces Ethan to invite the narrator to spend the night at his farm. Behind a closed door he hears a woman's voice droning querulously – who else can it be but the hypochondriac wife? As Ethan opens the door and the men enter, the voice stops. The sentence trails off inconclusively before the narrator triumphantly declares that 'it was that night that I found the clue to Ethan Frome, and began to put together this vision of his story'.[33] Three lines of elliptical dots follow, bringing the framework introduction to a close.

This vision, this reconstruction of events long past, is now presented in a nine-chapter sequence that ends with the broken lovers lying together at the foot of the hill following the failed suicide pact. The symmetry is precise: just as the vision was preceded, so too it is followed, by three lines of dots. We are being visually persuaded that this vision, the middle section of the triptych, belongs to a different order of imaginative experience from the two flanking panels – not less but more true, in the Keatsian sense of the authenticity of the imagination, the dream that Adam awoke from to find it real.[34] It is surely not to discredit the vision that it is so elaborately and carefully framed.

Only a few seconds of ordinary time have elapsed between these two sets of ellipses enclosing the long central section, yet in this briefest of intervals the nine-chapter-long story is told. The narrator, entering the room, sees for the first time its two female occupants, with as yet no knowledge of their identities. One of the women is presumably Ethan's wife, but which one? And who is the other? Not until after the narrator has told the story does Ethan introduce his wife and Miss Mattie Silver, the first time her name has been mentioned outside of the 'vision' section. The puzzle is: how could the narrator know this name before he heard it? And he hasn't heard it before Ethan's introduction which comes *after* the narrator's story. In all literature there is no more chilling introduction and the shock comes from the startling contrast between the two Matties – the laughing, dancing girl of the vision and the nagging paralytic of the squalid kitchen. But if we had not already met the younger Mattie and heard the story, there would be no contrast to shock us.

A remarkable stroke of authorial legerdemain has been practised upon us, to the extent that we never think to ask until afterwards how the narrator can tell a story about a woman who does not as yet exist for him. 'I had the story, bit by bit, from various people';[35] but the disjointed snippets he gets from Harmon Gow and Mrs Hale scarcely constitute a story – events without explanations do not qualify. Even when Mrs Hale consents to speak, she is misleading: 'Yes, I knew them both ... it was awful.'[36] This is hardly informative and is, in fact, deceptive: there is nothing in 'them' to indicate Mattie's existence, let alone that she was the other victim of the crash that occurred so long ago. Had the narrator known this before entering the farmhouse kitchen, he would at once have recognized the paralytic as Mattie and the other woman as Zeena. The bombshell of the introduction would have lost all of its force. The devastating revelation that the querulous voice belongs, not to the sickly wife but to the loving girl ('she ain't a fretter'[37] was Ethan's verdict within the vision) is a direct consequence of our completely confounded expectations. The reader is most certainly surprised by the introduction; the narrator is either equally surprised or he has taken great pains to withhold from us a vital piece of information already in his possession. Were this the case, the reader would have every right to feel indignant at the trick played upon him.

The narrator, emulating Mrs Hale, tells us no more about what happened that night in the Frome farmhouse, but shifts immediately to his landlady's sense of relief at his safe return, having feared him lost in the storm. Whether through happiness at his safety or surprise at where he spent the night, her tongue is loosened and she becomes much more communicative about those distant events –

redundantly, since the narrator has already recounted the story in the most meticulous and intimate detail. She knows (Jotham Powell is the obvious informant) that Zeena had dismissed Mattie and that Ethan had taken Mattie to catch the train. But she confesses her puzzlement as to what the pair were doing coasting on the hill when they should have been at the station – why did the accident happen at all? She speaks, finally, to reveal not what she knows but what she doesn't know, for by this point the reader knows that there *was* no accident, but an abortive suicide pact. So the narrator has told us, but how does he know? It is inconceivable that any one of the trio at the farm, tight-lipped for so many years, should suddenly, on a confessional whim, blurt out to a complete stranger secrets for so long and so jealously shielded. How, then, does the narrator come to know the story he tells?

Confusion arises from the book's perverse structure, obscuring as it does Mrs Hale's role, however inadvertent, in helping the narrator to achieve his vision. Prior to his final conversation with her, he has already seen the three prisoners of the dismal room and cannot have failed to see a connection between the crippled man and the even more crippled woman – the clue, surely, that enables him to begin putting together (his own words) his vision of what really happened. We do not usually think of a vision as being cumulative or incremental, but this one clearly does not come in a flash or as a whole – it is assembled in parts and at intervals. A crucial contribution is what Mrs Hale, in a final burst of unwonted candour, tells him in the concluding scene – only the *trompe l'oeil* of the book's structure prevents us from seeing this at once.

Mrs Hale continues to visit the Fromes (she tells him), far less often than after the accident, but at least twice a year. It is bad enough to see the two women together, but far worse when Ethan is present. She recalls how Mattie Silver (it is Mrs Hale's first mention of the name and only its second outside of the vision section) was carried from the accident scene to the room where the narrator now lodges. Mrs Hale (then Ruth Varnum) stayed the whole night with the unconscious girl who was to have been her bridesmaid. Toward morning Mattie awoke, looked straight at her friend and said ... We never know because at this point Mrs Hale retreats into her customary reticence. But it must have been something dreadful, since it caused Mrs Hale to tell the shocked minister that she wished her friend had died. She can understand the minister's horror, but, as she says in her own defence, 'he wasn't with me that morning when she first came to ...'.[38] The implication is clear: even he, listening to Mattie, might have agreed that death was better than life. Mattie's words, tantalizingly never revealed, are the final stimulant to the narrator's imagination. 'She [Mrs Hale] had been waiting, through all the years, for some one who should see what she alone should see.'[39] The narrator presents himself as a kind of confessor come, after a quarter of a century, to bring relief to a woman longing, but not daring, to speak, keeping for all those years her dreadful knowledge to herself.

The clue of the paralyzed woman in the farmhouse kitchen, followed by Mrs Hale's disclosures, permit the completion of the vision – it is simply that the reader has been misled because of the inverted sequence: textually, the vision precedes the meeting with Mrs Hale, when, logically, it must have come after. The narrator feels at liberty, with the help of Mrs Hale's hints, to assemble his own detailed reconstruction of the distant tragedy, especially since no one else seems to know the full story. Zeena, remarks Mrs Hale, was no help in unravelling the mystery – Mrs Hale 'never knew what Zeena thought', and doesn't to this day: 'Nobody knows Zeena's thoughts.'[40] Thus challenged, the engineer supplies a version of events in which Zeena's thoughts are made pellucidly clear; and his interpretation of her behaviour is completely at odds with the admiring view taken by Mrs Hale. For her, Zeena's recovery after the accident seems miraculous as she gallantly forgets her own infirmities in order to care for the injured couple: 'she seemed to be raised up just when the call came to her'.[41] The word, with its explicit religious overtones, is ironical, given the vindictive, spiteful wife of the narrator's vision. Mrs Hale exalts her as a heroine, providentially given the grace to care for her stricken family, valorously shouldering her burden for twenty-four years. The narrator, by contrast, presents her as a kind of vampire, battening upon the miseries of others, flourishing in proportion as others decline. If she has a call, it is from hell, not heaven. She laughs only once in the text, at Ethan's dismay on learning of her decision to fire Mattie, maliciously pretending that what worries him is the expense, when she knows that it is the pain of losing Mattie that torments him.[42] For the first time, Ethan sees her with loathing as she truly is, not the listless creature of the seven-year marriage, but 'a mysterious alien presence, an evil energy secreted from the long years of silent brooding'.[43] This is not the description of a sick woman, but of a malevolent succubus whose very weakness is stronger than the strength of those who try in vain to oppose her.

Zeena *is* sick, but it is the sickness of malice, of Satan leering at the lovers in Eden, of Claggart contemplating Billy, and her only recourse, too, is the diabolic one of infecting others. She thrives when others suffer; her vitality is that of the parasite. Mrs Hale's Zeena is a self-sacrificing heroine, nobly giving shelter to a homeless paralyzed girl. The narrator supplies an altogether more sinister explanation. Mattie, healthy, is driven out by Zeena as a threat. Crippled, she is readmitted as a mortifying daily reminder to Ethan of what went so terribly amiss. Not Christian charity but satanic spite explains her actions.

Mrs Hale characteristically fails to see the horror of the situation: 'It's a pity though ... that they're all shut up there'n that one kitchen.'[44] But the problem goes far beyond mere overcrowding and pity is too mild a term for what's going on in the Frome household. One might as appropriately regret the fact that Ugolino and Ruggieri were unfortunately obliged to share the same hole in hell or that Sartre's trio of tormented tormentors in *Huis Clos* could not find alternative accommodation.[45] If the narrator's vision is true, the farmhouse is as hellish as anything in Dante or Sartre. Mrs Hale unwittingly supplies the materials for the narrator's insight, describing the hell she does not see. When she pauses, the narrator remains silent, 'plunged in the vision of what her words evoked'.[46] It is the word he used at the entrance to the room where for the first and only time he sees all of the three main actors together. Deciding what 'vision' means is crucial to a proper understanding of *Ethan Frome*.

The book's construction continues to puzzle and mislead. In the final scene the narrator is still trying to break down Mrs Hale's reserve. What he hopes to gain from this is unclear: what could she possibly tell him that he doesn't already know? Why search for a key to a room lying wide open? He already knows the story down to the very motions of the characters' souls as only God or an omniscient author could know it. There is only one explanation: the final conversation with Mrs Hale is presented as epilogue to the vision when it must have been its prologue. There are two time schemes in the novel, one presented, the other concealed – the sequence of events as the text presents them and the sequence of events as they must have occurred. In the first, the narrator comes to Starkfield, sees Ethan Frome, talks with Harmon Gow, lodges and talks with Mrs Hale, meets Ethan, and is taken home by him during the snowstorm, all of this rendered in the frame introduction. The narrator then delivers a nine-chapter vision of what happened twenty-four years ago, displaying total knowledge of the inmost thoughts and motivations of those involved and ending with the thoughts of Ethan as he lies broken at the foot of the hill after the failed suicide attempt. The vision ended, the book closes with the frame conclusion: the entry into the Frome kitchen, the introductions to the two women and the final meeting with Mrs Hale.

In reality, the final section must have preceded the vision, since without the final section there could be no vision. Only after seeing the prisoners in the kitchen and absorbing the information supplied by Mrs Hale is the narrator in a position to conceive his vision, fleshing it out in all the detail that only his imagination could supply. How, for example, to take one instance from many, could he possibly know about the incident of the broken pickle-dish?[47] Who else, apart from Ethan or Mattie or Zeena, could have told him this? Did Ethan – and who else but he could know? – tell the narrator how his heart leapt at the thought that his wife might have been murdered by intruders?[48] Is it likely that Ethan, after a Trappist lifetime, should have unburdened himself to a stranger to whom he had been compelled to give a night's lodging? In any case, Ethan does not know his own story as intimately as the narrator does, because the latter knows Zeena and Mattie from the inside in a way never achieved by Ethan; the narrator knows Ethan better than Ethan knows himself. This inexplicable telegnosis is the problem.

Admittedly, the narrators of *Tess* and *The Secret Agent* are similarly omniscient, equally conversant with their characters' inmost desires and hidden motivations. But these narrators are not simultaneously characters within the texts. The convention governing these texts is that of the omniscient narrator: the reader simply accepts that the narrator knows everything and never questions how. The convention that *should* govern *Ethan Frome* is that of the internal, hence fallible, narrator, a participant in the action and, as such, liable to the same limitations and errors of judgement as any other actor. This convention is flouted. The narrator is an oxymoron – an omniscient participant, an actor who is also God, knowing everything about his fellow characters. Harmon Gow and Mrs Hale look and do not see; the newcomer looks and the stubbornly secretive events of long ago surrender their meaning.

Or do they? A natural reaction is to reply that the narrator cannot possibly know what he relates, that his story is a fiction, a hypothetical reconstruction of what *might* have happened many years ago.[49] The vision is simply his speculations concerning mysteries that other people unquestioningly accept: why didn't Ethan leave Starkfield, what were Ethan and Mattie doing on the hill, why did Zeena take on as a lifetime charge a paralytic whom she was brutally ejecting before the accident? The narrator (so it is argued) makes up a story in which all the mysteries are resolved, all the contradictory data made coherent. There is only one problem: the story is completely unverifiable – the narrator tells us what he cannot know and we cannot check. He invents rather than reports; everything he says is uncertain and unreliable.

His readiness to create is obvious from the outset as he calls attention to the linguistic and psychological deficiencies of his informants. They are, as he sees it, incapable of doing justice to the story they tell and so he must make good the shortfall. He refers derisively to Harmon Gow as the 'village oracle' and signals his shortcomings as an explicator: 'Though Harmon Gow developed the tale as far as his mental and moral reach permitted there were perceptible gaps between his facts, and I had the sense that the deeper meaning of the story was in the gaps.'[50] What Harmon does supply is a striking phrase to stimulate the narrator's imagination: 'Guess he's been in Starkfield too many winters.'[51] Winters, not years. Winter becomes a key concept in the book, reminiscent of Dante's woeful realm of ice in the *Inferno*, a place of desolation and despair. The narrator's curiosity is engaged. Why has Ethan remained for too many winters in Starkfield? Why did he never try to escape? The narrator has as yet an insufficient stock of fact upon which to put together his vision: he has to see the paralyzed woman, has to hear what Ruth Varnum saw and heard after the accident, before he can do this. 'Most of the smart ones get away,' chuckles Harmon and the joke has sinister undertones.[52] Despite being superior to Harmon in sensibility and education, Mrs Hale is handicapped by 'an insurmountable reluctance' to speak of Ethan or his affairs – voluble on everything else, she is 'unexpectedly reticent' on the one subject her lodger burns to discuss.[53] In any case, the true meaning is in the gaps, in what is unsaid. The narrator assumes responsibility for the creative in-filling of these gaps.

Since the local people lack the linguistic resources to tell the story as it deserves, the narrator comes to the rescue with a second language, a remedial discourse aimed at redeeming the crippled articulation that would otherwise prevail. This higher recreation of the actors' thoughts and words is, the narrator claims, the only way to reveal the true significance of what occurred. From Ethan's mouth it would be an altogether poorer thing. 'By nature grave and inarticulate', Ethan would have found it as difficult to express himself as to drag his broken body across the square.[54] When we read that 'Frome's heart ... had swung out over a black void', we know that he himself would never thus have described his sense of depression at seeing Mattie laughing with young Dennis Eadie.[55] The eloquence required to raise the story above the level of a rustic misadventure is beyond him. The potential for banality – it is the standing danger of Wordsworthian subject-matter – is already threateningly present in such things as broken pickle-jars, henpecked husbands, wives with false teeth and hair curlers, and the story has to be protected against this vulnerability.

Nowhere is the story more negatively Wordsworthian than in its lack of confidence in the real language of men. Wordsworth trusts his peasants to speak in words that enhance their dignity. In *Ethan Frome* the story would be demeaned without the narrator's intervention – he speaks for Ethan because Ethan cannot speak for himself. This deficiency is sometimes comic: 'he groped for a dazzling phrase, and brought out in a growl of rapture: "Come along".'[56] More often it is pathetic: 'He looked at her hair and longed to touch it again, and to tell her that it smelt of the woods; but he had never learned to say such things.'[57] It is the tragedy of the mute inglorious Milton, of the tongue-tied man who feels deeply. 'He wanted to say: "We shall never be alone again like this". Instead, he reached down his tobacco-pouch from a shelf of the dresser, put it into his pocket and said: "I guess I can make it to be home for dinner".'[58] It is at once comic and sad. Think of how diminished and denuded the story would be if the narrator did not come to Ethan's assistance. 'Her face changed ... like a wheatfield under a summer breeze. It was intoxicating to find such magic in his clumsy words, and he longed to try new ways of using it.'[59] But his hopes of being an artist with words are as doomed as his youthful dream of becoming an engineer. The simile of the wheatfield is verbally beyond him. The narrator speaks Ethan's longings, reveals what would otherwise be hidden and missed – we might carelessly mistake Ethan for a dumb ox, an unfeeling boor, were it not for the narrator's intuitive excavation of the real man: 'And this is Mr Ethan Frome.'

'His vocabulary being limited':[60] the narrator is referring to Jotham Powell, but the remark is applicable to all the characters; without the narrator's words, Ethan would be a nonentity, of little consequence. 'Ethan, a moment earlier, had felt himself on the brink of eloquence; but the mention of Zeena had paralysed him.'[61] To be forever on the brink – this is his misfortune. How to make a tragic hero out of a near-speechless man: it is the same problem that Büchner faced in *Woyzeck* and we see Edith Wharton tackling it in her own very different way in *Ethan Frome*. 'He vainly struggled for expression.'[62] Ethan is a man lost for words and the narrator is his saviour; it is he who intuits 'the poignant contrast between his outer situation and inner needs' and who brings all the resources of his art to reconcile this breach.[63]

In doing so, he reveals himself as a literary artist of the highest skill. We do not know how good an engineer he is; we do know that he is a highly accomplished story-teller, suspiciously every bit as good as Edith Wharton herself. Starkfield is just a cold, wintry place; the narrator transforms it into a Dantean landscape, nightmarishly forbidding: 'starved apple-trees writhing over a hillside', outcroppings of slate nuzzling up through the snow like animals pushing out their noses to breathe.[64] We might be in Dante's wood of the suicides or in the marsh of the slothful, the bubbles rising to the surface. Riding in Frome's cart, the narrator sees him as 'part of the mute melancholy landscape, an incarnation of its frozen woe', imprisoned in his own spiritual winter as the countryside is in its physical one.[65] His poet's eye is confirmed by his description of 'the devoted village' surrounded by the white tents of February storms and harassed by the wild cavalry of March winds, emerging after its six-month siege like a starved garrison capitulating without quarter.[66] These are the insights of a poet, not an engineer. Especially potent is his gift for rendering the sinister, the ugly and the squalid, as in his description of the farmhouse 'in all its plaintive ugliness'.[67] He sees, too, the parallel between the stunted house and its maimed proprietor, even before he meets the broken-backed woman within.[68] The house becomes an image, a metonym, for its three dwellers, recalling Poe's achievement with the House of Usher.

Every page reveals a sovereignty over words: a farmhouse mute and cold as a gravestone, a kitchen with the deadly chill of a vault, the spectral rocking of an armchair, a dead cucumber vine dangling from a porch like the crêpe streamer tied to a door for death (was phallic impotence ever more evocatively conveyed?), the inexorable facts closing in like prison warders handcuffing a convict.[69] The Starkfield countryside as he describes it is as cursed as anything in Browning's 'Childe Roland' or Eliot's 'Waste Land': 'certain lonely farm-houses where stricken creatures pined' – could Edith Wharton herself have done better?[70] Only a master craftsman could take the unpromising datum of a miserably poor, badly crippled, inarticulate New England farmer, trapped in a squalid domestic tangle with a vindictive slattern of a wife and her lamed, nagging cousin and turn it into so memorably bleak a tale. Comparing the vulgarly commonplace predicament of a sordidly loveless marriage to 'serpents shooting venom', he makes it at once more elevated and horrific, domestic tragedy to rival *Othello* or *Agamemnon*.[71] The beauty of the world is also acknowledged in his art, as when he tells how 'the iron heavens seemed to melt and rain down sweetness', or that 'field and sky spoke to him with a deep and powerful persuasion . . . a silent ache, veiling with sadness the beauty that evoked it'.[72] But, predictably, in a text designed to expose the horror of life in New England, the emphasis is on the bleak and the ugly, and it is, above all, in the depiction of these that the narrator demonstrates his genius.

This very genius, this imaginative gift, is what causes some critics to insist that the story he tells is simply a sinister fabrication. Clearly, the narrator does not employ the term 'vision' in any sense prejudicial to the story he tells – vision, for him, does not mean deception or illusion (the vision of Keats's 'Lamia'), but rather inspired intuition (the vision of Adam's dream). More important, however, is to decide what Edith Wharton means in using the term. The present argument assumes that she stands foursquare behind her narrator, supporting him all the way in his imaginative retrieval of the ancient story. This, down to the broken pickle-dish, is what actually happened, even if we have only the narrator's unverifiable word for it. His word is good enough, for it is really Edith Wharton's own word: his story is her story. We go astray if we read *Ethan Frome* as what it seems to be, internal narrator fiction. Normally, this type of narrator, doubling as a character in the text, is to be doubted and distrusted, certainly not simply to be accepted as telling the straightforward truth – see, for example, Melville's Delano and James's governess. The reader must take nothing on trust, must scrutinize every opinion offered, every assertion made, every sentiment expressed, to uncover the truth behind the appearance, the *parti pris*, the hidden agenda. There is no truth, simply perspective: the story we have heard is, of necessity, partial, limited, subjective.

Contrast the very different convention of a story like *Billy Budd*, with its significant subtitle, 'An Inside Narrative'. At the end we are given a radically different version of the events just recounted, in which Billy is a black-hearted villain, deservedly hanged, while Claggart is the upright officer, heinously stabbed to death for doing his duty. The reader knows that this 'News from the Mediterranean' is utterly false because he has already heard the true story, the inside narrative.[73] The reader accepts this as self-evidently true, never stopping to ask how the narrator knows everything about the characters, including things that they do not even know themselves. He's omniscient and that's all there is to it. But he is not a character within the story.

The problem of *Ethan Frome* is that it conflates two incompatible narrative conventions, blending old-fashioned story-telling with modernist technique, and so leading to a contradiction: a character who is omniscient. The assumption of the argument being advanced here is that Edith Wharton has no wish to undermine the narrator's credibility or to caution us against accepting what he says as true. The story of what happened to Ethan Frome is meant to be as convincing as the story of what happened to Billy Budd; the narrator is both reliable and truthful – what reader finds Mrs Hale's portrait of the self-sacrificing Zeena more convincing than the narrator's view of the malicious hypochondriac? But, if this is true, it points to something odd in the relationship between the author and her internal narrator. If he speaks for her, carries the seal of her unqualified approval, tells the story exactly as she wants it to be accepted, then why is he needed at all? How does *Ethan Frome* benefit from being told by him rather than by the omniscient narrator employed in *The House of Mirth*? He would indeed be redundant but for one crucial function: he is needed to make a bad story worse. Grim enough if told in the customary straightforward way, it becomes more harrowing still in the dramatically unusual mode selected by Edith Wharton. To achieve this harrowing effect, to make the reader grieve, is the book's prime purpose; its strange, contradictory structure is a proof of just how far she was prepared to go to attain this objective.

In its deliberate aim to shock and depress, it perfectly exemplifies the spirit of Vanni Fucci at work in modern fiction. Critics have wondered at its harshness: 'She has marred her work with no motive we can discover . . . the end of *Ethan Frome* is something at which we cover the eyes.'[74] Others seek a solution in art: 'Art for art's sake is the one justification of a piece of work as perfect in technique as it is relentless in substance.'[75] But *Ethan Frome* is not simply an exercise in technical virtuosity and there *is* a discoverable motive behind the work, although it may not be to our liking. Trilling was mistaken when he accused *Ethan Frome* of being merely a grim tableau devoid of any moral significance.[76] It has a moral purpose, albeit of a perversely negative kind: it presents the world as a vile place and life as a bad business. Edmund Wilson points us in the right direction in remarking a Puritanism in Wharton, causing her to insist that we must face the unpleasant and the ugly – to shirk this is the worst sin in her morality.[77] In *Ethan Frome*, this Puritanism, this sense of evil triumphant, is carried to a nightmare extreme. It is a fallen, a damned, world, with no hope of salvation. Ethan is as lost as any soul in the *Inferno* and to participate in his story is to share in his condition. The text says to the reader what the dead in the graveyard say to Ethan: 'We never got away – how should you?'[78]

It is inadequate to explain this bitterness as no more than a corrective rebuke to the sentimental views of the New England regionalist writers – as well explain the Slough of Despond as Bunyan's attack upon those responsible for maintaining roads in Bedfordshire. *Ethan Frome* transcends the occasion that produced it. This tale of wasted lives, mangled bodies and twisted souls secretes a venom out of all proportion to its almost trivial provocation. We must look deeper and elsewhere to find a motive commensurate with such a work.

Not Mary Wilkins and Sarah Orne Jewett, but America itself as the home and champion of a particular view of life: this is the real target in *Ethan Frome*. In 1911 America was still officially committed to a creed of cheerful gentility, still content to find reflected in its literature those smiling aspects of life prescribed by Howells as the special domain of American writers.[79] In debunking the myth of the rural idyll, Wharton was among the first to challenge this orthodoxy. Her book, she claimed, was born of an informed realism, aiming 'to draw life as it really was'.[80] She is what Saul Bellow fifty years later called a reality instructor and the defining characteristic of such instruction is the unpleasantness of its curriculum – life is a cesspit; informed people know this, simpletons don't. In the real New England villages, as distinct from the apple-pie fabrications, 'insanity, incest, and slow mental and moral starvation were hidden away behind the paintless wooden housefronts'.[81] *Ethan Frome* was written to drag these horrors into the open for all to see, shattering the daydreams, not simply of the New England arcadians, but of all who followed Howells in proclaiming the goodness of life.

Even in 1911 her book found a welcome among those who were tired of Howells and cheerfulness and who proposed a counter-doctrine in which smiling was a synonym for false, grim for true. Its very starkness commended it to such a readership – people proud of their ability to face the worst and eager for an opportunity to do so. Praising the book, they simultaneously praised themselves, while disparaging those weaklings who lacked the strength to face the truth. Only the hero can confront truth: it is the central axiom of our modern sensibility. That Edith Wharton was drawn to this dark outlook can be seen in the title she chose for her first commercial success, *The House of Mirth*: 'Sorrow is better than laughter ... The heart of the wise is in the house of mourning; but the heart of fools is in the house of mirth.'[82] Ecclesiastes is as relevant in New England as in New York: the Frome farmhouse is no house of mirth. Those proud of their elitist capacity for pain, at least in fiction, found the ideal challenge in a text exhibiting the triumph of disease, spite and despair over health, love and hope – here, precisely, is the source of its perverse allure as an anti-gospel, a bringer of bad news. In *A Backward Glance*, Edith Wharton tells us 'that life as it really was in the derelict mountain villages of New England [was] utterly unlike that seen through the rose-coloured spectacles of my predecessors'.[83] But the book is not simply a rebuke to the Polyannas. When she refers in the introduction to 'my granite outcroppings', there is a hint of stony inhumanity, of Medusa in the New World, and when the narrator describes Starkfield as 'the devoted village', it is in the Miltonic sense of the word:

> Defaced, deflowered, and now to death devote![84]

What, one feels like asking Edith Wharton, was the colour of her own spectacles?

For we have to keep reminding ourselves that *Ethan Frome* is as much a fiction as the fictions it attacked and that only the assumptions of the age, posing as truths, make us forget this. Sunny equals false, bleak equals true: this is what Hazlitt, in a very different context, called the spirit of the age. J.S. Mill informs us that 'ages are no more infallible than individuals',[85] but try telling this to the age you live in. That *Ethan Frome* seems more convincing than the fiction it attacks simply indicates how much we are in thrall to the *Zeitgeist*.

In *Ethan Frome*, a work of fiction, fiction is attacked, not only externally in the daydreams of regionalist writers, but internally in the escapism of its central character. Ethan exhibits the same evasiveness that his creator condemned in Wilkins and Jewett, becoming in a sense their surrogate within the text. Alone with Mattie when Zeena is away, Ethan 'set his imagination adrift on the fiction that they had always spent their evenings thus and would always go on doing so'.[86] Adrift is the warning word, implying a wilful abandonment of control, exactly the kind of wish fulfilment against which Freud cautions. Pleasure is presented as a drug, its withdrawal symptoms commensurate with the joy so transiently experienced, and Edith Wharton, again like Freud, would have us live without opiates: 'The return to reality was as painful as the return to consciousness after taking an anaesthetic.'[87]

The assumption that reality must be unpleasant is characteristic of our age. 'But why retreat to so much misery?'[88] It is Virgil's first question to Dante and it makes clear the assumption of Dante's age that happiness is what we were born for, our natural condition, while misery is the perverse choice we self-injuriously make. *Ethan Frome* inverts Dante: we were born for grief; joy may come but does not stay. Ethan swings between deluded joy and bleak reality: 'I've been in a dream, and this is the only evening we'll ever have together.'[89] Yet the 'vision of what life at her side might be' is too enticing to resist – 'the sense of unreality overcame him once more, and he could not bring himself to believe that Mattie stood there for the last time before him'.[90] Trapped between an evanescent joy and an unavoidable anguish, the best wisdom he can muster is evasion: 'don't let's think about it, Matt!'[91] But this solves nothing and dreams are hotel rooms, not permanent homes. Ethan's vision of an idyllic future with the girl he loves clashes with the final hideous tableau of the hellish kitchen, and it is the latter fiction that prevails: happiness is delusion, misery is truth. It is a sign of our modern bias toward pessimism that we call our happy fictions fiction and our harsh fictions reality: all fictions are fiction but some are more fictional than others.

What surprises is that a text so unsparing as *Ethan Frome* should come from the same author who had Lawrence Selden protest in *The House of Mirth*: 'Why do we call our generous ideas illusions, and the mean ones truth?'[92] Bellow makes a similar complaint against the reality instructors of today. One senses an authorial voice reinforcing Selden's protest, yet *Ethan Frome* might serve as a training manual for the reality instructors. It not only communicates its bad news, but contrives to do so in the most devastating manner. It meditates the worst possible outcome – neither life with love nor death with dignity, but a living death – and then brings it about. There is to be no escape, neither to California nor the grave; wintry Starkfield destroys love as surely as Orwell's Room 101, acquiring new captives for its frozen fastness. Ethan's hopes of a second chance are simply another refinement of torture; he ends up chained for life to the two women and to a farm bankrupt in every sense of the word. No glimmer of hope, no iota of comfort, remains: if ever a text was written to prove the world vile, it is surely *Ethan Frome*.

Sickness and death predominate. Zeena, so repulsive that Ethan has to put out the light to lie down beside her, embodies the sickness of a sick land. Passing the cemetery, Ethan senses the hostility of the spiteful dead, resolved to keep the lovers immured in Starkfield: 'We never got away – how should you?'[93] It is the spirit of Vanni Fucci, damned and wanting company. But where Dante escapes, Ethan surrenders: 'I shall just go on living here till I join them.'[94] Even worse, in a striking apostasy, he defects to the enemy side. The sight of the little graveyard gives him a sense of continuity and stability. He decides to make the best of the hell to which he is doomed and allies himself with the dead to detain Mattie as they would detain him: 'I guess we'll never let you go, Mattie.'[95] It is a revealing switch from prisoner to jailer and the plural pronoun incriminatingly associates Ethan with the spiteful, possessive dead: 'some day she'll lie there beside me'.

There is something profoundly perverse in this as the pinnacle of a lover's expectations – to share, not a bed, but a grave with his beloved – and it shows how dominant death is, infecting love itself. Ethan 'let the vision possess him', for 'he was never so happy as when he abandoned himself to these dreams'.[96] But dreams and vision verge dangerously on necrophilia, the love that cannot be consummated in life finding relief in the grave. What other lover in fiction (Poe's madmen excluded) has indulged such fantasies? 'O, that my love were in my arms and I in my bed again!' This, the normal, healthy aspiration of lovers everywhere, is beyond the desires, let alone the capabilities, of Wharton's defeatist hero. Marvell's opportunist sees grave and bed as irreconcilable opposites:

> The grave's a fine and private place,
> But none, I think, do there embrace.[97]

Ethan, by contrast, links bed and grave together as the heart of the heart's desire. Yet even this consummation the book pitilessly denies him. In a text where love is so subservient to death, it is fitting that even the suicide pact should so badly miscarry. In the end Ethan gets neither bed nor grave.

The engineered contrivance of the conclusion, the all-too-perceptible authorial determination to make it happen, are evident in the shaky motivation of the protagonist. Ethan is presented as a man not ruthless or selfish enough to leave his loathsome wife for the woman he loves. He is too concerned about Zeena to abandon her with an unprofitable farm which she could never sell. He is, it is implied, too scrupulously honourable for his own good. He decides to kill himself instead. The text is curiously silent as to how Zeena will be better off with a suicide rather than a runaway. His reason for not leaving her is that she will be destitute without him, yet it is difficult to imagine a more final farewell than suicide. Ethan, who cannot leave Zeena in order to live, is quite ready to leave her in order to die. The one forsaking will surely be as hard for her as the other – what difference to her if he's in the cemetery or in California? She will be just as penniless and abandoned, whatever his destination.

An obvious answer would be that Ethan is a cowardly weakling, dressing up his irresolution as a meritorious submission to duty – for if duty to Zeena is the true barrier to leaving her, it would be just as telling against suicide. The narrator, however, presents Ethan as a victim, pathetic, even heroic, hopelessly trapped in an inescapable situation, with everything, his own good nature included, conspiring against him – like Lily Bart, he loses because his enemy is ruthless and he is not. He remains in Starkfield, sacrificing his own ambitions and desires, because he cannot walk out on his successive obligations to father, mother and wife. He abandons his plan to trick the Hales into advancing him money as dishonourable and deceptive.[98] The narrator could so easily present him as cowardly or unscrupulous, but does not do so. The failures of Ethan Frome and Lily Bart are presented by Edith Wharton to exemplify the tragic destiny of the superior soul in the modern world, the doom of the pure in heart as they struggle, handicapped by virtue, against ruthlessly unscrupulous foes like Zeena and Bertha Dorset.

But this only serves to highlight the problem of Ethan's confused motivation. Edith Wharton does not want us to ask why a man unwilling to leave his wife alone and helpless is nevertheless willing to kill himself, for this question exposes the factitiousness of the finale. What Edith Wharton has set her heart upon is her three main characters locked up for life in the infernal farm. Ethan must attempt the botched suicide so that he and Mattie can live on in maimed despair with the malicious Zeena; yet, on Ethan's own reasoning, suicide should be as unacceptable as walking out on his wife. But what this shows is not a self-deceiving character, but an author bent upon getting her own way, regardless of how she gets it. The farmhouse finale had been planned from the outset and Edith Wharton is prepared to have Ethan behave inconsistently, provided that this end is achieved.

It links her, disconcertingly, with the malicious wife. The 'miracle' of Zeena's recovery, so wondered at by Mrs Hale, is no mystery for the reader. Zeena recovers because the final resolution is precisely the one she, too, would have chosen. Even better than driving Mattie away is having her permanently helpless on the premises, a daily reminder to Ethan of his wife's triumph. 'The one pleasure left her was to inflict pain upon him.'[99] The book ends with sadism triumphant, Ethan forced to see and hear every day the nagging cripple he once preferred to his wife, while she looks on with satisfaction. If he still looks forward to the grave, it is no longer with Mattie as his partner. The end that so suits Zeena is the one that Edith Wharton painstakingly plots to bring about – Zeena owes her victory to her creator.

'The book to the making of which I brought the greatest joy and the fullest ease was *Ethan Frome*.'[100] This is why its harshest critics are, paradoxically, without meaning it, her warmest eulogists. An early reviewer declared how hard it is to forgive Mrs Wharton for the bitter remorselessness of *Ethan Frome*, 'for nowhere has she done anything more hopelessly endlessly grey with blank despair'.[101] She would have taken this as the highest compliment because it is what she set out to do.

Her joy in the making of the book is clear from its careful construction as well as the meticulous craftsmanship of its dramatic ironies. In irony of this kind we listen to a speaker who does not understand, as we do, the painful significance of what he says. There is always an element of cruel superiority in hearing someone unwittingly talk himself to destruction: Duncan praising the castle where he will be murdered, Oedipus vowing to discover the sinner who has brought a curse upon the city.

Ethan Frome provides repeated examples of the treachery of words, the facility with which they turn against us. Ethan is tormented by the thought of being 'a helpless spectator at Mattie's banishment', but separation is not the fate to fear – he will look on impotently at a far grimmer spectacle.[102] 'I guess things'll straighten out.'[103] We hear the commonplace consolation, aware, as Ethan cannot be, of the negatively prophetic import of his words, for we have seen the speaker drag his contorted body across the village square and we know that things will never straighten out for the broken pair. Omit the frame introduction and it is an innocently trite remark; knowing what we do, it is chilling. The reader almost wishes that Ethan would take a vow of silence, since almost every word he speaks comes back to haunt him. 'I want to be there when you're sick and when you're lonesome.'[104] The wish will be hideously granted. Mattie extols the benefits of a suicide pact, 'so't we'd never have to leave each other any more', and the sadist author who rules the world of *Ethan Frome* decides to play along.[105] Ethan tells Mattie that this is 'the last time we'll ever walk together', and again he speaks, unawares, the truth, for Mattie will never walk again with anyone.[106] It is impossible to miss the cunningly crafted cruelty of these phrases and much of the creative joy acknowledged by Edith Wharton flows from her sense of superiority to these poor innocents ignorantly speaking such terrible words.

The 'awful mean time' that is Ethan's lot is as much the product of authorial contrivance as of 'informed realism'. The malevolent wife has a zealous accomplice in the author – the wife drives him to suicide, the author mercilessly keeps him alive. The 'fragments torn from his heart' reveal an especially sadistic surgery and the surgeon is Edith Wharton herself.[107] Ethan senses the tree 'waiting for us: it seems to know'.[108] It knows more than they do as it waits in superior, sadistic knowledge, synecdochic of the book itself. 'If she'd ha' died, Ethan might have lived.'[109] But Mattie is not dead, Ethan is not truly alive, and Zeena lives the life she craves, finding solace in tormenting others. It is the worst of all possible resolutions in the worst of all possible worlds. It takes inspiration to conceive so malevolent a design, but it is an inspiration that comes from below, not from above.

Some have sought an explanation of the book's animus in the author's unhappy marriage: Ethan's predicament is a disguised version of her own; his frozen world of emotional starvation and frustrated longing is the same as that in which she finds herself trapped. But the book's despair is not simply private or personal or it would have long since lost its impact and appeal. Unease comes from a suspicion that it goes too far in its gratuitous presentation of suffering, transgressing the boundary that separates sadism from art. Tragedy is always precariously poised on the verge of cruelty; what saves it is that it has an intention beyond itself. The depiction of suffering for its own sake is artistically inadmissible; the author must always stand ready to justify the pain inflicted upon the characters – to fail here is to risk association with the Marquis de Sade. *Ethan Frome* is a text dangerously close to the borderline. Whatever the various interpretations – a perverted fairy-tale in which Snow White turns into the wicked queen or Hansel and Gretel stay trapped for life in the witch's cottage[110] – there is a general consensus that it reveals Edith Wharton as lacking, perhaps even despising, the vocabulary of happiness. Here is tragedy in the mode of pain, suffering that is bleak, unnecessary and contrived.

There is no benediction in *Ethan Frome*. Words, written or spoken, cannot save – 'What good'll writing do?' cries Ethan in anguish when Mattie suggests they should write to each other when they are apart.[111] But words *can* condemn and damn. *Ethan Frome* is a striking example of the word as malediction. Vanni Fucci could not have done worse: if we do not grieve here, we are unlikely to grieve anywhere.

Chapter 5

Kafka

Vanni Fucci uses words to wound – they are his only weapon – and his heirs take up language as an instrument of chastisement and retribution. Dostoyevsky's narrator breaks off his story just as it becomes a verbal equivalent of the knout. In O'Connor's 'Revelation', the messenger from God knocks unconscious with a heavy book the insufferable pharisee in the waiting room. Waugh's Tony Last must read Dickens aloud till he dies. Miss Lonelyhearts' agony stems directly from the harrowing letters he can neither answer nor ignore. In all of these texts, words have become instruments for inflicting pain upon those compelled to read, speak, hear or feel them. But the most startling example in all literature of the word as punishment, of the letter that literally kills, is, without doubt, Kafka's short story, 'In the Penal Settlement': here Vanni Fucci's punitive word is carried to unmatchable perfection.

As with every other Kafka text, a critical debate has accreted round this strangely fascinating tale, but my present purpose is to focus upon the two elements already identified in the *Inferno*: the wounding power of words and the harsh but justified punishment of the guilty. The story was originally included in a volume to which Kafka gave the general title *Strafen* (Punishments) and it could be used to support his assertion that de Sade is the true patron of our age.[1] The 'great change of fortune' referred to in the text is not simply the substitution of one victim for another, the defeated Officer setting the condemned man free and voluntarily taking his place under the harrow.[2] It is a parable about the transition from one moral system to another, from torture to liberalism, from an ethos of vengeful retribution to one of compassion. Obvious in the larger structural sense, this is also reinforced in the many detailed allusions to religion. The Officer reveres the Old Commandant's writings as sacred scriptures, washes his hands before unfolding them, and will not allow them to pass into the profane possession, however temporary, of the Explorer. The two fine handkerchiefs, given to the condemned man by the New Commandant's ladies, recall Veronica's gift of her veil to Christ on his road to Calvary. The machine is equipped with jets of water to wash away the blood so that the message being imprinted is not blurred; this linking of blood and water evokes once again the Crucifixion. The Officer speaks of the dying man's transfiguration and of the radiance of the justice. The inscription on the Old Commandant's grave – the Explorer, significantly, must kneel to read it – exhorts his followers to 'Have faith and wait!' for the promised resurrection.[3]

Although not published until 1919, it was written in 1914, just as Europe was about to set in motion a war that, once begun, seemed to operate with a machine-like autonomy, regardless of the wills of those who began as its masters and soon found themselves its servants. Kafka's seems an anti-historical tale, describing the opposite of what actually occurred. In his attempt to recruit the Explorer as an ally against the reforms of the New Commandant, the Officer uses the term 'European' as a synonym for humane – the New Commandant will (he warns) try to enlist him as an eminent European, that is, an opponent of torture (long since abolished in Europe) in his campaign against the old, expiring regime.[4] Today this strikes us as being either ironic or laughably incorrect; far from moving toward greater liberalism, Europe was about to descend into a time of savage irrationalism. But Kafka's story ends with a prophecy of the resurrection and return of the Old Commandant, the repossession of the colony by his followers, and, presumably, the creation of new and even more abominable torture machines. No one with any knowledge of Kafka will accuse him of being too optimistic and some readers find in his story a prophecy of the catastrophe about to befall Europe. Others go further by arguing that Kafka's imagination is itself catastrophic, more attuned to the discords of hell than to the music of heaven, and caution against too easily assuming that he is necessarily on the side of the humane Explorer against the fanatical Officer. Nothing but harbour works, complains the latter at what he sees as the facile technological optimism of the new dispensation and it is far from certain that Kafka disagrees.[5] The failure of secular hopes is precisely the major theme of his writing. 'Earthly hope must be killed; only then can one be saved by true hope.'[6] Kafka obeys Kierkegaard's imperative to kill hope; but he does not follow him in his leap of Faith, that act of philosophical suicide denounced by Camus. Kafka's critical response to the social programme of the Prague Zionists shows his deep distrust of all earthly schemes of renovation and there seems no reason to think he would have made an exception in favour of the New Commandant's harbour works.[7] However hideous the machinery of salvation – *Heilsmaschinerie* is Nietzsche's term for what he saw as the religious exploitation of suffering, the age-old nexus between pain and religion – one suspects that Kafka would have preferred it to a society bereft of religious values and obsessed with technology. Nothing but harbour works! The exasperation is surely not confined to the Officer and the worthlessness of works in contributing to salvation is a recurring theme in Kafka's writing. His major indictment of modern European society is that it has no place for the Jews, but can only demand from them conformity and assimilation – it is, preeminently, a religious conception of life that Europe so disastrously lacks.

'This morning, once again after a long time, I took pleasure in imagining that a knife was being turned in my heart.'[8] This quotation from Kafka's diary, recalling Joseph's execution at the end of *The Trial*, should make us pause before too easily assuming that Kafka sympathizes with the Explorer rather than the Officer. 'In the Penal Settlement' can plausibly be presented as an attack upon the purely hedonistic conception of man found deeply embedded in the liberal, secularistic tradition of our Western world, a conception that Kierkegaard claimed was true only of what he called the aesthetic stage of human development. For Nietzsche, too, the defeat of the ascetic ideals by the Enlightenment qualities of humanitarianism, utility, welfare, sentimentality was a decadence – only through the rehabilitation of suffering and the purification it brings could Europe recover its soul. Kafka can be seen as an important member of a tradition that includes Kierkegaard, Dostoyevsky and Nietzsche, all of them thinkers who repudiate what they see as the shallow optimism that controls the conception of human destiny at the retarded aesthetic stage. Kafka's works have been mistakenly read through the spectacles of that same superficial humanism criticized in the New Commandant and his sentimental ladies, when the truth is that the Explorer, Joseph K and the superfluous land surveyor of *The Castle* are not at all the unqualified heroes they are often assumed to be.

It has been argued that 'In the Penal Settlement' is disguised autobiography, an allegory of the author's own sufferings in the penitentiary of his family, and the 'Letter to His Father' could be cited in support.[9] But the family setting is too restrictive, for the Earth itself is the penal settlement, as Schopenhauer (whom Kafka read) informs us: 'As a reliable compass for orientating yourself in life, nothing is more useful than to accustom yourself to regard this world as a place of atonement, a sort of penal colony.'[10] We know how fascinated Camus was by Kafka and, if Schopenhauer supplies the key to 'In the Penal Settlement', we can see how Camus may have found there the hint for his own early masterpiece, *The Outsider*, with its revelation that the world is a death cell where all await, condemned, their turn for execution.

More pertinent to the present argument is the reading of the story as a parable of the sufferings of the artist. Writing is shown as both revelation and torture, an ecstatic agony in which the discoveries achieved are in proportion to the pangs experienced. As so often in Kafka, guilt and writing are inseparably related. The Officer is paradoxically forced to defend his own procedures even as he denies the right of self-defence to the accused man: 'I have been appointed judge in this penal settlement ... My guiding principle is this: Guilt is never to be doubted.'[11] Such a system is a prosecutor's paradise – as Joseph remarks in *The Trial*, all that is needed is an executioner, and, indeed, the Officer is simultaneously judge and executioner. When the Explorer expresses his surprise, first, that the condemned man has not been told the sentence, and, second, that he has not been allowed to defend himself against the charge, the Officer calmly justifies the system. There's 'no point in telling him. He'll learn it corporally, on his person'[12] – he'll get the point, literally. And if, as Schopenhauer says, in the penal colony of Earth existence itself is the crime, what possible defence could there be? Our state (says Kafka) is sinful, irrespective of guilt: *il n'y a pas d'innocents*.[13]

What alone saves this from being simply abhorrent is the heroic consistency of the Officer in upholding it. Having so inexorably judged others, he appoints the Explorer as *his* judge, committing himself in advance to whatever verdict is pronounced – if the Explorer rejects the old ways, then 'I and the Old Commandant will be done for'.[14] When the judgment does go against him, he unhesitatingly does to himself what he is so ready to do to others in a perverted variant of the familiar gospel exhortation.

The machine that dominates this story of nameless men, of men as functions (officer, explorer, soldier, condemned man), is a writing machine – both an instrument of torture and an image of the artist's sufferings. The machine tortures by writing its sentence (the pun is not available in German) upon and finally through the body of the guilty man. At the end, just before its final disintegration, the machine is no longer writing but simply jabbing – literature has become sheer sadism, butchery, with no words being written and no sentence, no meaning, being communicated. The self-immolating zealot is simply being shredded by the machine he has so devotedly served. The narrator of *Notes from Underground* refers to penal correction, but this is a figure of speech. In Kafka, the metaphor becomes literal fact: the Officer is literally flayed, minced. This actualization of the figurative is not unusual in Kafka: St Augustine writes that his soul has become a spider; Gregor Samsa in 'Metamorphosis' is literally transformed into an insect as he awakens not out of but into a nightmare. 'I will give my law in their bowels and I will write it in their hearts.' What is trope in Jeremiah becomes appallingly factual truth in 'In the Penal Settlement'. He who refuses to hear must feel: the familiar German adage is hideously embodied as Kafka transposes proverb into fact. An idiom is literalized: the condemned man will get the point in the flesh.

'I have no literary interests, but am made of literature. I am nothing else and cannot be anything else.'[15] The words are Kafka's about himself, but they might easily have been spoken by the condemned man under the harrow, as he is processed from a living body into a piece of writing (from which the blood is continually washed to keep it legible) before being thrown into the grave. That Kafka saw writing as linked to guilt and punishment is indisputable: 'God does not want me to write, but I must.'[16] A pen takes the place of the forbidden fruit. He pursues this idea in words that anticipate Adrian Leverkühn's diabolic commitment to music in Thomas Mann's *Doctor Faustus*: 'Writing is a delicious reward. For what? ... for services rendered to the devil.'[17] He excuses his failure to marry by saying that he would prove a faithless husband, nightly deserting the marriage bed in adulterous intercourse with his writing. Writing, in yet another metaphor, becomes a hunt during which prey and predator can bewilderingly exchange identities. In the 'Letter to His Father', the latter accuses the son of having long tormented him and declares: 'If I am not very much mistaken, you are preying upon me even now with this letter as such.'[18] Kafka's denunciation of his father so easily turns into self-denunciation. Who is the tormentor, who the victim? The executioner of 'In the Penal Settlement' becomes, in the most natural of transitions, the condemned man.

'I am Literature.'[19] Kafka's self-description is the condition to which the condemned man will be reduced when he becomes an imprinted corpse, a dead letter. The machine writes after it has been programmed by the Officer who inserts the message and sets the needles to produce the prescribed result. The message to be inscribed upon the body of the disobedient soldier is 'Honour Thy Superiors', an imperative delivered too late to be acted upon since he will die without the opportunity to obey it. The victim's body is a blank sheet to be written on and the machine has been fitted with a glass reflector, so that the sentence can be read and meditated upon while it is being inscribed. The condemned man is simultaneously text and reader – the assertion 'I am Literature' vividly exemplified, he himself the page that he struggles to the death to comprehend: understanding and death coincide, arrive together. The sinner is punished not for but by his sin, in a *contrapasso* of which Dante himself would have been proud.

When the Officer fails to win the Explorer's support for the future of the machine and the whole fading system of bloodshed and discipline – at one time, the Officer nostalgically recalls, acid was used to wash away the blood, but the old ways are being irresistibly eroded by the conquering sentimentalists[20] – he decides that the honourable course is to set the condemned man free and take his place under the harrow. Silently, significantly, the Explorer agrees and so the Officer reprogrammes the machine with a new imperative, 'Be Just', and goes under its needles to suffer the fate that every violator of the law deserves. It echoes the sinner's demand for death in Arnold's poem, 'The Sick King in Bokhara', but Kafka characteristically takes the principle to a macabre extreme. In the Christian mystery of redemption the Word is made flesh to be crucified for the forgiveness of sins. In Kafka, the flesh is to be made words in a sacrifice that turns out to be without meaning or redemption, in flat rebuttal of the zealot's promise. The whole purpose and justification of the punishment – the promised enlightenment through pain – is apparently withheld from the fervent believer. The Officer had earlier described with excited reverence this moment of illumination for the dying criminal: 'how quiet he grows at just about the sixth hour! Enlightenment comes to the most dull-witted . . . A moment that might tempt one to get under the Harrow with him . . . the man only begins to understand the inscription, he purses his mouth as if he were listening. You have seen how difficult it is to decipher the script with one's eyes; but our man deciphers it with his wounds. To be sure, that is a hard task; he needs six hours to accomplish it.'[21]

It is literally a case of someone dying to understand, an exegesis rather than an execution: who other than Kafka would describe the process of dying as a slow, agonizingly terminal hermeneutics? Ironically, even as the Officer exhorts the Explorer to concentrate and understand – 'Can you follow it? The Harrow is beginning to write' – he himself signally fails to understand that the Explorer has decided against him: 'Had it dawned on the officer at last? No, he still did not understand.'[22] 'In the Penal Settlement' is a text about incomprehension, despite its promise that radiant understanding comes to every condemned man at the sixth hour of his death struggle. With such an expectation, the Officer, the verdict having gone against him, confidently strips himself naked to go under the harrow for his own illumination: 'Then the time has come.'[23] It seems the more cruel that so zealous a believer is apparently cheated. Despite his aversion to the machine, the Explorer is sufficiently intrigued to search the face of the corpse for any hint of the promised enlightenment, but 'it was as it had been in life; no sign was visible of the promised redemption; what the others had found in the machine the officer had not found.'[24] The sacrifice has been offered but not, it seems, accepted.

This failure of the irrational Enlightenment is no ground for assuming that Kafka endorses the rational one, the good works programme espoused by the New Commandant. Only those implacably hostile to the Officer will withhold all sympathy; mere revulsion is checked by the way he accepts the logic of his own fierce justice in condemning himself to death. His faith in the illuminative power of the machine is total and there is pathos, if not tragedy, when it proves, at least in his case, a cheat. For he possesses the virtues as well as the vices of the zealot and he does not exempt himself from the law he implements and the Moloch he serves. The new mild doctrines he genuinely regards as a decadence. He displays a dignity that sets him above the boors he deals with, and the coarse antics of the latter, the vulgarities connected with the torn trousers, serve to highlight the austere severity of his own conduct, the tragic hero made more conspicuous by the buffoonery of the clowns.[25] The reprieved man is a vengeful, uncomprehending brute – delighted to exchange fates with the Officer, he rushes superfluously to strap him in, unable to grasp that the Officer, like Christ at Gethsemane, is choosing his crucifixion. The soldier is not against the machine, so long as someone else is in it. Neither is the Explorer, his humane aversion to the machine notwithstanding, shown as unarguably superior to the man whose fate he decides. He comes close to fleeing the scene in a far from heroic, near-ignominious fashion; our last sight is of him threatening to scourge his pursuers.

It is not a question of presenting the Officer as the story's unqualified hero, rather to show how the story resists any simple, straightforward explication. It is as much about the difficulty of deciphering texts as about the clash between different regimes and moralities. In a text itself taxing to understand, the problem of understanding written words is repeatedly emphasized. The condemned man would not understand his sentence were it not written upon his body – even then it needs six hours of agonizing scrutiny before enlightenment comes. The Officer invites the Explorer to read the sacred scriptures of the old dispensation; despite his wish to say something appreciative, all the Explorer sees is a labyrinth of criss-cross lines. Where the believer finds meaning, the outsider sees only chaos. The Officer puts the papers away, conceding that 'it's no calligraphy for school children. It needs to be studied closely.'[26] How *can* it be a simple script when it's not supposed to kill a man until he has struggled for many hours to understand it? Dying under the harrow is the reverse of euthanasia: the intention is to prolong the agony. But, in the end, we understand; even the Explorer himself (so the Officer assures him) would make the breakthrough if he concentrated hard enough under the enlightening needles. No text is finally irresistible, however costly to unlock. For the moment, however, the Explorer remains uncomprehending, unable to read the new imperative, 'Be

Just', but diplomatically prepared to take the Officer's word for it as the self-styled infallible custodian of the text.

Only the initiate can read and understand. What seems to the Explorer a mere mess of squiggles and curlicues is really, like the detailed commentaries of the Talmudists, the key to ultimate truth. That the labyrinth of lines also resembles Kafka's own manuscripts reinforces the argument of those who would persuade us to accept 'In the Penal Settlement' as autobiographical and confessional. Kafka certainly felt that his writing was at once a torture to himself and a mystification to others, no calligraphy for school children. The story ends with yet more writing to be deciphered and understood, as the Explorer kneels to read the inscription on the Old Commandant's grave: God is dead, but his word survives. Perhaps this promise of a return and a repossession is simply to be smiled at, as the patrons of the tea house smile while the Explorer kneels and reads. But the Explorer does not smile: this is no calligraphy for school children. A law supported by illegible, incomprehensible writings; an illiterate prisoner who can read only through his wounds; an outsider to whom these scriptures are simply meaningless scrawls – only the believer can access them and we either take his word or reject the whole thing as idiot sadism: all this may be absurd, but it is no laughing matter. True, the Officer warns us that these texts are difficult and 'need to be studied closely'[27] – in *The Trial*, the commercial traveller Block labours for a day over a single page[28] – and only the most slothful of wooers demands surrender at the first asking. Here, however, is the key problem for the reader of Kafka. Increasingly, dismayingly, he comes to suspect that, however long and devoted his courtship, however patiently he curbs his desire for speedy gratification, he will, in the end, like the man from the country in his lifelong wait outside the door of the Law, be left frustrated, denied and unassuaged.

The text, despite the Officer's fideist assurance, is, in the end, impenetrable, unsolvable, invincibly resistant – it has many questions but no answers and we leave it more baffled, not less. Yet to attack Kafka for not providing answers is like attacking a fireman for not starting fires. The whole purpose of his art is to leave us stranded and perplexed outside the door of the Law. No more than the Officer under the harrow will Kafka's reader find redemptive enlightenment after his struggle with the text, simply an even deeper darkness than that in which he set out. Reading Kafka is, and is meant to be, a humiliation – we do not, as in Dante, emerge to see the stars.

'In the Penal Settlement' shows the reader as victim in the most vividly horrific way, but this simply carries to a macabre extreme a readerly punishment prevalent through all his work. The reader resembles Sisyphus, with one significant difference. Sisyphus knows from the outset that he labours to no end, that the boulder will forever slip from his grasp and roll back down the hill. Camus converts this fate into an image of stoic fortitude: it is the conscious acceptance of pain without remedy and toil without end that makes Sisyphus the existentialist hero. Any hint of optimism would sabotage this: 'Where would his torture be, indeed, if at every step the hope of succeeding upheld him?'[29] Sisyphus courageously sticks with his unaccomplishable task.

Something of this is inherent in Kafka's recurrent theme of non-arrival, of failure to reach the goal. All of his stories are anti-*Märchen*, recording the hero's inability to conclude the quest: Joseph vainly seeking his day in court, the land surveyor's repeated failure to contact the castle, the man from the country derelict outside the door of the Law, the gangs of labourers toiling over an unbuildable wall, the truth-seeking dog pursuing investigations that cannot succeed – all modern recreations of Sisyphus, experiencing the same agony of inconclusion, the same frustration of never having done. But, unlike Sisyphus, they all set out with high hopes, always confident, sometimes arrogant; only after repeated failure do they come to know the futility of their labours and the unattainability of their goals. The plebeian builders of the great wall never, indeed, recognize the hopelessness of the task – it's the narrator who comes to realize this – but they work to the death accepting the official fraud that they will bring the work to completion. The others, through bitter experience, grow into Sisyphus, but this is not their initial expectation.

The reader, too, sets out confident that all that is puzzling and obscure will be made clear. From darkness to light, from Dante's dark wood to the serene, shining stars: this is the time-honoured passage in traditional fiction. Just as Joseph is confident that he can find the court and clear his name, just as K is confident that the muddle over his appointment will soon be put to rights, so the reader waits patiently for all to be resolved. Why Joseph has been arrested, what really has happened to Gregor Samsa, who is in the right in the penal settlement dispute – secure in his implicit contractual agreement with the author, the reader trustingly reads on, convinced that he will know all. Every text, however difficult, must finally give up its meaning; it is the faith of the Officer in the penal settlement – Sisyphus will push his rock to the summit.

With Kafka we encounter something startlingly unique and unnerving: a writer whose purpose is *not* to be understood, who seeks to leave the reader not less but more perplexed.[30] As in the cathedral where Joseph meets the prison chaplain, darkness grows as the text proceeds.[31] Yet there is no mystification in the language. The reader cannot console himself with the thought that it is dark because he has failed to see, that if only he tries harder, is more attentive, all will be revealed. The humiliation is in the very lucidity of his incomprehension – he understands that he will never understand. Some texts need to be read twice – *Tom Jones*, 'Benito Cereno' – before they can be seen true. But we can re-read *The Trial* and *The Castle* from now to the world's end and be no closer to a cognitive breakthrough: these boulders were never meant to reach the summit. Yet no more than Sisyphus can the reader walk away. *Wovon man nicht reden kann darüber muss man schweigen*: be silent about what is not discussable.[32] It is the ostensibly sensible advice of Wittgenstein and his false heirs, the logical positivists. Applying it to Kafka, we might say give up trying to understand the incomprehensible. It is a seductive recommendation since, not the interpretation, but the immediacy of the work is what matters. 'The scriptures are unalterable and the comments often enough merely express the commentator's bewilderment.'[33] What the priest says about the parable of the man from the country is pertinent to Kafka's work as a whole. 'The reflections they give rise to are endless and chance determines where one stops reflecting.'[34] Thus Olga crushes K's hopes of wresting from the letters sent by the castle authorities a final, unchallengeable meaning: there is none. So why not have done with futile, unending exegesis, why not forsake interpretation and simply read on without trying to elicit meaning? Stick with the boulder but forget about reaching the summit.

It is excellent advice but for one flaw: Kafka won't allow it. Nothing is more important than the work that cannot be concluded: recognizing this is what makes Camus's Sisyphus a hero. Kafka's reader can no more leave the unmasterable text than Sisyphus the unmasterable rock: walking away is not an option. 'The whole art of Kafka consists in forcing the reader to re-read' – the link with the condemned man in the penal settlement is obvious. Camus continues with reference to *The Castle*: 'Each chapter is a new frustration.'[35] The hero runs in circles, going nowhere as he desperately seeks to break the impasse. But the reader is equally frustrated, condemned to re-read without hope of release or illumination, as trapped in the text as the character in the story.

If the reader is Sisyphus, the author is Vanni Fucci, a sufferer communicating his own suffering. Canetti identifies humiliation as Kafka's chief theme: humiliated himself, he humiliates the reader. Here is where modern literature so decisively parts from the *Inferno*: there is no final return to see the stars and Kafka is the most remorseless promoter of darkness. When Auden called the twentieth century the century of Kafka, he was calling attention to this power to darken and perplex, an art to gladden the heart of Vanni Fucci. There *is* a path out of hell and the Pilgrim, with Virgil's help, will find it. But the only guides in Kafka (Titorelli in *The Trial*, the Superintendent in *The Castle*) are there to prevent escape. Dante knows that art alone, however exalted, cannot bring the Pilgrim to his final destination – Virgil takes him only so far before handing him over to Beatrice, to Grace. Kafka's characters have no Beatrice to point the way; grace is absent and art has defected to the darkness.

It is all the more difficult if the reader regards Kafka as a great writer who, once read, cannot be forgotten. 'He over whom Kafka's wheels have passed has lost forever any peace with the world.'[36] Many readers will endorse Adorno's tribute – for it *is* a tribute, since Adorno clearly regards this as a peace well lost – and Kafka's fascination for many is his unique gift for creating situations replete with potential meaning, construable in many different ways, each interpretation carrying its own conviction. This *Vieldeutigkeit*, multivalency, requires a reader as prepared as Kafka himself to make friends with his ignorance, to stand uncommitted before a number of possible readings, rather than impatiently seizing upon one while dismissing the rest. What Coleridge says is good advice for the fit reader of Kafka:

'I warn all Inquirers into this hard point to *wait* – not only not to plunge forward before the Word is *given* to them, but not even to paw the ground with impatience.'[37] In Kafka's case, the warning is even more severe, because the wait is forever, with meaning as tardy as Godot.

Not every reader has the patience. From the rich harvest of competing exegeses, it is tempting to pick one and bid relieved farewell to the rest. And the explanations – political, psychological, autobiographical, metaphysical, religious – crowd obligingly forward. The lure of a single, exclusive exegesis is that it solves Kafka, puts him in a convenient box, and liberates us from fretting interminably over his meaning. There are some who think that this boulder is really an inconsequential pebble, not worth pushing at all. Kafka is a writer of no account who simply caters to the emotions of helplessness and self-contempt characteristic of the fainéant intellectuals of his time. His stories are about weaklings for weaklings: those who admire him as artist or guide merely condemn themselves.[38]

In calling Kafka the voice of his age, Auden meant something very different. Auden's Kafka is spokesman for humanity, not the pet author of a clique of faint-hearted intellectuals. Kafka himself (despite asserting that his work embodied the negative spirit of the time) denied that it was tied to any one historical period: 'This Fear (*Angst*) is after all not my private fear although it is in fact all that and terrible – but it is as much the Fear of all faith since the beginning of time.'[39] Kafka is claiming, in effect, that every age is an age of Kafka if only it knew it – it is simply that in our own time this realization has forced its way to the forefront of consciousness. The world as Kafka depicts it has always existed; it is just that previous ages were more happily deluded.[40]

Hence the link with Kierkegaard before and Camus after. All three claim to be making statements applicable to life everywhere and in all times, but the truth of which has only been revealed as a result of the spiritual crisis of the modern era. All men, says Kierkegaard, are in despair without knowing it. All men, says Camus, are condemned without knowing it. All men, so Kafka seems to say, are guilty without knowing it. That we have to qualify in Kafka's case is characteristic of the provisionality that attaches itself to almost any statement concerning him, but no one will dispute the centrality of guilt in Kafka's work. He agrees, too, with Kierkegaard that anguish is the essential human condition; what separates them is Kafka's lack of faith – Kafka's Officer is not transfigured. Kafka accompanies Kierkegaard beyond the aesthetic stage of human development, but stops short of the ethico-religious stage. He splits from Camus by not assuming with him that men are the wronged victims of an absurd universe. Camus's presumption in favour of human innocence puts him on the side of Meursault, even of Caligula and Martha: humanity has had a raw deal. The one place Camus will not sit is with the prosecutor – the late, startling example of *The Fall* apart, Camus always appears for the defence. This cannot be said of Kafka. Despite certain misreadings of his work it is far from clear that Kafka is on the side of George Bendemann or Gregor Samsa or the Explorer of the penal settlement or Joseph K or the would-be land surveyor –

he is not even consistently on his own side in the 'Letter to My Father'. The demon of ambivalence that presides over these writings forbids the adoption of any single exclusive reading – Kafka criticism is cluttered with the bodies of those who have fallen into the trap of interpretative exclusivity. There is always another word: exegesis is never-ending. If all we had was 'Before the Law', the parable near the close of *The Trial*, the key passage and mythic core of the book, this alone would be proof of Kafka's refusal to come to an end, his resolved inconclusiveness. Joseph starts off convinced that the meaning is crystal clear and ends up baffled and unsure: 'The simple story had lost its clear outline.'[41] But his blunder was to believe that there *is* such a thing as a simple story. It is the error that the investigating dog condemns in his incurious companions: 'their belief that it is simple prevents further enquiry'.[42] It is the mistake about life that we all make and Kafka's mission is to expose it.

Further enquiry forever: this is his goal. He bars our route to the haven of illusory certitude, he will not let us rest easy in mistaken knowledge. This explains the paradoxical nature of the praise lavished upon him by his admirers. They celebrate him for destroying our peace of mind. Adorno's tribute tells us that it is better to be grieved by Kafka's truth than comforted by a lie. Malcolm Bradbury salutes his ability to 'raise life to the level of high anxiety', and the verb implies an advance upon the life we lazily experienced before Kafka alerted us to our predicament.[43] Erich Heller refers to his 'power to perplex', and the phrase opens a window upon the peculiar nature of the modern situation.[44] Other ages hailed the light-bringers, those who solved problems and answered questions – Pope's lines on Newton record this gratitude for illumination.[45] Our age, in striking contrast, exalts the one who bewilders and disconcerts; it is the destabilizer who receives our homage. We have grown suspicious of answers and dread being deceived. The light that Kafka brings is that darkness visible identified by Milton as the property of hell: it enables us to see all too clearly that we cannot, and never shall, see. 'Despair is my business.'[46] To which one can only respond that no one ever knew it better.

Others whose business was despair invariably have an antidote: St Paul's grace, Schopenhauer's detachment. What they take away with one hand, they lavishly restore with the other. Kafka's uniqueness is that he gives nothing back. 'Never before has absolute darkness been represented with so much clarity and the very madness of desperation with so much composure and sobriety.'[47] Other writers plunge us into darkness so that they may lead us to the light. Not so Kafka. This is why, in reference to Kafka, Martin Buber speaks of a Paulinism of the unredeemed, of grace eliminated in a demonic world.[48] No other writer is so remorseless. Joseph K dies 'like a dog', the Officer dies untransfigured with the iron spike piercing his forehead, Gregor Samsa is swept away with the rubbish, George Bendemann drops defeated from the bridge into the river, K begins all over his futile round of trying to establish his identity and cure his homeliness. The message will never reach you and the one who sent it is long since dead: never was the cruel absurdity of life so calmly presented as in the single paragraph of 'A Message from the Emperor'.[49]

Torture and malice are at the heart of things for Kafka, leading some to impute to him an almost gnostic loathing for life – he is a 'religious' writer, but it is a forbidding religion, a bleakly negative theology. For Judaism, says Buber, God is hidden and this is our hope and consolation: 'Truly thou art a God who hides himself, O God of Israel, Saviour!' For to be hidden is to be there. But in Kafka God is not hidden but totally absent: the result is the Law without the law-giver, sin without God, an unredeemable world. The messianic theme is present in Kafka, but in a bleakly negative way in a succession of inadequate or perverse saviour figures. Schopenhauer denied the need for a Last Judgement in a world that is already one and Kafka seems to agree: 'There is nothing more diabolical than what exists.'[50] The prison chaplain is untroubled when Joseph objects that one of his interpretations entails an opposition between truth and reality: 'It is not necessary to accept everything as true, one must only accept it as necessary.' Joseph is understandably dismayed: 'A melancholy conclusion ... it turns lying into a universal principle.'[51] There is a hidden God in Kafka's world, who is the deceiving demon of Descartes' nightmare: no other writer has been so successful in terrestrializing hell.

We see now the blunder of identifying Kafka with his protagonists and why readers were so prone to make it after 1945. It was tempting to read *The Trial* as the work of a Jewish writer prophesying the advent of the evil regime that the Allies had just defeated. Read thus, the text is about the persecution of an everyday hero who resists to the end the tyranny of an arbitrary, inscrutable court, even though he cannot overcome its total power of life and death. Those who had just overcome Hitler hailed Kafka as a forerunner in his commitment to individual freedom against despotic power and celebrated his book as a prophecy of the fight against Nazism. Yet this is surely a reading imported into the text rather than found there. To read *The Trial* as a prophecy of political terror is both simplistic and wrong. What has Joseph's strange arrest got to do with politics at all? Compare it to what happens to the heroes of *Darkness at Noon* or *Nineteen Eighty-Four*. Kafka's protagonist is neither imprisoned nor detained. He rings a bell to summon his warders and they offer to fetch him breakfast from a nearby restaurant. He is *invited* to attend the first court meeting on a given Sunday but only if it suits him. Hitler's or Stalin's secret police were never so deferentially obliging. The court proceedings are conducted in the attics of old tenements; Joseph has to negotiate slum houses and lines of washing to find the court. His complaint about his treatment by the warders leads to *their* being punished – this is no prophecy of the world of death camps and gulags. The Whipper ('I am here to whip people, and whip them I shall') is sometimes taken as a proto-Eichmann, type of the amoral bureaucrat, ready to perform any act, however cruel, when ordered to do so because he has no life apart from his bureaucratic function.[52] But Joseph is, in fact, the character closest to Eichmann, especially to the Eichmann of the Jerusalem trial, genuinely perplexed as to how anyone could regard him as guilty. To the end he denied guilt, protesting that he was an innocent man unjustly abducted by enemy agents for judicial murder in Israel. Believing you are innocent and being so are not the same thing, as we must never forget when reading Kafka.

Not the Whipper's but Joseph's behaviour is what is so strange and singular. Why doesn't he summon help in a public building instead of testily ordering his subordinates to clean out the room? Whatever is going on, it is not political; either no 'real' beating has taken place or he is an accomplice after the fact. Is the trial actually occurring in a court within his skull? *Gerichtshof* (law court) was Kafka's word to describe the events in the hotel room when he listened in silence to the evidence against him in relation to his treatment of his fiancée. In the 'Letter to His Father' he refers to 'this terrible trial pending between us and you', and speaks of himself as a sinner irrespective of guilt: 'one was so to speak already punished before one even knew that one had done something bad'.[53]

The Trial takes place in a private, not a political, world. It can only be presented as the heroically doomed resistance of a helpless individual against an unjust world by ignoring important elements in the text. Camus's Sisyphus resists, knowing that it's hopeless – that's why he's a hero. But Kafka's characters *do* hope. Joseph seeks a *Freibesprechung* (complete acquittal), although such a verdict has never been handed down. Titorelli and the priest both rebuke him for what they regard as his irresponsible optimism.[54] We take leave of the aspiring land surveyor at the end of the text still hoping, all the rebuffs notwithstanding, to penetrate the castle. Joseph admittedly collaborates at the close with his killers when he suddenly apprehends 'the futility of resistance' and decides that 'there would be nothing heroic in it were he to resist'.[55] But, whether culpably confident or fatalistically submissive, he is not to be turned into a hero victim of totalitarian tyranny without a considerable frogmarching of the text. Straight after the bizarre incident of the Whipper, he stands looking through the window, trying 'to pierce the darkness of the courtyard', but the metaphysical darkness of the text presents a far greater problem; the reader, too, is in the dark.[56]

Not pleasant, of course, but if Kafka wants the darkness, it is not for us to insist upon introducing an inappropriate light. We must respect the text (as the priest cautions Joseph), even if it means suppressing our instinctive feeling that there can be no guilt without awareness, no sin without prior knowledge and consent. How can Joseph be guilty without knowing his crime? To ask this question, however reasonable, guarantees a misreading of the text. We end up regarding him either as the innocent victim of a corrupt court or as a sick soul with whom normal, well-adjusted people have nothing to do other than, possibly, to pity his condition. *The Trial* becomes a modern reprise of what some readers still imagine *Gulliver's Travels* to be: a case study of a neurotic individual. The pity we may feel for Gulliver and Joseph K is predicated upon our own sense of superiority: why else should it concern us if these blunderers make such a mess of things?

After 1945 it was, predictably, the first interpretation that found favour – so many innocent millions had been persecuted and killed in Europe between 1933 and 1945. 'Someone must have been telling lies about Joseph K, for without having done anything wrong he was arrested one fine morning.'[57] What else, in those years, could this be taken for but a prophecy of the political terror to come? The problem is that this is disguised first person being mistakenly read as omniscient narrator: this is *not* the magisterial author speaking – it's how Joseph thinks and feels when the arrest so inexplicably occurs. We have no grounds whatsoever for assuming that Kafka agrees. Joseph is executed at the close still ignorant of the charge against him and in our rational world of light this, in itself, is enough to prove his innocence; in Kafka's dark world we cannot be so sure. Bunyan's Mr Badman dies the tranquil death of the just man, unaware of the damnation in store, but his creator knows he is guilty; and if bewildered indignation is proof of innocence, Eichmann should have been acquitted.[58] Nescience is a synonym for innocence only for those who insist that there can be no sin without foreknowledge. We cannot be certain that Kafka held this view. '"I don't know this law", said K.' The warder is unimpressed: '"So much the worse for you".'[59] Even in the liberal West, ignorance of the law has never been an acceptable defence. Certainly, there is a difference between Mr Badman and Eichmann, on the one hand, and Joseph on the other, in that *we* know that the former are guilty and are being justly punished, whereas we are as bemused as Joseph with regard to his alleged, unspecified offence. Accordingly, so runs the argument, we must support his protestations of innocence and side with him against a crazy or sadistic court. This assumes, however, that what we know determines guilt and innocence, and precludes the possibility of our *learning* our guilt, as Oedipus and the man under the harrow do, each proceeding from a false conviction of innocence to a realization of sin. We instinctively tend to dismiss as absurd what we do not understand. 'All knowledge, the totality of all questions and all answers, is contained in the dog.'[60] We easily note the arrogance of the canine claim, but contrive to overlook it when man replaces dog. Because we and Joseph do not understand the court does not necessarily mean, at least as far as Kafka is concerned, that the court is meaningless. True, this conclusion leaves us in the same bewildering darkness as Kafka's character, but perhaps that's where Kafka wants us to be.

It is impossible to read Kafka and miss this intention to humiliate, for Kafka is Swift's greatest inheritor in continuing this tradition of humiliated man. Swift specializes in physical humiliation – man as Yahoo, noisome pest – but Kafka's is an intellectual humiliation: man as dunce, almost comically divorced from reality. Swift mortifies us in the body, Kafka in the mind – man's folly in regarding himself as the land surveyor, the measurer of all things.

Uniquely outrageous is his insistence that truth and explanation are incompatible, that to explain is to mislead: this is what we must understand if we are not to misunderstand. Kierkegaard defines maturity as understanding that you cannot understand and Kafka agrees. But where Kierkegaard introduces his Knight of Faith into the cognitive desert, Kafka demands no *sacrificium intellectus*, no submission to authority; he simply leaves us stranded in our incomprehension. In 'Investigations of a Dog' he presents the predicament of the modern mind as it attempts unilaterally, from its own unaided resources, to make sense of its condition. It is an impossible project. The investigating dog sees the scattered food and the little dogs floating in air, but cannot see the human hands that scatter and hold.[61] To seek truth in a fragmented world with fragmentary means is a doomed enterprise – it is impossible to distinguish between what is 'out there' and our consciousness of it; the only reality we can know is within our skulls. The conservative narrator of 'The Great Wall of China' refrains from asking the questions that would destabilize everything, so preserving for his less perceptive fellow citizens the tradition that he has seen through. But although the gangs of labourers continue enthusiastically at their unachievable task, the reader has been taken into the narrator's bleak confidence: the wall cannot be completed.[62] We labour in vain and for those who know this the choice is simple: be a good leper and preserve others from contagion or communicate the disease to all and sundry. Kafka chooses through his writings to expose this intellectual disinheritance, to reveal man as no longer being cognitively at home in the world: between reason and reality there is irreparable slippage.

It follows that Kafka does not provide an interpretation of the world and that, in turn, criticism cannot provide an interpretation of his work: how can you interpret a non-interpretation? What he does disconcertingly provide is an image of how experience looks when *all* interpretations are called into doubt. This underlies the virtuoso parody of rabbinical and patristic exegesis in the parable 'Before the Law', the obvious delight in the stunning exhibition of interpretative ingenuity, the play of the mind in negating itself, as each new interpretation, like the priests of some primitive rite, emerges to slay its predecessor. Too many meanings can be even more subversive of meaning than none at all; like plants competing for the same space they end up choking each other. Logic, Nietzsche tells us, is 'the conceptual understanding of existence ... logic calms and gives confidence.'[63] We should not look for this logic in Kafka – calm and confidence are not the commodities he deals in.

The reader who finally concedes the impossibility of understanding the text shows, in that very surrender, that he truly understands Kafka – the paradox is unavoidable. For Kafka the world is essentially turmoil, something non-rational; only the gratuitousness of the event, of the *contingit*, can reveal the essential absurdity of things – whatever is rational is wrong. The message is that there is no message. This devastating news is imparted in the most impassive way; the contrast is between the cool discipline of the writing and the latent anguish of the content, the clarity of the questions posed and the breathtaking refusal to provide answers. It is the lucidity of our incomprehension that is so chastening, for there is no obscurity in the language. Sentence by sentence everything that is happening seems perfectly clear; it is the whole that defies understanding. The narrative is intelligible; the world to which it refers is crazy.

In *The Trial* all the materials requisite for a tragic or pathetic view of existence are to hand – Camus's suffering hero, Hardy's pitiable victim. Joseph instinctively sees the man from the country as the dupe of a capriciously cruel door-keeper, understandably enough since Joseph regards himself as the victim of a parallel persecution. But the priest can account for the facts in an altogether different, equally coherent way: the man from the country may not be blameless, the door-keeper may not be a sadistic tormentor, Joseph may not be the innocent victim of his own imagining. The principle of being innocent till proven guilty may be the cornerstone of our legal system, but that does not make it a reliable guide to Kafka's fiction. There is an entry in Kafka's diary that implies that Joseph *is* guilty, but it does not say of what. Bachelorhood, says Philip Rahv, for Joseph is simply Kafka in disguise.[64] Others propose selfishness, isolation, careerism, bureaucratization: the charges fall over themselves in their eagerness to secure assent. But all of this is wasted endeavour, precisely the mistake of over-precision that fails to grasp what makes Kafka so uniquely himself, for it is exactly here that the adjective Kafkaesque comes into its own. In *Crime and Punishment*, Raskolnikov, knowing his guilt, seeks his deserved retribution: the offence seeks the punishment. In *The Trial* it is the other way around. Joseph behaves as if he were guilty without knowing why – an innocent man would have ignored the 'arrest' and carried on uninterrupted with his everyday life. Instead, he pursues his persecutors, protesting his innocence, but, in reality, searching for the offence that will make sense of the punishment: the punishment seeks the offence. There is no evidence to suggest that Kafka regards his protagonists as suffering heroes or blameless victims. More plausibly, they can be seen as comic dupes, prey to their own conceits and presumptions, fabricating their worlds and then ridiculously aggrieved that the world 'out there' does not conform to their expectations. This is certainly wounding to our dearest humanist prejudices, but we have no right to assume that Kafka shares them.

Man, for Kafka, is neither tragic nor pathetic: he is comic, a joke. If Kafka's ancestor is Swift, the heir is Beckett. When he finished reading the first chapter of *The Trial* to a group of friends, everyone burst out laughing, with Kafka joining in. In his cinema version, Orson Welles emphasized the comedy of the story. It comes as no surprise to learn that in Philip Roth's imagined filmscript of *The Castle*, Groucho Marx is cast as the land surveyor, with Chico and Harpo his two assistants. Kundera tells us that 'the comic is inseparable from the essence of the Kafkan', that 'in the world of the Kafkan, the comic is not a counterpart to the tragic ... as in Shakespeare; it's not there to make the tragic more bearable by lightening the tone; it doesn't accompany the tragic, not at all, *it destroys it in the egg* and thus deprives the victims of the only consolation they could hope for; the consolation to be found in the (real or supposed) grandeur of tragedy.'[65] That Joseph K and the self-styled land surveyor regard themselves as the piteous victims of a heartless conspiracy proves nothing – so, too, does Malvolio, but Shakespeare thinks otherwise. Naturally, they do not enjoy their predicaments. K is a janitor in a school that has neither need nor accommodation for one. He is a superfluous, totally unnecessary man, wanted for nothing, and, however personally mortifying, this is an essentially comic situation. Vainly seeking official confirmation of his appointment as land surveyor, he receives a letter from a Castle dignitary commending him for work he hasn't done.[66] It highlights the ironic humour of his position, but it would be too much to expect *him* to laugh. Yet it's funny for all that.

The basic pattern in Kafka is comic: a crisis leads either to a sense of guilt or a condition of alienation expressing itself in the arrogant demands made by the hero. Although he gradually trims these demands, he never completely abandons them and this greater modesty results from his gradual discovery of an overarching system he can neither control nor understand. Man is not the measure of things. K assumes he is the land surveyor, but the Castle will not confirm it; initially assured of his place in the world, he finds himself houseless in existence. The mind's futile attempt to transcend its own condition – the claim to be the land surveyor – is as futile as the efforts of the investigating dog to comprehend its incomprehensible world. The dilemma is that the evidence of experience points to dimensions of experience which transcend experience. Kafka subverts the rational assumption that there is reciprocity and congruity between the world as intelligible entity and the inquiring mind; on the contrary, there is mismatch, slippage, discordance – reason is not the instrument with which to engage an irrational world. In *The Trial*, Titorelli tells Joseph that the court is completely impenetrable (*unzugänglich*) by argument, and the Castle proves equally resistant.[67]

In another's hands, it might be tragic; in Kafka's, it is high comedy, a prolonged *boutade*. A world in which nothing can be said that cannot be immediately contradicted is an essentially comic world. 'The right perception of any matter and a misunderstanding of the same matter do not exclude each other.'[68] Who, reading this for the first time, is not taken aback by the effrontery of the proposition? The instinctive reaction is to think that Kafka is joking, followed by puzzled indignation when we realize he is completely serious. Joseph, for whom it literally is a matter of life and death, is not to be blamed for missing the comedy in the priest's Wittgenstein-like dictum that 'it is not necessary to accept everything as true, one must only accept it as necessary'.[69] The victims of this comic outrage cannot be expected to see the comedy (Shylock, Malvolio, Alceste, etc.), but neither are they to be taken at their own valuation. Kundera speaks of the Kafka hero as 'trapped in the joke of his own life like a fish in a bowl; he doesn't find it funny . . . a joke is a joke only if you're outside the bowl; by contrast, the Kafkan takes us inside, into the guts of a joke, into the *horror of the comic*.'[70] We cannot avoid the oxymoron in speaking of the experience of reading Kafka.

The reader begins to worry that he, too, is inside the bowl, that the joke's on him and that he shares in the character's humiliation. The commercial traveller, Block, suffers the most graphic humiliation in *The Trial*. Exasperated at the hold-up in his case, Joseph decides to dismiss his advocate and act for himself. At the advocate's house he meets and has a long, instructive talk with the much more experienced commercial traveller. Joseph's case is a mere infant of six months, whereas Block, in his own phrase, has been carrying his burden for five years.[71] Joseph's initial contempt for his new acquaintance gives way to a desire to learn all he can from this highly experienced man. And he learns much: that when the men in the court offices stood up in what he thought was respect to him, it was really for the Attendant. They had instantly recognized Joseph, not merely as an accused, but as a guilty man – the look on his face made this clear. (The chapter anticipates Winston Smith in the Ministry of Love, with the link between Kafka's facial guilt and Orwell's facecrime so obvious as to scarce need remarking.) Joseph learns, too, that any combined action against the court is impossible: there can be no solidarity of the accused. As with death in Pascal, so with accusation in Kafka: it is a solitary fate, despite the number of the accused. He learns about hedge advocates, those lowest of lawyers to whom some accused, desperate for a judgment, turn in betrayal of their official representatives. He hears, significantly, for the first time of the possible existence of an elite of great advocates, guarantors of acquittal, but in the next breath is cautioned against believing in them or, at least, of hoping to gain access to them: 'Don't give way to that temptation ... I don't believe they can be got at.'[72] As such they are simply another source of torment – inaccessible saviours, redeemers who might as well not exist. Belief in acquittal, hope in salvation, *le sale espoir*: this, as the man from the country learns too late, is the greatest anguish of all. Yet, once mentioned, how can the great advocates be dismissed from mind? 'Unfortunately one can never quite forget about them, especially during the night' – that is, when we are most weak and vulnerable.[73]

Yet Block continues himself to dream of salvation and sleeps every night in the advocate's house lest he should miss it, for at any moment he may be summoned and he must be ready. Ready for what? To be rebuffed and humiliated, for, despite all his efforts, he never comes at the right time even when he responds instantaneously to the summons. He does all he can and it is worthless. Given the religious context, it seems to be a comment on the futility of works in the economy of salvation. Grace is what he needs, but *The Trial* is a text without grace: for Block, for the man from the country, for Joseph himself. Joseph's education is furthered as Block becomes a visual aid in a lesson pitilessly staged for Joseph's instruction. When the advocate learns that Joseph intends to dismiss him, he responds that he has treated Joseph too well ('I'd like to show you how other accused men are treated'[74]) and he summons Block to show Joseph what might so easily have been done to him. Here, above all, *The Trial* anticipates Orwell's Room 101, but Kafka's is a subtler depiction of humiliation and abasement, dispensing with the *grand guignol* elements of Orwell's presentation. Winston is felled by a blow from a truncheon; Block staggers at a simple question. This Ministry of Love has no need for rats. 'You were called for ... and yet you've come at the wrong time ... You always come at the wrong time.'[75] The sadistic cat-and-mouse treatment cannot be missed: this is a master impossible to please. Block is as ready as Winston to un-man himself, to crawl and lick the tormentor's hand, to offer up his new-found friend Joseph as a victim in his place. Outraged at what he judges to be an insult, not just to Block, but to mankind (all men fall in Block as they did in

Adam), Joseph tries to persuade him to act with decency, but is thwarted by the desperate man's determination to degrade himself – Block refuses to see that the advocate is abusing *him* simply to bring Joseph to heel.

What most depresses Joseph is the realization that this is all part of 'a well-rehearsed dialogue', a long-established ritual, that it has happened many times before and will happen many times in the future.[76] It is the equivalent of Orwell's boot in the face forever but, again, the greater subtlety of the earlier text is what catches attention. As in *Nineteen Eighty-Four*, the religious dimension is impossible to ignore. Leni's role in the ritual provides an opportunity to criticize the cult of the Virgin (although Leni is far from virginal), especially the Catholic doctrine of Mary as mediatrix of all grace. The spectacle of the greybeard businessman shamelessly begging a girl to intercede for him scandalizes Joseph, is 'humiliating even to an onlooker'.[77] The shame is not simply Block's but spills over to pollute us all: there *is* a solidarity, after all, but it is one of debasement. 'The client ceased to be a client and became the Advocate's dog.' Grovelling before the advocate, Block is treated like a cur when Leni warns him to behave by jerking on his collar. This exhibition of abasement links Kafka with Orwell's Ministry of Love. 'We shall squeeze you empty.'[78] O'Brien's promise to Winston could so easily apply to the abject commercial traveller.

So revolted is Joseph that he cannot bear to look at Block; it is the fear of becoming what nauseates him that makes him turn away. Indeed, if the aim was to bring Joseph back into line, then the lesson seems to have misfired. He is more opposed to the court than ever; the treatment of Block angers as well as sickens him. Hence the importance of the following chapter. No one can say if Kafka would have approved of the way in which his literary executor, Max Brod, arranged the chapter sequence of *The Trial*. What is indisputable is that the chapter following the humiliation of Block is exactly where it should be, depicting as it does the different but equally devastating humiliation of Joseph himself. 'In the Cathedral' makes transparent the links between Joseph, Block and the man from the country. If Block seems guilty of Mariolatry, Joseph is rebuked by the priest for relying too much on women. Block spends a whole day trying to understand the difficult scriptures (echoes of 'In the Penal Settlement') without getting past the first page; Joseph is ensnared by the priest in a labyrinthine exegesis, with as much hope as Sisyphus of reaching a conclusion. Block lives like a dog, Joseph dies like one. All three – Block, Joseph, the man from the country – consume their lives waiting for a judgment that never comes. Could there be a greater humiliation?

Joseph is humiliated in the mind, made to confess how little he knows, even about his own affairs. He goes – more accurately, is brought – to the cathedral to be shown how ignorant he is about himself and the world he lives in. Why is he in the cathedral at all? He believes, mistakenly as it turns out, that he is there to give a guided tour to an Italian, an important customer of Joseph's bank – a task assigned him at the last minute when the Manager, the original guide, capriciously changes his mind. Pressed for time, the Italian suggests to Joseph that they restrict the tour to the cathedral rather than the city and fixes a time for their meeting. The whole affair is haphazard from start to finish – Joseph would have been in the bank but for the Manager's sudden unexplained change of mind or in another part of the city but for the Italian's casually fortuitous proposal of the cathedral. So, at least, it seems to Joseph; his presence in the cathedral is simply the contingent conclusion of a series of accidents – he could so easily have been somewhere else.

It is not the view taken by Leni when he tells her by phone of his cathedral appointment. Surprised to begin with, she interrupts his attempted explanation with a magisterial summation of what's really going on: 'They're driving you hard.' It's a contagious insight, for he finds himself agreeing: 'Yes, they're driving me hard.'[79] What first appeared mere accident is now seen as careful design. 'They' – it is the same unspecified pronoun that Hemingway's stricken hero in *A Farewell to Arms* employs to convey his sense of the forces conspiring our destruction – have arranged the meeting in the cathedral, *not* with the expected Italian (he is simply the ruse to get Joseph there), but with the prison chaplain. Beneath what Joseph thinks is true is what really is true, beneath what he thinks he is doing is what is really being done: there is a destiny that shapes our ends, rough-hew them as we will – but it is a far more baffling business for Joseph than it is for Hamlet.

The priest tells Joseph that he has had him summoned, and, when Joseph understandably replies that he has come to meet an Italian, the priest brusquely dismisses this as irrelevant: what do Joseph's intentions have to do with it? 'They' want him in the cathedral and here he is. And where, for that matter, is the Italian if the visit really is for his sake? Joseph is made to recognize that he has no more dignity than a pawn on a board, but the pawn is at least spared the delusion of believing itself a free-choosing agent. Without this power to imagine and enact the future, to choose to act or abstain, human beings, says Spinoza, would simply be falling stones. Joseph has been battling to maintain a minimum degree of control over his life; shown that even this is a hoax, he capitulates and the chapter ends with him dully resigned to the execution that awaits him.

Nor is this the full measure of his humiliation; it is not simply that he does not manage his own life, neither does he understand it. This is the purpose of the priest's story of the man from the country: to replace certainty with doubt, knowledge with confusion, light with darkness. If Joseph (and the reader) can go astray in misunderstanding so apparently simple and straightforward a story, how can we ever be sure of being right? At first hearing, Joseph has no doubt as to what it means – it is, after all, his own story. The man from the country is another blameless victim of a cruel jest, of irrational persecution and moronic injustice. By the time the priest has spun his web of intricate exegesis (he only finishes because he has run out of time), Joseph wearily concedes that he is no longer sure of anything and will debate no more: how can you stand on ground that won't stay still? It is impossible to know for sure, yet just as impossible to live unperturbed in that state of suspense that Swift condemned as the life of a spider.[80] To need, yet be unable, to know: it's the nadir of cognitive degradation.

The lesson that miscarried in the episode with Block is successfully concluded in the meeting with the priest. Joseph is demoralized: his seeming choices are not really his at all, his reading of events is merely one among many, each as unstable as the next. Descartes found in the *cogito* the unchallengeable fact of personal identity; Kafka finds there the irrefutable conviction of personal insignificance, of nonentity: I think, but to what purpose? Better to be the pawn or the falling stone, for, if they are impotent, it is without knowing and being embarrassed by it.

Kafka is at once the most powerful of Vanni Fucci's heirs, yet scarcely an heir at all. There could be no more devastating account of human life than the one presented in his pages: here, if anywhere, is cause to grieve. But there is no sense of malice in Kafka's work, of an author out to get us as there is in Hardy, Conrad or Wharton. In the humiliations of Tess, Winnie, Ethan, one senses an authorial hostility toward character and reader alike: some enemy hath done this, as the lord of the field says. There is contrivance in the disposals of Tess, Winnie and Ethan – not so much the way things are as the way they are crafted to be. We sense nothing of this in Kafka.

It is not – the mistake of his early readers – that he lines up with his harassed protagonists or tries to enlist our sympathies for them: whatever compassion we find in these texts we have imported. This work occupies a space between tragedy and satire – man as victim or as fool – closer to the second, but lacking the punitive impulse native to satire. There is, rather, a disconcerting neutrality, a detachment, almost an indifference to the harrowing fates presented, whether it be George Bendemann, Gregor Samsa, the Officer in the penal settlement or Joseph K in *The Trial*. These texts reveal, on the surface, all the unemotional factuality of a police notebook: there is no heartache, sorrow, no relish or satisfaction at the events recorded. Below the surface it is another story. Precisely because it is not overt propaganda for any particular world-view, it is the more powerful in its impact. There is no manipulation or rigging of events to resent or react against. If we grieve, it is not because of the palpable intentions of the author.

Every reader of Kafka remarks on the fact that, however bizarre, considered in isolation, the discrete events may be, they assume a strangely compelling force when they come together as an integral whole: the individual details may tax belief, but the overall design commands our acceptance. We move from an initial remonstrative incredulity ('this is impossible') to a sense of unshakeable conviction ('this is true'). It is a tribute to Kafka's uncanny narrative power that at the close of these perplexing texts one should be reminded of Bishop Butler's words: 'Things and actions are what they are, and the consequences of them will be what they will be; why then should we desire to be deceived?'[81] Disagreeing with Kafka seems almost like quarrelling with nature.

Chapter 6

West

Since his death in a car crash in 1940, the transformation in Nathanael West's reputation has been arresting. Aged 37, the author of four neglected fictions, he was better known as a Hollywood script-writer and best known, to the obituarists, as the husband of his recently acquired actress wife. It was she, also killed in the crash, who claimed most of the newspaper attention; they misspelled his name and got the titles of his books wrong. Today, despite the early death and curtailed output, West is recognized as one of the most intriguingly original of modern writers, the key figure, for some critics, in linking the radicalism of the 1930s with that of the 1960s. Ignored in life, West has become, sixty years after his death, an indispensable interpreter of the modern world.

The parallel with Kafka is compelling. In the case of both men, events after their deaths were to justify what had been initially rejected as eccentricity, if not perverseness. 'I'm a comic writer and it seems impossible for me to handle any of the "big things" without seeming to laugh or at least smile.'[1] West's striking blend of savagery and fun, of insanity and laughter, scandalized many in the years of the Depression, of grave commitment to all the noble causes of the anti-Fascist front. He seemed deplorably irresponsible, displaying altogether too great an affection for what Swift (another great forerunner) had celebrated as *la bagatelle*. He was at once too apocalyptic and too facetious – an unforgivable combination to the sternly sober gladiators of the revolutionary left. He joked about despair; and to be a jesting mortician in America, land of mandatory optimism where happiness is a constitutional fiat, is to be guilty twice over.

What injured him then exalts him now. Precisely his scandalous intuition of the world's non-interpretability, his presentation of the absurdity of a fantastic reality (seen, not imagined), of life as a fractured picture: this is what makes him speak so pertinently to our condition.[2] Writing in 1975 Philip Roth grieved over the dilemma of the American writer, vainly trying to understand, describe and then *make credible* much of American reality.[3] America puts to shame the writer's meagre imagination and forever mocks his inventive talents: anything you can do, I can do better. The mind finally balks at the descent into unreality entailed in the depiction of everyday life. How to compose fiction in a society that is the most monstrous fiction of all? 'For a writer of fiction to feel that he does not really live in his own country ... must seem a serious occupational handicap. For what will his subject be?'[4]

Forty years earlier West supplied the answer. In his fiction alienation is grasped artistically, impotence turned to account – if you cannot destroy a hostile reality, you can always ridicule it. West boldly enters the American menagerie, engages the fantasy head-on. His books are about dreams and the dangers of disenchantment, the fantasy life of mass man and its revenges. West's abiding theme is how dreams become nightmare: political nightmare in *A Cool Million*, religious nightmare in *Miss Lonelyhearts*, aesthetic nightmare in *The Dream Life of Balso Snell*, cultural nightmare in *The Day of the Locust*. From Dr Johnson to Yeats the warning has rung out against destructive dreams, the imagination that preys upon life. Yeats reminds us of the dire consequences of feeding on fantasy: 'The heart's grown brutal from the fare.'[5] In *The Day of the Locust* (originally entitled *The Cheated*) West depicts the apocalyptic violence that must erupt when brute reality revenges itself on failed utopia, when promises that should never have been made and cannot be kept are ineluctably broken.

But *The Day of the Locust* is a book with a specifically American matrix dealing with a peculiarly American problem – though, admittedly, one increasingly available for export in our own century. Even yet, however, we lack, as Europeans, equivalents for the American Dream and for the cheated who go to California only to discover the fraud. *Miss Lonelyhearts*, by contrast, its New World setting notwithstanding, has an application as universal as the *Book of Job*, dealing not simply with the problem of suffering, but with the still more bafflingly intractable problem of innocent, inexplicable suffering. It is the suffering of those who, in Ivan Karamazov's phrase, have never eaten the apple that turns West's protagonist from a callous young careerist into a melancholy depressive, self-tormentingly brooding upon the broken bastards who write to him.[6] 'What did I do to deserve such a terrible fate?'[7] The anguished cry of Job in the mouth of a 16-year-old New York girl born without a nose destabilizes Miss Lonelyhearts' world. Not his own pain, but the infectious pain of others, especially of women and children, those innocent victims (see Keats and Dostoyevsky[8]): this is what pierces his heart and sets his feet on the *via dolorosa* of his own quasi-farcical martyrdom.

Pain is the link with Dante. From the moment he enters hell, the Pilgrim is aware of the omnipresence of pain. *La citta dolente*: the sorrowful, the aching city – it lives up to the name over its gate. Soon after entering, the Pilgrim hears the sound of inconsolable anguish and he turns, perplexed and frightened, to his guide for an answer:

> What souls are these so overwhelmed by grief?[9]

Even the explanation that the cries are from people getting their just deserts, that this is what they have chosen, fails to put Dante's mind at ease. For much of the *Inferno* a struggle is waging within Dante between a rational acknowledgement that all this is the will of God, hence, by definition, irreproachable, and a contrary emotional involvement in the surrounding suffering. The deeper the descent, the louder the lamentation; as the circles narrow, the grief increases. This 'strife with the pity' (most noticeable in the meeting with Francesca da Rimini and later with the deformed soothsayers) continues almost to the close, culminating in Ugolino's challenge:

> If you are not weeping now – do you ever weep?[10]

The *Inferno* is a terminal ward whose inmates go on dying forever.

West seems to have been as well acquainted with hell as his great predecessor. Auden declares that 'West's descriptions of Inferno have the authenticity of first-hand experience; he has certainly been there, and the reader has the uncomfortable feeling that his was not a short visit.'[11] *Miss Lonelyhearts* and *The Day of the Locust* are transplantations of hell to the New World, as the Devil in Hawthorne's 'Earth's Holocaust' so gleefully predicts.[12] Like the Pilgrim, Miss Lonelyhearts lives in a world of ubiquitous, incurable pain, in which he and everyone he meets are among the damned. The letters open his eyes to a world of unrelievable torment, always there but never previously noticed. He, too, like the Pilgrim, is stricken by the cries of the afflicted, although he *reads* rather than hears the pain. But he is far less fortunate than Dante, for, where the latter had Virgil and Beatrice to assist him, he has Shrike and Betty. Moreover, *his* Virgil is also doubling up as Vanni Fucci, relieving his own pain by making others suffer. Far from guiding him out of hell, Shrike wants to lead him deeper in.

Betty, too, is a poor substitute for Beatrice. The initial superficial resemblance masks profound differences. They seem to share an indifference, an imperviousness, to the suffering that overwhelms their menfolk. In answer to Virgil, Beatrice makes it plain that, in every sense of the word, she is 'above' the evil that encompasses them. She is immune to the pangs of hell, to the extent of feeling no sympathy with the sufferers:

> God gave me such a nature through His Grace,
> The torments you must bear cannot affect me.[13]

Domiciled among the blessed, she cannot even begin to imagine what it feels like to be in hell and has no wish to; spiritually, she remains in heaven even when she leaves it on this unique errand of mercy. She wants to save her admirer Dante, but there the solicitude ends; naturally (or supernaturally), she feels nothing for the ruined souls through whom his journey to salvation takes him. Let the damned stay damned, provided Dante escapes: it is exactly Betty's attitude toward the letter-writers and Miss Lonelyhearts. Hers is a pragmatically commonsensical view of hell: get out of it as quickly as you can, or, failing that, ignore it. The unforgivable folly is to ruin your own life because you cannot save another's, and this is the course that she sees her lover perversely pursuing. Where's the good of a pity that destroys the subject without helping the object?

One of the texts underlying *Miss Lonelyhearts* is Melville's short story, 'Bartleby'. At its close, after the death of the forlorn young scrivener, the narrator reports a rumour that Bartleby had once been a clerk in the Dead Letter Office in Washington. He seizes upon this as the clue to the nature of the strange character whose story he has just told. 'Dead letters! does it not sound like dead men?'[14] No job, he reflects, could have been more harmful to a man so peculiarly constituted – 'a man by nature and misfortune prone to a pallid hopelessness, can any business seem more fitted to heighten it than that of continually handling these dead letters'.[15] The letters had brought pardon for those who died in despair, hope for those who died unhoping, good tidings for those who died stifled by unrelieved calamities: 'On errands of life, these letters speed to death. Ah, Bartleby! Ah, humanity!'[16]

The rumour, if correct, may help to explain Bartleby's depression, his anhedonia, to use William James's term. People destroyed simply because of an unlucky miscarriage in the postal service – the thought might well thrust a temperamentally sad man toward total melancholia. Bartleby, then, may be a man destroyed by letters; Miss Lonelyhearts certainly is. But his predicament has no element of accident or mischance about it. *His* letters reach their proper destination to uncover problems without solution; their writers are damned by the very nature of things, not by some unlucky lapse in communication. 'Ah, humanity!' Miss Lonelyhearts deliberately echoes Melville's narrator as he muses upon the irremediable plight of those who appeal to him as saviour;[17] but, unlike Melville's narrator, he does not survive, and it is his failure to survive that is the key to the book's meaning.

The lawyer in 'Bartleby' survives by keeping compassion in check. No one has more penetratingly charted the process whereby pity turns into revulsion than Melville in his depiction of the pale young scrivener, 'forlornest of mankind', who first moves his employer to compassion before becoming a 'millstone', an 'intolerable incubus', someone to be, by whatever means, discarded.[18] The story is a chilling parable of how pity, driven to an unbearable extreme, turns into irritation, revulsion and repudiation. It shows how the law of kill or be killed applies to the gentlest of men in the most civilized of situations. The lawyer is neither cruel nor callous; he simply pleads that he had no choice.

> Up to a certain point the thought or sight of misery enlists our best affections; but, in certain special cases, beyond that point it does not. They err who assert that invariably this is owing to the inherent selfishness of the human heart. It rather proceeds from a certain hopelessness of remedying excessive and organic ill. To a sensitive being, pity is not seldom pain. And when at last it is perceived that such pity cannot lead to effectual succor, common sense bids the soul be rid of it. What I saw that morning persuaded me that the scrivener was the victim of innate and incurable disorder.[19]

This discovery precipitates the lawyer's resolve to separate forever from his incurable clerk. True, he cannot bring himself to 'commit his innocent pallor to the common jail' – but he is content to let others do it for him.[20] The 'wasted' scrivener is led off to die in prison; suffering is made invisible, taken where the sensitive lawyer need no longer see it. Out of sight, out of mind: it is the solution recommended by Betty to Miss Lonelyhearts. It is easy to condemn the lawyer's conduct, but in that case we must confront his question: what would *you* do if Bartleby turned up on your doorstep?

The problem of Bartleby and of Miss Lonelyhearts' letter-writers is closely linked to the current debate on euthanasia. We demand not only that we shall not suffer, but that the sufferings of others, when carried beyond a certain point, shall be removed from our gaze. In 'The Old Cumberland Beggar', Wordsworth speaks of the beggar's value to the community in providing an opportunity for the exercise of charity and compassion, but our modern definition of value is more strictly economic – there are no deformed beggars on our streets; we find the spectacle too painful.[21] The misery of others can so easily become offensive, even revolting. 'That dislike and even disgust should be felt by the fortunate for the unfortunate . . . is not only natural, but desirable for any society, whether of man or brute.'[22] Butler's unashamed brutality openly avows the secret sentiments of many who do not dare to speak them aloud. So, too, does Nietzsche's denunciation of Judaism, Christianity and socialism as dysgenic forces, promoting unhealth in their perniciously misplaced concern for society's losers. For Butler and Nietzsche alike, to feel pity for the misbegotten is simply to swell their ranks. Had West's text been available, they could have cited it in confirmation and Nietzsche would doubtless have asked what else we should expect from a book written by a Marxist Jew whose chief character is the son of a Christian preacher.

At bottom, Betty's attitude differs from that of the lawyer in 'Bartleby'. He is protecting himself against an injurious pity; when you try to help the damned you join their company – it is Virgil's warning to Dante in the meeting with the soothsayers, repeated when he rebukes the Pilgrim for becoming too obsessed with the business of hell:

> Keep right on looking,
> a little more, and I shall lose my patience.[23]

There is no evidence that Betty is similarly fending off a self-destructive pity; she simply has no time for unfortunate people, looks through them as though they were glass, and wonders why her lover cannot do likewise. It is, however, undeniable that he ruins himself by failing to take the prophylactic measures against pity adopted by Melville's lawyer. Had he put protective distance between himself and the incurables, he would have survived; but, overwhelmed by compassion, he goes down into hell and perishes, for, had it not been the Doyles who destroyed him, it would have been someone else. Beware of pity: he pays the price for not heeding the warning.

Initially, he takes the job of agony aunt for selfish, indeed callous, reasons. He wants promotion, it is a step up the journalistic ladder, and it will be an amusing experience, affording ample opportunity for mocking the fools who genuinely hope to solve their problems by writing to the papers. Miss Lonelyhearts prepares to have a successful and hilarious time; instead he is destroyed. Only two months into the job, already receiving up to thirty letters a day (Beatrice Fairfax, a well-known agony aunt mentioned in the text, got up to 1,400 letters a day), he is consumed with pity for the broken bastards, deprived and uneducated, who turn to him for help.[24] The fact that these appeals are laughably illiterate, vulgarly plebeian, grotesquely absurd, simply intensifies their pathos. It is one thing to listen to Lear or to Job raging magnificently against the injustice of the universe in tongues that match the enormity of their fates – complaint is inspired. But the inarticulate letter-writers are in humanity's basement, just sufficiently human to make what happens to them seem even more unjust: how unfair that people so poorly equipped to cope with their agonies should nevertheless be forced to endure them – their very protests make them ridiculous. But Miss Lonelyhearts soon ceases to see the joke. A man apparently on the verge of death staggers into a cinema to see a cretinous romantic film; a woman with a Brobdingnagian goitre rummages excitedly through a garbage-can to unearth a moronic love magazine.[25] It would be comic were it not sad. Even illiterate, inarticulate, unattractive people can suffer and dream. *The Day of the Locust* makes the position clear. 'It is hard to laugh at the need for beauty and romance, no matter how tasteless, even horrible, the results of that need are. But it is easy to sigh. Few things are sadder than the truly monstrous.'[26] And again: 'Feeling is of the heart and nerves and the crudeness of its expression has nothing to do with its intensity. Harry suffered as keenly as anyone, despite the theatricality of his groans and grimaces.'[27] Miss Lonelyhearts quickly learns the truth of Wordsworth's assertion that 'men who do not wear fine cloaths can feel deeply'.[28] And people who write illiterate letters can suffer the torments of hell. 'The letters were no longer funny.'[29] It dawns upon him that the agonies of the assembly line, vulgar and standardized, are still agonies – proletarians hurt the same as princes and if you prick them they, too, bleed. Pain is not the privilege of an elite – before West, Büchner with *Woyzeck* and Gogol with the anti-hero of *The Overcoat* had urged the same point. Raw suffering is like raw sewage: however nauseating, it must be treated. Betty holds her nose, averts her gaze and steps round it; Shrike wants to party on top of it. Miss Lonelyhearts deserves credit for recognizing the problem even if he does not know the solution.

In a process reversing Gulliver's, Miss Lonelyhearts moves from cynic to lover of humanity, especially in its most downcast, degraded condition. The great tragic sufferers from Oedipus to Lear have a prodigious inner strength with which to confront calamity: they elicit admiration more than pity. But West's victims have only Hollywood, cheap magazines and agony aunts to help them through their crucifixions – only a triumph of the sympathetic imagination enables us to see them as appropriate recipients of our compassion at all. We have to overcome a temptation to despise or ridicule before we can give them our pity.

So it is to his credit that Miss Lonelyhearts changes as he does. Whatever else is in dispute, it is undeniable that he is a better man after his change of heart than he was before it, just as Gulliver at the close is preferable to the crass, complacent jingoist who set out on the last voyage. Even if we find fault with their solutions, they deserve praise for identifying the problems. The young man cynically prepared to exploit other people's suffering to advance his own career is morally inferior to the zealot who, however mistakenly, wants to replace Christ as Redeemer. We need to hold this in mind in view of the strange detours that criticism of West's book have sometimes taken. The parallel misreadings of *Gulliver's Travels* may prove instructive. We sometimes encounter in Swift criticism a curious notion that if only we can somehow succeed in discrediting Gulliver (something not too taxing to accomplish) – show him as fool, madman, naif, incarnation of the very pride he attacks, and so on – then we have got to the heart of the book and solved the problem it propounds. Yet Swift said that he wrote his *Travels* to vex the world, not to target one single delinquent.[30] Even conceding Gulliver to be any or all of the things listed above, this leaves untouched, never mind unsolved, the problem of the odious little vermin, namely ourselves, condemned by the Giant King. Supposing Gulliver a fool or a madman does not, of itself, make the world a better place to live in – the Yahoo continues to exist whether or not Gulliver is in his senses. The idea that Swift wants us to excuse the world and condemn its accuser will not stand scrutiny, however often and devastatingly the critics demolish Gulliver.

There is a comparable fallacy in what might be described as the anti-religious interpretation of *Miss Lonelyhearts* – a strangely skewed and distorted reading which would have us believe that the chief aim of the text is to expose and attack religious mania.[31] On this view, the book indicts the folly of born-again religion, of the Christ complex, mocked by Shrike and deplored by Betty, that destroys the protagonist without bringing help to anyone else. West is showing that there is no place for the Christ vision in the modern world, that Miss Lonelyhearts is a sick Jesus freak, and that Christianity is pathological, intensifying the ills it fraudulently claims to cure. Miss Lonelyhearts (we are advised) *selects* the letters that permit him to indulge his messiah fantasies – which is why he ends up a victim of his own *mis*representation of the world.[32] The text is about the unmasking of the religious masquerade and its key purpose is to denounce the solacing fantasies of religion.

Undeniably, there is abundant evidence, within and without the text, to show that West had no confidence in religion as the answer to the ills of life. The glimpses given into the hero's experiences as boy and young man are disquieting and distasteful, in no sense complimentary to religion. The son of a Protestant minister, he remembers how shouting the name of Christ in his father's church triggered off an unhealthy, irresistible hysteria.[33] He recalls how he and some fellow students at college, all very drunk after a long night of theological argument, bought a lamb and destroyed the poor creature in a hideously botched sacrifice – he returned to the bloody scene later to smash in the dying animal's head with a stone and put it out of its misery.[34] It is a Lucretian insight: *tantum religio potuit suadere malorum*. His re-conversion after reading the letters shows religion in no better a light. He rants ridiculously to the totally uncomprehending Doyles about how the love of Christ can exalt their otherwise squalid lives – with what success can be seen from the fact that she sends her husband out for gin and tries to seduce Miss Lonelyhearts for the second time. At the end of the book he retreats into a state of beatific imbecility, in stupefied detachment from the world, and West is clearly being ironical when, using William James's phrase, he refers to Miss Lonelyhearts as having a religious experience.[35] No friend of religion or, more specifically, Christianity could be happy with the treatment it gets in the text. 'I read your column and like it very much.'[36] Shrike's mocking letter to Christ places him in the shady company of all the other charlatans who are busy exploiting the woes of ignorant, credulous people. Christ is, for Shrike, the Miss Lonelyhearts of Miss Lonelyhearts and, as such, equally bankrupt – if the one is a bogus messiah, what reason is there to trust the other?

Nevertheless, it remains true that West was strongly attracted to, even if he could not believe in, the Christ dream, and, in a paradoxical way, the book betrays a kind of inverted homage to the salvific power of religion: Christ would be the answer if only he were not a delusion. It is the same kind of baffling antinomy sometimes encountered in Kafka. But, in any case, the anti-religious reading of *Miss Lonelyhearts*, however valid, is irrelevant to the chief concern of the book. Whether the hero is a sick fanatic or Christianity a grotesque disease is not really the central issue – the text is not about the false answers (of which Christianity may well be one) to the mystery of suffering; it's about the insolubility of this mystery. Its subject is not misconceived faith but irremediable despair. Exposing religion as a false cure leaves intact the problem of the real disease. Any reading that identifies the hero's Christ complex as the core of the book has failed to take its measure. The text is not primarily an attack upon religion any more than upon all those other escapes – South Seas, pastoralism, hedonism, art, self-realization – conceived in the fertile mind of man. It presents a damned world and, as such, confirms St Paul's gloomy conditional: if Christ is not risen, we are the most miserable of men. St Paul's mistake is to believe that Christ *is* risen. 'If he could only believe in Christ . . . then everything would be simple and the letters extremely easy to answer.'[37] But since he cannot believe, the letters are unanswerable. *Miss Lonelyhearts* is not, of course, religious propaganda, but it lends itself all so easily to the propagandistic purposes of a dialectician like Pascal. Here is that world of man without God that Pascal so powerfully presents in order to prepare the reader for that acceptance of faith which is our only remedy. Anyone who reads *Miss Lonelyhearts* without prior prejudice will concede that its implicit message is that with Christ we are saved, without him lost; it concludes that our only hope of salvation is hopeless. Those eager to attack Miss Lonelyhearts as a fake messiah (which he is) would have us believe that faith is the disease, but this is not so: life is the disease and there is no cure, religion included.

There is no hint of Feuerbachian optimism, no confident atheism, in West; most certainly he does not regard religion as the answer to our distress, but just as surely he does not think that we solve our problems merely by getting rid of God: if the simple denial of God meant the abolition of misery, who would not be an atheist? West shows, in a demonstration unlikely to endear him to dogmatic atheists, that we can discard God without improving our condition in the slightest. The letters remain and, with them, the problems and these are as troubling for West (and should be for us) as they are for Miss Lonelyhearts. They do not vanish simply because Miss Lonelyhearts is a religious maniac. Marx's optimistic anticipation that the misery produced by a bad society will automatically be dispelled by a good one rests on two assumptions: that all misery is socially produced and that all misery can be cured. There is not the slightest evidence that West agrees.

The challenge of the text is not to catch out the protagonist; it is to answer the letters, since they are addressed to the reader as well as to Miss Lonelyhearts. Convicting him of error or worse – that can as easily be done with Miss Lonelyhearts as it can with Gulliver or the Modest Proposer. Exposing their wrong answers is one thing, providing the right answer is altogether different. We refuse (are meant to refuse) to accept cannibalism as the solution to Ireland's ills; but this leaves the really important task untackled: what do *we* propose instead? This holds good for Miss Lonelyhearts too. We are under no obligation to accept the proposals of Betty, Shrike or Miss Lonelyhearts, but, as with the lawyer and Bartleby, we are obliged to say what *we* would do. How will we answer the girl with no nose, the armless boy who wants to play the violin, and all the other broken bastards when they turn to us for advice? Granted that Miss Lonelyhearts has no answer: do we? The letters reveal a reality not to be evaded or ignored; and we, as readers of the book, are in exactly the same case as Miss Lonelyhearts as reader of the letters. The letters trouble him and the book should trouble us: it is our quandary too.

West himself does not know, any more than his protagonist, how to answer the letters: the challenge is to do better than just sympathize. Neither Betty nor Shrike, the two opposing spirits engaged in this Everyman-style struggle for the hero's soul, likes his solution, and each offers an alternative. Forget the damned and save yourself, urges Betty. Torment the damned and divert yourself, counsels Shrike. These are the three main solutions to the problem of suffering advanced in the text: self-destructive compassion; self-preserving detachment; and sadistic exploitation. The problem for the reader is that none of them is finally acceptable.

Despite the universality of the problem propounded by *Miss Lonelyhearts*, its relevance to life in every time and place, the text can best be apprehended within its own American matrix. The two great tutelary presences behind the text – there are unmistakable allusions to each of them – are Hermann Melville and William James. The importance of Bartleby for West's story has already been demonstrated, but Melville's chapter on the two sides of a tortoise in his essay on the Encantadas, as well as the dialectical debate on the same theme in 'The Try-Works' chapter of *Moby Dick*, also provide insights into the argument of *Miss Lonelyhearts*. The same is true of two chapters in James's *The Varieties of Religious Experience*, one on the Sick Soul, the other on the Religion of Healthy-Mindedness. Together, Melville and James will help us to understand better the issues raised by West's parable.

Melville's entire *oeuvre* is an attempt to wean the reader away from a one-eyed view of existence, exclusively single, whether optimistic or pessimistic – life is double, but not to the heirs of Polyphemus. In his Encantadas meditation he reminds us that there are two sides to a tortoise: a dark side when the creature is right side up and a light side made visible only when it rests upon its back. What we must do, if we would be comprehensively truthful, is not to insist bigotedly that the tortoise is either all-black or all-white, for it is both: truth is binary. 'Enjoy the bright, keep it up perpetually if you can, but be honest and don't deny the black.'[38] Equally, don't deny the bright either; acknowledge the doubleness of things.

Melville's application of this little lesson in natural history to the moral life is evident enough: life is neither evil nor good, but a blending of both. This is made even more explicit in 'The Try-Works' chapter of *Moby Dick*. Ishmael dozes off at the tiller and awakes disoriented to find himself staring into a scene from hell. Without realizing it, he has swung round to face the try-works where the ship's three harpooners are working in the fiery darkness with their spears, extracting oil from blubber. The truth suddenly dawns on him: those he mistook for devils are his own shipmates and, when morning comes, what looks like hell by night will be seen for what it really is – a part of the ship that is his home.

He at once draws the moral. If we look too long in the fire, we risk becoming fixated with evil and forgetting the existence of 'the glorious, golden, glad sun, the only true lamp – all others but liars!'[39] The world becomes hell to those hypnotized by its hellish elements. It is Virgil's rebuke to Dante when he chides him for being transfixed by the spectacle of evil. Nevertheless, evil is also real and, from celebrating the good, bright sun, Ishmael moves, Hegelian-style, to its antithesis in the desolate, godforsaken regions of the globe: Virginia's Dismal Swamp, Rome's accursed Campagna, wide Sahara, and the ocean itself, the dark side of this earth and accounting for two-thirds of its surface, none of which the blessed sun hides from view. Hell is not the whole world, but it is part of it and we should not forget this. Ishmael–Melville comes close to revealing that it is the dark side that really attracts him – not the golden sun but the gloomy ocean: 'So, therefore, that mortal man who hath more of joy than sorrow in him, that mortal man cannot be true – not true, or undeveloped ... the truest of all men was the Man of Sorrows.'[40] Brightness, joy, optimism: these, we infer, are the lightweights, the minority shareholders in the concern. Melville even expresses his contempt for the evasive optimist: 'But he who dodges hospitals and jails, and walks fast crossing graveyards, and would rather talk of operas than hell; calls Cowper, Young, Pascal, Rousseau, poor devils all of sick men'[41] – such a man is clearly being classed as a fugitive from reality. Compelled to choose, Melville would prefer the pessimist to the optimist – his stinging criticisms of what he sees as Emerson's naive innocence would lend support to this view. After all, when the tortoise is in its natural, normal position, nothing can be seen but black.

Nevertheless, Melville is not partisan in this preference, since his whole endeavour is to strike an equilibrium, maintain a dialectic, between the contending claims of the light and the dark – between an empty innocence, resolved to ignore the fact of evil, attributable either to immaturity or spiritual cowardice, and a fascination with evil so entrenched that it declines to know good at all. Melville wants us to shun these two extremes of childish optimism and of a pessimism at risk of becoming evil's accomplice.

These are the extremes contending for Miss Lonelyhearts' soul. Betty primly turns away from evil, skirts held high, and would have him follow. Shrike, in cynical collusion with darkness, wants his young colleague to join them. In *The Varieties of Religious Experience*, William James draws a distinction, in terms reminiscent of Melville's contraries, between what he calls the Sick Soul and the Religion of Healthy-Mindedness. That James was in West's mind when he wrote *Miss Lonelyhearts* we need not doubt. The title of the last chapter is an open plagiarism from James. Earlier in the text, sitting alone in a speakeasy, Miss Lonelyhearts overhears some colleagues discussing him and one remarks that 'even if he were to have a genuine religious experience, it would be personal and so meaningless, except to a psychologist'.[42] In the opening chapter of his book, James, disclaiming any expertise in theology, history of religion or anthropology, declared that it was as a psychologist that he was examining the different forms that the religious life took in different types of person.[43] In the wider context of West's book, we can see how profoundly un-American he is in challenging what James calls the Mind-cure movement as an important subdivision of the Religion of Healthy-Mindedness. James declares that 'the extremely practical turn of character of the American people has never been better shown than by the fact that this, their only decidedly original contribution to the systematic philosophy of life, should be so intimately knit up with concrete therapeutics.'[44] West was certainly no lover of traditional religion, but this new, specifically American religion provoked in him nothing but contempt. 'America has her own religions,' cries Shrike, in a mixture of serio-comic rebuke to a woman who wants to discuss Aquinas.[45] Indeed America has, and West despised above all the Mind-cure, New-Thought creed that James identified as so quintessentially American. It should not surprise us that in *Miss Lonelyhearts*, West provides striking dramatizations of the two contrasting psychological types referred to by James as the sick soul and the devotee of healthy-mindedness.

Betty is an extreme embodiment of the latter religion; in her, optimism has become pathological. She has no sympathy for what she regards as Miss Lonelyhearts' morbid preoccupation with the letters – he is simply making a fool of himself, being perversely obstinate, remaining in hell when he could so easily ascend to her apple-pie heaven. He *wants* to be sick, insisting on making a giant of his misery, when all the time evil is merely a superficial nuisance, easily put to rights by someone with a mind to do so. How can I be saved? It is the recurring cry of the spiritual hypochondriac. Luther, with his doctrine of justification by faith, Wesley, with his belief in acceptance of free grace, make the same reply: you are saved the instant you believe it.[46] The cure is in the mind. As soon as you stop worrying and relax, salvation comes; precisely the morbid fretting over salvation keeps it away. Salvation likes good cheer and equability; it will not come to stay with sullen, neurotic company.

Betty is a believer in the mind-cure: forget the letters and get well. To go on poring over them is to imitate those who are forever scanning their sick souls. Why ruin your life because you cannot save another's? As well put out your eyes because you cannot make the blind see. Nobody can save the damned. She adamantly declines to acknowledge the existence of evil. There are no moral problems, only medical ones, nothing that will not yield to the intake of aspirin and hot soup. There is only sickness, brought on in Miss Lonelyhearts' case by too long an immersion in the stressful city. She persuades him to take a trip to the countryside, confident (it is the American assurance) that geographical relocation and a change of air will scatter all his troubles, and he agrees to go, even as he laughs at her faith in 'the curative power of animals'.[47] The excursion begins well enough but ends in failure, as she might have been warned had she read James: 'No alteration of the environment' can heal the Sick Soul.[48] The patients in a terminal ward do not recover simply by switching beds. Baudelaire knew this, too, as his poem 'Anywhere Out of This World' demonstrates. The poet suggests to his soul various escape routes: Lisbon, Holland, Batavia. His soul explosively replies: *'N'importe ou! pourvu que ce soit hors de ce monde*!'[49] It turns out to be the only escape available to the trapped protagonist of West's tale.

But if Betty can easily forget the letter-writers – Betty the Buddha, with her smug smile, serenely above the woes of the world[50] – Miss Lonelyhearts lacks the gift of this convenient amnesia. Betty keeps herself *virgo intacta* in every sense (it comes as no surprise to learn that she is virgin physically to complement her spiritual immaturity) by screening off unpleasant reality and by arbitrarily limiting experience.[51] Miss Lonelyhearts has every right to regard his own confusion as significant in contrast to her carefully censored order. She will not understand that the soul can have its ailments as can the body, that aspirin is no more helpful to Miss Lonelyhearts than it would have been to Lady Macbeth. Cans't thou not minister to a mind diseased? Betty considers it a disgrace to possess such a mind at all. Miss Lonelyhearts, knowing that his sickness is psychosomatic, a ruse of the body to relieve pressure on the soul, feels angry with himself for ever having considered marriage to Betty as the answer to his problems. However grim the hell in which he finds himself stranded, it is preferable to the bland mendacities, the dumbed-down world of advertising agency, children, picket fence and gingham curtains, that Betty would have him embrace: better to be damned than saved by this.

Betty's salvation comes at a price: regression to adolescence or even childhood. She straightens lives as she straightens ties, like any mother sending her boy to school. The regression becomes even more pronounced when she feeds the submissive invalid with a spoon: unless you become a little child, you cannot enter into Betty's kingdom. It is, revealingly, just when he is trying to exclude the horrors of the letters that she comes into his mind, and this calls attention to what she is: a shield against reality.[52] He who appeals to experience renounces faith – so says Feuerbach.[53] But he who appeals to Betty renounces experience, as West plainly shows. It is better, she declares, to go blind and deaf into the heaven of married domesticity than to go lynx-eyed and prick-eared into the hell of the letters – Miss Lonelyhearts decides otherwise. Go west: it was Horatio Alger's advice to the ambitious young American and West claimed to have obeyed it by changing his name from Weinstein.[54] Betty's is a different command: go back, either to infancy or adolescence. In the chapter called 'The Party Dress', Miss Lonelyhearts reverts to being a college freshman on a first date, strawberry sodas and all, in order to mollify his aggrieved girlfriend – Betty can tolerate anything except maturity. It is an appropriate concluding irony that she should unwittingly bring about his death when the panic-struck cripple mistakenly thinks she is cutting off his escape.

Just as Shrike is a negative Virgil, so Betty is a negative Beatrice to West's Pilgrim. Beatrice leads Dante, with the poem's total endorsement, to the paradise of complete, perfected experience. Betty, in a text severely critical of her, wants to take Miss Lonelyhearts to a limited, limiting heaven to which the entrance fee is intellectual suicide. Beatrice resides in Paradise and, before condemning her lack of charity toward the damned, we should perhaps wait until we, too, experience the Beatific Vision. But Betty lives in New York and her paradise is a crass, retarded enclave in the middle of Inferno, owing its existence to a mean instinct for self-preservation. Even Miss Lonelyhearts, with Virgil and Beatrice to assist, might have survived; with Betty and Shrike, he is a lost soul from the start.

Between them both, the sick soul Shrike and the devotee of healthy-mindedness destroy the hero. To Betty, epitome of healthy-mindedness, the sick soul is simply a morbid loser. To Shrike, the healthy-minded person is shallow, immature and uninformed. Having tried impartially to describe both types, James, like Melville before him, comes down in the end in favour of the darkness. 'There is no doubt that healthy-mindedness is inadequate as a philosophical doctrine, because the evil facts which it refuses positively to account for are a genuine portion of reality; and they may after all be the best key to life's significance, and possibly the only openers of our eyes to the deepest levels of truth.'[55] West joins their company in *Miss Lonelyhearts* because there can be no question that he sides with the protagonist against his incorrigibly optimistic girlfriend. Melville, James and West, in the final analysis, prefer the sick soul to its upbeat adversary; the Church of old may have ranked presumption and despair as sins of equal gravity, but in our own time presumption has become by far the more serious offence. West invests something of himself in Miss Lonelyhearts and in Shrike as he splits himself into compassionate sympathizer and cynical joker, but there is nothing whatever of him in Betty.

Shrike and Miss Lonelyhearts are both sick souls; they differ only in their reactions to the predicament. Shrike's solution is to join the torturers. Abused himself – 'I too suffer,' he cries in an unguarded moment and there is no cause to disbelieve him – his remedy is to become himself an abuser in a cycle altogether familiar and predictable.[56] His name reveals his identity: he is the butcherbird that impales its prey the more conveniently to devour it – but it is crucial to see that this is revenge, retaliation, that he is doing to the world what the world first did to him. He inflicts pain because he is in pain. He is a sufferer resolved to make others suffer: the malevolent leper, the spiteful HIV victim, Vanni Fucci. West's own self-projection as Shrike has to do with betrayed idealism venting itself as cynicism; when Shrike ridicules a shoddy mass culture, best typified by Hollywood, he simultaneously speaks for his creator. Yet Shrike is no saviour; against Betty's sentimental pastoralism, he stands for the city, the evil, heartless city of Romantic tradition proceeding from Wordsworth through Baudelaire to Eliot.

He needs, however, to be located even more in a religious than in a socio-economic context. He is the tempter, the seducer, a type of the loosed Satan who heralds the final catastrophe.[57] He is the master rhetorician who prevails in contrast to the master rhetorician who fails, the Satan of *Paradise Regained*. He is an anti-Christ; when he proclaims 'the gospel according to Shrike', he anticipates the sneering monologist of *The Fall*.[58] Beneath the jeering banter is a deadly serious message: this is hell and we are the damned. The only item for discussion is how we are to pass the time.

Shrike is West's grandest creation, a rhetorician of the abyss in the tradition of Sabbatian nihilism.[59] He plays the role of a wise-cracking, stand-up American Satan to Miss Lonelyhearts' fallen American Adam, with the idiom of Groucho Marx recruited for the service of hell. The reader does not witness the Fall. The hero has already been ruined by the power of Shrike's satanic rhetoric before the story begins; Betty is the sole, trivial connection with the lost, inadequate Eden. But again we must note that Shrike is his own first victim: the parallel with Satan holds. He is consumed by religious hysteria, tormented by an ache for God that has turned, through repeated disappointment, into venomous rancour; in this sadism of thwarted passion, he lives only to hurt the God who has hurt him. 'How can I believe, how can I have faith in this day and age?'[60] The mocking cannot conceal the pain, for he wants desperately to believe and would willingly barter all the jibes for the gift of faith, if only he could. The baffled lover has become jeering desecrator, but it is the protracted, barren waiting, the repeated delays and postponements, that have brought about the change. Perhaps also operative here is a peculiarly Jewish rage against that long longed-for, eagerly expected, inexcusably tardy messiah, pleaded with and prayed to for millennia, but still, inexplicably, refusing to come. But the Christians, too, have their own dilatory redeemer. How long, O Lord, how long? In *The Day of the Locust*, Tod Hackett listens, with the other mourners, to Bach's yearning appeal to Christ, but Christ himself shows no sign of having heard it.[61] Shrike, in a retaliatory strike, turns the traditional Judaeo-Christian position upside down: it is not we who have betrayed God, it is He who has betrayed us, by keeping us waiting far too long.

Defensive mockery is Shrike's response to this slowcoach saviour. It is a humour that hovers on the brink of what ancient gnosticism called the *Kenoma*, the cosmological emptiness, a *Galgenhumor* that quarries its materials from the abyss.[62] Shrike is the assassin of dreams, polluting before despatching them. Knowing that we are in hell, he will not allow anyone to dream of heaven. Human beings have a penchant for dreams of escape and salvation; Shrike appoints himself the debaser of dreams, so befouling them that they are henceforth unusable. He leaves us like Cordelia after her sisters have degraded the language of love and loyalty; the effect is to debar these words from the currency of honest debate and to make them the property of rogues and liars. Only cretins can continue to cling to these exploded fantasies. The South Seas asylum, the return to pastoral innocence, the salvific power of art, hedonistic self-realization: all wither irrecoverably before the blast of Shrike's scorn. But the greatest, the nonpareil, of all dreams is the Christ dream and it is to besmirch this that Shrike summons up his greatest satanic powers.

'I feel like hell.'[63] The commonplace idiom masks a starkly literal truth that links him yet again with Milton's Satan ('myself am hell') and in his determination to make Miss Lonelyhearts like himself, he is following in the steps of his great predecessor. Spying upon the lovers in Eden, Satan resolves that they shall join him in hell:

> Accept your Maker's work; he gave it me,
> Which I as freely give.[64]

In a similarly sharing spirit, Shrike communicates his own ruin to his young colleague. He is a vandal of spiritual needs, a deflater of dreams, a dweller in despair's basement, and his chief concern is not to live there alone.

It is a malice born of impotence and disappointment. The jeers hide heartache. His favourite ruse throughout is a double-talk in which the mournful truth is spoken under the camouflage of cynical nonchalance. 'Life for me is a desert empty of comfort.'[65] Reality masquerades as jest under cover of grandiloquent words. 'How was it you first came to believe?'[66] The yearning he dares not express directly emerges as sarcasm. Yet, in ridiculing others, he betrays himself. In mock rebuke to a colleague he supplies the key, not only to himself, but to his creator. 'You cannot believe, you can only laugh.'[67] West tells us that when belief is impossible, only laughter remains; but such laughter is inseparable from anguish and is only availed of because the alternative is to weep. The mocker is in torment: Shrike buries his face, like the blade of a hatchet, in a woman's neck; sleeping with his wife is like a knife in the groin.[68] Whether as agent or sufferer, subject or object, he is always associated with violence and pain.

In a world of lost souls, he is the most forsaken, the living proof of Melville's caution against looking too long into the fire lest we become enamoured of evil, agents of Satan. His is an anti-gospel of bad news and he rejoices to find and to augment pain. 'O the pity of it,' cries Othello to Iago, who is secretly scheming to make things as bad as possible. Shrike is a worthy recruit to a fraternity that includes Satan, Vanni Fucci, Iago, the Underground Man, Uplandtowers and Jean-Baptiste Clamence. 'I am his disciple,' he mockingly claims, just prior to betraying Miss Lonelyhearts by reading aloud to the company the cripple's letter accusing him of trying to rape his wife.[69] We know, in that case, which disciple he is. Dante places Judas in the lowest circle of hell. West agrees that it is the right place for the traitor.

Yet the fear persists that Shrike may be right, because he is not refuted; his response to the problem of incurable suffering is as good (or as bad) as any other within the text. Compassion is Miss Lonelyhearts' way, but the text shows how futile and self-destructive this is. Disregard, advises Betty, but West is surely not recommending such self-concern among the pangs of the damned. Mockery, insists Shrike: ridicule the pain you cannot cure or lessen. We instinctively protest, but remember, even as we do so, that this is the very strategy employed by West himself as writer. What Shrike as character does within the text, West does as its creator. As so often in modern fiction, evil is given the last word; that, in West's case, it is also a funny one is scant consolation.

A Cool Million shows how resolved West is to be a comedian, whatever the material, whatever the cost. He has no other way of dealing with life – deprive him of laughter and you leave him naked to the world. 'Some people have funny ideas of what's fun,'[70] says Homer in *The Day of the Locust*; but it would be a mistake to include West among them – some people make jokes because otherwise they would weep. 'Even clowns must grow serious,'[71] says Lemuel, but he is assassinated before he can do it. West fought shy of seriousness all his life. *A Cool Million* is like *Animal Farm*; neither is the light-hearted burlesque it purports to be. West and Orwell may appear simply to be having fun; they are, in fact, engaging a reality that would otherwise be unbearable. From *Animal Farm* Orwell moved to *Nineteen Eighty-Four*, a bleak, nightmarish text from which all the gaiety of the earlier book has completely haemorrhaged. West's next book after *A Cool Million* (like Orwell's it, too, was his last) was *The Day of the Locust*, the gravest and least humorous of all his writings.

West's final book deals with a problem touched upon briefly by the narrator of *Notes from Underground*: the problem of boredom and of the violence that inevitably comes in its wake. The Underground Man lays all the blame for his condition – suffering, jealousy, anger, self-laceration – upon boredom: 'And all out of boredom, gentlemen, all out of boredom.' It is why he tortures himself and others: 'if I take my revenge, it is purely out of resentment'.[72] In this he is no different from the rest of us, but he is superior by virtue of his greater self-awareness: he knows why he acts as he does. Cleopatra liked to stick golden pins into the breasts of her slaves and took pleasure in their screams; but, if challenged, she might well have lacked the insight (possessed by the Underground Man) to explain that this was her revenge upon life for being such a let-down.[73] This is why the Underground Man is so sure that the Crystal Palace must fail. Certainly, human beings will strive to get there because they love the journey. But they do not like the arrival. Once they are domiciled in the Crystal Palace, it will quickly start to pall and will thereafter become intolerably boring. At that point, the disenchanted will rise up, smash it to pieces and start all over again.[74]

The Day of the Locust describes what happens when the Crystal Palace is relocated in California. America provides an ideal laboratory for studying the associated problems of boredom and violence. If dream and disenchantment are so inseparably related, if the depth of the disillusion is in proportion to the lavishness of the promise, then America, so preeminently the land of the dream and the promise, is peculiarly prone to the sadistic ennui of Dostoyevsky's Cleopatra. Boredom explains everything that happens in the text, including the existence and *raison d'être* of Hollywood itself. The barber in Purdue, worn out from cutting hair all day long, needs a break from the tedium or he will stop barbering altogether.[75] He goes to the cinema, not to see his own drab life but to find glamour and excitement – it's the price he demands for turning up at work the next day. Without dreams how can he endure? Life must be intensified, augmented, enhanced, if it is to be lived at all. And so the foodstuffs in the supermarket are bathed in exotically alluring colours – pale green fish, rose steaks, ivory eggs, and so on – rather than set out in their own everyday, unadorned, natural hues, because nature cannot satisfy, reality will not suffice: unembellished life cannot match the level of our desires and the demands of our expectations.[76] How to keep the barber in Purdue working? This is the problem that America (first in the field here as in so much else) has to solve. The solution is the continual ratcheting up of nature in order to gratify desire – it explains the perversions, the pornographic movies, the brothels, the cockfights, the female impersonators, the hideous imitation horse at the bottom of the pool, the daily sensationalism of the media, the banal stimulations of the cinema, the ghoulish haunting of funereal parlours, the feverish excitement of film premieres, the craved osmotic proximity of celebrities, the overall insatiable search for new experiences: anything that confers an assurance, however unstable and short-lived, that one is really alive, that life is not just dully, insignificantly ebbing away.

The same pernicious attraction to fantasy is responsible for the individual, private cruelties inflicted by people on each other. Precisely the realization that Homer is in thrall to her makes the desire in Faye to hurt him irresistible:[77] bores create sadists – it is Cleopatra and her slaves all over again. Harbouring the grotesquely extravagant dreams of Hollywood as Emma Bovary before her cherished the exalted loves of romantic fiction, how could Faye ever live at ease with Homer any more than Emma with Charles? Reality is simply not good enough. Tod, even as he so expertly analyzes the fantasies of others, fantasizes himself about stalking Faye, knocking her unconscious and raping her: unsatisfied desire turns him into a thought criminal.[78] Homer, too, has a similar effect upon him as upon Faye: Tod wonders why his initial sympathy for Homer should have turned into irritation and malice.[79] Had he read 'Bartleby', he would have understood how pity can change into revulsion and callousness.

The unsatisfied desires of the dreamers, the actors, the performers confront the fierce resentments of those who have seen through the cheat. From the beginning Tod is struck by the division between the performers and the spectators. The first group includes the actors, the would-be actors, the failed actors, all those connected, however tenuously, with the entertainment industry, even if only to the extent of dressing in some outlandish way designed to catch the attention of others. The fact that they are performers does not mean that they do not suffer. Harry Greener, peddling his polish from door to door, clowns continuously: 'it was his sole method of defence'.[80] He carries around in his pocket an old newspaper clipping lauding him for his stage role as the suffering victim: 'The pain would be unbearable if it were not obviously make-believe. It is gloriously funny.'[81] Nothing could be more mistaken. On or off stage, Harry is the same; despite the third-rate routine, he plays his part in the same anguished pantomime and he dies the same death as Lear from the same heart failure, alike in this if in nothing else. Clowns can be casualties, too. The injuries suffered when the screen-set Waterloo collapses are not less real because the event is make-believe and the battlefield lathe and plaster. The vaudeville critic is completely wrong: the pain *is* unbearable even if the pratfalls are rehearsed. The gap between life and art is closed. Faye is not a fake in the usual, uncomplicated sense: 'she didn't know how to be simpler or more honest.'[82] She acts what she is and is what she acts: she is (the oxymoron is unavoidable) naturally artificial, self-deceived, first victim of her own shoddy dreams. 'Any dream was better than no dream and beggars couldn't be choosers.'[83] So Tod interprets her outlook and, for those in a generous mood, she might rightly take her place, however menial, in a tradition that runs from Keats's 'Lamia' to Fitzgerald's *Gatsby*: she is Emma Bovary at a cruder, more vulgar level. What is remarkable is that so many years ahead West should have so presciently anticipated Marilyn Monroe.

From Cervantes on, the novel has dealt with the risks of dreams and the destruction of dreamers. West's special contribution is to focus upon the cheated society rather than the deluded individual, to examine what happens when all the barbers in all the Purdues discover that they have been duped. From the outset Tod is uneasily aware of the army of shiftless nomads on the streets of Los Angeles who seem to be waiting for something, anything, to happen, so that their emptiness will be somehow filled. They loiter on corners, nothing to do, staring at the passers-by, but if anyone stares back, 'their eyes filled with hatred', and Tod senses coming from them, like a bad smell, a vicious, acrid boredom that trembles on the verge of violence.[84] Yet they are his salvation as an artist, for in them he finds a new, worthy subject matter, a reason for going on working. He had been on the point of abandoning painting as too facile, trivially reproductive, unrewardingly realistic (one recalls the barber in Purdue), when into his life come these strange, menacing people, arrived not from some far-off galaxy, but from the American Midwest. Despite earning his living in Hollywood, Tod's real work is his nightmarishly surrealistic painting, 'The Burning of Los Angeles' (Goya is the master), and he may well be speaking for West himself when he reflects how some of his friends reproached him for selling out to the movies.

The book describes how Tod gradually unpicks the mystery of these people: who they are, what they represent. At one point he wonders if he is perhaps exaggerating their importance, projecting upon them a significance they do not deserve, but, in a series of encounters culminating in the final riot, he comes to see how instinctively right he was to fix upon them as the prime subject of his art. On the street, in the funeral parlour, in the churches where he sketches them, he pieces together the jigsaw of their existence. America has its own religions. So Shrike shouts in parodic patriotism. In a meeting place of yet another zany sect, Tod watches, fascinated, a skeletal Midwesterner raging against modern America with all the fervour of a fanatic from the Dark Ages denouncing the decadence of Rome and prophesying the wrath to come. It is a crazy jumble of religion, economics and diet, but 'Tod didn't laugh at the man's rhetoric. He knew it was unimportant. What mattered were his messianic rage and the emotional response of his hearers.'[85] There is, indeed, no cause to laugh, since the very title of West's book comes from the same tradition of biblical commination. Here is a people ready to kill and burn: this is what matters, not the flimsy rationalizations in which they clothe their fury.

But why are they as they are? Not till the last pages is the explanation explicitly given. The book's original title was *The Cheated*. As with Dostoyevsky's Cleopatra, boredom becomes psychopathic. The one thing worse than unsatisfied desire is satisfied desire: the frustration of not getting what you want is as nothing compared to the frustration of getting what you want only to find that you don't want it. The despair of hell is posited on a lost heaven; how much worse the despair of a heaven won and found to be a fraud. 'The Burning of Los Angeles' depicts a revenge upon failed utopia; the flames are fed by the fury of disappointed expectations. Deep in hell, Vanni Fucci dreams of revenge. West reveals an army of Vanni Fuccis, occupying heaven – California is 'paradise on earth' – and outraged at the swindle practised upon them.[86] The Promised Land is a cheat; they have crossed Jordan only to be disenchanted. Oranges, avocado pears, passion fruit, the unfailing sun, the waves of the Pacific – all quickly lose their transient charms; what remains is the potentially explosive combination of insatiable desire and *un ennui atroce* – it is Flaubert's dilemma democratized, all citizens endowed with the right to life, liberty and disillusionment. Nothing happens and they burn with resentment, a mob of Cleopatras, individually impotent, collectively irresistible. Disappointment gives way to a simmering rage at the broken promises, the breached contract: as with Fitzgerald's Dutch sailors speechless at the promise of the New World, it is America itself (like Fitzgerald's Daisy, like West's Faye) that is held guilty of reneging. The false woman is synecdochic of the deceitful culture. Heaven becomes hell. An itch for chaos grows. Watching the mob at the premiere, Tod knows he was right all along: they are *not* simply harmless curiosity seekers. They are addicts of mayhem and, if the airplane won't fall out of the sky with the regularity required, they will create calamities for themselves. A veritable bedlam, says the inflammatory newsman at the premiere, speaking truer than he knows, for these are the damned and, in traditional satanic fashion, they seek relief from their own torment in tormenting others.[87] Los Angeles will be put to the torch by people too bored to live without flames. No longer bored or jaded, they sing and dance joyously in orgiastic destruction, and Tod, with no hint that West disagrees, sees the incineration of the city as prelude to a nation-wide conflagration.

Art is the one fruit of catastrophe. The riot enables Tod to complete his painting as it enables West to complete his book. But West is no art-for-art's saker any more than is Tod, despite his half-hearted attempts at self-deception. Reflecting upon the impending débâcle, Tod tries to comfort himself with the thought that 'he was an artist not a prophet. His work would not be judged by the accuracy with which it foretold a future event but by its merit as painting.'[88] Revealingly, however, he also finds a strong satisfaction in his role as Jeremiah, and Jeremiah was certainly no devotee of art for art's sake. Later, puzzling over his divided attitude to Homer, Tod tries to solve the problem by dismissing it: 'He had never set himself up as a healer.' But West, too, was, like Jeremiah, a prophet and he wanted to be a healer.[89] Evidence of this ambition, however oblique and disguised, can be detected in his books. But, superb diagnostician though he is, the cure for the disease eludes him; and if he laughs when telling us we are incurable, it's because he doesn't know what else to do.

Chapter 7

Camus

Compare these two passages:

> I agree that Copernicus's opinion need not be more closely examined. But this! It affects our whole life to know whether the soul is mortal or immortal.[1]

> Whether the earth or the sun revolves around the other is a matter of profound indifference. To tell the truth, it is a futile question. On the other hand, I see many people die because they judge that life is not worth living. I see others paradoxically getting killed for the ideas or illusions that give them a reason for living ... I therefore conclude that the meaning of life is the most urgent of questions.[2]

The first is Pascal, the second Camus – the apologist of Christianity and the apostle of the Absurd – yet what is striking is their unanimity as to what is and what is not important, in particular, their joint dismissal of science as a help in interpreting human existence. Thereafter agreement ends. Pascal exhorts us to wager upon the soul's immortality, for, even if it turns out to be the wrong bet, we shall have lost at most only a few years of suspect pleasures that, with any good sense, we should have shunned in any case. Camus, by contrast, demands that we abandon the pernicious dream of immortality: 'If there is a sin against life, it is not so much to despair of life, as to hope for another life and to lose sight of the implacable grandeur of this one.'[3] If we follow Pascal and he turns out to be wrong, we shall have lost everything.

Despite the contradictory lessons, they are, nevertheless, both moralists, both teachers, and their paramount purpose is to tell us how to live right. No other modern writer has been so explicitly, dedicatedly didactic as Camus. His work is inspired by a desire to be avenged upon the false religion into which he was born and which he soon repudiated. With its promise of eternal life and everlasting happiness, Christianity is, for Camus, the cruellest of all the deceptions ever practised upon man. In play, novel, essay, he takes on the task of replacing this fraud with a true account of the human condition. Whether in his own voice, as in *The Myth of Sisyphus*, or through the utterances of his protagonists (Caligula, Martha, Meursault), he pursues this curriculum of bleak enlightenment. Kafka has but one lesson to teach: that we do not and never can know – we learn that there is nothing to learn. Camus is a teacher of a very different kind: he knows where we have gone wrong and he comes to tell us how to go right – we are to learn from him how to live.

The epigraph from Pindar preceding *The Myth of Sisyphus* alerts us to the nature of this instruction: 'O my soul, do not aspire to immortal life, but exhaust the limits of the possible.' Yet this essay, so anti-Pascalian in its championship of earthly life, begins by telling us that suicide is the most pressing philosophical problem of our time. Why do we go on living when the case for self-destruction seems so unopposably clear? Perhaps Camus had in mind the passage in *The Castle* where K is told that no one is detaining him in the village, that he is free to go whenever he wishes: no one is forcing us to go on living.[4] A more probable ancestor is Dostoyevsky. In Camus's dramatization of *The Possessed*, Kirilov admits to being puzzled as to why there are not many more suicides and searches for 'the reasons why men don't dare kill themselves'. Stavrogin, in the same play, is likewise tormented by the question, 'should one live or should one destroy oneself?'[5] In the end, he chooses the latter.

The Myth of Sisyphus sets out to refute Kirilov and Stavrogin, but only after first conceding the potency of their arguments. Having initially admitted that 'it is legitimate and necessary to wonder whether life has a meaning', Camus moves quickly to repair any possible damage: 'even if one does not believe in God, suicide is not legitimate.'[6] It is the apodictic nature of the assertion that commands attention – Camus is as authoritarian as the Church in his ban upon self-destruction; thou shalt not kill thyself – it is the first commandment of the new creed. At the same time, he reminds us, as remorselessly as the Ash Wednesday service, about the cruel mathematics that govern our condition: precisely because we are fated to return to the dust, we must commit to living now because it is the only life we have.

Denying eternal life, Camus is just as categorical as Christianity in forbidding suicide: 'even within the limits of nihilism it is possible to find the means to proceed beyond nihilism'.[7] Not everyone who reads *Caligula* or *Cross Purpose* will agree that he succeeds, but this is undeniably the challenge he accepts in *The Myth of Sisyphus*: finding a reason for living in a world that provides none, discovering a meaning where none exists. The difference between Camus and Christianity is not that he is libertarian and it is dogmatic; *The Myth* is a text crammed with instructions and commands. You must not commit suicide, you must not commit intellectual suicide by making the leap of faith across the gulf of the Absurd, you must not equate being deprived of hope as being in despair, the work of art must respect the injunction of the Absurd not to sacrifice to illusion or arouse hope, you must not hope, you must imagine Sisyphus happy.[8] Camus has commandments aplenty, as binding as those brought down from Mount Sinai. Strenuously, Camus insists that life 'will be lived all the better if it has no meaning' – a convenient conclusion, given that he starts from the premise that it has none.[9] Even in a world bereft of hope and meaning, one where 'there is no future', Camus is as vehement as Christianity in forbidding a do-it-yourself euthanasia: 'the important thing is not to be cured but to live with one's ailments' – the fact that there is no cure for these ailments is no excuse for putting an end to them.[10] It is the identical argument of Christianity, save that submission to the will of God has been omitted. At the same time, Camus prohibits any pact with life that involves an intellectual sell-out. 'It is essential to die unreconciled and not of one's own free will.'[11] Any Christian who defected to Camus in order to obtain a release from dicta and dogma would be sorely mistaken.

In two images – the collapsed stage and the painted screens – Camus takes us to the heart of his instruction.[12] The stage sets collapse when the emptiness of existence suddenly dawns upon a man and he realizes that there is nothing to live for. The world becomes, in Camus's word, a desert, akin to the wilderness in which Christ was tempted by Satan just before the beginning of his mission. The man suddenly confronted by the Absurd must similarly overcome a temptation: 'he is asked to leap.'[13] Christ, too, was asked to leap from the pinnacle of the temple to prove that he was the Son of God. The absurd man is tempted to leap in order to solve his problem. Both refuse, though for very different reasons. Christ, as Son of God, knows that it is wrong to put the Father to the test. The absurd man, as son of Earth, knows that there is no Father to rely on, and he prefers to stay in the desert rather than take refuge in the dream. It is better to despair than to leap: 'a determined soul will always manage.'[14] It is a secular equivalent of St Paul's assurance that grace is always sufficient. Had Christ refused the leap of faith as he refused that other leap, he would have been spared that terrible moment when he cried out in anguished protest to the God who had so unaccountably abandoned him. The absurd man, despite knowing the finality of death, remains loyal to Earth. He disdains the little painted screens used by priests in the past to prevent the condemned man from seeing the gallows, for he is strong enough to confront his pointless existence and inexplicable annihilation.[15] Throughout his entire work, Camus's aim is to remove the painted screens that hide the truth from condemned humanity.

Strangely, despite the openly apodictic nature of his own work, Camus attacks the Christians for teaching a doctrine: 'it is a doctrine they bring, and one must subscribe to it'[16] – as though he himself were not doing exactly the same thing. In denouncing those who make the leap or hide behind the painted screens, Camus is as intolerant as any inquisitor of old. To describe *The Myth* as a text replete with dogmas and instructions is not to condemn it, for that's what it set out to be. But why should someone so unmistakably a teacher attack other people for being teachers – not simply *false* teachers, but teachers at all? 'What counts is not the best living, but the most living.'[17] What is this if not a doctrine? 'One must imagine Sisyphus happy.'[18] What is this if not a command? We read Camus's warning against the seductively 'stirring lyricism' of Kierkegaard and then arrive at the rousing peroration of *The Myth*: 'I leave Sisyphus at the foot of the mountain! ... The struggle itself towards the heights is enough to fill a man's heart. One must imagine Sisyphus happy.'[19] Kierkegaard might have justifiably raised an eyebrow at being rebuked for lyricism by someone who could write like this.

The final command has a smack of *credo quia impossibile* about it. Easy enough to imagine Sisyphus happy, if, as the Church teaches, he will one day find relief in heaven from his temporary, earthly, back-breaking toil. But Camus's Sisyphus must strain forever at a task he can neither forsake nor complete. 'Sisyphus is the absurd hero ... the whole being is exerted towards accomplishing nothing.'[20] There could be no crueller fate, which is why Camus proposes him as the stoic hero. We are to celebrate the fortitude that triumphs over necessity: 'there is no fate that cannot be surmounted by scorn'.[21] Knowing you're a loser and continuing to fight is nobler than continuing to fight in the hope of victory: 'crushing truths perish from being acknowledged'.[22] In such a spirit Hemingway's hero walks away from his dead wife at the close of *A Farewell to Arms*.

But Hemingway neither promoted his book as 'a manual of happiness' nor insisted that we regard his stricken hero as happy.[23] When Camus does say these things and declares a life without meaning to be preferable to a life with it, we feel that we have left the world of common sense for a realm of almost mystic exaltation, that these are the accents of faith, not the conclusions of reason. There is, too, just a whiff of self-congratulation in the triumph over disaster: 'the nobility of my soul make[s] me conclude that all is well'.[24] What defines hell for Dante is that it excludes hope, closes the door upon the future and for more than two millennia people in the West agreed.[25] Camus's aversion to hope marks his book as a text for our times. 'There is so much stubborn hope in the human heart.'[26] In the new creed, hope occupies the deplorable position that sin did in the old one: get thee behind me, Satan. Camus talks about hope as of some kind of addiction, ruinous as heroin, corrupting its victims. *Le sale espoir*: only in our twentieth century could this adjective and this noun (it is Anouilh's collocation) consort together. Those so sick of hope that they would be rid of it forever may warm to Camus's new doctrine; those who continue to side with Dante will not.

Yet it would be incorrect to find in *The Myth* the spirit of Vanni Fucci, for it is free of spite or malice. Camus simply wants to liberate us from the harmful delusion of a future life so that we may fully commit to the only life we shall ever possess. Once we have accepted his view of the world as a desert, Camus invites us to live and to create in the very midst of this wasteland, inventing a reason for living because there is none to be discovered. *The Myth* might easily be criticized for being, at the close, too romantic or utopian but it begins its journey in that wasteland so familiar to our modern sensibility and, for many readers, it never succeeds in leaving it.

The Outsider is a fictional exploration of this same territory. The climax is the showdown between Meursault and the prison chaplain in the death cell, when Meursault's previous indifference to religion turns into a fierce hostility on his realization that religion is the foe of life and of all he now believes in. His initial lack of interest in religion is plain from the outset when he describes the events at his mother's funeral as though they were the rites of some remote primitive tribe. He obviously cares little for his mother who has been in a home for three years, in the last of which he has hardly seen her. Visiting her 'would have meant losing my Sunday', and in the following chapter we learn what this loss would have entailed:

a long lie in bed after his Saturday night girlfriend has left, a day spent lounging on the balcony watching the business of the streets, dinner and, finally, back to bed in preparation for return to work on Monday.[27] Clearly, he is not a religious man – the Lord's day has no religious significance for him.

But neither is he antagonistic to religion; though slightly taken aback by the priest's salutation of 'my son', he is too uncaring to object – what does it matter? In Part Two, however, following his arrest his attitude gradually hardens into one of opposition, deepening into an almost Voltairean intensity: *écrasez l'infâme*. The first hint is in the meeting with the examining magistrate who tells Meursault that, with God's help, he means to save him.[28] The reference to God seems gratuitous, but Camus wants to set the scene for a confrontation between religion and paganism. The magistrate histrionically produces a crucifix and waves it intimidatingly at the prisoner, demanding if he knows what it is. It seems an improbable interrogation procedure, but, however far-fetched, this behaviour is designed to fit into the ideological confrontation – the magistrate behaves as he does because Camus wants him to do so. He assures Meursault that the worst of sinners can repent and be forgiven, all the while brandishing the crucifix before the prisoner's eyes. He succeeds only in startling Meursault.

When Meursault denies believing in God, the magistrate reacts with outraged incredulity – all men believe in God, even those who deny it, because, without such belief, life would have no meaning. '"Do you wish," he asked indignantly, "my life to have no meaning?".'[29] Meursault apologetically replies that he doesn't see what his wishes have to do with it nor does he see why one man's disbelief should have such catastrophic consequences upon another man's faith.

Baffled by what seems to him stony impenitence, the magistrate gives up in despair and never mentions God again. The result is that relations between them improve. The magistrate continues to call Meursault Mr Antichrist, but he does so jocularly and pats him on the shoulder.[30] Yet the joke is close to the truth.

Meursault's unconcern toward religion hardens into enmity as he comes to appreciate what is at stake between him and it. Three times he refuses to see the chaplain and even when the chaplain gatecrashes the cell, Meursault remains politely indifferent. He declines the priest's invitation to sit beside him on the bed, but 'not because I had anything against him; he seemed a mild, amiable man'.[31] Not the man but what he embodies and preaches – this is what finally provokes the normally placid Meursault to explode with rage.

The chaplain follows the magistrate in insultingly refusing to take the prisoner's word for it as to his disbelief in God. Yet again, the easygoing Meursault declines to be offended and mildly replies, in refutation of Pascal, that whether God does or does not exist is 'a question of so little importance'; but his patience at this point is in stark contrast to what will follow.[32] Let men who wish to turn to God in their distress do so – he, for his part, has no such inclination. When the priest, still angling to save this lost soul, declares that every human being is under sentence of death, not just those condemned to the guillotine, Meursault politely demurs: it is not at all the same thing, he replies, and is certainly no consolation to the occupant of the death cell.

The priest is an actor, a trickster, 'an old hand', using every ploy and stratagem to get his way: looking the sinner straight in the eye, dropping his gaze, expressing his sorrow for the miscreant, and all the other tricks of the trade.[33] Meursault feels the onset of boredom, but little else. When the priest tells him that every condemned man, however abandoned, finally sees Christ's face on the walls of the cell, Meursault counters that the only face he longs to see is the face of Marie, 'a sun-gold face, glowing with desire'.[34] Mournfully, the chaplain plays his last card: does Meursault really love these things so much? Does he not wish that there was an afterlife? It is a high-risk strategy and it completely miscarries. Of course, Meursault replies, everyone, if only intermittently, feels a longing for heaven, but wishes and facts have nothing to do with each other – religion is a shabby exploitation of human desires that, in the very nature of things, cannot be satisfied. Marie is reality, Christ a fantasy: this life is what matters, not the undisciplined dreams to which we sometimes surrender. Questioned as to what he desires in the grave, Meursault, finally losing patience, bawls defiantly, 'a life in which I can remember this life on earth'.[35] For what could be more precious than this life on earth?

With mounting anger, he tells the badgering priest that he is not *his* Father, that he is sick of his company, and that he has no time of the little left to him to waste on God. His former indifference gives way to a fierce intolerance, born of his newly apprehended intuition of what it means to be alive. What he had always vaguely sensed, he now knows with startling clarity, and it breaks upon him with all the force of a religious revelation – as surely as the saints and prophets, he knows the meaning of salvation. His previous nonchalant attitude to religion has vanished: to choose religion is to be recreant to earth. It is the creed of the Absurd as promulgated in *The Myth* and Meursault is as fanatical for the new faith as was any zealot for the old.

He spurns the priest's God and his 'rotten prayers', and, with uncharacteristic aggression, assaults the man he had described as mild and amiable, showing far more violence and anger now than when he shot the Arab.[36] What most enfuriates him is the cocksure attitude of his opponent, 'yet none of his certainties was worth one strand of a woman's hair'.[37] The irony is that he attacks the priest for being too sure of himself while simultaneously expressing an unshakeable conviction of his own infallibility: 'I'd been right, I was still right, I was always right.'[38] Gone is the previous diffidence – in its place a positiveness that the most ultramontane of Popes might have envied. 'Nothing, nothing had the least importance, and I knew quite well why.'[39] There is no arguing with such certitude. Christians are right and pagans are wrong: Meursault simply inverts the terms of *The Song of Roland* and appropriates its infallibility for himself. He has corrected the Church's error in proclaiming the resurrection of the body and the life to come; and, emptied of this hope, he feels how 'the great rush of anger had washed me clean', flushing away simultaneously the delusion of heaven and disloyalty to Earth.[40] Camus characteristically repudiates the old religion with its own imagery, with Meursault's commitment to Earth presented as a counter-sacrament, a secular baptism. He is cleansed, not of sin but of faith, he is saved *from* religion, not *by* it. It is what we expect from the author of *The Myth of Sisyphus*.

It is instructive to contrast the two meetings of Joseph K and Meursault with their respective priests – much as Camus admired Kafka, it shows the gulf between them. Kafka stays aloof from the discussion in the cathedral, refusing to endorse any interpretation of the parable or to tell us how it is to be resolved. We are, as always, left in the dark – it is Kafka's way. But it is not Camus's way. We know exactly where he stands, whose side he takes and expects us to take. In *The Myth* he is unequivocal: 'I start here from the principle of innocence ... there may be responsible persons but there are no guilty ones.'[41] Kafka is never so forthright. We are never told if Joseph K is guilty or innocent, culprit or victim – he himself doesn't know. The contrast with Meursault's total self-assurance could not be greater. How fortunate for Kafka's priest that he did not meet a character like Meursault – but, then, there are no characters like Meursault in Kafka's dark, problematic world. 'What does eternity matter to me? To lose the touch of flowers and women's hands is the supreme separation.'[42] When we find Camus's own words being used by Meursault to fend off the persuasions of the priest, we know that he is the spokesman for his creator, and this alone shows how distant we are from the deliberately indeterminate world of Kafka.

Kafka is a teacher without a syllabus; Camus, by contrast, knows precisely what he wants us to learn and is prepared to torture us into enlightenment. Those who have been schooled by Camus must expect to suffer – as much as the religion he rejected, he sees suffering as the gate to salvation; he proclaims happiness, but only after the probationary, purgatorial pain. *Caligula* is, above all, a play about education; the fact that the dominie is an emperor simply empowers him to implement his education programme. What his sister's death has so painfully taught him – that men die and are not happy – he feels impelled to communicate to everyone else. Like Lepidus, our initial reaction is to tell the young visionary that he is proclaiming as a revelation what the world has known since time began. Caligula's response is that our conduct is strangely at odds with our knowledge: we decline acquaintance with death and behave as though we were immortal.

Men die and they are not happy. It is an inaccurate assessment. If it were true, Caligula's mission would be unnecessary. The truth is that men die and are, nevertheless, unwarrantably, reprehensibly happy, or, at least, uncaring. This is what sticks in his craw and he resolves to devote his energies to destroying this offensive, irrational happiness. Pascal was similarly outraged at the inexplicable paradox of a creature at once carefree and condemned. Speaking of his own miserable condition (which is that of all men), he comments: 'I marvel that so wretched a state does not drive people to despair.'[43] How can men, in so desperate a plight, contrive to be happy, amusing themselves with trifles on the scaffold?

Caligula is a Pascal turned murderous, so enraged at the blindness of men that he turns to terror to make them see: he means to open eyes even if it entails cutting throats. Most teachers have only words to persuade their pupils. Caligula, the all-powerful emperor, has dungeons and thumbscrews. 'I wish men to live by the light of truth. And I've the power to make them do so. For I know what they need and haven't got. They're without understanding and they need a teacher; someone who knows what he's talking about.'[44] What cries out to be communicated is his discovery that life is absurd. Only unforgivable frivolity prevents men from seeing this and from being the desolate creatures they ought to be. They must be taught, whatever the cost, the grim truth of their condition. Scipio describes the gentle, pre-enlightenment emperor: 'He often told me that the only mistake one makes in life is to cause others suffering.'[45] Now, illuminated, he is resolved to multiply and inflict suffering, because only thus do men learn; without it, they will remain trapped in a state of blinkered, unearned happiness. Caligula's is the ruthlessness of the dismayed idealist. He decides to become a force of nature – an earthquake, a storm, a famine – to bring home to men the slaughter they so calmly, complacently accept as routine reality. Just as deliberately, he resolves not to spill blood by going to war. War is normal, 'rational', a matter of human choice, and its deaths have been humanly willed. Natural disasters – flood, plague and so on – come upon us, by contrast, completely uninvited, without consultation or permission, and we submit to them as things completely beyond our control: what else can we do? When Caligula startlingly announces that famine begins tomorrow, the shock is as though a volcano were to announce its intention to erupt. Men, unlike famine, must have a reason to kill and without any such reason it is absolutely intolerable – the victims are less willing to accept arbitrarily from the hands of a man what they supinely submit to from God or nature or fate.

This is what Caligula is banking on – he wants to drive his frightened, outraged subjects to rebellion against himself and, more importantly, against life itself. If they will not submit to arbitrary, random slaughter from himself, why bow down to it from any other quarter? Political revolt will lead to metaphysical revolt: so Caligula hopes. Warned by Scipio of the plot to kill him, he replies, 'I've done everything needed to that end.'[46] If his tuition succeeds, he will be killed: that's his plan. He wants to train absurd men, rebels against the human condition, a nation of Sisyphuses. With this in mind, the programme of educative murder is launched.

His new creed is inimical to Christianity and humanism alike. When Cherea, spokesman of humanism, advocate for life as it is, begs him to temporize – 'since this world is the only one we have, why not plead its cause?' – the reply is sternly uncompromising: 'Lies are never guiltless. And yours attribute importance to people and to things.'[47] Caligula's truth, that 'the world has no importance', is even more unpalatable to the atheist than it is to the believer, if only for the obvious reason that the atheist has nowhere else to go. Cherea's dagger is his only argument. When he argues that Caligula must be killed because he is making life no more significant than a speck of dust, he sounds like a brother to Meursault's indignant magistrate and his solution – execute the offender – is identical. Caligula, as armed prophet with the power to enforce his terrifying ideas, is much more dangerous than Meursault, but they are alike in two respects: the threat they pose to received belief and the alarm they provoke in their opponents. They are to be killed, not confuted.

Scipio's plea to Caligula is that of the peace-loving conservative to the disruptive agitator in all ages. Caligula claims to have discovered a new truth but its promulgation will lead to turmoil – why impose it upon men who would otherwise be tranquil and happy? The reply is fiercely uncompromising: men have no right to be deludedly happy – their very tranquillity is an affront. Truth is paramount. Asking Caligula to keep his revelation to himself would be like asking St Paul to leave the Ephesians in peace with Diana. Suetonius's Caligula is a monster of depravity; Camus presents him as the hero of existentialist truth.

The new religion takes over the rituals of the faith it has come to supplant: 'Make known to us the truth about this world – which is that it has none. And grant us the strength to live up to this verity of verities.'[48] No one can miss this parody of a Christian prayer which Caligula orders his senators to recite much as traditional believers recite the catechism. Writing in 1945, Camus was anxious to deny that Caligula was intended to be a portrait of Hitler. The truth is that neither is it a portrait of Caligula, for it is not a historical play at all. Its true matrix is not Imperial Rome but late nineteenth-century Europe and the fall-out from the religious catastrophe of that time – Camus's Caligula has been reading Nietzsche on the death of God and brooding on Ivan Karamazov's assertion that everything, consequently, is permitted. This, not Drusilla's death, lies behind his curriculum of educative terror. The old, consoling religious interpretation of life is his chief target. Caesonia, his mistress, assures him that his enemies will not succeed because heaven will come to his aid. He replies with withering contempt, 'There is no heaven, my poor dear woman!'[49] It is the first lesson in Caligula's classroom and Caesonia's blunder is unforgivable – he strangles her, unsurprisingly, soon afterwards. There was never a harsher, more punitive dominie: 'A man is guilty because he is one of Caligula's subjects. Now all men are Caligula's subjects. Ergo ...'[50] Even the dullest dullard will easily complete the syllogism. Some teachers speak hyperbolically of making their pupils learn even if it kills them. With Caligula it is literal fact.

Yet he dies a pedagogical failure. He achieves the minor goal of making his pupils rebel against him, not the major one of making them rebel against life. Cherea acknowledges the seductive power of his ideas and his skill in expounding them: 'He forces one to think.'[51] But this is over-generous: there is no evidence that Caligula forces anyone (reader apart) to think. The senators oppose him out of sheer animal self-preservation. Cherea himself had already been a thinker before Caligula turned educator, with a strong hankering for the nihilistic ideas that Caligula now expounds. Cherea kills Caligula because he threatens traditional ideas about the meaning of life, the others kill him because he threatens their own skins. The great education experiment is a flop: it makes no converts and ends in the teacher's assassination.

Caligula himself, just before dying, seems to disavow his own project: 'I have chosen a wrong path, a path that leads to nothing. My freedom isn't the right one.'[52] One wishes him preserved if only to hear him explain how any path chosen in existentialist freedom can be described as objectively wrong; or how, within the context of the Absurd, we are to distinguish true from false freedom. It seems more compatible with traditional morality. A wrong kind of freedom: it is exactly what Christians say caused the loss of Eden.

'Killing is not the solution.'[53] Caligula is now talking like Christ. It is, Scipio tells us, what Caligula believed before Drusilla died, what he scornfully rejected in the light of the new, superior knowledge that that death purportedly supplied.[54] Caligula's recantation (if that's what it is), his unexplained reversion to beliefs he had trenchantly dismissed as claptrap, threatens the integrity of the play.

Caligula says he has gone wrong, but does not specify where. Cherea has already conceded the impossibility of refuting him – he has to be killed because he cannot be intellectually overcome. But now he collapses internally. Are we to conclude that the first enlightenment following his sister's death was bogus, that the play is simply the staging of an individual aberration? Is this death-bed conversion simply due to a loss of nerve, a faltering purpose, an evaporating confidence? It seems a lame conclusion to so momentous a debate. The problem is that Camus has taken pains to make us side with Caligula, at least within the world of the play. It is precisely Rousseau's complaint against the tragic theatre that it makes us sympathize with characters whose actions would horrify us in life.[55] Told beforehand about the deeds of Macbeth or Medea, we would turn away in disgust: it's the stage that dazzles and seduces us. Caligula might easily stand in confirmation of this thesis. Having been so powerfully persuaded to take Caligula's experiment seriously, even sympathetically, not just as a madman's delirium, there is a sense of being cheated when Caligula himself, without any warning or preparation, abruptly tells us to treat it all as a mistake. It's as if Meursault were in the end to send for the priest and make an act of contrition.

Camus is clearly trying to find a way out of his own impasse, to detach us and himself from a too compromising connection with the murderous protagonist. We agree, of course, that killing is no solution, but this seems a moral absolute of the old-fashioned kind that existentialism had come to destroy. Not Caligula's anti-climactic change of heart, but his earlier, unsettling, nihilistic insights: this is what remains with us from the play. Cherea killed the man because he could not defeat the insights; the trouble is that the insights continue to plague us after the man is dead.

Cross Purpose is yet another metaphysical play similarly haunted by the spectre of death. It is the blackest of Camus's works, depressingly claustrophobic, a product in part of the period of confinement (1942–3) spent by the author in central France, exiled from his home in Algeria. When Martha complains of the 'shut-in valley ... this dreary town where it's always raining ... this land of shadows', and longs for the space and sunshine of the south where people have no souls but 'bodies that shine like gold', it is impossible not to detect an authorial longing seconding these sentiments.[56] Martha's desire to escape and final sense of entrapment are shared by her creator – the only difference is that he was actually born in that golden land to which she can only aspire.

The story of the play had haunted Camus for years. In his prison cell Meursault finds an old newspaper clipping which he reads again and again. It is the story of a crime. After many years abroad a man returns with his wife and child to the village in Czechoslovakia where he was born and where his mother and sister still live. Wishing to surprise them, he leaves his wife and child in a hotel and goes incognito to the old home, intending to play a joke before revealing himself. But he incautiously flaunts his money and, while he is asleep, his mother and sister kill him with a hammer and throw his corpse into the river. Next morning his wife turns up and the dreadful truth emerges. The mother hangs herself, the sister throws herself down a well. So ends the report. Meursault concludes that the traveller got what he deserved for monkeying about: 'you should never play games'.[57] As to the fates of the three women, Meursault has nothing to say.

Camus's changes in the play are significant. He leaves out the child and introduces the crucially important figure of the old servant. In the newspaper the murder is a spur-of-the-moment affair, with the women surrendering to the temptation of easy money. In the play they are serial killers who intend this to be their last murder in a long, carefully planned campaign to amass the money needed for their escape to the south. They do not bludgeon him to death, but drug him and throw his unconscious body into the river, just as they had done with all their previous victims, thus permitting them to claim that they are really providing a service – death as a release – and are, echoing Caligula, less cruel than life itself. The mother joins her son in the river, the sister hangs herself after viciously telling the appalled widow that her foolish husband got what he deserved, a view she shares with Meursault – the real victim of the whole misunderstanding is, as she sees it, herself.

The newspaper account is grim enough, the stage version even more so, but Camus was still not satisfied. We speculate (surely justifiably) that *The Secret Agent* and *Ethan Frome* are shaped as they are, given the peculiar constructions they possess, to make them as harrowing as possible – there seems no other plausible explanation for these authorial decisions. But with *Cross Purpose* no speculation is necessary: we *know*, without possibility of contradiction, that Camus's sole purpose was to make us grieve and that he altered the original version to make us grieve even more. The revised 1958 text has no other object than to make an already horrific story more horrific still. In the original version the old supposedly mute servant watches the frightful drama unfold without trying to stop it – he knows what the women plan to do, but makes no attempt to warn or intervene. This indifference seems bad enough, but not, apparently, for Camus. In the revision the old man does intervene at decisive points in the action, but only to ensure that the calamity is *not* averted. He is present when the women discuss the projected crime, he sees Jan and Maria together but hides so that they won't spot him, he deliberately interrupts Martha on the point of examining the passport, he removes the passport when she drops it and brings it back to make sure that she reads it only *after* the murder has been committed. In the original version he could be seen as a village idiot, slow and retarded, but in the later version he logically, cold-bloodedly plans to facilitate the murder. If, as seems undeniable, he is meant to be a representation of God – the final scene with Maria is intelligible only on the basis of such a supposition – then the difference between the two versions is trenchant: it is the difference between the gods of Arnold's 'Mycerinus', 'careless of our doom', but not going out of their way to contrive it, and the gods of Shakespeare's Gloster, killing us for their sport, the difference between apathy and sadism. What might have been construed as mischance in the original can be seen only as malefic design in the revision. The world of the play, already bleak enough, is made immeasurably more so by the alterations and it is incontestable that Camus's motive is the same as Vanni Fucci's.

The old servant, mute until the last line of the play, is, despite his relatively minor role, the most important character, symbolically speaking, for it is he who reveals the true nature of the world we live in, he who confirms Martha's final message to Maria, bringing home to even the most thoughtless the bleak fact of abandonment. As much as the *Inferno*, this is a text about damnation, and the rage of Vanni Fucci at the God who has condemned him pervades the play in a form suitably adapted for an unbelieving age. Atheistic it may be, but the hurt of a lost salvation is as palpable here as in any of the Dantean circles. The fact that neither Hardy nor Camus believed in God does not prevent Him from appearing in their dramatis personae: Hardy's President of the Immortals, tormenting Tess, Camus's mute given a voice to reject Maria's appeal with such curt brutality.

The names of the characters reveal the religious matrix. It is surely no coincidence that in this story of a dead man and two sisters – Martha calls Maria sister just before she goes to hang herself – the names should be taken from one of the most celebrated episodes in St John's Gospel, the raising of Lazarus; the only change is that the dead man should ironically be given the name of the Evangelist. In St Luke we read that Martha was aggrieved at being left to do all the housework while Mary simply enjoyed herself, but that when she complained to Jesus, he was unsympathetic. Mary (this was his answer) was doing the one thing needful – loving the Lord – while Martha, fretful, always busy, was dissipating her energies in secondary and, finally, unimportant chores. Many readers of the gospel feel, nevertheless, that Martha got something of a raw deal. The same opposition of life and work occurs in the play, with the two women still playing their gospel role. Camus's Martha is likewise bitterly resentful at her exhausting life in the dreary north while her brother and his wife have enjoyed a life of pleasure in the sun-drenched south – her constant theme is the unfairness of it all, although it is not to Christ that she complains.

In John's Gospel, Martha implicitly rebukes Jesus for coming too late: 'If you had been here, Lord, my brother would not have died. But I know that even now God will give you whatever you ask him for.' When Mary afterwards meets Jesus, she repeats Martha's first sentence but omits the second. Camus separates the biblical Martha's statement into two parts and distributes them between the two women. If God existed, the world would make sense and Jan would not have died: the biblical Martha reproaches God for being absent from Bethany – Camus's Martha resents him for being absent from existence. Underlying the play is a nostalgia for the lost God; as the mother wearily says before her suicide, the world does not make sense and this is directly attributable to the discrediting of the old religious answers.[58] It is this interpretation of the world as meaningless, one forced upon the mother and Martha by the unacceptability of any religious solution, that brings about Jan's death, at once paradoxically willed yet undesired. If the Lord had been present in Bohemia as in Bethany, Jan need not have died. But he could not be present, because he does not exist. Camus's Martha, so different from St John's, is left to curse a forsaken world in which our wishes are forever frustrated and our intentions always undone.

Camus's Mary, who believes with her biblical namesake that love is the one thing needful, is assigned the gospel Martha's prayer, which is that, even now, with all seemingly lost, a miracle of redemptive love can put all to rights. She prays to God for a sign of His mercy and love. St John's Martha is blessed because she speaks to the Saviour, the lover of mankind. Maria, by contrast, is cursed, because her appeal is to Descartes's demon, a vindictive and malevolent spirit, startlingly shown as such at this final moment of the play and clarifying, in retrospect, much that has previously occurred. The mystery of the old man's behaviour is finally to be resolved. Earlier, Martha tells her brother that the old man is not a mute, that he talks, but only when it is necessary. It makes the final breaking of silence all the more significant. Maria must be disabused of her last illusion, her trust in the God of love. God speaks, but there is no love in His words.

As unmistakably as *King Lear*, *Cross Purpose* is a play about theodicy: the prayers made and the answers received, the moral order of the world and God's role therein, what life does to us and how we should react. It is plain that the religious interpretation of life is Camus's chief target. The mother and daughter have exchanged only a few words when religion is gratuitously dragged in so that it can be derided. The mother, longing for peace, confesses, with an ashamed laugh, that sometimes she almost feels like taking to religion. Shocked at so craven a surrender, the daughter rebukes her, but the mother replies that she is, of course, only joking.[59] Religion is, clearly, the last bolt-hole of those too cowardly to face life as it is, the leap so roundly condemned in *The Myth of Sisyphus*: no self-respecting person would consent to this degradation.

The son, by contrast, *is* religious; it is an integral part of the folly with which he is associated from the outset. Even his wife, herself an innocent, cannot understand his peculiar behaviour, his absurdly roundabout way of reintroducing himself to his family, his vague discontent with happiness. His intention, as a successful prodigal son, is to rescue those left behind, but, uncertain as to his reception, he plans to ease his way in before revealing himself. But, instead of feasting on the fatted calf, he *is* the fatted calf and the two women slaughter him. The forgiving father of the parable is missing: we have been abandoned by God. After the calamity, when the mother grieves for her dead son, Martha speaks in the jealous, resentful accents of the stay-at-home son who feels himself slighted in favour of the runaway. The parable story is clearly present, but with its elements morbidly transformed.

Meursault and Martha agree in seeing Jan as the play-acting fool who provokes his own destruction – even his devoted wife declares at the close that his indirect ways were bound to be punished[60] – yet his folly is inseparable from his faith that in the end all shall be well and this, in turn, rests upon his trust in God. He is the conventionally good man, subordinating happiness to duty, doing the right thing, and it is unthinkable that God would allow any evil to befall someone so laudably engaged: 'I'm not in any danger, as you seem to fear.'[61] So he reassures his worried wife and he dies drugged and unaware that this trust in God is pure delusion. His folly springs from a conviction that earthly happiness is not enough (the cardinal sin for the creed expounded in *The Myth of Sisyphus*), that 'no one can be happy in exile or estrangement' (the rationale for Pascal's Christian commitment), and that a man 'needs to find his true place in the world' (by which he does not mean the bed of the river).[62] The words transcend any simple naturalistic exegesis; the characters, without realizing or intending it, speak metaphysically, and in the end Jan dies for his false metaphysics, a victim of misplaced faith. Camus could have told him that exile is forever and that the task is to live homeless in the universe, an eternally displaced person.

Maria's religion is love and she leaves her husband with a blessing: 'Then – good-bye! And may my love shield you from harm.'[63] It might have alarmed her, had she known *King Lear*, to realize that she is echoing the last futile prayer uttered by Albany just before the king enters carrying Cordelia's corpse: 'The gods defend her!' Neither in *King Lear* nor in *Cross Purpose* do the gods seem concerned to protect those who love and believe, but Camus is far more partisan in campaigning for a malevolent universe. Gloster's view of the sadistic gods is only one among a number of competing theodicies in *King Lear*; it is unopposably dominant in *Cross Purpose*, as it is at the close of Hardy's *Tess*.

Jan's total incomprehension – a Candide without an indulgent Voltaire to see him through – is emphasized throughout, from his own mouth and from the others after his death. He tells his killers of feeling at home in the murder-house, exasperating his sister to an injudicious rudeness that would have driven any other guest away. So deaf is he to the warnings and half-threats of his hosts that he seems to be colluding in his own murder; in the end they kill him almost reluctantly as a man determined to die. His sentimental delusions undo him: so stunned is he at being called 'my son' that he misses the ominous words that follow when the old woman says that her hands are still strong enough to hold up a man's legs, a strange claim for a hotel-keeper to make.[64] An alert man might have wondered as to what kind of hotel he was in, but he's too preoccupied with his prodigal son image to notice what's going on around him. Short of telling him outright what they mean to do (surely they did not behave like this with their previous victims?), the women could scarcely have done more to drive him away. The mother muses over his refusal to understand Martha's words: 'But why must this man be so bent on dying?'[65] To his killers this innocence, this gullibility, is culpable. Innocence (as Dostoyevsky recognizes in *Notes from Underground*, as Melville in *Billy Budd*, as Graham Greene in *The Quiet American*) can perversely become a provocation, a lure to its enemies – Billy destroys Claggart as surely as Claggart destroys him. Martha is particularly incensed at the man's behaviour: 'this traveller is really too confiding, his innocence is too much of a good thing', and it leads her to a proto-feminist outburst at the stupidity of men in general.[66] Agamemnon walking onto the carpet is no more of a legitimate target than Jan strolling trustingly into the snare. Such innocence is almost a request for crucifixion (see the humanitarian pacifist of *The Fall*) and the world is always ready to oblige.[67] Paradoxically, just when Martha has almost decided against the murder, Jan ensures his destruction by his lyrical celebration of the land from which he has come and to which she so ardently aspires. All qualms about killing the simpleton vanish: she has her own salvation to achieve.[68]

From early on, Camus makes it plain that the world of his play is not to be comprehended naturalistically, that much more is at stake than a series of gruesome misunderstandings in a dark Bohemian village. When Jan talks to himself in his hotel room of the 'fear of the eternal loneliness, fear that there is no answer', we know that more is involved than a breakdown in room service, that the room is a symbol of the world itself.[69] The same is true of Martha's rebuke to his sentimentalism: 'Remember you are in a house where the heart isn't catered for.'[70] Nowhere in existence is such a service provided. The play's conclusion shows that Jan is not fearful enough, for what worries him is that there might be no answer in a mute universe. Maria's experience is far worse: she receives an answer, but the silence of those infinite spaces so feared by Pascal would be infinitely preferable. Jan encounters the old man as simply a failure or refusal of communication: 'He neither moves nor speaks ... The bell works, but *he* doesn't speak. That's no answer.'[71] But far better no answer than the one given to Maria.

The religious echoes persist, always with an anti-religious purpose. Looking at her drugged son, the mother remarks that it's still only sleep, not death.[72] The child is not dead but sleepeth: these are the words of Jesus before he performs the miracle of restoring her to life. In Camus the reverse movement occurs: from sleep to death, and there is no resurrection. The houses symbolizes the world itself – 'nobody's home', as Martha declares, and the dead man has only himself to blame for mistaking it for anything else.[73] Martha cheats, however, in claiming to have taught Jan the truth about the world, for he simply passes from sleep to death, as innocently ignorant as ever. It is his wife who is the doubtful beneficiary of

Martha's instruction. Martha, however, only teaches what she herself has been taught – Camus is equally remorseless toward all the characters, because they are all equally guilty of believing that the world can be made to serve their desires: whether by relying on God (Jan), on love (Maria) or on self (Martha). The final act shows how woefully mistaken they all are.

The revelation of the dead man's identity affects the killers in very different ways: shocked remorse in the mother, angry defiance in Martha. 'My hell has begun.'[74] The mother's words are the sinner's traditional response to awareness of sin. Weary from the start, she abandons all desire to live, brushing aside her daughter's protests as she goes out to join her son in the river. Martha, by contrast, repudiates all responsibility, ironically using Cain's words to deny she is Cain: 'What concern was it of mine to look after my brother? None whatever. And yet now I'm an outcast in my own land.' She presents herself as the real victim of the whole affair and concludes, apropos of her harsh, unrewarding life, 'that must be paid for'.[75] One responds to the cruelty of life with a matching cruelty. Like Vanni Fucci, she longs for revenge and for this she needs someone upon whom to displace her own suffering; Maria's arrival is timely. Like Vanni Fucci again, Martha continues to be defiant. All that has happened is the fault of a narrow land where one is 'reduced to gazing up at God'.[76] But this she will not do, will not bend the knee or express contrition – why should she when it is she who has been abused? 'To moan, to weep, to pray is equally cowardly': Vigny would have been pleased with Martha who refuses to do any of these things.[77] And when she speaks of the need to die unreconciled, she is echoing Meursault and Camus himself in *The Myth of Sisyphus*.

She is the play's truth-teller, even if the truth she tells is frightful, confirming yet again the link with Vanni Fucci. It makes the advice and instruction she offers to Maria a matter of the most crucial significance. When, in the last moments of her life, she turns educator, she must be heeded – not simply because of the words of a dying person tradition, but also because she has become, clearly, the play's spokeswoman. The instruction is unbearably hideous, but it is what Maria demanded: 'Tell me quite clearly what I want to know quite clearly.'[78] So she has no cause to complain at the news of her husband's face being gnawed away or of how revolting her tears are to her sister-in-law. Martha's pity is reserved for herself – 'my lot is worse' – and again, speaking with authority, she insists that the real crime is against *us* – 'we're cheated' – with those perceptive enough to see, suffering the most.[79]

What is paramount is that we should not weep at our fate but instead despise it: the power that torments us must not be given the satisfaction of our tears. Vanni Fucci's twofold aim is to defy God and to drive Dante to despair. Dante's last sight of him is of his making, despite his agony, an obscene gesture to heaven:

> Throughout the circles of this dark inferno
> I saw no shade so haughty towards his God[80]

Martha is a kindred spirit, both in her rebellion and in her desire to communicate despair: 'I have yet to drive you to despair,' she tells her appalled sister-in-law.[81] Her mission, in the short time left her, is to destroy Maria's hope, in particular her illusion that love is not futile. In a kind of metaphorical defloration, Maria is to be shown the blunder she shares with her Gospel namesake: her trust in love as the one thing needful. As to why she cannot simply leave Maria with her illusions, Martha, if pressed, would give the same answer as Caligula gives to Scipio: no one has the right to remain hopefully nescient or blissfully deceived. The truth-teller cares only for the message, nothing for the anguish it brings. That Martha communicates her message vindictively highlights its malevolence without discrediting its truth.

Her final tuition is how to deal with the disaster. The choice is between suicide and stony insensitivity: 'Pray your God to harden you to stone' – it is what He Himself is and how He endures.[82] Martha chooses suicide and goes out, leaving Maria to decide for herself, but not before testing Martha's hypothesis of a wilderness world and a God of stone who rules it. She cries out to her own God, the God of love who comforts the afflicted and guarantees happiness, the God of the Christians. 'Oh God, I cannot live in this desert.'[83] It is the word used in *The Myth*, a word integral to the whole Christian experience of trial and testing, the place where Jesus spent forty days before commencing his redemptive mission. Maria is objecting to the desert as a place of permanent residence – passing through is a very different thing from living in it. She calls upon her God in the time-honoured, approved, traditional manner: ask and you shall receive, says Christ; 'In my distress I called to the Lord and he heard my voice.'[84]

But that is the Psalm and this is Camus. Her prayer *is* heard, but it is a demon who answers. Martha as teacher is completely justified. What else but demon can we call a God who hears our appeal but savagely rejects it, who could so easily save but prefers to destroy? Camus must have hated the Christian position very much to conceive so appalling a refutation; so intent is he on dispelling the myth of heaven that he is prepared to turn the Earth into hell to achieve his goal. We leave Maria helplessly confronting the demon.

Camus seems to have realized belatedly the enormity of what he had done – how else are we to explain the unbelievably puerile exculpation of the play that he offers? In an utterly unconvincing attempt to evade its nihilistic implications, he tries to persuade us that it is positive and even optimistic: it declares in favour of openness, it upholds an ethic of sincerity. Jan is the chief violator of this ethic; had he listened to his wife and simply and sensibly announced who he was, there would have been no tragedy and all would have been well.[85] This rivals the description of *Othello* as a play about the need to look after one's linen, but, at least, it wasn't Shakespeare who said this.[86] Camus apparently realized that his attack upon religious hope had gone so far as to threaten any viable idea of human existence, including the humanism upheld in *The Myth of Sisyphus* and *The Plague*. The final scene between Maria and the old servant had, after all, been conceived from the outset as the fit conclusion to the action. But if the world is as bad as this – 'quand les choses s'arrangent mal, on ne peut rien à faire' – if it is simply a machine designed to torture us, then we are all, believers and unbelievers alike, in the same forlorn predicament and there is, bluntly, nothing to be done.

Cross Purpose is a far darker play than *Caligula*. Caligula attempts to become the incarnation of the Absurd, made flesh and dwelling among us, but he himself confesses the failure of the experiment. Cherea, too, is an opponent who understands and challenges him. No comparable figure exists within *Cross Purpose*. The enemy is not an unhinged emperor, not a human being at all, but a malign world of which the old servant is merely the delegate. Maria can do nothing but cower helpless and uncomprehending before such malice: there is no other action possible.

Camus's attempt at sanitizing his play is simply a badly failed case of damage limitation. Is it really the case that all would have been well if only Jan had been more direct? Presumably, he could have bought air tickets for all of them and carried his sister off to that ideal land for whose sake she has become a multiple murderess. We can, in that case, forget all the other dead men, so long as Jan lives and Martha is happy. Even to state it is to see how absurd this is. Anyone who knows the play knows, too, that Martha was never meant for happiness. Camus recoils from his own insights because they are too terrible to be borne, trying to mend with his heart what he has ruined with his intellect: how else are we to account for the eccentric vindication he offers?

To begin with, it makes Jan the centre of the action when he so clearly isn't – even if it were (which it isn't) a psychological drama, Martha would have a better claim to that distinction. But the play does not turn upon a personal or psychological issue. The action flows from an evil world, not a character defect, such as Jan's perverse indirection when simplicity is all that's needed. It's not that kind of play, for at its core is metaphysics, not psychology – Aeschylus, not Euripides, is the master. Nor is Jan its sole victim, because, through his own folly, he is not recognized; no one – it is Martha's magisterial summation – is ever recognized: that's the kind of world it is, regardless of individual behaviour.[87] The title is misleading, because non-recognition and mischance are the norm, not the aberration: the wrong order of things is 'right', after all.

It is breathtakingly unfair of Camus to fault Jan's behaviour for the tragedy, when Jan clearly behaves as he does at Camus's behest – Jan *has* to be indirect, because otherwise he would not be killed and there would be no play. We need not linger too long over the complicated reasons Jan gives for concealing his identity; he conceals it because that's what Camus wants – the motivation is imposed from without. Jan's mother and sister are marked down to kill him and they would not do so if they knew who he was, ergo they must be prevented from knowing it. We accept this for the sake of the story, but jib when Camus tries to pass the buck, blaming the character for doing what the author so clearly designed.

But, even on an inappropriate psychological reading, it is wrong to put all the blame on Jan. The old servant is even more culpable. He sees Maria with Jan and yet unaccountably fails to tell his employers that the man is accompanied, hence ineligible for killing. In the revised version, he actually hides, because if Jan and Maria see him, Jan could not pretend to be travelling alone and so the murder would not take place. At crucial points, the old man acts so as to ensure both that Jan will be murdered and his employers undone. It is pointless to search for psychological reasons for his behaviour or to ask what he is going to do at the close, having wantonly destroyed his employers and put himself out of a job, for he is not to be understood in these terms. He is, like Satan, an enemy of humankind and they are all, finally, his victims: the murdered man, the killers, last of all the widow. He is not, like Caligula, a human being, however monstrous; he is the opposite of the Word made flesh, the anti-Word, the nay-sayer, and he comes to tell Maria that there will be no raising of Lazarus. In this reprise of the gospel story of a pleading woman and a loved, dead man, the old servant is, like Jesus, the power from above, but a power that annihilates rather than revives. He is, simultaneously, the key character and no character at all, for he exists on an entirely different plane from the others. Camus's original title for his play was 'Dieu ne répond pas', echoing his debt to Vigny's poem, 'Le Mont des Oliviers', a study of Christ in agony abandoned by his putative Father. But Camus intensifies the torment, carries it to a deeper level, for, if we are appalled at a father who abandons his children, what shall we say of one who sadistically torments them?

Cross Purpose is a didactic play, with three teachers collaborating to deliver its frightful syllabus: Martha, the old servant and Camus himself. Maria is the recipient of this dread instruction. Martha informs her as to the nature of the world we live in; the old servant confirms this lesson and tells her not to look for help from above; and Camus, as head of the faculty, ensures that all is for the worst in this worst of all possible worlds.

Chapter 8

Waugh

The religious counter-attack in modern literature was entirely predictable. Just as the revolutionary terror of Saint Just and Robespierre begot the counter-revolutionary terror of de Maistre, so the attack upon the Christian view of the world, explicit in Hardy and Camus, implicit in Conrad and Kafka, provoked a religious backlash clearly discernible in the work of Evelyn Waugh and Flannery O'Connor. There is the same implacable resolve to punish culprits – only their identity is altered. Believers had been attacked for their credulous trust in Providence, non-believers are now criticized for their even more credulous trust in themselves. Only when it is too late do Hardy's Tess and Camus's Maria learn that there is no God of love watching over them; only when it is equally too late do Waugh's Tony Last and O'Connor's ironically miscalled Sheppard realize that unassisted man is bound to fail. In both sets of writers there is the same merciless treatment of the misguided, with no concessions made for good intentions or high misconceptions. Believing in the goodness of humanity now calls down the same condign retribution as believing in the goodness of God had once done.

The Christian writers are as ruthless as their atheist counterparts, just as unsparing in chastising the self-destructive follies of their deluded protagonists. They have absorbed Virgil's dictum that there must be no sympathy for the damned and the damned include the simpletons, the uninstructed. Jean-Baptiste Clamence in *The Fall* recounts with relish the fate of the philanthropic fool who hung a sign over his door in unqualified welcome to all who wished to enter: 'Who do you think answered that noble invitation? The militia, who entered and made themselves at home, and disembowelled him.'[1] Quite right, too, is the implication: trust equals credulity. Orwell similarly finds the moral of *King Lear* to be not to give away your power in the first place, or, if you do, not to complain when those to whom you have given it proceed, as they surely will, to abuse you – what else can you expect?[2] The argument is so uncomfortably close to the self-justifications advanced by the wicked daughters that this alone might have dissuaded Orwell from repeating it; that he nevertheless did so is simply another sign of the unsentimental atmosphere of the age – we are all realists now.

The Christian writers are just as unforgiving toward folly as Conrad and Camus. Tony Last and Sheppard are neither bad nor ill-intentioned. They misjudge, they go astray, but they do not wilfully sin against the light. They blunder in the dark and are prime candidates for that plea made by Christ to the Father: 'forgive them for they know not what they do'. The sinner is an ignoramus, a dunce. But, even if true, this supplies no explicit instruction, no indubitable directive, for dealing with sin or the sinner. Nevertheless, despite the words just quoted, Christ seems to speak ambiguously on the subject. If we heed his dying utterance (and how can we ignore words spoken at so crucial a moment?), it can only mean that those who do wrong unintentionally must not be held accountable. Where there is no premeditated malice, no will to evil, there can be no guilt, hence no condemnation. Yet the same Christ tells the cautionary story of the Fool who spent a lifetime gathering wealth in the deluded confidence that he would be spared to enjoy it. It was a blunder, but by no means a choice of evil for its own sake. Yet, far from being pardoned, it was for being a fool that he was condemned. The same holds true of the foolish virgins who were, at worst, careless and unforeseeing but not, surely, malicious: they erred but there ends their culpability. Yet they were damned for being dunces.

They would have wasted their breath pleading ignorance in mitigation – how can the offence be the excuse? Convictions would cease altogether if ignorance of the law secured automatic acquittal. The response to such a plea is itself automatic: you ought to know the law and if you don't, so much the worse. This is the unsympathetic, irreproachably legal reply of the warder to Joseph K.[3] There is little point in the Fool's pleading that he had no idea that death was so close when it's for not knowing that he is being punished. Those who disapprove of Christ's dying plea as a charter for fools to run amok, subverting our courts and systems of justice, have a very different recommendation: punish ignorance, chastise incomprehension. It is this mentality that sustains and shapes the fiction of Waugh and O'Connor.

Waugh's is an especially interesting case, because we can trace in his fiction a shift from the indulgent treatment of folly prayed for by the dying Christ to the far harsher attitude of those who call for retribution. The subject matter of the early novels remains recognizably constant; it's the author's attitude that undergoes a transformation. Stephen Spender calls Waugh a comedian who turns serious.[4] One need only contrast the treatment of Paul Pennyfeather, the hero of *Decline and Fall* (Waugh's first novel) with the very different treatment meted out to Tony Last, the luckless protagonist of *A Handful of Dust,* his fourth book. After a series of bizarre misadventures, Paul incredibly lands on his feet, ready to resume his life as it was before his disasters began. Tony's is an altogether different fate as he ends up a prisoner for life in the Amazon jungle. Yet, folly for folly, Tony is no more flagrantly at fault than his fortunate predecessor. Waugh would have been hard put to explain why he is so lenient toward the one, so severe toward the other. Paul's gullibility over Margot is as reprehensible as Tony's over Brenda. Both men are imprisoned for their blunders, but, while Paul's release is all arranged for him without his lifting a finger, Tony must remain with Mr Todd forever. Why? The only answer is that Waugh himself has changed, has come to take a far more censorious view of the things he had previously beheld with a detached, nonchalant amusement. The letters stop being funny. Something similar happened to Waugh as happens to Miss Lonelyhearts: it simply isn't funny any more. In two poems written by those close friends, Alexander Pope and Jonathan Swift – 'The Rape of the

Lock' and 'The Journal of a Modern Lady' – a similar spectrum of frivolities and follies is surveyed, but in a manner completely different. Pope's Belinda and Swift's modern dame spend their hours, objectively considered, in much the same way, but Pope's delight in his subject stands in sharp contrast with Swift's disgust. The same behaviour provokes very different reactions. The passage from *Decline and Fall* to *A Handful of Dust* recapitulates this transition from Pope to Swift: from good-humoured tolerance to pitiless condemnation.

The change is not in the material. Removed from its comic context, what happens in *Decline and Fall* is as unsavoury as anything in Zola – Chesterton, a fellow convert to Catholicism from an older generation, was bewildered as to how this could be classed as comedy. A child is shot in the foot, has to have it amputated, and dies of gangrene poisoning. The obtuse hero is jailed for trafficking unawares in white-slave prostitution on behalf of his socialite fiancée. A religious maniac, in prison for murder, decapitates the chaplain with tools obligingly supplied by the trendy governor. Despite all this, the text is imbued with a spirit of irresistible fun, and demands that it be read as uproariously absurd comedy.

Folly is paraded in all its different forms. The prison governor is a fool of the murderous kind, newly graduated from some modern equivalent of Swift's Academy of Lagado. His aspiration to be the pioneer of artificial sunlight in prison is a harmless enough lunacy, less so his insistence that prisoners with skin diseases should work in the prison kitchen, and criminally imbecile is his belief that the best therapy for homicidal maniacs is to supply them with sharp tools. This springs from his conviction that crime results from a repressed desire for aesthetic expression. Waugh's conversion to Catholicism was two years in the future, but already original sin seems to him a more plausible explanation.

Paul Pennyfeather is the fool as *ingénu*, as victim, and his highly improbable preservation throughout the text simply reflects his creator's indulgent forbearance. For a time he could be mistaken for a transatlantic cousin of Lemuel Pitkin, destined for the same unhappy end as the All-American Boy. Waugh, however, is not writing a savagely subversive skit on an unjust society, rather a *jeu d'esprit* in which the spirit of nihilistic fun overwhelms every other consideration. At the close, Paul, unscathed, is in exactly the same situation as when his story began. *In circuitu impii ambulant*? Not in the least. These are not the circles of the damned, more a kind of farcical merry-go-round. In Tony Last's case, by contrast, Augustine is entirely applicable as the captive of Mr Todd goes round forever in the novels of Dickens – comedy shades darkly into painful satire, painful to author, character and reader alike. But anarchic comedy reigns in *Decline and Fall*; in a work of such irresponsible levity it would be incongruously inappropriate if the dolls were suddenly to weep real tears.

The world of *Vile Bodies* may superficially resemble that of *Decline and Fall*, but it reveals, to closer inspection, a shift from comedy to judgement. There is no hilarity in the title taken from the *Epistle to the Philippians* – Paul Pennyfeather and the Apostle to the Gentiles share nothing but a name. The anguished cry to be rescued from our vile bodies is no laughing matter. The England of the bright young things may shut its eyes to the fact, but the sickness unto death, the crooked and perverse nation, the denunciation of those whose God is their belly and who mind only earthly things: beneath the Pascalian distractions, all these are as fully present in the novel as in the epistle.[5] 'I'd give anything in the world for something different.'[6] This is the young hero, after sex with his girlfriend, echoing the Underground Man's protest against the pointless monotony of existence. These *are* the circles of the damned that Augustine invites us to exchange for the Jacob's ladder of Christian direction. Who shall deliver me from the body of this death? It would be absurd to expect Adam, the young hero, to couch his appeal in these terms, but in the depths of the book the cry is, nevertheless, implicitly there. *Vile Bodies* presents a once-powerful civilization, now drifting rudderless, at ever increasing remove from its religious and cultural backwaters.

The well of Edwardian certainty is choked with the debris of modernity; under the frenetically brilliant surface is corruption, chaos and despair. Oh, Bright Young People! interjects the narrator, in parodic echo of Miranda's ecstatic cry.[7] (How, one wonders, did she fare when she left the island and settled in Milan? Did it continue to be a brave new world or did delighted innocence give way to disenchanted knowledge?) Miranda would have been sorely tested in the vile world of *Vile Bodies*, rife with political and sexual corruption among young and old alike. Lady Metroland is still procuring, Miles Malpractice is homosexual, Mrs Panrast is lesbian. It is the same malodorous subject matter as in *Decline and Fall*, but the stench is stronger. Revulsion against the vile, suffocating flesh touches Manichaean point in the frantic, moronic activity of the massed parties. While the young mindlessly pursue pleasure in dirigibles and windmills, the old meditate the lurch toward destruction without any clue as to how to halt it. All trust in tradition is ruthlessly subverted. Lord Metroland finds a spurious stability in the old classic books in his library.[8] The young, however, know nothing of England's cultural heritage. The heroine's new husband, looking down from their honeymoon plane, is vaguely reminded of some words he once read in a blue poetry book about 'sceptr'd isle, earth of majesty, something or other Eden, precious stone set in the silver sea'.[9] Nina corrects him; it comes, she says, from a play, but Ginger sticks to his guns – they may have put it in a play since, but *he* certainly read it in a blue poetry book. So much for Shakespeare's influence upon the young barbarians of Mayfair; what Metroland relies on for national survival means nothing to the new generation. So much, too, for the 'sceptr'd isle', as Adam looks out from his hotel window on canal, factory, rubbish dump, derelict perambulator – the depressing landscape of modern England, already unearthed by Eliot, soon to be revisited by Larkin.[10] Near the book's end, Adam and Nina awake from their adulterous sleep to the sound of bells ringing the Christian summons: 'Come all to church, good people; good people come to church.'[11] They neither go nor think of going. The débâcle in morals, culture and religion is complete; the old world is in ruins and savages now madly cavort where gravitas and decorum once held sway.

In his next novel, *Black Mischief*, Waugh temporarily leaves the sophisticated Yahoos of Mayfair to survey their literally savage brethren in Africa under their westernized Emperor Seth, Chief of the Chiefs, Tyrant of the Seas, Bachelor of Arts at the University of Oxford – the bathos is that of Swift ridiculing the Emperor of Lilliput and the spirit of our greatest, darkest satirist pervades the whole book.[12] Cannibalism is now part of the comedy. There is an increasing aversion against modern life, an increasing exasperation with fools of every kind: Waugh is becoming savage himself in his rage against folly. 'I am the New Age. I am the Future.'[13] This imbecilic hubris is the more damning because the future so ardently appropriated is one that Waugh detests: abortion, birth control, vivisection, building in steel and vita glass, the telephone acclaimed as a symbol of education and progress. When Bishop Sprat published his *History of the Royal Society* in 1667, the frontispiece displayed emblems, including gunpowder, the compass and the printing press, as irrefutable proofs of modern superiority to all previous ages. Swift despised this as noxious nonsense and in *Gulliver's Travels* exposed these touted emblems as simply convenient channels for Yahoo filth.[14] A similar contempt for progressive fatuities pervades Waugh's pages. Seth's has been a ruinous stay in Oxford. He now knows why cannibalism exists ('it's want of education') and looks to Montessori for a cure.[15] He is yet another instance (Quixote and Emma Bovary are among his predecessors) of a mind ruined by reading – turning him loose in a library is like sending a child into an arsenal with a blowtorch. His is a lethal innocence, but, unlike the prison governor in *Decline and Fall*, he destroys himself as well as others. The mood change between the two novels is unmistakable: the fate of innocence in a corrupt world has ceased to be purely a matter of amusement or diversion – levity is in retreat as Waugh turns serious.

Yet nothing he had previously written could have prepared us for the pitiless treatment of the fool in *A Handful of Dust*, justly recognized as the first work of Waugh's maturity. Again, the comparison with Swift is instructive. In the Academy of Lagado Gulliver encounters a succession of zany projectors with crackpot schemes for extracting sunbeams from cucumbers, calcining ice into gunpowder, softening marble for pillows, and so on. But all this is the height of good sense in comparison with what he later finds in the Academy's department of political science. Here are even more extravagant dreamers: people who think to persuade monarchs to choose favourites on the grounds of their wisdom, capacity and virtue, to teach ministers to consult the public good, to instruct princes to act in the best interest of their subjects, 'with many other wild impossible chimeras, that never entered before into the heart of man to conceive'.[16] Believing that you can extract sunbeams from cucumbers may be crazy, but what word, in that case, are we to use for those enthusiastic enough to believe in the possibility of good government? Swift has no doubt as to which set of fools deserve the dunce's cap.

Throughout the early novels we can watch Waugh tracing Gulliver's steps through the school of the zany projectors. Sir Wilfred Lucas-Dockery, with his plans for artificial sunlight, is eminently qualified to take his place on the faculty of

Lagado. Plato argues that justice means denying a madman a knife, even when it's his own;[17] Sir Wilfred presses knives into the hands of demented psychopaths. Seth, with his Montessori cure for cannibalism and his preposterous slogans – through sterility to culture, Women of Tomorrow demand an empty cradle – is equally appointable. But if Sir Wilfred and Seth are unquestionably fools, what term shall we employ to describe the hapless protagonist of *A Handful of Dust*, the last person to know of his wife's infidelity and even then only because she writes to tell him? 'But it was several days before Tony fully realised what it meant. He had got into a habit of loving and trusting Brenda.'[18] A bad habit and the more fool he: this is the uncompassionate message of this dark and bitter book.

Swift trawls the depths of his despondency when he ranks belief in good government as an imbecility beyond credence, more fatuous still than the follies of the scientific projectors. Waugh likewise tells us that the dreams of artificial sunlight are sober realism when set against the idiocy of trusting other people. The harshness of the treatment he receives shows that Tony is the king of fools. This is why the very different conclusion written for the American serialized edition of *A Handful of Dust* – Tony escapes from Mr Todd, returns to England and gives Brenda a taste of her own medicine by setting up a London flat for his own newly acquired mistress – is so completely wrong. Waugh wrote the book to punish the fool for his folly, not to allow him to elude its consequences in the end.

This folly can be summarized in a word that comes easily to hand: humanism. It is Waugh himself who says so; *A Handful of Dust*, he declared, was his last word on the subject of humanism, a blow from which it could not recover.[19] Tony Last is the good pagan, the humanist hero of a certain exemplary type: kind, courteous, considerate, dignified, a gentleman possessing the full set of virtues associated with that very English term. He has but one single defect, unfortunately, however, a fatal one: a total inability to understand his fellow human beings and the world they live in. A newborn infant left alone to survive in an equatorial jungle would have as good a chance of pulling through. There is no malice in him, simply ignorance, but of so culpable a kind, as Waugh sees it, that it justifies all the disasters that crowd on his luckless head. He is helpless before the world's barbarism, but, far from being his excuse, this impotence is his condemnation.

Only five years after the publication of Waugh's novel, a book appeared written by Rosalind Murray called *The Good Pagan's Failure*.[20] It was as though she had read *A Handful of Dust* and found in the hero's particular predicament the paradigm of a general cultural crisis. She herself was the daughter of a highly distinguished good pagan – her father was Professor Gilbert Murray, the well-known classical scholar – and she had been educated in her father's values until her conversion to Christianity. She wrote about these values from a position of sympathetic insight, but her sorrowful conclusion was that the good pagan's day was over and that his values could not survive in an increasingly barbarized world. He is the most polite, self-disciplined and agreeable of human beings, but all of this is nullified by the hollowness of his *Weltanschauung*, the illusions upon which his whole outlook rests. He is a good man in a bad world, without the faintest clue as to how to deal with it. Unlike the religious believer, educated to expect evil and forewarned as to the frailties of human nature, the good pagan is completely unprepared for the incursions of barbarism – when they come (as come they must), he is dismayed and helpless, because what he sees and hears is so violently at odds with his civilized picture of the world: chaos is come again. He, not the believer, is the chief victim of barbarism – it is he who suffers most and is most completely overwhelmed. In shirking the reality of evil and preferring an ideal world of his own imagining to the real world of death and betrayal, he sets himself up for pain and disappointment. It is because evil cannot be avoided that we should equip ourselves in advance for its onslaught. This is what the good pagan so singularly fails to do and this is why, in a world relapsing into savagery, his sun has set. He has disarmed himself before his unscrupulous, opportunistic enemies by turning away from God, and his values, unsupported and fragile, cannot survive. *A Handful of Dust* anticipates the problem at the core of *Nineteen Eighty-Four*: the helplessness of the humanist in a world where humanism is as discredited as religion.

The pertinence of this to the hero of *A Handful of Dust* is self-evident – the major difference is that where Rosalind Murray treats her good pagan with sympathy, a gentleman adrift amid a savage rabble, an aristocrat among the tumbrils, Waugh presents him as a simpleton who colludes in his own destruction. The clue to the book's meaning is in its conclusion. Waugh had already written a short story, 'The Man Who Loved Dickens', based on his own experiences while travelling in South America. In Brazil he had spent some time as guest of a rancher, a Mr Christie, who turned out to be a religious maniac. It struck Waugh how completely he was in the madman's power and his story depicts the predicament of a traveller just as helpless, but far less fortunate than, himself.[21] The religious fanatic is transformed into an illiterate with a mania for Dickens, possessing all the beloved texts but not, alas, the ability to read them. (Hadn't Arnold predicted that as religion waned, art would steadily replace it as a source of comfort and spiritual instruction? Mr Todd is simply an example, admittedly extreme, of this transition.[22]) To gratify his appetite he needs a captive reader forever on call; Waugh sends him one in the shape of a lost traveller strayed out of the jungle into this space where the madman's word is law.

But the subject, even when written, would not go away. The story focused upon the madman, not his reader; but the question now nagged Waugh: how had the traveller come to be lost at all, what brought him to the jungle in the first place? 'I wanted to discover how the prisoner got there, and eventually the thing grew into a study of other sorts of savages at home and the civilised man's plight among them.'[23] The novel was written to answer these questions. He knew in advance the hero's destination; all that was needed was to trace the route. Tony Last, without knowing it, had always lived in a jungle: the second one, his final home, is simply a punishment for failing to perceive the first.

We first meet him ensconced in his humanist Eden at Hetton Park, his ancestral country home, where he lives in ostensible bliss of the gentry kind with his wife and child. But it is, in fact, a brittle, unstable paradise, about to be invaded, not by a serpent, but by a beaver. A casual, off-the-cuff invitation brings a young social parasite down from London to ruin paradise. It is the standard Jane Austen theme: the noble house threatened by the incursion of moral waifs from the trendy, corrupt city; but, whereas in Austen, the noble house and all it stands for, though shaken, prevails over the barbarian assault, in Waugh the opposite occurs. Tony's problem is that there is a barbarian within in the shape of his bored, restless wife, and it is she who welcomes the external vandals and becomes one of their number. But, though true, this is incomplete. *A Handful of Dust* is not the tragic tale of a noble man undone by corrupt enemies; it is the savage satire of a simpleton who aided and abetted his foes and who ends up in the jungle because that's where he deserves to be.

Tony's immaturity is revealed from the outset. He still sleeps in the room he occupied as a child when he was the victim of nightmares (but truly foretelling his fate); it remains preserved in its original puerile condition, all the trophies of boyhood and adolescence lovingly retained.[24] The room is the external representation of Tony's inward condition. When I was a child I thought as a child, but now that I am a man I have put away childish things. Tony has not grown up as St Paul insists we should – he has simply added to the childish things his own singular set of adult fantasies. Among the books on his shelf, strangely out of place among the juvenile productions, is a copy of Hemingway's *A Farewell to Arms* which tells of how a man lost his wife and child. Hemingway has advice on how to deal with life's disasters, but Tony knows nothing of that stone-faced stoicism that Hemingway recommends as our only shield against atrocity and can envisage no circumstance where such an ethic might be needed in a world customized to our requirements.

Waugh's contempt for Tony's facile creed explains the care with which he emphasizes the emptiness of Tony's religious professions. Despite his deliberately paraded traditionalism, it is, significantly, Tony who puts a stop to the long-established practice of joint prayers for family and servants in the household chapel.[25] His own carefully continued attendance at Sunday service in the local church is no more than mindless conformity with an ossified ritual. 'The more severe practices of his parents' have dwindled to an empty formalism, ceremonies drained of significance.[26] Renan spoke of living on the perfume of an empty vase, but in Tony's case the very aroma has almost completely evaporated. Brenda (who does not accompany him to church) twits him about his pose as a believer and, far from being offended, he joins in the joke. He actually enjoys the charade. When Beaver offers to go with him, Tony hastily puts him off: 'You wouldn't enjoy it. I only go because I more or less have to.'[27] But this isn't true, for he likes posing as a believer much as little boys like pretending to be pirates – the child's escapism carried on into the adult's life.

Yet the service he attends might have been salutary for a grown-up with ears to listen: 'Enter not into judgement with Thy servant, O Lord.'[28] Tony sees not the least application to his own case – what need has he of God's forbearance? – and so when his troubles come, he is left inadequately alone to solve them. Physically present as the words are being read, Tony is mentally elsewhere, planning a future of bathrooms and lavatories, too preoccupied to hear the words of salvation. Yet he has no future, at least none at all to do with the renovation of Hetton. Emerson praised the American attitude to life by likening it to the nonchalance of boys assured of a dinner;[29] it is precisely this lack of a sense of life's precariousness that Waugh condemns as his hero's worst shortcoming. Yet in Tony's own wider social world things are falling apart: broken marriages, failed relationships, adulteries, crumbling values, a disintegrating upper class desecrating its wood panels with chromium and learning its fortunes from foot reading. Living among this, Tony contrives not to see it or its significance – which explains why he alone is stunned by his wife's adultery while everyone else accepts it as unexcitingly routine. Eyes are wasted on Tony, for he doesn't know how to use them.

To be always surprised suggests an inability to learn. In a Houyhnhnm we might admire this bewilderment in the face of evil, in a man it is surely reprehensible – the gullibility of a simpleton who gets what he deserves. This authorial bitterness is arguably attributable, if only in part, to Waugh's own distressing divorce: Tony is the fictional fool, created so that he can be whipped, in surrogate retribution, for the author's own shortsightedness – he, too, had been the butt of society's jokes, the last to know of his wife's betrayal. Evelyn Waugh and Tony Last have a good deal in common.

Brenda is the internal vandal, cuckolding her husband, neglecting her child, modernizing, which is to say ruining, their house. From the perspective of contemporary society (it is shared by the society of Restoration Comedy), she is perfectly right to do all this; her husband is the 'old boy' (he is just over 30), embodying, in however mild a form, the shackles of domestic repression, while she and Beaver represent the spirit of sexual liberation.[30] This is not, of course, Waugh's view, but it is interesting, given the autobiographical element, that he is not more wholeheartedly on the side of the duped husband. That Tony is, almost by definition as a husband, made into an object of ridicule by Brenda and her cronies does not automatically make him an object of sympathy for the reader – Waugh prevents this from happening and that's what is revealing. Brenda may be worthless, but Tony is too foolish to deserve pity, let alone respect. When the clique conspires to procure a lover for Tony (thus retrospectively justifying Brenda's own adultery), the scheme misfires; it's the child, not the father, who falls for the egregious Jenny Abdul Akbar. Mournfully, Brenda sums up: 'The trouble is I've become such a habit with him – he won't take easily to a new one.'[31] Waugh uses the same noun when describing the devastation wrought upon Tony at the news of his wife's infidelity: 'He had got into a habit of loving and trusting Brenda.'[32] Brenda being what she is, it was, clearly, a very bad habit to have acquired.

The status and problem of trust are at the book's core. When Brenda vents her fear to her brother-in-law that Tony may suspect her, the reply is blithely reassuring: 'Lord, no. It's the last thing that would come into his head.'[33] Is this a compliment or an indictment? There are those who would say that it is better to trust and be betrayed than to go through life as though it were a minefield, wary and suspicious, on guard against every man as a potential rogue, every woman as a potential cheat. Nevertheless, it is far from evident that Waugh is asking us to admire Tony because it never once crosses his mind that someone he loves might let him down. If this is virtue, it is that vacuous kind that Milton disparaged: 'a youngling in the contemplation of evil . . . a blank vertue, not a pure; her whitenesse is but an excrementall whitenesse'.[34] If Milton is right in insisting that we can know good only through knowing evil, then Tony is disqualified from knowing anything at all. He takes his wife for granted and in the world of Waugh nothing can be taken for granted; this, if we can believe Orwell, is also the lesson of *Lear*. This does not, of course, absolve Goneril or Brenda, but it does mean that Lear and Tony cannot claim to be entirely faultless victims. They suffer, but only because they collaborate with their tormentors; they share responsibility.

This question of responsibility is yet another point where Dickens's influence on Waugh's text is apparent. Our last word from Amazonia is of Mr Todd singing the praises of *Little Dorrit* and we know that this book's original title was *Nobody's Fault*. According to John Forster, the book originated from a notion Dickens had of a leading man for a story who would bring about all the mischief in it, lay it all on Providence, and intone at every fresh calamity, 'Well, it's a mercy, however, nobody was to blame, you know.' Although Dickens abandoned this title, the original intention is sustained in a series of chapter titles: 'Nobody's Weakness', 'Nobody's Rival', 'Nobody's State of Mind', 'Nobody's Disappearance' – plainly, Dickens meant the reader to see that nobody was most certainly somebody. Dickens also omitted the projected character, but the idea the character embodies is subsumed in the dominant concept of 'nobody's fault' being 'everybody's fault'.[35]

It is inconceivable that Waugh did not have *Little Dorrit* in mind while writing certain sections of *A Handful of Dust*. The specific reference at the end generates its major irony from the fact that Tony's pitiless jailer weeps sentimental tears over Dickens's great prison novel, that Mr Todd is wilfully guilty in life of the very injustice he grieves over in fiction. There are, too, unmistakable echoes of Dickens throughout the episode of John Andrew's death in the reiterated insistence that it was nobody's fault – the characters veritably queue up to tell each other that the child's death was sheer accident, an unlucky fluke. It is this repetition that calls attention to the humanist imperative to ascribe all our misfortunes to random events over which we have no control and for which we bear no responsibility. In the text the repetition is counter-productive: the reader would never have thought the death anything other than sheer accident but for the almost hectoring way it is drummed into him. 'Everyone agreed that it was nobody's fault.'[36] This unanimity reflects the humanist project to substitute a random world for a fallen one, a fault-free life for one of responsibility and duty. Had Tony studied his copy of *A Farewell to Arms* more closely (in some ways it parallels his own situation) he would have discovered a very different cosmology being proposed – the idea of a universe of hostile forces vindictively conspiring our destruction: 'They threw you in and told you the rules and the first time they caught you off base they killed you.'[37] It is not, in Waugh's view, a true philosophy of life, but it is manifestly superior, in its honest confrontation of evil, to the evasive creed of a facile humanism.

The death of John Andrew can only be accommodated within a humanist ethic as a stroke of atrociously bad luck; in a senseless world, death – especially sudden, violent death, more devastating still when it happens to a child – strips away our meagre defences to leave us the poor, shivering, naked wretches that Lear encounters on the heath. Mrs Rattery, like a goddess descending from the heavens in her plane, can create order from chaos when she plays patience, but life is not a card game and the structures we impose upon it, however elaborate and impressive, are fictions that collapse in ruins at the touch of death.[38] 'It just happened,' says Jock and Tony readily agrees.[39] There are events but there is no meaning. In *Three Sisters*, Masha pleads with Toozenbach: 'Isn't there some meaning?' He simply tells her to look out of the window at the falling snow: 'What's the meaning of that?'[40] None, obviously, and the death of the child for Tony has no more significance than the fall of snow for Toozenbach. It just happened.

Tony has nothing but the pathetically inadequate code of the gentleman to sustain him: the guests must be attended to, their comfort secured. 'Were you having a good day?', he asks, ironically echoing the black joke of Mrs Lincoln's being asked how she enjoyed the play, but Tony is heartbroken.[41] 'It's awful for the girl … I hope I was all right to her.'[42] The courtesy and considerateness are exemplary in their way, but in the circumstances they seem artificial, mechanical, even inhuman, mere devices for evading unbearable reality. One thinks of how the death of Princess Diana polarized opinion in Britain between those who supported the Windsors in their reticent, stiff upper-lip attitude to the blow of bereavement and those others who favoured a less inhibited, more tear-stained response to the catastrophe. While not strictly coterminous with class divisions, it is nevertheless true that the self-disciplined mourners were mainly on the royal, aristocratic, elitist side, while the less restrained grievers exhibited a kind of democratic, populist abandon. Certainly, this division can be seen in Waugh's text. Tony, typically upper class, keeping his emotions firmly in check, seems heartless to the servants. The footman who enters the room to find Tony and Mrs Rafferty clucking away at the absurd card game reports this outrageously callous behaviour to a scandalized kitchen: 'and the little fellow lying dead upstairs'.[43]

To his working-class employees Tony seems a monster, but Waugh knows how unjust this is and presents him instead as a victim of class incomprehension. There is a parallel incident in Scott's novel *The Antiquary*, where the misunderstanding works in the contrary direction.[44] The middle-class protagonist, on a mission of condolence to the newly bereaved fisherman, is shocked to find him working at his nets, with his drowned son barely taken from the sea – he ought, surely, to be mourning, not working. The fisherman senses the disapproval and retorts that a working man must work; the fact that he has lost one son doesn't mean he should let his other children starve. The mistake comes from inappropriately applying the conventions of middle-class mourning to a working-class situation: the fisherman must work though heartbroken. *Pari passu*, the same holds true for Tony. He *is* devastated by his son's death even though his employees think otherwise; it is the class gulf that creates the misunderstanding.

Some may find here simply another instance of that snobbery for which Waugh has so often (and sometimes justly) been accused. Cyril Connolly deplored the early chapters of *A Handful of Dust* – it first appeared in serial form – as revealing a snobbery ruinous to Waugh as a writer.[45] Yet it is surely incorrect to say that in this book Waugh shows us the upper class behaving well and the lower orders behaving badly. The text defies any such simple antithesis. True, the lower-class Baby is rude simply because she's cold and her friends are apparently well used to this, expecting no better from her.[46] But, balancing this, the prostitute who accompanies Tony to Brighton for the bogus adultery is a better, more caring mother than the daughter of Lady St Cloud. Tony's self-control may be icily inhuman, but Brenda has about as much self-discipline as an alley cat. Waugh *was* a snob, but *A Handful of Dust* presents the English upper class as decadent and corrupt – it is precisely his failure to see this that leads to Tony being singled out for such strikingly unusual chastisement.

Under the world's savage tuition, Tony remains incorrigibly unteachable. He tells Mrs Rattery that Brenda will be devastated when she learns of her child's death – he could not, as it turns out, be more appallingly mistaken.[47] The most harrowing moment in the book (and, possibly, in modern fiction as a whole) comes when the mother thanks God that it is her child, not her worthless lover (it is her own valuation), who has been killed. 'Poor little boy,' she says much later when the momentary relief has subsided, but at the decisive moment when it counts Brenda would rather kill her child than lose her lover, and this is the woman for whom Tony had been so laughably concerned.[48] He tells Mrs Rattery that he and she scarcely know each other, but the real stranger is the woman to whom he has been married for so many years. He is so cocksure that he knows his wife, knows, too, how desolate she must be. Mrs Rattery tries to caution him against being too sure of anything: 'You can't ever tell what's going to hurt people.' He brushes the warning aside: 'But, you see, I know Brenda so well.'[49] But he knows her not at all and to be so ignorantly assured undermines whatever sympathy we may feel for him. To be both convinced and wrong is an inherently comic situation.

Not till she rubs his face in the noisome truth does he bring himself to admit it. Days after the disaster, with Brenda pointedly refusing to come home, he is still excusing her, still insisting to Jock, of all people – Jock who alone with the reader heard her joyful reaction to the news that it was her child, not her lover, who died – that the death has hurt her far more than him. He has not a shred of evidence for this apart from the wife he has invented to blot out the woman who exists. Uniquely situated to know just how wrong Tony is, Jock remains tight-lipped: the choice is to be silent, to lie or to tell the appalling truth. Tony doesn't query this silence, almost as though his subconscious mind cautions him against any dangerous questions best left unasked. So between Tony's too vehement assertions and Jock's stonewall silence, Brenda's reputation as a distraught mother remains intact, so far as her deluded husband is concerned.

Even after the confessed adultery, he continues, surprisingly, to trust her. Ever the irreproachable chevalier, he still gallantly tries to protect her: 'it was thought convenient that Brenda should appear as the plaintiff' – convenient, that is, for her. Tony is prepared to become a fake adulterer in order to provide his wife with a remunerative divorce. The lawyer, a circumspect man who has not contracted Tony's self-injurious habit of loving and trusting Brenda, tries to warn him against the possibly perilous consequences of such an agreement, but Tony, typically, sweeps aside this good advice as cavalierly as he had earlier dismissed Mrs Rattery's: 'Lady Brenda's word is quite good enough.'[50] However impressively gallant, it is suicidally knuckleheaded when the word being trusted is Brenda's – why should he believe anything she says after what she has done? There may be an element of closing upper-class ranks against professional hirelings such as the lawyer, but the exchange confirms our impression of Tony's unintelligence – in time, even he comes to see what a double-dealer his wife is.

But only because she so obligingly reveals her corruption. She tells him that she understands he is prepared to connive at her affair with Beaver provided only that she is discreet.[51] She has been misinformed, but it is another proof of her moral obtuseness that she should believe him capable of such an arrangement. It is the much less serious offence of winking at their relatives' adultery that brings the hero of *Mansfield Park* finally to see through the depravedly meretricious charms of Mary Crawford.[52] It is significant that only Tony seems unaware of his wife's true nature. Polly Cockpurse correctly predicts that the child's death will mean the end for Tony and this is, indeed, true; but to be known by such a woman (as Brenda is) is in itself an incrimination – it is to be, in effect, of her sisterhood.[53] Tony is ignorant, not because Brenda is devious, but because he is blind, the walking incarnation of Rosalind Murray's well-meaning, totally uncomprehending good pagan. Murray's account of the impact of evil upon this naif is reflected in Tony's bewildered reaction to his misfortunes:

> for a month now he had lived in a world suddenly bereft of order; it was as though the whole reasonable and decent constitution of things, the sum of all he had experienced or learned to expect, were an inconspicuous, inconsiderable object mislaid somewhere on the dressing-table; no outrageous circumstance in which he found himself, no new, mad thing brought to his notice, could add a jot to the all-encompassing chaos that shrieked about his ears.[54]

It is, as it turns out, too extravagant a claim: Tony (for these are plainly his thoughts) would have done better to recall the wise words of Edgar in *King Lear*:

'the worst is not so long as we can say "This is the worst".' Mr Todd and the jungle wait just round the corner, an 'outrageous circumstance' that finds Tony as unprepared as ever. Yet it is merely an exchange of jungles and there were signs enough, for someone able to read them, of the savagery in England before the savagery of Brazil. The repeated animal allusions, the vicar's absurd Christmas sermon, John Andrew's bizarre speculations concerning the monkey woman;[55] beneath the grotesquerie is truth: Tony was lost in a metaphorical jungle before he became trapped in a literal one.

His inability to learn is revealed in his continual surprise at his wife's behaviour. He is dismayed to hear that she has been telling the world that he's a drunken adulterer: 'He had imagined during the preceding week-end that nothing new would surprise him.'[56] By now Brenda has shown herself ready to sacrifice anyone and anything for her own gratification – why he should assume that she shares his own veneration for Hetton simply highlights his stupidity. He cannot believe it when Reggie, sent to negotiate, makes it clear that Brenda expects him to sell the house so that she can hold on to an increasingly reluctant lover. Wife, child, house: everything is to be taken from him. Reggie has already parted painlessly with his own ancestral home and accuses Tony of being unreasonable and spiteful in not following his example. The sale has left Reggie 'free to go where I liked',[57] but for Tony and Waugh this is not freedom but deracination, nomadism – Tony's values are those expressed by Yeats in 'A Prayer for my Daughter'. An archaic, aristocratic ethos is being betrayed from within by renegades like Reggie who have joined with rancorous political egalitarians to pull the great houses down. Between his unfaithful wife and her recreant brother, Tony is a kind of tragi-comic Samson delivered into the hands of his enemies.

A Samson who cannot see through Delilah: he still refuses to believe that Brenda could ask him to sell Hetton. Reggie has to become brutal: Brenda is not asking but demanding – Tony must sell so that her gigolo will stay. Reggie is insolent enough to tell Tony that Beaver is the brains behind the stratagem; the conspirators have the dupe over a barrel. For the only time in the text, Tony becomes decisive, heroic, forsaking his role as fool. His salvation is the absurd arrangements he entered into with the prostitute to give Brenda her grounds for divorce – his good-natured compliance in allowing Millie to bring her daughter along becomes his incontestable argument for refusing the divorce. Courteously, he tells the flabbergasted Reggie what his new intentions are and bids him a polite goodbye. The rogues are defeated, the simpleton has triumphed, but at a cost: the abandonment of a lifetime's dreams. 'His mind had suddenly become clearer on many points that had puzzled him. A whole Gothic world had come to grief ... there was now no armour glittering through the forest glades, no embroidered feet on the green sward; the cream and dappled unicorns had fled.'[58] It turns out to be a premature, over-optimistic assessment.

It would be bad enough if a grown, twentieth-century man were, in fact, saying farewell to so insubstantial a dream – how did he ever embrace it at all? – but the truth is that Tony remains an incorrigible dreamer. He does not forsake but simply re-locates his dream: where Renaissance man once hoped to discover Eldorado, Tony aspires to find the City called 'Shining' or 'Glittering' – the very words recall the dream he is supposed to have abandoned.[59] He dreams of discovering a transfigured Hetton, Gothic in character, straight out of Malory, in the heart of the Amazon jungle – compared to this, Eldorado is sober calculation. In Augustinian terms, he is still fixated on the City of Man. His recovery from Brenda is partial and temporary; in the jungle he dreams of how they will greet each other when reunited. His victory over his tissue of fantasies, wife and home alike, is short-lived; his brief heroic stand over, he reverts to type, the fool cosseting the same folly: 'I am looking for a city.'[60]

The remainder of the book shows the fate of those who pursue so futile a quest. Yet not so much the search itself as where he conducts it – this is for Waugh the core of Tony's error. In *Helena* Waugh supplies a sketch of what the City really means.[61] Even when it exists on Earth, it does so as no more than a faint, imperfect adumbration of another city beyond space and time. Tony's city, however, is rooted in earth, which is why it can never suffice. He is now 'the explorer', but is as big a failure here as in all his other avocations: husband, father, country gentleman. He is searching in the wrong place and Waugh clearly uses the search as a symbol of humanist inadequacies and pretensions.

Tony's trust in Dr Messinger recapitulates his blunder over Brenda. His meeting with Messinger seems another instance of the randomness so much alluded to in the matter of John Andrew's death. Tony, long intending to cancel his membership of the club, keeps forgetting to do so – a fateful omission since it is there he meets Messinger just as the latter is about to set out for Brazil. But here at least Tony resembles his wife: had it not been Beaver, it would have been someone else, and the same is true of Tony and Messinger – one way or another, Tony is marked out for destruction. From the start Messinger is a false guide: his choice of a small boat so as to avoid all 'that hideous nonsense of deck games' is no good augury of his perspicacity.[62] He is wrong about the river system, completely misjudges the effect of the toy mice, only has to deny that the situation is desperate for us to know that it is.[63] Amazonia is simply Hetton in a different location. There are blood-sucking parasites in the jungle as there are Beavers in London. Dr Messinger describes the ritual of his initiation into the tribe: buried up to the neck in mud, the women all spitting on his head.[64] It seems uncomfortably akin to what happens to Tony (and Waugh) in their messy divorces. When Jock says that 'the whole world is civilised now', Waugh means that the whole world is reverting to barbarism.[65] Ten o'clock on the Waurupang river is question time at Westminster, with pigs the first item of business in both locales – roast pig in the jungle vies with Board of Trade regulations. In Anchorage House and at the party in the Indian village the same vile bodies are present.

Betrayed by Brenda, misled by Messinger, Tony has simply exchanged jungles. He lurches feverishly into what appears to be the long-coveted city – 'gilded cupolas and spires of alabaster shone in the sunlight'; it is in fact the squalid hamlet of the mad Mr Todd.[66] Amid the ravings, insight dawns: 'There is no City. Mrs Beaver has covered it with chromium plating and converted it into flats.'[67] As so often in Waugh, the twin declines, architectural and moral, go hand in hand. Todd and Mrs Beaver, the primitive and the modern, the natural Yahoo and his sophisticated counterpart, together destroy Tony's humanist dream. Those who would set up heaven on Earth end up in hell: it is the warning that religion is forever sounding. Waugh has now shown how the trapped man – the image from which he set out – has come to be where he is. 'My name is Last.'[68] So Tony greets the last of the savages he meets and gives, in casual response to the question as to whether he can read, the answer that damns him forever.

The theme of reading and torture, of reading as torture, so prominent in Dostoyevsky, Kafka and West, receives its own singular treatment in *A Handful of Dust*. Tony had enjoyed reading to Brenda in happier days until she confessed that 'it was a torture to her', and the everyday hyperbole recalls the diabolic machine of the penal colony and the excruciating letters sent to Miss Lonelyhearts.[69] Once Brenda's unintentional torturer, Tony is now Mr Todd's chosen victim, a prisoner of print, trapped within texts without hope either of release or of a liberating last word: there is no last word for Tony Last. Mr Todd's appetite for Dickens is insatiable; to read to him is, in every sense, a life-long sentence. Even here Tony is characteristically slow to recognize his predicament. A more perceptive, warier man, told by the illiterate of the black man who read to him every day until he died, might have heard a warning bell, sensed the uneasy parallel with Scheherezade. Tony is the black man's replacement, a new reader risen from the grave to minister to the madman's obsession. Still in the dark, Tony expresses doubt as to whether he will have time to finish *Bleak House*, only to be ominously reassured: 'You will have time to finish it, my friend'; Dickens will finish Tony, not vice versa.[70] Not until he finds within the pages of *Martin Chuzzlewit* the note promising to let the black man go does Tony wake up to the peril of his position, but, as with his wife's adultery, he has to be told. His attempted rebellion in the jungle is as ineffective and short-lived as was his brief defiance back home. Read or die: it is the ultimatum to Scheherezade, although Mr Todd is a master far easier to please, for he demands no new inventions to keep him amused, simply a never-cloying repetition of the same old familiar, cherished texts.

Christopher Sykes tells us that Waugh read and re-read the novels of Dickens, but, we can be sure, not in the spirit of the Brazilian maniac. Love of Dickens makes Todd a monster. What he claims to find and admire in the great Victorian is a belief in God and, inseparable from this, a conviction that all must turn out well. Applied to this Earth, it is an article of humanist, not religious, faith – what Christian ever held that everything must turn out well here below? It is anti-Christian, for the Christian knows that things can and do go monstrously wrong on Earth, that only in the life to come is felicity promised.

'I suppose so. I've never really thought about it.'[71] Tony's reply to Mr Todd's question as to whether he believes in God is misleading, if not dishonest. What he truly thinks has already been revealed in his comment on the vicar's unwelcome attempt to bring religious solace following the child's death, when all Tony wants him to do is arrange the funeral. 'It was very painful ... after all the last thing one wants to talk about at a time like this is religion.' This is the view of a completely secularized man: if religion is dumb before death, when should its voice be heard? Tony, clearly, doesn't believe in God in any meaningful, let alone traditional, sense. Mrs Rattery puts in a word for the religion so easily dismissed: 'Some like it', but Tony is not to be ranked among them.[72] His is the mindset of the heroine of *The Sun Also Rises* when, at a moment of desolation, Jake attempts to console her with thoughts of God: 'Some people have God ... Quite a lot.' Brett is not to be comforted: 'He never worked very well with me.'[73] Tony, in honesty, would have to say the same thing.

Mr Todd thinks a lot about God, but only courtesy of Dickens – God comes with the novelist's guarantee. It will all turn out well, the madman assures Tony, because Dickens has said so. There has, surely, never been a stranger theodicy and it is at once both sentimental and ruthless. As much as Brenda, Todd is ready to sacrifice other people to gratify himself. Reading Dickens has, in his case, become not just a substitute for moral, but a justification for immoral, action. He weeps over the fictitious misery of Tom-all-Alone's so that he can behave like a criminal in life; he grieves over *Little Dorrit*, the great prison novel, while keeping Tony captive. Fielding's Parson Adams loves Aeschylus, but lets the text burn while he rushes to help Fanny;[74] Mr Todd, by contrast, prizes texts above people. 'Poetry excites us to artificial feelings – makes us callous to real ones.'[75] We are the more attentive to Coleridge's stricture precisely because it is a great poet who makes it, and Mr Todd perfectly exemplifies the dictum. He anticipates those sentimental monsters who served the death camps, exterminating by day, spending their evenings with Beethoven and Goethe. With sadistic glee, he kills off forever Tony's hopes when he reports the visit of the search party as though he does not comprehend its import – they left, he says, after he showed them the black man's grave and Tony's wristwatch. Tony is now officially dead; no one will ever come for him again – he is Todd's forever. In the light of such sadism, one ponders just what kind of God Mr Todd believes in.

Yet at the close Mr Todd has a collaborator in Waugh himself, a colluder in his cruelty. The reader is reading about Tony reading to Todd and the experience is not, is not meant to be, pleasant. Especially cruel is the encouragement of Tony's hopes only to crush them. When he succeeds in passing a message to a transient prospector, hope revives, but it is *le sale espoir*, the filthy hope, described by Anouilh. There will be no return home, no reunion with Brenda, no happy ending. Rescue, the last of Tony's dreams, is as empty as all the others: he is a fool for life. 'Tony endured the day for hope of what might happen on the morrow.'[76] But tomorrow is simply today prolonged: he will be as lost then as he is now.

In the last chapter we return to Hetton and to *le mythe animal*. Horses have been replaced by silver foxes and the rabbits they feed on. The foxes are treacherous and dangerous; it is 'unwise to rely on them' – people have been badly bitten.[77] We think, inevitably, of Tony. People are animals, too, and Tony's blunder, the blunder of humanism, is that he trusts and relies upon them – not until he is damned does he confront the fact of evil. To discover the real lesson of *A Handful of Dust* we have to trek back through the centuries to the conclusion of Chaucer's *Troilus and Criseyde*. In the palinode Chaucer instructs us how to interpret the tale we have just heard: 'Swich fyn hath, lo, this Troilus for love! ... Swych fyn hath false worldes brotelnesse!'[78] Tony and Troilus are both casualties of female inconstancy. Chaucer begs his younger readers in particular to learn from the sad example of Troilus:

> O yonge, freshe folkes, he or she
> In which that love up groweth with your age,
> Repeyreth home fro worldly vanyte
> ... and thynketh al nys but a faire
> This world, that passeth soon as floures faire.[79]

The world of *A Handful of Dust* is as much a Vanity Fair, as abandoned and astray, as the pagan world of Chaucer's poem; and the command to turn away from it is just as stringent, if less explicit, as that delivered by Chaucer in his closing stanzas. The great difference is that Chaucer unequivocally tells us where salvation lies:

> And loveth hym, the which that right for love
> Upon a crois, oure soules for to beye,
> First starf, and roos, and sit in hevene above;
> For he nyl falsen no wight, dar I seye,
> That wol his herte al holly on hym leye.
> And syn he best to love is, and most meke,
> What nedeth Feynede loves for to seke?[80]

Love God and He will never betray you; love human beings and the outcome is problematic. Without the anchor of divine love we shall be adrift and lost if and when our human affections founder and fail.

The application to Tony's case is obvious. A godless man, despite his routine ritualism, he has invested all his love, contrary to Chaucer's injunction, in earthly things – wife, child, home – and when these are taken away, he is defenceless against disaster. Unlike Chaucer, Waugh does not explicitly tell us that God is our recourse, but only a careless reader will miss the implied message. Troilus, now secure and at peace, looks down from heaven. Tony, by contrast, is as lost as Orwell's Winston Smith and for the same reason: each believes he can survive unassisted in the jungle. It is a mistake that provokes the severest chastisement.

Chapter 9

O'Connor

Waugh seems almost benevolent when set beside Flannery O'Connor. It is as though Vanni Fucci had switched employers and gone to work as God's enforcer, a religious terrorist intent on causing the maximum damage to the Lord's enemies. She was Catholic by birth and belief, but her God is the Old Testament God of her native Bible Belt, a wrathful figure bringing not forgiveness but retribution; it is Christ the Tiger who prowls her pages. Like Milton, she reports from the wars of truth and she has not the slightest doubt as to where truth resides.[1] Christians are right and pagans are wrong: it is this return to the dogmatic certitude of *The Song of Roland* that makes her work so implacably severe. Her fiction has been described as having an axe-murder feel to it, but it would be more accurate to connect it with de Maistre's idea of the executioner, for it is the blade of justice that she claims to wield.[2] De Maistre's paradox is that, since men instinctively prefer evil, punishment is providential: abolish the state executioner and chaos is come again. The most unnerving passage in all Dante is the explanation over hellgate:

> Justice it was that moved my great creator;
> Divine omnipotence created me,
> And highest wisdom joined with primal love.[3]

Omnipotence, wisdom, love – the attributes of the three persons of the Trinity. Shelley condemned hell as vengeance embodied, but Dante insists that love, wisdom and power all contributed to its creation, with Father, Son and Spirit all equally involved. Any attempt along Blakean lines to split the Godhead into an irascible old Nobodaddy and a loving, compassionate Son is stopped in its tracks by this assertion of the shared responsibility for hell. O'Connor follows Dante in denying a division in the Deity: those condemned by God have no other advocate toward whom to turn. Christ has already come to plead for sinners; next time it will be to judge and O'Connor's pages anticipate that second coming.

True, Christianity, as O'Connor well knows, is above all a religion of the second chance: 'There is something in us ... that demands the redemptive act, that demands that what falls at least be offered the chance to be restored.'[4] 'Demands' is a strange word to use in relation to God's grace, but this simply emphasizes O'Connor's sense of the importance of another opportunity, a second chance. But, for her, our present life *is* this second chance and there will be no third if we squander it. *This* is our last warning: ignore it and we are lost forever. Nowhere is the ethic of the *Inferno* more vividly dramatized than in O'Connor's fiction. The prohibition of pity for the contumacious sinner is straight out of Virgil's rebuke to the Pilgrim in Canto XX of the *Inferno*.

And for O'Connor the sinner beyond grace is the Pharisee. The Publican is saved, despite his sins, because he fears damnation; the Pharisee is damned, despite his virtues, because he is too sure of salvation. The first shall be last and the last shall be first: a proposition no self-respecting Pharisee can abide. O'Connor's only target is the Pharisee and she finds him in every rank and in every state of belief or disbelief – atheist Pharisees, religious Pharisees, Pharisees who care nothing about religion one way or the other. She ferrets him out, wherever he lives, whatever he believes. She finds him, predictably enough, in his traditional habitat, among the whited sepulchres, the *unco guid*. Ruby Turpin censoriously surveys the waiting room and sincerely thanks God that she is not like other people. Mrs May looks on disapprovingly at the ecstatic convulsions of her white-trash neighbour and knows that her own rigid self-control finds favour in the Lord's sight.[5] But this assumption of superiority is not a monopoly of believers; the sense of belonging to an elect far above the graceless rabble can as easily exist in atheistic minds. The central characters of 'Everything That Rises Must Converge', 'The Enduring Chill' and 'The Comforts of Home' are all unmistakably Pharisees, though theirs is a secular rather than a religious triumphalism – they belong to a cultural elite, but are as much a chosen people as any in the past and they pray the same prayer: I give thanks that I am not like other men. It is what O'Connor, following Christ, cannot forgive.

She employs two parables, that of the Fool, that of the Pharisee and the Publican, conflating them to wreak the maximum retribution upon the culprits. The young, spoiled man-child of 'Everything That Rises Must Converge', smugly convinced of his superiority to both his mother and his world, is cruelly cut down to size at the close. He wants his mother to be taught a lesson she will never forget (the word dominates the story); but O'Connor ruthlessly kills the scatterbrained mother to teach the pretentious son a lesson *he* will never forget. People do learn in O'Connor's school, but there was never an academy with higher tuition fees, as the central character in 'Greenleaf' would surely agree, could she speak from the grave. Ostensibly Christian, she despises her poor white neighbours for living like the lilies of the field in contrast to her own anxious, neurasthenic overwork, ignorant of or indifferent to the fact that Jesus was commending, not reproving, the lilies for their trustful unconcern. She worries over having no insurance if the bull should kill Mr Greenleaf; as for herself, 'I'll die when I get good and ready.'[6] It is the blindness of the Fool in the parable, for she has no future to worry about – the bull kills her and she loses not simply all her money to the Greenleafs in damages but life itself to another creditor altogether; this night I require thy soul of thee.

Mrs Turpin in 'Revelation' is yet another of the tribe of Pharisees, contemptuous of the human trash around her, odiously grateful to God for having made her the exemplary person she is. She takes too high a place at the table and is predictably demoted. Her discomfiter is appropriately named Mary Grace, for the story is an anti-Annunciation in which God's messenger comes to tell Mrs Turpin not that she is blessed among women but is an old wart-hog from hell. Despite her feeling of outrage, Mrs Turpin knows that this is not just some insensate assault by a crazy girl – this *is* how God sees Mrs Turpin and, in a room full of worthless people, the injustice of it all rankles. Mrs Turpin goes on the offensive, challenging God: 'Who do you think you are?'[7] It is the most startling, comic blasphemy ever hurled at the One who said I am who am – not even Vanni Fucci, the most defiant of all the souls who rebelled against God, could improve upon this.

What distinguishes the story is the hint of redemption: Mrs Turpin abandons her own way of seeing to look, if only momentarily, through God's eyes. She raises her arms in a 'gesture hieratic and profound' (she has come a long way from the vulgar exhibitionism of the waiting room) and 'a visionary light settled in her eyes'.[8] What she sees is the radical, destabilizing vision of primitive Christianity: I tell you solemnly, the tax gatherers and prostitutes are entering the kingdom before you; the first shall be last and the last shall be first. It is as shocking in Georgia as it was in Galilee. But, watching the anarchic procession as it moves through the heavens, Ruby Turpin knows her true place at last: a Pharisee is miraculously saved. There are not many such moments in O'Connor.

All of O'Connor's work is a deliberate affront to the modern world, but it is in her 'happy' stories that she is especially offensive. The endings of 'The River', *Wise Blood* and 'A Good Man Is Hard to Find' are an intentional scandal to a modern sensibility. A neglected child drowns as he seeks the kingdom of Christ; a man befuddled by religion blinds himself and dies; a family of three generations is slaughtered by a psychopath. For a modern reader there is nothing here but lunacy and horror, yet O'Connor truculently presents these as images of grace. Compromise is impossible; there can be no accommodation between the modern temper and the values implicit in these stories. We can easily describe them as stories by a freak about freaks, but this simply invites her response that the real freaks are those who condemn her. She knows that many of her readers will be hostile but this only makes her the more pugnacious. When people are deaf, she says, you have to shout to be heard; it is no different when the deafness is spiritual.[9] Hence the dramatic, heightened, almost histrionic nature of her art, intensified to a pitch where only the most blind will not see and the most deaf not hear.

In 'A Good Man Is Hard to Find' two worlds catastrophically collide – the lightweight, comic world of the Grandmother and the sinister, nightmarish world of the Misfit; it is as though a woman out of Thurber were to meet a man out of Dostoyevsky, as though the Porter in *Macbeth* were suddenly to be handed the tragic role. The story begins as comedy in the everyday sense of the word and ends as comedy in the provocative sense employed by O'Connor. The same material is deployed in both halves of the story, but with a shift from levity to seriousness as the Grandmother searches for the elusive good man, first with the sociable restaurant boss, then with the brooding Misfit. When the first bemoans his own benevolence and asks why he foolishly trusts other people, the Grandmother obligingly supplies an answer designed to please: 'you're a good man'.[10] Sammy's wife (presumably better informed) looks hard at him before echoing St Paul's dark view that there is not one who does good, that nobody can be trusted.[11] A good man is not so much hard as impossible to find. The two benignly complacent Pelagians, Sammy and the Grandmother, think otherwise. Having pondered her words, Sammy gravely concurs with the Grandmother's judgement: he *is* a good man. Later, desperately clinging to life, she screams the same compliment at her captor. Taking just as long to consider the words, the Misfit (playing a perverse Publican to Sammy's Pharisee) gives an ominously different answer.[12] Here is the match she never found in her son, a man she cannot cajole or manipulate. Surely, she declares, he would never shoot a *lady* (it almost makes murdering a *woman* sound acceptable); he unsmilingly replies that he would certainly hate to have to do so. It grimly echoes the authorial observation in the comic part that, even when not telling the truth, the Grandmother wishes she were.[13] Tell lies, commit murders – Misfit and Grandmother will each do whatever needs to be done to serve their own interests.

She starts out as a selfish old woman, fond of her own way and always scheming to get it. She fails to persuade the family to switch the holiday from Florida to Tennessee, but she covertly brings along her contraband cat and, having tempted the children, blackmails her long-suffering son into taking the fatal diversion. But for her trickery (the cat causes the accident in a place they should never have been) they would not have met the Misfit; she next guarantees their annihilation by rashly blurting out his identity. With the Misfit's entry the story changes. The hearse-like automobile slowly cruises into view, the line of woods gapes like a dark open wound: the imagery of death and blood signals the shift from the world of trivial chit-chat to that of nihilistic terror.[14] The story now has a Pauline character to match its Pauline title.

'Either one is serious about salvation or one is not.'[15] The Misfit meets O'Connor's stipulation, albeit in a terrifyingly negative sense. He is deadly serious about salvation; no one ever so fully exemplified the Pauline alternatives: either Christ is risen or we are the most miserable of men. The Misfit, choosing misery, kills out of disbelief. If only he had been there in Galilee when it all allegedly happened, he would have known for sure.[16] Instead, he walks the way of despair predicted by Paul, a metaphysical murderer slaying because the world is absurd, like Camus's Caligula. After killing the old woman, he rounds upon his laughing cohort who thinks that slaughter is fun – there is, he insists, no pleasure but meanness; he kills in revenge for betrayal.[17] Job, tormented by the randomness of suffering, turns psychopath: 'Does it seem right to you, lady, that one is punished a heap and another ain't punished at all?'[18] Pained at life's purposelessness, he imitates Vanni Fucci and deals out pain to others. A lost theodicy has made him an outlaw. His is the world of Ivan Karamazov where, God being dead, everything is permitted, the world of Svidrigaylov who asks, a simulated levity masking his grief, 'Now tell me, why on earth should I restrain myself?'[19] The longing is almost palpable: if only there were a reason for self-restraint.

The Misfit is Kierkegaard's demonic man, close to grace in the sense that he lives on the same level as the saint, not in the basement with the unthinking mob who muddle through life, indifferent to its mystery. Insofar as we do good or evil, we are human; it is therefore better to do evil than to do nothing: thus Eliot explicating Baudelaire.[20] In choosing evil, 'meanness', the Misfit fulfils Baudelaire's prescription, thereby becoming the most complete representation of Vanni Fucci in modern fiction. No pleasure but meanness: it is a slogan Dante's villain would have been happy to adopt. The paradox is that the Misfit is simultaneously the unwitting instrument of salvation for the woman he kills. O'Connor tells us that her stories always include an action indicating the offer of grace and that 'frequently it is an action in which the devil has been the unwilling instrument of grace'.[21] She does *not*, she insists, insert these actions into the stories but discovers them there, and she claims that this free act, this offer and acceptance of grace, is what makes the story work for her. In 'A Good Man Is Hard to Find' she informs us that this act is 'the Grandmother's recognition that the Misfit is one of her children'.[22]

The Misfit's unconscious mission is to test the old woman, to reveal what she bears within to take with her into eternity – he is as much God's messenger to the Grandmother as is Mary Grace to Ruby Turpin. At the close the Misfit remarks with black humour that she would have been a good woman if there had been someone there to shoot her every minute of her life. Not just someone, anyone – it needed *him* as Christ needed Judas – but there is truth in what he says without his realizing it. 'It is the extreme situation that best reveals what we are essentially.'[23] It is a conviction O'Connor shares with Conrad and Hemingway, although she puts a Christian spin upon it. In crisis we reveal ourselves and the Grandmother's situation could not be more critical. Her sudden grace-given insight into the Misfit's anguish causes her to forget her own peril. 'The grandmother's head cleared for a moment.'[24] What vacates it is her own frantic self-concern and mounting panic in the face of death. She has tried everything to stay alive: appealing to his goodness ('you're a good man'); begging him to pray ('Jesus will help you'), but with a mind set more on her own survival than his conversion; even repudiating Jesus if it will save her ('Maybe He didn't raise the dead') – and when she chants His name it sounds like cursing.[25] The moment her head clears is the moment of grace toward which the whole story moves – the search for a good man has ended in the revelation of the good woman. The panic-stricken woman amazingly forgets herself (grace is self-forgetfulness, says Bernanos[26]) and reaches out in love toward the anguished man, as though the Pilgrim had tried to embrace Vanni Fucci: 'Why you're one of my babies. You're one of my own children!'[27] It is a fatal recognition. The Misfit recoils as if stung by a snake (recalling Vanni Fucci in the circle of serpents) and shoots her three times: there is no place for compassion in a nihilist world. But the Grandmother finds the life she loses – the whole authority of the ending supports this conclusion. She lies sprawled, her face smiling up at the cloudless sky, victorious over the death she feared; it is her killer who looks 'pale and defenseless-looking'.[28] O'Connor leaves us with only two choices: to accept this as a happy death or to stay adamantly loyal to the uncomprehending modern world. She despises those who ask her to make the choice a little less abrasive.

Wise Blood poses a similar dilemma. O'Connor tells us it is a happy book, written with zest and meant to be read that way – but it is just as undeniably designed to scandalize the modern world.[29] When she described it as 'a very hopeful book', she was following Hardy when he attached the subtitle 'A Pure Woman' to his contentious novel, *Tess*; just as much as he, she knew how outrageously unintelligible her description would be to sensibilities nurtured upon altogether different values.[30] Sally Fitzgerald tells us that when we truly understand O'Connor's stories, we shall find more happy endings than we might otherwise have noted, and this is doubtless true.[31] Nevertheless, the general disapproval and incomprehension among critics suggest that we need a very different definition of happiness from that current among us today if we are to begin to understand, let alone agree with, O'Connor's claim. By any normal or natural definition of the word as understood by the average modern reader, *Wise Blood* is neither happy nor hopeful. But then we recall with some unease that Hazel's landlady made the same complaint about his behaviour – that it was not normal or natural – and blamed it upon the Jesus nonsense in which he was embroiled.[32] Not many readers will wish to line up with the landlady against her lodger, and this in turn may give rise to doubts about so summarily dismissing O'Connor's description of the book as a whole.

The instinctive modern reaction is to read it as a story about a crazy man moving among crooks and hypocrites in situations totally irrelevant to modern life and everyday concerns. The citizens of Taulkingham look at Hazel 'as if he were in a booth at the fair', but it is the city itself that is the monstrosity, the lost city of Baudelaire and Eliot in which no one, Hazel apart, was paying any attention to the sky.[33] 'Do you people care anything about the truth?'[34] Hazel's challenge to the citizens of Taulkingham is just as surely O'Connor's challenge to us. It is all too easy to see Hazel as the freak at the fair, but the book insists that the real freaks are on the outside looking in. The prostitute whom Hazel visits shortly after arriving in the city is 'so well adjusted that she didn't have to think any more'.[35] How well adjusted are you? It is O'Connor's question to us.

When she described *Wise Blood* as a comic novel about a Christian *malgré lui*, she was using the term in the same sense as it is used in *The Divine Comedy*.[36] Both texts begin with alienation and record a homecoming. Going home is the phrase with which *Wise Blood* begins and ends. Hazel is described at start and finish as having eyes like passages leading somewhere and his search for truth ends in triumph. 'I see you've come home,' says the landlady, but he corrects her: 'I want to go where I'm going', and this is what the book shows him doing: going home to Christ, because 'there's no other house nor no other city'.[37] Belief in Christ is a requirement of the text or else the story is simply that of a man who blinded himself in a fit of madness, lost all interest in life, was beaten up by the police and died. The landlady is right and the prostitute is justified.

But if Hazel is a madman, so, too, were Christ and St Paul before him, for they, too, lived lives that most people today would consider unnatural and abnormal and they, too, believed things that would today cause them to be classified as delusional or schizophrenic. Paul is, of course, the template against which Hazel's life is to be aligned. Saul, the fulminating foe of Christ, was on his way in his chariot to Damascus to persecute Christ's followers when he was briefly blinded before becoming Paul, the passionate apostle of the one against whom he had warred. Hazel similarly rages against Christ, frenziedly trying to exorcise the mad, stinking image from his mind, denouncing him in the streets of the city to anyone prepared to listen. Christ is redundant: 'Nobody with a good car needs to be justified,' Hazel declares, and he, too, is in his car, on his way like St Paul to another city to wage war against Jesus when his mission is interrupted by policemen who stop him and push the car over a cliff.[38] As with Paul, the beginning of a new life is accompanied by blindness, in Hazel's case self-inflicted. Like Oedipus and Gloster, when he has eyes he goes astray, is spiritually blind; only when he is physically blind does he see true. Those who decry this as mystical mumbo-jumbo in O'Connor should tell us why it is spiritual insight in Shakespeare and Sophocles.

True, the landlady is baffled by Hazel's behaviour, but that proves only her own limitations. There seems no compelling reason to accept her as an internal guide to the text or to defer to her assessment of what is normal and natural. She tries to trick the blind man into marriage with the bogus argument that we must be saviours to each other, when the true aim is to get hold of his money. Her chief source of bewilderment is his total unconcern for money, but she is also mystified by his penitential exercises and even more by his attempt to explain them. There is only one kind of clean, she unbrookably insists; for her, purity means hygiene and anything else is anti-American, Romish superstition, a view unlikely to endear her to O'Connor.[39] 'She was not religious or morbid.'[40] It may look like third person narration, but this is plainly the landlady's own voice and these are her synonyms, not the author's. 'She liked the clear light of day. She liked to see things.'[41] For blind Hazel it is now unending night, but what the text says is that his darkness is light, her light darkness. At the close we leave her struggling with a half-intuition that perhaps it's not just some kind of scam, that perhaps there is in Hazel some secret beyond her power to uncover. It is not a perplexity that the perceptive reader would wish to share with the spiritually obtuse landlady and her view of what happens to Hazel is certainly not the one that O'Connor wants us to adopt.

'The River' is yet another text in which O'Connor does her best to quarrel with the modern reader by presenting as a happy story what the latter instinctively construes as a tale of misguided, disastrous fanaticism. Certainly, there is nothing to prevent any reader determined enough from interpreting 'The River' as a caution against the dire consequences of failing properly to vet prospective childminders, but it would not be the tale O'Connor tells. It is about sickness and healing, at the spiritual even more than the physical level. When the hungover father calls from the darkened bedroom to the new babysitter, 'for Christ's sake, fix him!', he unintentionally supplies the key to the tale's significance.[42] The newly hired minder does exactly as she is bid: she takes her charge to a river baptism and there, literally for Christ's sake, he is fixed forever.

From the outset the child is shown as unloved and neglected, shunted aside so that his alcoholic parents can rest up for their next binge – he jumps as if shot at his father's unexpected words of affection.[43] Mr Paradise, faithfully attending the revivalist meetings to jeer at the believers and to parade his untreatable, cancerous ear, is the most obvious of those who need to be healed. But the child's parents, too, are spiritually maimed. What's her trouble? the child is asked about his mother.[44] Withdrawal symptoms is, of course, the immediate answer and it fills the disbelieving Mr Paradise with glee to hear it, but alcoholism is symptom, not cause, and the true significance of the question does not go away. 'Will he heal me?' asks the little boy and the challenge posed by the story is to say how and if this question is answered.[45]

From the new sitter the child learns that he was made by a carpenter called Christ, whereas his parents had told him it was a fat doctor named Sladewall – not much doubt as to which version O'Connor favours.[46] The child concludes that the parental version must be a joke, since everything at home is a joke. The contrast with the young, dignified preacher, austerely promising no miracles, gravely stressing the need for a change of heart, could not be sharper. The giggling boy is made to realize that the preacher is no clown and that what's happening in the river is no laughing matter. The reader, too, must take it seriously or else dismiss the whole business as callous, farcical deception: alcoholics, fanatics, tricksters and a poor, abused, finally destroyed child. Either Harry, re-baptised Bevel, is the victim of irresponsible parents and his escape to the river is genuine, or he is the victim of a crazy zealot and the trip to the river is his undoing. There is nothing in the text to support this second reading and only a reader coming to it resolved to indict religion as a swindle could consider it true. There can be no doubt as to which reading O'Connor wants us to accept. The child prefers death in the river (which is life) to life in the apartment (which is death). Only those ignorant of or hostile to the Christian paradox of losing life to find it will consider this repugnant or incomprehensible.

'Where he lived everything was a joke. From the preacher's face he knew immediately that nothing the preacher said or did was a joke.'[47] The story exists to vindicate the child's judgement. The preacher is clearly no crook and the text supplies no reason to regard him as deluded. When, after baptising the boy, he tells him that now for the first time he counts, it sounds both offensive and nonsensical to a modern ear, a piece of deplorable superstition long outgrown – which is precisely why O'Connor has him say it. Not for her the strategy favoured by her fellow Christians in the adverse circumstances of the modern world of going on tiptoe in the hope of not attracting the attention of the atheist bullies; don't antagonize them and they may leave you in peace. O'Connor, by contrast, stands prominent as she can, arms akimbo, shouting at the top of her voice her retrograde faith, taunting her enemies, challenging them to do their worst. She strides into town like God's gunslinger, ready to shoot it out with any adversary who comes against her.

Next morning, his parents again sleeping off their drunkenness, the boy awakes and prepares a makeshift breakfast before setting out on his last earthly journey to the river. In taking no suitcase – 'there was nothing from there he wanted to keep' – he acts with the maturity of the exemplary Christian leaving the world for eternity.[48] It is what Bunyan's hero does in shedding all secular baggage before setting out for the Celestial City. It is what the Fool in the parable so conspicuously fails to do, when, clinging to his worldly goods, he loses his immortal soul. It is the Fool who is childish, the child who is mature, because he knows that it's not so much a case of you can't take it with you – you shouldn't even want to.

The child means to waste no more time dawdling with middlemen; he intends to go straight to the kingdom all by himself. Entering the water, feeling its resistance – it seems at first that the river is rejecting him – he thinks he's the victim of yet another joke, the frivolity of the apartment replicated in the river. Mr Paradise comes charging after him (as the pig had earlier done) in an attempt to save that would, in fact, be the reverse of rescue. Far from being a saviour, Mr Paradise, as the associated pig imagery makes clear, is one of the possessed. He reminds the boy of the pig that chased him and is described in pig-like terms; echoes of the Gadarene swine, both from Luke's Gospel and Dostoyevsky, place him unmistakably for the attentive reader.[49] Our final vision is of the pig-man, frustrated and bested, standing 'empty-handed', with 'dull eyes', as the escaping boy is carried along on the life-giving waters.[50] 'The waiting current caught him like a long gentle hand' – so unlike the uncaring hands of the apartment; when he 'knew that he was getting somewhere, all his fury and fear left him'.[51] This drowning is clearly meant to be seen as a baptism, a spiritual rebirth. The world of peace and purposeful direction entered by the child stands in sharp contrast to the drunken purposeless round of the parents' existence: *in circuitu impii ambulant*.

O'Connor undeniably presents the drowning as a happy event, even if the modern world, with Mr Paradise acting as its spokesman, responds with angry incomprehension to what it can only understand as obscurantist nonsense. Hers is a belligerent, unaccommodating faith that seeks no truce with, makes no concession to, the enemy. The choice is stark: life in the apartment versus death in the river, with no milder, more acceptable alternative allowed between these extremes. It is a disturbing choice, but that's what O'Connor means it to be.

This crusading mentality, these knight-errant excursions to champion the faith, are best of all exhibited in her attacks upon the ultimate enemy: the Pharisee as militant atheist. In her challenge to the modern world she targets its arrogant assumptions about the discreditable origins of religious belief and carries the war straight to the enemy with her counter-investigations of the psychology of atheism.

When religion ruled, believers branded atheists as licentious people who denied God in order to live immoral lives – *a fare il porco* (to play the pig).[52] Disbelief is simply debauchery in disguise. When atheists gained the upper hand, they retaliated by dismissing religion as the invention of poltroons too weak to confront truth. If there were no cowards, there would be no God. It follows that atheists are brave, resolute people, and it seems not to trouble the atheist that, in so describing himself, he might be risking a charge of smug pharisaism. Such an atheist, like the Pharisee, is a praiser of himself.

This is O'Connor's starting point in her war with the Pharisee atheist. Not for her the old, all too easily refutable jibe that they are simply rogues in disguise – she attacks them where they are really vulnerable, in their smug assumption of superiority. Modern disbelief is too often an exercise in self-congratulation. Cowards believe, heroes don't. The whole mindset reeks of pharisaism. In 'Good Country People' and 'The Lame Shall Enter First' O'Connor presents the comic and tragic versions of this ruinous vanity.

'Good Country People' (the very title is pharisaical) is a comic story about pride and retribution that might easily have taken its place as a fabliau in *The Canterbury Tales*. The central figure is a conceited atheist who takes for granted her superiority to the believing bumpkins around her – her deserved comeuppance at the end is endorsed by author and reader alike. Unlike her male counterpart in 'The Lame Shall Enter First', she harms only herself and this is what keeps the story within the bounds of comic nemesis. But she squanders the fund of sympathy we feel for her at the start: a 32-year old woman who lost a leg when she was a child, now a PhD in philosophy trapped among the rednecks, an intellectual snared among banal, cliché-ridden people – good country people, as they smugly, infuriatingly describe themselves. Her immediate companions, her mother and a female employee, Bouvard and Pecuchet with a sex change and a New World setting, would drive a saint to blasphemy with their inane, self-congratulatory chatter and Hulga, the crippled philosopher, is far from being a saint. Exasperated beyond endurance by her mother's cheerful prattle, she pointlessly quotes Malebranche to the uncomprehending woman.[53] When her mother comes across the book open at the passage on Nothingness, she hastily thrusts it away as though it were something perversely witless and foul.[54]

Hulga is in these red hills among these good country people from necessity, not choice. She has a heart condition; but for this she would be working in a university, talking to people who appreciate her merits, instead of being, as she is, a pearl among swine. She belongs to a standard recurring type in O'Connor, a person who thinks herself too good for her surroundings and companions: Julian in 'Everything That Rises Must Converge', Mrs May in 'Greenleaf', Thomas in 'The Comforts of Home', Mrs Turpin in 'Revelation', Asbury in 'The Enduring Chill', all pharisees, whether of the comic or tragic kind. Denied her deserved position in the world, Hulga decides to make the worst of things, changing her name from Joy to Hulga ('her highest creative act') in a deliberate choice of ugliness:[55] if the world has treated her badly, she will reply in kind. Her philosophy does not seem to have helped much and there is a case for her mother's view that it would have been better if 'the child had not taken the PhD'.[56] A child with a PhD is what she certainly is and, although the mother may be a fool, she is right in her assessment of her daughter as brilliant but without a grain of sense. Even in her own specialism she goes woefully astray. 'Malebranche was right: we are not our own light. We are not our own light!'[57] Had she read more deeply in the Bible she will not tolerate in the parlour, the words about motes and beams might have saved her from blundering, for, correct though she is in seeing the application of Malebranche to her mother, she completely misses the application to herself: it is for smugly trying to be her own light that she comes so badly unstuck. Her mother's folly is beside the point, because O'Connor is not hunting the mother; it is the arrogant atheist whom O'Connor is out to get and, assisted by the young Bible salesman, she succeeds.

'I want to devote my life to Chrustian service.'[58] The pronunciation marks him as a yokel, the ambition as a simpleton. A dolt serving dolts, he seems to incarnate the superstitious folly and provincial backwardness among which she finds herself so excruciatingly trapped. He is, in reality, Tartuffe, pretending to be a fool the better to exploit fools. He sees in a flash the mother's vulnerability to the good-country-people line, but what endears him to the mother alienates the daughter and his aim, still hidden, is to dupe the two. Hulga decides to seduce him intellectually, dazzling the hayseed with her cerebral gymnastics. She despises him as a cretin, but since 'true genius can get an idea across even to an inferior mind', she sets out to deflower him and afterwards take away all the shame he will undoubtedly feel, turning it into 'something useful'.[59] She sees herself as both educator and redeemer (a delusion she shares with Sheppard in 'The Lame Shall Enter First' and Rayber in *The Violent Bear It Away*), but it is a redemption not from sin but from religion – when the boy is stricken with foolish remorse, she will stoop down, an atheistic Lady Bountiful, and show him how misguided his guilt is.

Her plan is based on twin assumptions: she is clever, he's a fool, or, in other words, she's an atheist, he's a Christian. The story reveals him as far too clever for her – he's the seducer in every sense. And just as he knows how to trick the mother, so he traps the daughter by pretending to be awestruck by her exhibitionist impiety. When she invites him to admire her Promethean intelligence, he plays along, but even as she surveys him with that gaze of derisive pity reserved by the atheist for the believer, she is unwittingly digging her own pit. *Sapientiam sapientiae perdam*. Hulga is wise only in her own deluded eyes, but that's enough to incite O'Connor. 'Then you ain't saved?' asks the salesman, blending shock with admiration as he cunningly reels her in.[60] It is just the bait to catch an uppity intellectual, confirming her in her thoroughly mistaken view of the relationship between herself and her Bible-Belt compatriots straight out of Mencken; but a southern follower of Mencken can expect no sympathy from O'Connor.[61]

There is, of course, a perverse and spiteful element in her seducer – this is not the stereotypical opportunist salesman, nor is it just sexual gratification he wants.

As in Restoration Comedy, the sex is disturbingly contaminated with elements of triumphalism and revenge, a plebeian desire to hoodwink the educated superior. He schemes to humiliate her in as public a fashion as possible: to steal her artificial leg and to leave her, seduced and stranded, in the loft. To be rescued she will have to cry out to the world her folly and this is what the salesman sadistically intends. But O'Connor forbids any hint of sympathy for the abused woman on the stern biblical principle that you reap what you sow. It is as hard an ethic as that impressed on Dante by Virgil as he leads him through hell. No pity for God's foes: it holds equally true in Georgia.

Nevertheless the salesman, however abhorrent in himself, belongs to a tradition long established in Christian thought: that of the scourge of God, whereby a sinner, the unconscious instrument of God, following his own wicked ways, is nevertheless simultaneously used by God to punish other sinners. The victims get their just deserts, even if justice is the last thing on the avenger's mind. However different their motives, O'Connor (consciously working for God) and the salesman (unconsciously working for God while pursuing his own debased agenda) are united in their joint aim to humiliate Hulga. O'Connor wants to uphold religion against a conceited atheist, while the salesman, at heart as contemptuous of religion as the woman he deludes, wants revenge for her insufferable condescension. O'Connor has no objection to making a temporary pact with the salesman – indeed, it simply augments her sense of satisfaction to use the one atheist to degrade the other.

'I don't have illusions. I'm one of those people who see *through* to nothing.'[62] The vanity, the pretentiousness and pomposity, simply cry out to be punished. What O'Connor thinks of Hulga is made plain when she removes her glasses and it makes no difference since 'she seldom paid any close attention to her surroundings'.[63] She is too busy seeing through to nothing to notice what's going on under her nose. Patiently, the salesman waits for the moment of revenge. When she boasts to him about her degrees, it simply inflames him to debase her and the reader, too, joins in this desire to see her humbled – for who ever deserved it more? 'You poor baby ... It's just as well you don't understand ... We are all damned ... but some of us have taken off our blindfolds and see that there's nothing to see. It's a kind of salvation.'[64] To be proud of seeing nothing – it's exactly how Holy Willie would speak if he ever turned atheist, for it is the same spiritual elitism, the same claim to possess a salvation denied to the rabble of ordinary men. Poor eyesight is the least of Hulga's problems, for it's her soul that is blind.

It was Malvolio's lording it over the others that provoked them into humbling the upstart; this, rather than sexual conquest, is the salesman's motive too. Author and character combine to make the pretentious woman a laughing-stock, leaving her in every sense without a leg to stand on. (It is another instance of O'Connor's penchant for turning metaphor into fact, as when she has Mary Grace throw the book at Mrs Turpin.) Hulga, losing not her heart but her leg to the travelling salesman, pays dearly for despising religion.

The irony is that she is duped by a fellow atheist, resentful at being treated as a country bumpkin. 'You're just playing me for a sucker,' he complains, as he carefully sets the trap.[65] Like all tricksters he knows the power of flattery. 'You ain't like anybody else.'[66] It is what she herself thinks and it sounds all the sweeter in the context of the unappreciative hillbilly trap in which she finds herself caught. She is struck that a simpleton should so easily stumble upon the truth of her uniqueness, while all the time he craftily tells her the flattering lie she wants to hear. Thinking herself 'face to face with real innocence', she is, in fact, in the company of low cunning.[67] In the fable the fox tells the crow what a sweet singer he is in order to get the cheese; the salesman employs a similar tactic to get the leg. Both succeed because vain simpletons are so easily taken in.

O'Connor turns the screw by having the credulous woman surrender to the seducer in the language of the religion she condemns: 'it was like losing her own life and finding it again, miraculously, in his'.[68] The miracle that is absurd in the old religion becomes somehow credible with a secular face-lift. It is as Pascal says: unbelievers are the most credulous. They believe in Vespasian's miracles, in order not to believe in those of Moses.[69] Hulga, proud of having risen above all superstitious nonsense, rejects the true saviour only to fall for a fraudulent one and O'Connor clearly means this to have an application far wider than the case of a foolish woman and a sexual conman. This, we infer, is what happens to all those who are arrogantly self-sufficient, who, disregarding Malebranche's warning, think they are their own light.

The removal of Hulga's leg by the salesman is described in the reverent discourse of religious ritual, but the celebrant is a backwoods Tartuffe. It is a seduction reminiscent of the Underground Man's exploitation of Liza, seen this time, however, from the viewpoint of the duped woman. In both cases, the man's brutality is revealed once the seduction is over. For Hulga the bombshell is the salesman's revelation that he, too, is an atheist. Despite having pretended to be a believer in order to seduce her, there is a genuine indignation in his rebuke: 'I hope you don't think ... that I believe in that crap!'[70] A PhD would not use this expression, but it is Hulga's sentiment if not her idiom. O'Connor's point is that you don't need a PhD to be an atheist. The notion that only highly educated people, those who have laboured for years to be able to see through to nothing, can be atheists is the chief reason for the predicament she now finds herself in – atheistic conceit is her undoing.

Atheists are intelligent – that's why they're atheists. Believers are simpletons – it's what makes them believers. 'Good Country People' confounds these impertinent, simplistic assumptions. Hulga is a well-educated simpleton, a PhD with no sense. The salesman is an uneducated hillbilly, devious and manipulative. Both are atheists, but he has become so without the charge of Hulga's expensive, laborious education and this is what incenses him against the condescending intellectual: 'You ain't so smart. I been believing in nothing ever since I was born.'[71] Who needs Heidegger in order to deny God? The boast in his mouth is intended to make Hulga ask herself what she has to be so conceited about.

His final insult is to call her by the name she regards as her creative masterpiece, mouthing it 'as if he didn't think much of it'.[72] The name and the leg are, as she sees it, the two items that set her above and apart. The patronized yokel disparages the first and steals the second, leaving her stranded, physically and spiritually, in the loft. Her mother watches him leave, 'that nice dull young man that tried to sell me a Bible yesterday' – a simpleton, of course, but the world would be a much better place with more of such simplicity in it.[73] Casanova regarded as one of his greatest exploits the simultaneous seduction of a mother and daughter together. Soon Hulga will be forced to call for help to people she despises, thereby publishing to the world her shame and stupidity, and the mother will realize just how much she, too, has been taken in by this Georgia Casanova. Getting a replacement leg will be easy enough, but Hulga now needs a replacement life, because there is no way she can simply resume the old one after what has happened. It's a swingeing price to pay for being a Pharisee atheist, but it's a no-holds-barred contest when you go into the ring with God's champion.

Yet Hulga escapes lightly when we contemplate the fate of the protagonist of 'The Lame Shall Enter First'. In this story we see O'Connor at her most punitive, not to say vindictive; it illustrates perfectly her chilling statement (echoing Tertullian) that 'judgement is just as much a matter of relishing as condemning'. The story is her most overt challenge to the main movement of Western intellectual history since the Renaissance, denying the key assumptions of humanism: that man controls his own destiny, that every problem has a rational solution, that science is the infallible route toward the earthly paradise. In a world totally amenable to the restructuring of the social engineers, the priest, embodiment of the old philosophy of helplessness, has been made redundant, his place taken by the scientists as the new lords of creation. The old ideas of salvation and damnation succumb to the new categories of technology and progress. The story shows, in the persons of its two chief characters – social worker and demonic delinquent – these two worlds in collision and it is our world, the modern scientific world, that is shown as inadequate and mistaken.

Sheppard – social worker, militant atheist, scientific zealot – embodies everything O'Connor finds most detestable in modern life. He is not the good shepherd but a foolish one who invites the wolf into the fold to devour his lamb. He is the most consummate expression of the Pharisee atheist in O'Connor's pages, as she herself tells us. It is 'about a man who thought he was good and thought he was doing good when he wasn't ... I don't know, don't sympathise, don't like Mr Sheppard in the way that I know and like most of my other characters ... the empty man who fills up his emptiness with good works.'[74] Just how much she dislikes and wants to punish him is shockingly revealed at the tale's conclusion.

From the outset we know he is a fake redeemer, the more ironic because he clearly doesn't know it. He is a highly selective saviour, for only the intelligent merit salvation and the rest, his own child included, can be discarded as trash. He is a sombre version of Mrs Jellyby, trying to save the world while her home collapses around her. Burke's description of Rousseau – a hater of his kindred and a lover of mankind – will serve, provided that we qualify it as intelligent mankind.[75] The IQ assessment is the new sacramental sign and so pains must be taken with Rufus because of his high IQ and 'great potential'. Norton, by contrast, is valueless and can be metaphorically dumped in the same garbage cans from which Rufus must be literally rescued. Sheppard is a type of that unfeeling rationalism condemned by the Romantics, in particular by Wordsworth and Hawthorne, for violating the sanctity of the human heart.

Yet, far from having no feelings, he is an enthusiast, a fanatic committed to science and progress, an Abraham of technology as ready to sacrifice his son to the new God as the patriarch was to the old one. That it is a rival religion is made clear from the imagery: the hair like a halo brush, the ascetic-looking iron bed, the office like a confessional; but he rescues bodies, not souls, and he easily assumes his superiority to a priest. He doesn't forgive sins, he denies them, and, unlike the priest, he is 'trained' for what he does.[76] The claim is grimly ironical in the light of what he achieves. By their fruits you shall know them. The appalling conclusion is no testimonial to his vaunted expertise. Norton, he cavalierly assumes, is not 'bright' enough to be harmed, and the folly is only matched by the arrogance. Rufus is right when he scornfully accuses him of not knowing his left hand from his right, for he sees only what he wants to see: that when the crippled boy slights and ignores him, he doesn't really mean it; that, despite the boy's contemptuous denial, he is secretly thirsting for scientific knowledge; that the orthopaedic boot *must* make Rufus a new person. Sheppard knows everything – people included – even better than they know themselves; it's a god-like omniscience to which he lays claim. Rufus's cry of outraged surprise – 'he thinks he's Jesus Christ!'[77] – doesn't do justice to this conceit, for he thinks he's incomparably better than Christ, a bringer of true salvation, not a pedlar of mumbo-jumbo. The new religion has its own attested miracles – orthopaedic boots, telescopes, space rockets – as well as its own heaven in the distant stars soon to be conquered by man. Redemption through gadgets: it would be simply laughable were its consequences not so disastrous.

The new religion is, at best, a pig philosophy that would reduce human life to a well-run sty. It is the thought of the high IQ boy rooting in garbage cans that upsets Sheppard and he thinks that if he gives him bread all will be well; it is the destitute boy who protests that man does not live by bread alone and, in a dramatic gesture, crams the holy pages into his mouth to prove it. The fallacy of materialism is signalled by the contrasting lifestyles of the two boys. Norton's material needs are tended, but this is scant compensation for the emotional abuse he suffers, the emotional blackmail and bullying of a father who tries to make him feel guilty for eating while others go hungry. Rufus has never known a father, but better none at all than one like Sheppard. Raised by a poverty-stricken grandfather who beats him every day, his mother in prison, scouring the trashcans for scraps of food, Rufus lives in a state of gross material deprivation. Norton has his own bedroom in a comfortable house with a pink-tiled bathroom, his father is City Recreational

Director, yet it is not so clear that Rufus is the loser. 'Your daddy gives you everything you need and want.'[78] Just when you think that Sheppard has touched rock-bottom in stupidity, he surprises you by reaching a lower depth still: he actually tells his weeping son he should rejoice that his mother is dead rather than in prison. He rebukes the child for selfishness in a monstrous display of egotism, all the more unpardonable because he is genuinely unaware of what he's doing: the words 'I, me, my' occur six times in four lines in what is an attack upon another person's selfishness.[79] And his foolish attempt to coerce the child into philanthropy shows that, so far as he is concerned, Dickens might as well never have created Mrs Pardiggle.

Rufus, selected to be its star pupil, becomes the enemy of the new religion and he marshals the concepts of the old one – heaven, hell, salvation, damnation – against it. The story begins as an attempt by a rationalist to rehabilitate a potentially brilliant juvenile delinquent, but it soon becomes a contest between the two, the boy upholding fundamentalist religion, the man scientific progressivism, the fought-over prize being the man's mentally retarded child. The man's failure to mould the delinquent to his own purposes provokes a loathing for the perversely unteachable boy. It echoes the situation in 'Bartleby' when the lawyer, recognizing the unsaveable nature of his forlorn clerk, wants nothing so much as to be rid of him, but cannot muster the courage to dismiss him once and for all. So, too, with Sheppard. Rufus deliberately provokes him – 'nobody can save me but Jesus', he taunts this rival messiah, this competing saviour, and Sheppard experiences that hatred that the reformer comes to feel for what resists him, that temptation to liquidate and have done with what is refractory and perverse.[80] Yet, like Melville's lawyer, he lacks the courage to eject the nonconformist and yearns instead for him to leave the house of his own accord.

The reader sides with Rufus in spurning the impertinent conclusion that he is as he is only because he is crippled and that, but for this, he would be the reformer's replica. Rufus is in direct descent from the Underground Man: he is, he insists, what he is by choice, what he wants to be, he is proud of his perversity and he will not be dragooned, by reason, logic or scientific coercion, into anyone's crystal palace. 'Is your trouble in your foot or in your head?' asks the exasperated salesman.[81] In neither, Horace, St Paul and Dostoyevsky could all have told him, but in his will: Rufus wants to be what he is. Sheppard is hurt at his personal failure to recover the lost sheep: 'the failure of his compassion numbed him'.[82] It is the occupational hazard of every thwarted reformer and the rival of Christ is no exception. He loses his temper with the contumelious sinner as Rufus taunts him with the Bible, which Sheppard has ridiculed as a text for weaklings and which, he insists, the boy cannot possibly believe. In repudiating this impertinence, Rufus upholds not just the Bible but freedom itself. Man does not live by bread alone, he defiantly declares, wonder transforming his face as he devours the printed words. Behind Sheppard and the whole tribe of social engineers stands Dostoyevsky's Grand Inquisitor, father of all moulders and manipulators, confident that in any choice between bread and freedom, men will always choose bread. Rufus refuses to do so. Rejecting bread and stars, the two symbols of modern scientific materialism, he chooses instead the bread of heaven, Ezekiel's food.

He is undeniably perverse. He deliberately gets caught by the police in order to ruin the tin Jesus by falsely accusing him of homosexual advances, all in eager earshot of the prurient newspaper reporter. But it is poetic (if no other) justice that Sheppard should be destroyed by the very perverseness he will not acknowledge. From the moment he gives the key of the house to Rufus – assuming that decent treatment *must* redeem the worst of sinners (the delusion of *Les Misérables* ridiculed by Camus in *The Fall*) – he puts himself in the boy's power. Visited briefly by the truth of things, he feels a dull despair at being 'faced with some elemental warping of nature that had happened too long ago to be corrected now';[83] he has almost stumbled upon Newman's classic formulation of the Fall.[84] But he quickly 'recovers' and feels angry that obscurantist ideas of hell and damnation should linger on into the space age, as though sin were a matter of chronology and ceased with the invention of rockets. His parting words to Rufus reveal this basic blunder: 'you're not evil, you're mortally confused'[85] – but Rufus claims his inalienable, God-given right to be evil rather than merely confused. His bad foot is not the excuse for his anti-social behaviour that Sheppard would have it be. Far from being a handicap, it is his claim to precedence: the lame shall enter first.

With Rufus and the police gone, Sheppard speaks in his own defence words that irreprievably condemn him: 'I have nothing to reproach myself with ... I did more for him than I did for my own child.'[86] As with St Peter denying the Lord, it is only on the third repetition that the dreadful significance of the words breaks upon him. He is a guilty soul, fallen into the power of that Satan in whom he had not believed. If T.S. Eliot sensed the power of evil in 'Barbara of the House of Grebe', what would he have thought of 'The Lame Shall Enter First'? We know from her own words that O'Connor was fully aware of the diabolism in her story: 'The thing I am writing now is surely going to convince Jack [Hawkes] that I am of the Devil's party.'[87] Writing to Hawkes himself, she concedes that her story 'will add fuel to your theory though not legitimately, I think. You haven't convinced me that I write with the Devil's will or belong to the romantic tradition ... there is a difference in our two devils.'[88] His is the romantic rebel of Shelley, hers is the fiend who roams the world to destroy souls – he makes a singularly repulsive appearance near the end of *The Violent Bear It Away* and none but the most abandoned of paedophiles would wish to belong to *his* party.[89] Hawkes is surely wrong when he tries to recruit her as a follower of Satan. Nevertheless, the Devil is in the story and he triumphs, as O'Connor's own words somewhat uneasily acknowledge. Just as Milton comes dangerously close to approving, however unconsciously, the libertarian sentiments he puts in Satan's mouth, so O'Connor, in her zeal to punish the Pharisee, risks a compromising association with something suspiciously akin to sadism.

The cruelty of the conclusion has a satanic smack to it. In a flash of searing insight the deluded father finally realizes how shamefully he has treated his son and rushes to make amends. But to the end Sheppard is a pathetically inept saviour, a 'good' man doing more harm than a villain could have schemed to achieve. There is to be no second chance (or, according to O'Connor's numbering system, *third* chance), no new beginning – what Victorian fiction up to the advent of Hardy had always so liberally supplied is now ruthlessly refused. Insight comes too late to be of any practical service to the man or his son; 'grace' is given simply so that, terrifying paradox, he may be the more damned. It is as though Mrs Jellyby were reborn as Lear. The fallen telescope, the hanging boy, the jungle of shadows, the flight into space (but so hideously parodied and perverted!) – all the symbols come together in a devastating climax, almost as appalling to the reader as to the character.

Rufus wants revenge on Sheppard and succeeds brilliantly. 'The lame'll carry off the prey!' he screeches as the police take him away (it had been the story's original title) and Norton's sad launch into space to find his dead mother vindicates the prophecy.[90] But behind Rufus is a foe more unsparing, more implacable still. We watch O'Connor setting out to snare *her* prey with cold precision, just as we simultaneously watch Sheppard striding like a blind man toward a precipice. He almost deserves what happens to him, but the end is savage retaliation and, even though Virgil scolds us, we cannot help but weep when we see the fate of the sinner.

Admittedly, every reader knows that, with every word and deed, Sheppard is laying up punishment for himself. 'Why try to make him superior? Heaven and hell were for the mediocre, and he was that if he was anything.'[91] Sheppard's resigned reflections on his retarded son were bound to be taken by O'Connor as a personal insult, certain to exact revenge. All of O'Connor's stories exhibit a kind of moral inflation in which the cost of truth becomes progressively steeper the longer people put off acquiring it and Sheppard puts it off to the last possible moment. We know he is going to pay dearly, but we never dreamed it would be so exorbitantly.

The conclusion is as cruel, as relentless, as anything in Hardy or Wharton, Conrad or Camus – the religious writer can be as merciless as any unbeliever when disposing of a defeated enemy. What is especially painful is that she destroys Sheppard at the very moment he forsakes pharisaism and is on the verge of what might be called 'conversion': kicking a man when he's down is, perhaps, the appropriate colloquialism. For the first time in the text Sheppard uses the word 'salvation' in its traditional, unironic way.[92] His contrition is genuine, as is his resolve to sin no more, to begin anew, to love and protect the hitherto neglected child. The closest parallel is Albany's prayer near the close of *Lear*: 'The gods defend her.' The villain Edmund, dying, has repented and wants Cordelia to be saved; a comic coda is apparently about to be superimposed on the dark, horrific action. It is Shakespeare who will not have it so. No more will O'Connor. Like Lear enlightened, apprised of the worth of the child he spurned, Sheppard rushes off to put all to rights, only to learn that it is too late, that both he and the child are lost.

Behind the stricken character stands the appalled reader and one would have to be as pitiless as O'Connor herself to believe that there is nothing excessive here, that the match between offence and retribution is a fitting one. No doubt it can be argued that, even after this catastrophe, Sheppard can recover, going on to receive and accept salvific grace; but many will justifiably doubt the possibility of such a comeback for such a man in such a situation. Certainly, this story cannot be included among the 'happy' stories such as *Wise Blood*, 'The River' and 'A Good Man Is Hard To Find', because it lacks that moment of redemptive grace so prominent in them. 'Grace' comes to Sheppard simply as a prelude to damnation, grace is subordinated to damnation. The denier of heaven finds himself trapped in hell. There is no evidence within the text to suggest that Sheppard is saved and we would have to project the story beyond its legitimate confines to speculate gratuitously about such an outcome. What we can say is that the conclusion of 'The Lame Shall Enter First' is harrowing enough to rival anything in the dark pages of twentieth-century fiction, taking its ambiguously deserved place alongside such grim finales as those of *The Secret Agent*, *Ethan Frome* and *Nineteen Eighty-Four*. Our century has been in so much of its distinctive fiction the golden time of Vanni Fucci; we bring to a close this survey with a fiction that consummately fulfils his resolve to make us grieve.

Notes

Introduction

1. Dante Alighieri, *The Divine Comedy: Volume 1 – Inferno*, trans. Mark Musa (Penguin Classics: New York, 1984), 291. (All future references to this edition.)
2. John Keats, 'Ode on a Grecian Urn', *The Poems of John Keats*, ed. Miriam Allott (Longman Group Limited, W.W. Norton and Co. Inc.: New York, 1970), 534–5.
3. *Inferno*, 292.
4. Ibid., 292.
5. Ibid., 293.
6. Tertullian, *De Spectaculis*, trans. T.R. Glover (Harvard University Press: Cambridge, MA, 1931), 279, 297–301.
7. *Inferno*, 317.
8. Ibid., 293.
9. Ibid., 217.
10. Ibid., 297.
11. Ibid., 293.
12. George Orwell, *Nineteen Eighty-Four* (Penguin: Harmondsworth, 1954), 208–9.
13. *Inferno*, 160–1.
14. Dante Alighieri, *The Divine Comedy: Volume 3 – Paradiso*, trans. Mark Musa (Penguin Classics: New York, 1986), 204.
15. T.S. Eliot, *The Complete Poems and Plays of T.S. Eliot* (Faber & Faber: London and Boston, 1969), 258.
16. Dietrich Bonhoeffer, *Ethics*, ed. Eberhard Bethge (SCM Press: London, 1955), 328, 326–34.
17. Saul Bellow, *Herzog* (Penguin: Harmondsworth, 1965), 36.
18. Karl Popper, *The Myth of the Framework: In Defence of Science and Rationality*, ed. M.A. Notturno (Routledge: London, 1994), 132.
19. Samuel Taylor Coleridge, 'The Rime of the Ancient Mariner', *Poems*, ed. John Beer (Everyman, J.M. Dent: London; Charles E. Tuttle: Vermont), 1798, 233.
20. Fyodor Dostoevsky, *The Devils*, trans. David Magarshack (Penguin: Harmondsworth, 1953), 655.
21. *Nineteen Eighty-Four*, 213.
22. *Revelations of Divine Love Recorded by Dame Julian of Norwich*, ed. Grace Warrack (Methuen: London, 1901), 57.
23. Edith Wharton, *Ethan Frome* (Collier Books, Macmillan: New York, 1986), 175.
24. Ibid., 137.
25. Jonathan Swift, *Gulliver's Travels*, ed. Peter Dixon and John Chalker (Penguin: Harmondsworth, 1967), 174–5.
26. Frederic Taber Cooper, 'The Bigger Issues and Some Recent Books'. *The Bookman*,

XXXIV, no. 3 (November 1911), 312.
27. Quoted in Christopher Ricks, *Tennyson* (Macmillan: New York, 1972), 49.
28. Thomas Hardy, *Tess of the d'Urbervilles: A Pure Woman*, intro. A. Alvarez, ed. David Skilton (Penguin: Harmondsworth, 1978), 170–1.
29. *Inferno*, 93.
30. Ibid., 93.
31. Ibid., 252.
32. Ibid., 252.
33. Quoted in *The English Auden: Essays and Dramatic Writings, 1927–1939*, ed. Edward Mendelson (Faber & Faber: London, 1977), 375.
34. George Woodcock, *Anarchism: A History of Libertarian Ideas and Movements* (Penguin: Harmondsworth, 1963), 288–94.

Chapter 1 Dostoyevsky

1. Joseph D. Frank, *Dostoyevsky: The Miraculous Years* (Princeton University Press: Princeton, NJ, 1995), 69.
2. Sigmund Freud, 'Dostoyevsky and Parricide', *Collected Psychological Works*, ed. James Strachey (Hogarth Press: London, 1961), vol. XXI, 177–94. Trans. D.F. Tait, rev. J. Strachey.
3. Nikolai K. Mikhailovsky, *A Cruel Talent*, trans. Spencer Cadmus (Ardis: Ann Arbor, 1978).
4. Quoted in *Dostoyevsky: A Collection of Critical Essays*, ed. René Wellek (Prentice Hall: Englewood Cliffs, NJ, 1962), 3–4.
5. Fyodor Dostoyevsky, *Notes from Underground*, trans. and intro. Jessie Coulson (Penguin: Harmondsworth, 1972), 116.
6. Robert Lord, *Dostoyevsky: Essays and Perspectives* (University of California Press: Berkeley and Los Angeles, 1970), 166–7.
7. *Notes from Underground*, 44.
8. Ibid., 63.
9. Ibid., Introduction, 10.
10. *Selected Letters of Fyodor Dostoyevsky*, ed. Joseph D. Frank and David I. Goldstein, trans. Andrew R. MacAndrew (Rutgers University Press: New Brunswick and London, 1987), 173.
11. *Collected Essays, Journalism and Letters of George Orwell*, ed. Sonia Orwell and Ian Angus (Penguin: Harmondsworth, 1970), II, 169; IV, 465.
12. Fyodor Dostoyevsky, *The Insulted and Injured*, trans. Constance Garnett (Grafton Books, Collins: London, 1987), 251.
13. Ibid., 243.
14. Ibid., 243.
15. Ibid., 245.
16. Ibid., 244.
17. Ibid., 246.
18. George Orwell, *Nineteen Eighty-Four* (Penguin: Harmondsworth, 1954), 223.
19. *The Insulted and Injured*, 251.
20. Michael Holquist, *Dostoyevsky and the Novel* (Northwestern University Press:

Evanston, IL, 1977), paperback edn 1986, 39.
21. *Notes from Underground*, 23.
22. Fyodor Dostoyevsky, *Crime and Punishment*, trans. David Magarshack (Penguin: Harmondsworth, 1951), 167.
23. David Hume, *A Treatise of Human Nature*, ed. L.A. Selby-Bigge (Clarendon Press: Oxford, 1978), 416.
24. *Volpone* 111, VII, 204–5, in Ben Jonson, *Three Comedies*, ed. Michael Jamieson (Penguin: Harmondsworth, 1966), 114.
25. Charles Dickens, *Hard Times*, ed. and intro. David Craig (Penguin: Harmondsworth, 1969), 302–3.
26. *The Tempest* V, 1, 275.
27. *Notes from Underground*, 29.
28. Franz Kafka, 'Letter to His Father', in *Wedding Preparations in the Country and Other Stories* (Penguin: Harmondsworth, 1978), 32.
29. D.H. Lawrence, quoted in Wellek (ed.), *Dostoyevsky: A Collection of Critical Essays*, 90–7.
30. Nikolai G. Chernyshevsky, *What Is to Be Done?*, trans. Michael R. Katz, annot. William G. Wagner (Cornell University Press: Ithaca and London, 1989), 187. See Richard Peace, *Dostoevsky's 'Notes from Underground'* (Bristol Classical Press: London, 1993), 84–9.
31. Ovid, *Metamorphoses*, trans. and intro. Mary M. Innes (Penguin: Harmondsworth, 1955), 168.
32. *Notes from Underground*, 31.
33. Ibid., 32.
34. *A Spinoza Reader: 'The Ethics' and Other Works*, ed. and trans. Edwin Curley (Princeton University Press: Princeton, NJ, 1994), 267–8.
35. Joseph Conrad, *The Secret Agent: A Simple Tale*, ed. Martin Seymour-Smith (Penguin, Harmo[illegible] [illegible]986), 103.
36. *Selectea* [illegible] [illegible]. Frank and Goldstein, 191. See also William J. Leatherbarrow, *Fyodor Dostoye*[illegible] (Twayne Publishers, G.K. Hall: Boston, 1981), 67.
37. *Notes from Underground*, 42.
38. Ibid., 43.
39. St Augustine, *Confessions*, trans. and intro. R.S. Pine-Coffin (Penguin: Harmondsworth, 1961), 21.
40. *Notes from Underground*, 43.
41. Ibid., 43.
42. Herman Melville, *Billy Budd, Sailor and Other Stories*, ed. and intro. Harold Beaver (Penguin: Harmondsworth, 1967), 351.
43. *Notes from Underground*, 44.
44. Ibid., 44.
45. Ibid., 45.
46. Ibid., 45.
47. Ibid., 45.
48. Ibid., 45.
49. Ibid., 45.
50. Ibid., 45.
51. Ibid., 46.
52. Ibid., 46.

53. Ibid., 46.
54. Ibid., 49.
55. Fyodor Dostoyevsky, *Winter Notes on Summer Impressions*, trans. Richard Lee Renfield (Criterion Books: New York, 1955), 101–17.
56. Quoted in *Winter Notes*, 109.
57. Francis Fukuyama, *The End of History and the Last Man* (Penguin: Harmondsworth, 1992), XI–XXIII.
58. *Winter Notes*, 114.
59. Ibid., 116.
60. Ibid., 117.
61. *Notes from Underground*, 49.
62. Ibid., 61.
63. Ibid., 61.
64. Ibid., 61.
65. Fyodor Dostoyevsky, *The Brothers Karamazov*, trans. and intro. David Magarshack (Penguin: Harmondsworth, 1958), 276.
66. *Selected Letters*, ed. Frank and Goldstein, 173.
67. *Notes from Underground*, 78.
68. Ibid., 85.
69. Ibid., 85.
70. James Joyce, *Dubliners* (Penguin: Harmondsworth, 1956), 95–6.
71. *Notes from Underground*, 90.
72. Ibid., 91.
73. Ibid., 95–6.
74. Ibid., 98.
75. Ibid., 100.
76. Ibid., 100.
77. Ibid., 101.
78. Ibid., 107.
79. *Winter Notes*, 146.
80. *Notes from Underground*, 112.
81. Ibid., 114.
82. Ibid., 115.
83. Ibid., 115.
84. Ibid., 115.
85. Ibid., 116.
86. Ibid., 116.
87. Ibid., 113.
88. Ibid., 117.
89. Ibid., 117.
90. Ibid., 118.
91. Ibid., 119.
92. Dante Alighieri, *The Divine Comedy: Volume 1 – Inferno*, trans. Mark Musa (Penguin Classics: New York, 1984) 198.
93. *Notes from Underground*, 120.
94. Ibid.,121.
95. Albert Camus, *The Fall*, trans. Justin O'Brien (Penguin: Harmondsworth, 1963), 108.

96. *Notes from Underground*, 122.
97. Ibid.,122.
98. Ibid., 60.
99. Ibid., 122–3.
100. Dostoyevsky's 'Preface' to *Notes from Underground*, 14.
101. *Notes from Underground*, 123.
102. Ibid.,123.
103. Ronald Hingley, *The Undiscovered Dostoyevsky* (Hamish Hamilton: London, 1962), 79.
104. *Notes from Underground*, 122.

Chapter 2 Hardy

1. Virginia Woolf, 'The Novels of Thomas Hardy', *The Second Common Reader* (Harcourt, Brace: New York, 1932). See also *Victorian Literature: Modern Essays in Criticism*, ed. Austin Wright (Oxford University Press: New York, 1961), 174.
2. Thomas Hardy, *Tess of the d'Urbervilles: A Pure Woman*, intro. A. Alvarez, ed. David Skilton (Penguin: Harmondsworth, 1978), 40 (hereafter *Tess*).
3. Quoted in Ian Gregor and Brian Nicholas, *The Moral and the Story* (Faber & Faber: London, 1962), 135–6.
4. *Tess*, 39.
5. Quoted by Donald Davidson, 'The Traditional Basis of Hardy's Fiction', in Albert J. Guerard, *Hardy: A Collection of Critical Essays* (Prentice Hall: Englewood Cliffs, NJ, 1963), 17.
6. George Orwell, *Homage to Catalonia* (Penguin: Harmondsworth, 1962), 46.
7. Dorothy van Ghent, 'On *Tess of the d'Urbervilles*', in Guerard, *Hardy*, 77–90.
8. Arnold Kettle, *An Introduction to the English Novel*, vol. 2 (Hutchinson Library: London, 1953), 49.
9. See Davidson, 'The Traditional Basis of Hardy's Fiction', in Guerard, *Hardy*, 10–23.
10. Gregor and Nicholas, *The Moral and the Story*, 143.
11. Kettle, *Introduction to the English Novel*, 56.
12. *Tess*, 60, 332.
13. Ibid., 62.
14. Ibid., 63, 64.
15. Ibid., 62.
16. Ibid., 123.
17. Ibid., 62.
18. Ibid., 400–1.
19. T.H. Huxley, 'Science and Culture', in *The Norton Anthology of English Literature*, 6th edn, vol. 2 (W.W. Norton: New York and London, 1993), 1448.
20. *Tess*, 441.
21. Ibid., 91.
22. Ibid., 93.
23. Patrick Reilly, *George Orwell: The Age's Adversary* (Macmillan: Basingstoke and London, 1986), 30–58.
24. *Tess*, 119. But see p. 434 where Hardy seems to uphold this idea of retribution.

25. Ibid., 170.
26. Ibid., 174.
27. Reilly, *George Orwell*, 59–93.
28. *Tess*, 150.
29. Ibid., 119.
30. Aldous Huxley, 'Wordsworth in the Tropics', *Do What You Will* (Chatto & Windus: London, 1931), 113–29.
31. *Tess*, 123, 134.
32. Ibid., 137.
33. Ibid., 142.
34. Ibid., 151.
35. Ibid., 187.
36. Robert Browning, 'Caliban on Setebos', *The Poems*, ed. John Pettigrew (Penguin: Harmondsworth, 1981), vol. I, 811; II, 256–7.
37. *Tess*, 151.
38. Ibid., 158.
39. Ibid., 158.
40. Ibid., 214.
41. Ernest Hemingway, *A Farewell to Arms* (Penguin: Harmondsworth, 1958), 252.
42. Franz Kafka, *The Trial* (Penguin: Harmondsworth and London, 1953), 237.
43. *Tess*, 180.
44. Aeschylus, *The Oresteian Trilogy*, trans. Philip Vellacott (Penguin: Harmondsworth, 1966), 48. William Shakespeare, *King Lear*, II, iv, 160–1.
45. *Tess*, 180–1.
46. Ibid., 176.
47. Ibid., 182.
48. Ibid., 325, 61–2, 119, 149, 486.
49. Ibid., 314.
50. Samuel Beckett, *Endgame* (Faber & Faber: London, 1972), 37.
51. *Tess*, 410.
52. Ibid., 410.
53. Fyodor Dostoyevsky, *Crime and Punishment*, trans. David Magarshack (Penguin: Harmondsworth, 1951), 482.
54. *Tess*, 411.
55. Ibid., 418.
56. Ibid., 474.
57. Ibid., 467.
58. Ibid., 411.
59. William Wordsworth, *The Prelude*, XI, 142–4.
60. *Tess*, 449, 309.
61. Ibid., 467.
62. Ibid., 486.
63. Ibid., 234.
64. Ibid., 488.
65. Hardy's preface to *Tess*, 38.
66. Florence Emily Hardy, *The Later Years of Thomas Hardy, 1892–1928* (Macmillan: London, 1930) 57–8.

67. *Tess*, 148.
68. John Henry Newman, *Apologia Pro Vita Sua* (Collins: Glasgow, 1977), 278–9.
69. *Tess*, 70.
70. A. Alvarez, introduction to *Tess*, 18–19.
71. John Milton, 'Comus', *Milton: Complete Shorter Poems*, ed. John Carey (Longman: London, 1981), 209.
72. *Pall Mall Gazette*, 8 July 1891. See Michael Millgate, *Thomas Hardy: His Career as a Novelist* (Random House: New York, 1971), 290.
73. Quoted in Michael Millgate, *Thomas Hardy: A Biography* (Oxford University Press, Oxford and Melbourne, 1982), 316. See *Pall Mall Gazette*, 10 July 1891.
74. *Pall Mall Gazette*, 10 July 1891. See Millgate, *Thomas Hardy: His Career as a Novelist*, 290.
75. Millgate, *Thomas Hardy: His Career as a Novelist*, 290.
76. Thomas Hardy, 'Barbara of the House of Grebe', *Selected Stories of Thomas Hardy*, intro. John Wain (Macmillan: London and Basingstoke, 1966), 182 (hereafter 'Barbara').
77. George Orwell, *Nineteen Eighty-Four* (Penguin: Harmondsworth, 1954), 203.
78. Ibid., 232.
79. 'Barbara', 207.
80. Ibid., 214.
81. Orwell, *Nineteen Eighty-Four*, 236.
82. T.S. Eliot, *After Strange Gods: A Primer of Modern Heresy* (Faber & Faber: London, 1934), 56–8.

Chapter 3 Conrad

1. Joseph Conrad, *The Secret Agent: A Simple Tale*, ed. Martin Seymour-Smith (Penguin: Harmondsworth, 1986), 37.
2. Ibid., 38.
3. Ibid., 39.
4. Ibid., 43.
5. Ibid., 42.
6. Ibid., 42.
7. John Keats, *The Letters of John Keats*, ed. Hyder Edward Rollins (Cambridge University Press, 1958), vol. 1, 193.
8. *The Secret Agent*, 38.
9. Ibid., 41–2.
10. Ibid., 39.
11. Thomas Mann, 'Joseph Conrad's "The Secret Agent"' in *The Secret Agent: A Casebook*, ed. Ian Watt (Macmillan: London and Basingstoke, 1973), 99–112, 106.
12. *The Secret Agent*, 41.
13. Ibid., 41.
14. Ibid., 38.
15. Flannery O'Connor, *Mystery and Manners: Occasional Prose*, ed. Sally and Robert Fitzgerald (The Noonday Press, Farrar, Straus & Giroux: New York, 1961), 75.
16. Ibid., 76.

17. *The Secret Agent*, 99.
18. Ibid., 201.
19. Ibid., 222.
20. Ibid., 162.
21. Ibid., 48.
22. Ibid., 49.
23. Ibid., 72.
24. Ibid., 72.
25. Ibid., 179.
26. Ibid., 38.
27. Ibid., 105.
28. Ibid., 211.
29. Ibid., 81.
30. Ibid., 64.
31. Ibid., 128.
32. Bertrand Russell, *Portraits from Memory and Other Essays* (George Allen & Unwin: London, 1956), 82.
33. *The Secret Agent*, 215.
34. Ibid., 154.
35. Ibid., 224.
36. Ibid., 254.
37. Ibid., 220.
38. Ibid., 183.
39. Ibid., 219.
40. Ibid., 186.
41. Ibid., 246.
42. Ibid., 204.
43. Ibid., 87, 85, 175.
44. Ibid., 87.
45. Ibid., 185.
46. Ibid., 192.
47. Thomas Mann, in Watt (ed.), *The Secret Agent: A Casebook*, 108. *The Secret Agent*, 66.
48. Ibid., 77.
49. *The Collected Letters of Joseph Conrad*, ed. Frederick R. Karl and Laurence Davies (Cambridge University Press, 1996), vol. V, 358.
50. *The Secret Agent*, 102.
51. Ibid., 121.
52. Jonathan Swift, *The Prose Works of Jonathan Swift* (16 vols), ed. Herbert Davis *et al.* (Basil Blackwell: Oxford, 1939–68), vol. 1, 180.
53. *The Secret Agent*, 70.
54. Jonathan Swift, *The Poems of Jonathan Swift* (3 vols), ed. Harold Williams (Clarendon Press: Oxford, 1937, rev. 1958), vol. 2, 571.
55. *The Secret Agent*, 85.
56. Ibid., 216.
57. Ibid., 213.
58. Ibid., 129.

59. Ibid., 213.
60. *The Secret Agent*, 224, 227.
61. Ibid., 214–15.
62. Ibid., 221.
63. Ibid., 252.
64. Ibid., 226.
65. *Epistle to the Romans*, v. 6–8.
66. *The Secret Agent*, 226.
67. Ibid., 255.
68. Dante Alighieri, *The Divine Comedy: Inferno*, trans. Mark Musa (Penguin: New York, 1984), 151.
69. *The Secret Agent*, 255.
70. Ibid., 147.
71. Ibid., 222.
72. Ibid., 62, 156.
73. Ibid., 168.
74. Ibid., 169.
75. Ibid., 167.
76. Ibid., 118.
77. Ibid., 191, 172.
78. T.S. Eliot, 'Burnt Norton', in *The Complete Poems and Plays of T.S. Eliot* (Faber & Faber: London and Boston, 1969), 172.
79. *The Secret Agent*, 236.
80. Ibid., 185.
81. Ibid., 211.
82. Ibid., 202.
83. Ibid., 58.
84. Ibid., 177.
85. Ibid., 181.
86. Ibid., 183.
87. Ibid., 182.
88. Ibid., 254.

Chapter 4 Wharton

1. Edith Wharton, *The House of Mirth*, intro. Cynthia Griffin Wolff (Penguin: Harmondsworth, 1986), 252.
2. Ibid., 301.
3. Ibid., 321.
4. Quoted by Alfred Kazin, 'Edith Wharton', in *Edith Wharton: A Collection of Critical Essays*, ed. Irving Howe (Prentice Hall: Englewood Cliffs, NJ, 1962), 90.
5. Stevie Smith, 'Exeat', in *The Norton Anthology of English Literature*, 6th edn, vol. 2, ed. M.H. Abrams (W.W. Norton: New York and London, 1993), 2225–6.
6. Lionel Trilling, 'The Morality of Inertia', in Howe (ed.), *Edith Wharton*, 139. Cynthia Griffin Wolff, intro. to *Ethan Frome* (Signet, Penguin: New York, 1987), XV–XVIII. *New York Times Book Review*, 8 October 1911, in *Ethan Frome*, ed. Kristin O. Lauer

and Cynthia Griffin Wolff (Norton Critical Edition, W.W. Norton: New York and London, 1995), 113–15. *Saturday Review*, 18 November 1911. Ibid., 119–20. Frederic Taber Cooper, *Bookman*, November 1911. Ibid., 120–1.

7. *The House of Mirth*, 219.
8. Ibid., 318.
9. Quoted in *The House of Mirth*, Introduction, VIII.
10. *New York Times Book Review*, 8 October 1911. *Ethan Frome*, Norton Critical Edition, 113–15.
11. *Bookman*, November 1911. Ibid., 121–2.
12. Trilling, 'The Morality of Inertia', in Howe (ed.), *Edith Wharton*, 138–40.
13. Edith Wharton, *Ethan Frome* (Collier Books, Macmillan: New York, 1986), 60–1 (all subsequent references to this edition).
14. Ibid., 142.
15. Ibid., 180.
16. 'Michael: A Pastoral Poem', in *Wordsworth and Coleridge: Lyrical Ballads*, ed. Derek Roper (Collins: London and Glasgow, 1973), 11. 1–2.
17. Ibid., 14.
18. *Ethan Frome*, 9.
19. Ibid., 14.
20. Ibid., 138.
21. Matthew Arnold, 'Preface to First Edition of Poems' (1853), *Selected Prose*, ed. and intro. P.J. Keating (Penguin: Harmondsworth, 1970), 42.
22. *Ethan Frome*, 6.
23. Ibid., 177.
24. Ibid., 180.
25. Ibid., 6.
26. Christopher Marlowe, *Doctor Faustus*, ed. Roma Gill (Ernest Benn: London; Norton: New York, 1965), 19.
27. Dante Alighieri, *The Divine Comedy: Inferno*, trans. Mark Musa (Penguin: New York, 1984), 364.
28. Ibid., 374.
29. *Ethan Frome*, 181.
30. *The Divine Comedy: Inferno*, 373.
31. *Ethan Frome*, 15.
32. *The Divine Comedy: Inferno*, 374.
33. *Ethan Frome*, 25.
34. John Keats, *The Letters of John Keats*, ed. Hyder Edward Rollins (Cambridge University Press, 1958), vol. 1, 185.
35. *Ethan Frome*, 3.
36. Ibid., 10.
37. Ibid., 33.
38. Ibid., 180–1.
39. Ibid., 177.
40. Ibid., 178.
41. Ibid., 179.
42. Ibid., 115.
43. Ibid., 118.

44. Ibid., 180.
45. *The Divine Comedy: Inferno*, 366, 370–3.
46. *Ethan Frome*, 179.
47. Ibid., 85–6.
48. Ibid., 52.
49. Cynthia Griffin Wolff, Introduction to *Ethan Frome*, XV.
50. *Ethan Frome*, 7.
51. Ibid., 6.
52. Ibid., 6.
53. Ibid., 10.
54. Ibid., 68.
55. Ibid., 43.
56. Ibid., 44.
57. Ibid., 155.
58. Ibid., 99.
59. Ibid., 91.
60. Ibid., 105.
61. Ibid., 84.
62. Ibid., 48.
63. Ibid., 17.
64. Ibid., 19.
65. Ibid., 14.
66. Ibid., 9.
67. Ibid., 20.
68. Ibid., 20–1.
69. Ibid., 134.
70. Ibid., 73.
71. Ibid., 111.
72. Ibid., 33.
73. Herman Melville, *Billy Budd, Sailor and Other Stories*, ed. and intro. Harold Beaver (Penguin: Harmondsworth, 1967), 406–7.
74. *Saturday Review*, 18 November 1911, in *Ethan Frome*, Norton Critical Edition, 119–20.
75. *Bookman*, November 1911. Ibid., 121–2.
76. Trilling, 'The Morality of Inertia', in Howe (ed.), *Edith Wharton*, 137–46.
77. Edmund Wilson, 'Justice to Edith Wharton', in Howe (ed.), *Edith Wharton*, 24.
78. *Ethan Frome*, 50.
79. William Dean Howells, *Selected Literary Criticism*, vol. 2, 1886–1897, intro. Donald Pizer (Indiana University Press: Bloomington and Indianapolis, 1993), 336. See Andrew Hook, *American Literature in Context, III: 1865–1900* (Methuen: London and New York, 1983), 94, 84–99.
80. Edith Wharton, *A Backward Glance* (Appleton-Century: New York, 1934), 293, in *Ethan Frome*, Norton Critical Edition, 79.
81. Ibid., 79.
82. *Ecclesiastes*, vii. 3.
83. *A Backward Glance*, 293.
84. *Ethan Frome,* Author's Introduction, VI. *Paradise Lost*, ed. Alastair Fowler (Longman

Group Limited: London, 1971), Book IX, 901.
85. J.S. Mill, *On Liberty*, ed. and intro. Gertrude Himmelfarb (Penguin: Harmondsworth, 1974), 78.
86. *Ethan Frome*, 90.
87. Ibid., 95.
88. *The Divine Comedy: Inferno*, 69.
89. *Ethan Frome*, 95.
90. Ibid., 151. See Frederik L. Rusch, 'Reality and the Puritan Mind: Jonathan Edwards and *Ethan Frome*', *Journal of Evolutionary Psychology*, vol. 4 (August 1983), 238–47.
91. *Ethan Frome*, 94.
92. *The House of Mirth*, 70.
93. *Ethan Frome*, 50.
94. Ibid., 50.
95. Ibid., 50.
96. Ibid., 50.
97. Andrew Marvell, 'To his Coy Mistress', *Andrew Marvell: The Complete Poems*, ed. Elizabeth Story Donno (Penguin: Harmondsworth, 1976), 51.
98. *Ethan Frome*, 143.
99. Ibid., 131.
100. *A Backward Glance*, 293. Quoted in *Ethan Frome*, Norton Critical Edition, 78.
101. *Bookman*, November 1911. Ibid., 121–2. But see Howe on the book's purpose as being 'to shock and depress', in *Edith Wharton*, 5.
102. *Ethan Frome*, 139.
103. Ibid., 137.
104. Ibid., 159.
105. Ibid., 165.
106. Ibid., 163.
107. Ibid., 166.
108. Ibid., 170.
109. Ibid., 181.
110. Blake Nevius, *Edith Wharton: A Study of Her Fiction* (University of California Press: Berkeley, 1953). Cynthia Griffin Wolff, *A Feast of Words: The Triumph of Edith Wharton* (Oxford University Press: New York, 1977). Marlene Springer, *Ethan Frome: A Nightmare of Need* (Twayne Masterworks: New York, 1993). Elizabeth Ammons, *Edith Wharton's Argument with America* (Georgia University Press: Athens, GA, 1980). See also Bruno Bettelheim, *The Uses of Enchantment: The Meaning and Importance of Fairy Tales* (Alfred A. Knopf: New York, 1976), 119–215.
111. *Ethan Frome*, 158.

Chapter 5 Kafka

1. Erich Heller, *Kafka* (Fontana, Collins: London, 1974), 28, 35.
2. Franz Kafka, 'In the Penal Settlement', *Metamorphosis and Other Stories*, trans. Willa and Edwin Muir (Penguin: Harmondsworth, 1961), 194.
3. Ibid., 198.
4. Ibid., 181, 185.

5. Ibid., 188.
6. Kierkegaard, quoted in Albert Camus, *The Myth of Sisyphus*, trans. Justin O'Brien (Penguin: Harmondsworth, 1975), 120.
7. Ronald Gray, *Franz Kafka* (Cambridge University Press: London and New York, 1973), 134–5.
8. Quoted in Heller, *Kafka*, 88.
9. *The World of Franz Kafka*, ed. J.P. Stern (Weidenfeld & Nicolson: London, 1980), 20–1.
10. Arthur Schopenhauer, *Essays and Aphorisms*, ed. R.J. Hollingdale (Penguin: Harmondsworth, 1970), 49.
11. *Metamorphosis and Other Stories*, 175.
12. Ibid., 174.
13. Emil Henry, quoted in Benjamin R. Barber, *Superman and Common Men: Freedom, Anarchy and the Revolution* (Penguin: Harmondsworth, 1972), 29. See also *The Anarchist Reader*, ed. George Woodcock (Fontana, Collins: Glasgow, 1977), 193.
14. *Metamorphosis and Other Stories*, 186.
15. Quoted in Heller, *Kafka*, 62.
16. Ibid., 64.
17. Ibid., 64.
18. 'Letter to His Father', in *Wedding Preparations in the Country and Other Stories* (Penguin: Harmondsworth, 1978), 75.
19. Quoted in Heller, *Kafka*, 13.
20. *Metamorphosis and Other Stories*, 184.
21. Ibid., 180.
22. Ibid., 187.
23. Ibid., 191.
24. Ibid., 197.
25. Ibid., 192–3.
26. Ibid., 178.
27. Ibid., 178.
28. Franz Kafka, *The Trial* (Penguin: Harmondsworth and London, 1953), 215.
29. Albert Camus, *The Myth of Sisyphus*, 109.
30. Peter Heller, 'On Not Understanding Kafka', in *The Kafka Debate: New Perspectives for our Time*, ed. Angel Flores (Gordian Press: New York, 1977), 24–41.
31. *The Trial*, 225, 233.
32. Ludwig Wittgenstein, *Tractatus Logico-Philosophicus* (Routledge: London and New York, 1981), 26, 188.
33. *The Trial*, 240.
34. Franz Kafka, *The Castle*, trans. Willa and Edwin Muir (Penguin: Harmondsworth, 1957), 216.
35. *The Myth of Sisyphus*, 112.
36. T.W. Adorno, quoted in Malcolm Bradbury, *The Modern World: Ten Great Writers* (Penguin: Harmondsworth, 1989), 259.
37. Quoted by George Steiner, *Real Presences: Is There Anything in What We Say?* (Faber & Faber: London and Boston, 1989), 224.
38. *Kafka: A Collection of Critical Essays*, ed. Ronald Gray (Prentice Hall: Englewood Cliffs, NJ, 1962), 94.
39. Quoted in Gray (ed.), *Kafka: A Collection of Critical Essays*, 20.

40. Milan Kundera, *The Art of the Novel*, trans. Linda Asher (Faber & Faber: London and Boston, 1988), 106.
41. *The Trial*, 243.
42. *Metamorphosis and Other Stories*, 111.
43. Bradbury, *The Modern World*, 258.
44. Heller, *Kafka*, 26.
45. *The Poems of Alexander Pope*, ed. John Butt (Methuen: London, 1968), 808.
46. *Wedding Preparations in the Country and Other Stories*, 53.
47. Erich Heller, 'The World of Franz Kafka', in *The Disinherited Mind* (Penguin: Harmondsworth, 1961), 177.
48. Quoted in Gray (ed.), *Kafka*, 157.
49. *Wedding Preparations in the Country and Other Stories*, 136.
50. Heller, *Kafka*, 94.
51. *The Trial*, 243.
52. Ibid., 97.
53. *Wedding Preparations in the Country and Other Stories*, 41.
54. *The Trial*, 171, 233.
55. Ibid., 247.
56. Ibid., 98–9.
57. Ibid., 7.
58. John Bunyan, *Grace Abounding and The Life and Death of Mr Badman*, intro. G.B. Harrison (Everyman's Library, Dent: London, 1956), 298.
59. *The Trial*, 12–13.
60. *Metamorphosis and Other Stories*, 97.
61. Ibid., 102–3.
62. Ibid., 69, 74.
63. Friedrich Nietzsche, *The Gay Science*, trans. Walter Kaufman (Vintage Books: New York, 1974), 328.
64. Philip Rahv, quoted in John Peter, *Vladimir's Carrot: Modern Drama and the Modern Imagination* (Methuen: London, 1988), 160, 159.
65. Kundera, *The Art of the Novel*, 104–5.
66. *The Castle*, 115.
67. *The Trial*, 167.
68. Ibid., 238–9. See Steiner, *Real Presences*, 103–4.
69. *The Trial*, 243.
70. Kundera, *The Art of the Novel*, 104.
71. *The Trial*, 190.
72. Ibid., 197.
73. Ibid., 198.
74. Ibid., 209.
75. Ibid., 210.
76. Ibid., 213.
77. Ibid., 214.
78. George Orwell, *Nineteen Eighty-Four* (Penguin: Harmondsworth, 1954), 203.
79. *The Trial*, 224.
80. Jonathan Swift, *The Prose Works of Jonathan Swift* (16 vols), ed. Herbert Davis *et al.* (Basil Blackwell: Oxford, 1939–68), vol. 1, 244.

81. Bishop Joseph Butler, *Fifteen Sermons*, preached at the Rolls Chapel and *A dissertation upon the nature of virtue*, ed. W.R. Matthews (George Bell: London, 1953). See also Gray (ed.), *Kafka*, 6.

Chapter 6 West

1. Alistair Wisker, *The Writing of Nathanael West* (Macmillan: Basingstoke, 1990), 17.
2. John Hawkes, 'An Interview', *Wisconsin Studies in Contemporary Literature*, Wisconsin, 1965.
3. Philip Roth, in *The Novel Today: Contemporary Writers on Modern Fiction*, ed. Malcolm Bradbury (Fontana, Collins: Glasgow, 1977), 34.
4. Ibid., 35.
5. Samuel Johnson, *The History of Rasselas, Prince of Abyssinia*, ed. and intro. D.J. Enright (Penguin: Harmondsworth, 1976), 133–5. 'On Those That Hated "The Playboy of the Western World"', 1907, *Poems of W.B. Yeats*, intro. A. Norman Jeffares (Macmillan: Basingstoke, 1988), 291.
6. Fyodor Dostoyevsky, *The Brothers Karamazov*, trans. David Magarshack (Penguin: Harmondsworth, 1958), 278.
7. Nathanael West, *Miss Lonelyhearts and A Cool Million* (Penguin: Harmondsworth, 1961), 8.
8. John Keats, *The Letters of John Keats*, ed. Hyder Edward Rollins (Cambridge University Press, 1958), vol. 1, 292. *The Brothers Karamazov*, 277–88.
9. Dante Alighieri, *The Divine Comedy: Inferno*, trans. Mark Musa (Penguin Classics: New York, 1984), 90.
10. Ibid., 371.
11. W.H. Auden, 'West's Disease', in *Nathanael West: Modern Critical Views*, ed. Harold Bloom (Chelsea House: New York, 1987), 43. See also W.H. Auden, *The Dyer's Hand and Other Essays* (Random House: New York, 1962), 238–45.
12. Nathanael Hawthorne, 'Earth's Holocaust', *Mosses from An Old Manse* (Fields, Osgood: Boston, 1870), vol. 2, 188–9.
13. *The Divine Comedy: Inferno*, 82.
14. Herman Melville, *Billy Budd, Sailor and Other Stories*, ed. and intro. Harold Beaver (Penguin: Harmondsworth, 1967), 99.
15. Ibid., 99.
16. Ibid., 99.
17. *Miss Lonelyhearts*, 11.
18. *Billy Budd, Sailor and Other Stories*, 80, 83, 90.
19. Ibid., 79.
20. Ibid., 91.
21. William Wordsworth, 'The Old Cumberland Beggar', *Selected Poetry and Prose*, ed. Philip Hobsbaum (Routledge: London and New York, 1989), 95–8.
22. Samuel Butler, *Erewhon*, ed. and intro. Peter Mudford (Penguin: Harmondsworth, 1970), 104.
23. *The Divine Comedy: Inferno*, 347.
24. Randell Reid, *The Fiction of Nathanael West: No Redeemer, No Promised Land* (University of Chicago Press: Chicago and London, 1967), 101.

25. *Miss Lonelyhearts*, 50.
26. Nathanael West, *The Day of the Locust* (Penguin: Harmondsworth, 1963), 11–12.
27. Ibid., 80.
28. *Wordsworth and Coleridge: Lyrical Ballads*, ed. Derek Roper (Collins: London and Glasgow, 1973), 400.
29. *Miss Lonelyhearts*, 7.
30. *The Correspondence of Jonathan Swift* (5 vols), ed. Harold Williams (Clarendon Press: Oxford, 1963–5) 111, 102.
31. Kingsley Widmer, 'The Religious Masquerade', in *Nathanael West* (Twayne: Boston, 1982), 26–50.
32. James W. Hickey, 'Freudian Criticism and *Miss Lonelyhearts*', in *Nathanael West: Modern Critical Views*, ed. Harold Bloom (Chelsea House: New York, 1987), 61–88.
33. *Miss Lonelyhearts*, 15.
34. Ibid., 16–17.
35. Ibid., 70.
36. Ibid., 46.
37. Ibid., 36.
38. *Billy Budd, Sailor and Other Stories*, 138.
39. Herman Melville, *Moby Dick, or The White Whale* (Signet, Penguin: Harmondsworth, 1980), 405.
40. Ibid., 405.
41. Ibid., 405.
42. *Miss Lonelyhearts*, 22.
43. William James, *The Varieties of Religious Experience* (Collins: Glasgow, 1977), 26.
44. Ibid., 108.
45. *Miss Lonelyhearts*, 13.
46. James, *The Varieties of Religious Experience*, 119, 122.
47. *Miss Lonelyhearts*, 46.
48. James, *The Varieties of Religious Experience*, 143.
49. *Baudelaire*, intro. and ed. Francis Scarfe (Penguin: Harmondsworth, 1972), 190–2.
50. *Miss Lonelyhearts*, 19.
51. Ibid., 18.
52. Ibid., 18.
53. Ludwig Feuerbach, *The Essence of Christianity*, trans. George Eliot (Harper & Row: New York; Hagerston: San Francisco and London, 1957), 239.
54. See Wisker, *The Writing of Nathanael West*, 1.
55. James, *The Varieties of Religious Experience*, 169.
56. *Miss Lonelyhearts*, 30.
57. J.R. May, 'Words and Deeds', in *Nathanael West's 'Miss Lonelyhearts': Modern Critical Interpretations*, ed. Harold Bloom (Chelsea House: New York, 1987), 53–60.
58. *Miss Lonelyhearts*, 67.
59. Gershom Scholen in Bloom (ed.), *Nathanael West: Modern Critical Views*, 2.
60. *Miss Lonelyhearts*, 46.
61. *The Day of the Locust*, 91.
62. Scholen in Bloom (ed.), *Nathanael West*, 4.
63. *Miss Lonelyhearts*, 46.
64. *Paradise Lost*, ed. Alastair Fowler (Longman Group Limited: London, 1971), Book IV,

380–1.
65. *Miss Lonelyhearts*, 46.
66. Ibid., 55.
67. Ibid., 55.
68. Ibid., 14, 30.
69. Ibid., 66.
70. *The Day of the Locust*, 113.
71. *A Cool Million*, 174.
72. *Notes From Underground*, 26–7.
73. Ibid., 32.
74. Ibid., 39–41.
75. *The Day of the Locust*, 25.
76. Ibid., 42.
77. Ibid., 107, 111.
78. Ibid., 144.
79. Ibid., 127.
80. Ibid., 30.
81. Ibid., 31.
82. Ibid., 61.
83. Ibid., 62.
84. Ibid., 10, 89.
85. Ibid., 107.
86. Ibid., 101, 148.
87. Ibid., 146–7.
88. Ibid., 78.
89. Ibid., 127.

Chapter 7 Camus

1. Blaise Pascal, *Pensées*, trans. and intro. A.J. Krailsheimer (Penguin: Harmondsworth, 1966), 82.
2. Albert Camus, *The Myth of Sisyphus*, trans. Justin O'Brien (Penguin: Harmondsworth, 1975), 11–12.
3. Ibid., 137.
4. Franz Kafka, *The Castle*, trans. Willa and Edwin Muir (Penguin: Harmondsworth, 1957), 75.
5. Albert Camus, *The Possessed*, trans. Justin O'Brien (Penguin: Harmondsworth, 1970), 104, 142.
6. *The Myth of Sisyphus*, 7.
7. Ibid., 7.
8. Ibid., 111.
9. Ibid., 53.
10. Ibid., 40–1.
11. Ibid., 55.
12. Ibid., 19, 84–5.
13. Ibid., 52.

14. Ibid., 43.
15. Ibid., 84–5.
16. Ibid., 83.
17. Ibid., 59.
18. Ibid., 111.
19. Ibid., 111.
20. Ibid., 108.
21. Ibid., 109.
22. Ibid., 109.
23. Ibid., 110.
24. Ibid., 109.
25. Dante Alighieri, *The Divine Comedy: Inferno*, trans. Mark Musa (Penguin Classics: New York, 1984), 161.
26. *The Myth of Sisyphus*, 94.
27. Albert Camus, *The Outsider*, trans. Stuart Gilbert, intro. Cyril Connolly (Penguin: Harmondsworth, 1961), 15, 29–32.
28. Ibid., 71.
29. Ibid., 73.
30. Ibid., 75.
31. Ibid., 113.
32. Ibid., 114.
33. Ibid., 115.
34. Ibid., 116.
35. Ibid., 117.
36. Ibid., 118.
37. Ibid., 118.
38. Ibid., 118.
39. Ibid., 118.
40. Ibid., 120.
41. *The Myth of Sisyphus*, 64, 65.
42. *Essais d'Albert Camus* (Bibliothèque de la Pleiade, Gallimard: Paris, 1965), 65–6 (my translation).
43. Pascal, *Pensées*, 88.
44. Albert Camus, *Caligula*, trans. Stuart Gilbert, intro. John Cruickshank (Penguin: Harmondsworth, 1965), 35.
45. Ibid., 36.
46. Ibid., 70.
47. Ibid., 40.
48. Ibid., 65.
49. Ibid., 94.
50. Ibid., 55.
51. Ibid., 83.
52. Ibid., 97.
53. Ibid., 97.
54. Ibid., 36.
55. Jean Jacques Rousseau, 'Lettre à M. d'Alembert', *Oeuvres Complètes* (Gallimard: Paris, 1995), vol. V, 1–125. See Lionel Trilling, *Sincerity and Authenticity* (Oxford

University Press: London, 1974), 63.
56. Albert Camus, *Cross Purpose*, trans. Stuart Gilbert, intro. John Cruickshank (Penguin: Harmondsworth, 1965), 103, 105.
57. *The Outsider*, 82.
58. *Cross Purpose*, 143–5.
59. Ibid., 102.
60. Ibid., 151.
61. Ibid., 111.
62. Ibid., 111.
63. Ibid., 112.
64. Ibid., 120.
65. Ibid., 121.
66. Ibid., 122.
67. Albert Camus, *The Fall*, trans. Justin O'Brien (Penguin: Harmondsworth, 1963), 11.
68. *Cross Purpose*, 127–8, 139.
69. Ibid., 130.
70. Ibid., 120.
71. Ibid., 130.
72. Ibid., 137.
73. Ibid., 140.
74. Ibid., 144.
75. Ibid., 145.
76. Ibid., 148.
77. Alfred de Vigny, 'Le Mont des Oliviers', *Oeuvres Complètes* (Gallimard: Paris, 1986), vol. 1, 149–52.
78. *Cross Purpose*, 151.
79. Ibid., 153, 155.
80. *The Divine Comedy: Inferno*, 297.
81. *Cross Purpose*, 154.
82. Ibid., 155.
83. Ibid., 156.
84. St Luke, xi. 9, Psalm 18.
85. See Olivier Todd, *Albert Camus: A Life*, trans. Benjamin Ivry (Chatto & Windus: London, 1997), 186.
86. William Shakespeare, *Othello*, ed. Kenneth Muir (Penguin: Harmondsworth, 1968). Thomas Rymer's criticism of the play is quoted in the introduction, 12.
87. *Cross Purpose*, 154.

Chapter 8 Waugh

1. Albert Camus, *The Fall*, trans. Justin O'Brien (Penguin: Harmondsworth, 1963), 11.
2. *Collected Essays, Journalism and Letters of George Orwell*, ed. Sonia Orwell and Ian Angus (Penguin: Harmondsworth, 1970), IV, 340–1.
3. Franz Kafka, *The Trial* (Penguin: Harmondsworth and London, 1953), 13.
4. Stephen Spender, *The Creative Element: A Study of Vision, Orthodoxy and Despair Among Some Modern Writers* (Hamish Hamilton: London, 1953).

5. St Paul, 'Epistle to the Philippians', ii.15; iii.19; iii.21.
6. Evelyn Waugh, *Vile Bodies* (Penguin: Harmondsworth, 1938), 192.
7. Ibid., 29.
8. Ibid., 134.
9. Ibid., 199.
10. Ibid., 156–7.
11. Ibid., 213.
12. Jonathan Swift, *Gulliver's Travels*, ed. Peter Dixon and John Chalker (Penguin: Harmondsworth, 1967), 79.
13. Evelyn Waugh, *Black Mischief* (Penguin: Harmondsworth, 1938), 16.
14. See Patrick Reilly, *Jonathan Swift: The Brave Desponder* (Manchester University Press, 1982), 91–3.
15. *Black Mischief*, 40–1.
16. *Gulliver's Travels*, 232.
17. Plato, *The Republic*, trans. and intro. Desmond Lee (Penguin: Harmondsworth, 1977), 66.
18. Evelyn Waugh, *A Handful of Dust* (Penguin: Harmondsworth, 1951), 125.
19. Evelyn Waugh, 'Fan-Fare', *Life*, XX, 1946, 60.
20. Rosalind Murray, *The Good Pagan's Failure* (Fontana, Collins: London and Glasgow, 1962.
21. Evelyn Waugh, *Ninety-Two Days* (Duckworth: London, 1934), 88.
22. Matthew Arnold, 'The Study of Poetry', *Essays in Criticism*, intro. G.K. Chesterton (Everyman's Library, Dent: London; Dutton: New York, 1969), 235.
23. 'Fan-Fare', 58.
24. *A Handful of Dust*, 15–16.
25. Ibid., 35–6.
26. Ibid., 30.
27. Ibid., 31.
28. Ibid., 32.
29. Ralph Waldo Emerson, 'Self-Reliance', *Anthology of American Literature*, ed. George McMichael, 4th edn, vol. 1 (Macmillan: New York, 1985), 1092.
30. *A Handful of Dust*, 65, 57.
31. Ibid., 82.
32. Ibid., 125.
33. Ibid., 96.
34. John Milton, 'Areopagitica', *Prose Writings*, intro. K.M. Burton (Everyman's Library, Dent: London; Dutton: New York, 1965), 158.
35. Quoted in J.C. Reid, *Dickens: Little Dorrit*, Studies in English Literature (Edward Arnold: London, 1967), 11.
36. *A Handful of Dust*, 105.
37. Ernest Hemingway, *A Farewell to Arms* (Penguin: Harmondsworth, 1958), 252.
38. *A Handful of Dust*, 110.
39. Ibid., 106.
40. Anton Chekhov, 'Three Sisters', in *Chehov Plays*, trans. and intro. Elisaveta Fen (Penguin: Harmondsworth, 1951), 282.
41. *A Handful of Dust*, 107.
42. Ibid., 106–7.
43. Ibid., 113.

44. Sir Walter Scott, *The Antiquary*, intro. W.M. Parker (Everyman's Library, Dent: London; Dutton: New York, 1969), 307.
45. Cyril Connolly quoted in Christopher Sykes, *Evelyn Waugh: A Biography* (Collins: London and Glasgow, 1975), 138.
46. *A Handful of Dust*, 138–9.
47. Ibid., 109.
48. Ibid., 118, 119.
49. Ibid., 109.
50. Ibid., 129.
51. Ibid., 128.
52. Jane Austen, *Mansfield Park*, ed. and intro. Tony Tanner (Penguin: Harmondsworth, 1966), 441–2.
53. *A Handful of Dust*, 120.
54. Ibid., 137–8.
55. Ibid, 44, 60.
56. Ibid., 148.
57. Ibid., 149.
58. Ibid., 151.
59. Ibid., 159, 160.
60. Ibid., 153.
61. Evelyn Waugh, *Helena* (Penguin: Harmondsworth, 1963), 39–40.
62. *A Handful of Dust*, 164.
63. Ibid., 180, 189.
64. Ibid., 159.
65. Ibid., 172.
66. Ibid., 203.
67. Ibid., 207.
68. Ibid., 205.
69. Ibid., 210.
70. Ibid., 211.
71. Ibid., 208
72. Ibid., 115.
73. *The Essential Hemingway* (Penguin: Harmondsworth, 1967), 188.
74. Henry Fielding, *Joseph Andrews*, ed. R.F. Brissenden (Penguin: Harmondsworth, 1977), 156–7.
75. Quoted by George Steiner in *Real Presences: Is There Anything in What We Say?* (Faber & Faber: London and Boston, 1989), 144.
76. *A Handful of Dust*, 215.
77. Ibid., 221.
78. 'Troilus and Criseyde', *The Works of Geoffrey Chaucer*, ed. F.N. Robinson (Oxford University Press: London, 1957), 479.
79. Ibid., 479.
80. Ibid., 479.

Chapter 9 O'Connor

1. John Milton, 'Areopagitica', *Prose Writings*, intro. K.M. Burton (Everyman's Library, Dent: London; Dutton: New York, 1965), 181.
2. Jesse Hill Ford, *Nashville Tennessean*, 4 September 1966.
3. Dante Alighieri, *The Divine Comedy: Inferno*, trans. Mark Musa (Penguin: New York, 1984), 89.
4. Flannery O'Connor, *Mystery and Manners: Occasional Prose*, ed. Sally and Robert Fitzgerald (The Noonday Press, Farrar, Straus & Giroux: New York, 1995), 48.
5. Flannery O'Connor, *Everything That Rises Must Converge* (Faber & Faber: London, 1966), 191, 31.
6. Ibid., 37.
7. Ibid., 216.
8. Ibid., 218.
9. *Mystery and Manners*, 33–4.
10. Flannery O'Connor, *A Good Man is Hard To Find and Other Stories*, intro. Lisa Alther (The Women's Press: London, 1980), 15.
11. Ibid., 15. St Paul, 'Epistle to the Romans', iii.10.
12. *A Good Man*, 24.
13. Ibid., 16–17.
14. Ibid., 20.
15. *Mystery and Manners*, 167.
16. *A Good Man*, 29.
17. Ibid., 29.
18. Ibid., 28.
19. Fyodor Dostoyevsky, *Crime and Punishment*, trans. David Magarshack (Penguin: Harmondsworth, 1951), 482.
20. T.S. Eliot, *Selected Prose*, ed. John Hayward (Penguin: Harmondsworth, 1953), 194.
21. *Mystery and Manners*, 118.
22. Ibid., 116.
23. Ibid., 113.
24. *A Good Man*, 29.
25. Ibid., 28, 27.
26. George Bernanos, *The Diary of a Country Priest*, trans. Pamela Morris (Fontana: London, 1977), 251.
27. *A Good Man*, 29.
28. Ibid., 29.
29. *Mystery and Manners*, 114.
30. Quoted by Sally Fitzgerald in *Three by Flannery O'Connor: Wise Blood, The Violent Bear it Away, Everything That Rises Must Converge* (Signet, Penguin: Harmondsworth, 1983), Introduction, xiv.
31. Ibid., xxxiv.
32. Ibid., 116–17.
33. Ibid., 76, 18.
34. Ibid., 75.
35. Ibid., 31.
36. *Mystery and Manners*, 114.

37. *Three by Flannery O'Connor*, 120, 118.
38. Ibid., 58.
39. Ibid., 116.
40. Ibid., 109.
41. Ibid., 113.
42. *A Good Man*, 30.
43. Ibid., 31–2.
44. Ibid., 45.
45. Ibid., 33.
46. Ibid., 38.
47. Ibid., 44.
48. Ibid., 50.
49. St Luke, viii. 32–6. Fyodor Dostoyevsky, *The Devils*, trans. and intro. David Magarshack (Penguin: Harmondsworth, 1953), 20. See also 647–8.
50. *A Good Man*, 52.
51. Ibid., 52.
52. Jonathan Swift, 'An Argument Against Abolishing Christianity', *The Prose Works of Jonathan Swift* (16 vols), ed. Herbert Davis *et al.* (Basil Blackwell: Oxford, 1939–68), vol. 2, 38. James Boswell, *The Life of Johnson*, ed. Christopher Hibbert (Penguin: Harmondsworth, 1979), 110.
53. *A Good Man*, 176.
54. Ibid., 176–7.
55. Ibid., 174.
56. Ibid., 175.
57. Ibid., 176.
58. Ibid., 180.
59. Ibid., 186.
60. Ibid., 189.
61. *Mystery and Manners*, 59, 164, 201.
62. *A Good Man*, 191.
63. Ibid., 191.
64. Ibid., 191.
65. Ibid., 192.
66. Ibid., 192.
67. Ibid., 192.
68. Ibid., 192.
69. Blaise Pascal, *Pensées*, trans. and intro. A.J. Krailsheimer (Penguin: Harmondsworth, 1966), 100.
70. *A Good Man*, 194–5.
71. Ibid., 195.
72. Ibid., 195.
73. Ibid., 195–6.
74. Flannery O'Connor, *The Habit of Being: Letters of Flannery O'Connor*, ed. and intro. Sally Fitzgerald (Farrar, Straus & Giroux: New York, 1979).
75. Edmund Burke, *Reflections on the Revolution in France and Other Writings* (The World's Classics, Oxford University Press: London, 1958), 300.
76. *Everything That Rises Must Converge*, 149.

77. Ibid., 161.
78. Ibid., 146.
79. Ibid., 147.
80. Ibid., 180.
81. Ibid., 176.
82. Ibid., 181.
83. Ibid., 150.
84. John Henry Newman, *Apologia Pro Vita Sua* (Collins: Glasgow, 1977), 278–9.
85. *Everything That Rises Must Converge*, 188.
86. Ibid., 189.
87. *The Habit of Being*, 449. See also John Hawkes, 'Flannery O'Connor's Devil', *Sewanee Review*, 70, Summer 1962, 395–407.
88. Ibid., 456.
89. *Three by Flannery O'Connor*, 260–1.
90. *Everything That Rises Must Converge*, 189.
91. Ibid., 166.
92. Ibid., 190.

Bibliography

Primary texts

Camus, Albert, *The Outsider*, trans. Stuart Gilbert, intro. Cyril Connolly (Penguin: Harmondsworth, 1961).

______, *The Fall*, trans. Justin O'Brien (Penguin: Harmondsworth, 1963).

______, *The Myth of Sisyphus*, trans. Justin O'Brien (Penguin: Harmondsworth, 1975).

______, *The Possessed*, trans. Justin O'Brien (Penguin: Harmondsworth, 1970).

______, *Caligula and Cross Purpose*, trans. Stuart Gilbert, intro. John Cruickshank (Penguin: Harmondsworth, 1965).

______, *Essais d'Albert Camus* (Bibliothèque de la Pleiade, Gallimard: Paris, 1965).

Conrad, Joseph, *The Secret Agent: A Simple Tale*, ed. Martin Seymour-Smith (Penguin: Harmondsworth, 1986).

Dante Alighieri, *The Divine Comedy*, trans. Mark Musa (Penguin: New York, 1984).

Dostoyevsky, Fyodor, *Notes from Underground*, trans. and intro. Jessie Coulson (Penguin: Harmondsworth, 1972).

______, *Fyodor Dostoyevsky: Notes from Underground*, ed. Michael Katz (Norton Critical Edition, Norton: New York and London, 1989).

______, *The Insulted and Injured*, trans. Constance Garnett (Grafton Books, Collins: London, 1987).

______, *Crime and Punishment*, trans. David Magarshack (Penguin: Harmondsworth, 1951).

______, *The Brothers Karamazov*, trans. and intro. David Magarshack (Penguin: Harmondsworth, 1958).

______, *The Devils*, trans. David Magarshack (Penguin: Harmondsworth, 1953).

______, *Winter Notes on Summer Impressions*, trans. Richard Lee Renfield (Criterion Books: New York, 1955).

______, *The Diary of a Writer*, trans. Boris Brasol (Charles Scribners: New York, 1972).

Hardy, Thomas, *Tess of the d'Urbervilles: A Pure Woman*, intro. A. Alvarez, ed. David Skilton (Penguin: Harmondsworth, 1978).

______, 'Barbara of the House of Grebe', *Selected Stories of Thomas Hardy*, intro. John Wain (Macmillan: London and Basingstoke, 1966).

______, *The Life and Work of Thomas Hardy by Thomas Hardy*, ed. Michael Millgate (Macmillan: London and Basingstoke, 1984).

Kafka, Franz, *The Trial* (Penguin: Harmondsworth and London, 1953).

______, *The Castle*, trans. Willa and Edwin Muir (Penguin: Harmondsworth, 1957).

______, 'In the Penal Settlement', *Metamorphosis and Other Stories*, trans. Willa and Edwin Muir (Penguin: Harmondsworth, 1961).

______, *Wedding Preparations in the Country and Other Studies* (Penguin: Harmondsworth, 1978).

______, *Letters to Felice*, ed. Erich Heller and Jürgen Born, trans. James Stern and Elizabeth Duckworth (Penguin: Harmondsworth, 1978).
O'Connor, Flannery, *Everything That Rises Must Converge* (Faber & Faber: London, 1966).
______, *A Good Man Is Hard To Find and Other Stories*, intro. Lisa Alther (The Women's Press: London, 1980).
______, *Three by Flannery O'Connor: Wise Blood, The Violent Bear It Away, Everything That Rises Must Converge* (Signet, Penguin: Harmondsworth, 1983).
______, *The Habit of Being: Letters of Flannery O'Connor*, ed. and intro. Sally Fitzgerald (Farrar, Straus & Giroux: New York, 1979).
______, *Mystery and Manners: Occasional Prose*, ed. Sally and Robert Fitzgerald (The Noonday Press, Farrar, Straus & Giroux: New York, 1961).
Waugh, Evelyn, *Decline and Fall* (Penguin: Harmondsworth, 1937).
______, *Vile Bodies* (Penguin: Harmondsworth, 1938).
______, *Black Mischief* (Penguin: Harmondsworth, 1938).
______, *A Handful of Dust* (Penguin: Harmondsworth, 1951).
______, *Helena* (Penguin: Harmondsworth, 1963).
______, *Ninety-Two Days* (Duckworth: London, 1934).
______, 'Fan-Fare', *Life*, XX, 1946.
West, Nathanael, *Miss Lonelyhearts and A Cool Million* (Penguin: Harmondsworth, 1961).
______, *The Day of the Locust* (Penguin: Harmondsworth, 1963).
Wharton, Edith, *Ethan Frome* (Collier Books, Macmillan: New York, 1986).
______, *Ethan Frome*, ed. Cynthia Griffin Wolff (Signet, Penguin: New York, 1987).
______, *Ethan Frome*, ed. Kristin O. Lauer and Cynthia Griffin Wolff (Norton Critical Edition, W.W. Norton: New York and London, 1995).
______, *The House of Mirth*, intro. Cynthia Griffin Wolff (Penguin: Harmondsworth, 1986).
______, *A Backward Glance* (Appleton-Century: New York, 1934).

Secondary texts

Abrams, M.H. (ed.), *The Norton Anthology of English Literature*, 6th edn (W.W. Norton: New York and London, 1993).
Aeschylus, *The Oresteian Trilogy*, trans. Philip Vellacott (Penguin: Harmondsworth, 1966).
Ammons, Elizabeth, *Edith Wharton's Argument with America* (Georgia University Press: Athens, GA, 1980).
Amory, Mark (ed.), *The Letters of Evelyn Waugh* (Weidenfeld & Nicolson: London, 1980).
Anders, Günther, *Franz Kafka*, trans. A. Steer and A.K. Thorlby (Bowes & Bowes: London, 1960).
Andreach, Robert J., 'Nathanael West's *Miss Lonelyhearts*: Between the Dead Pan and the Unborn Christ', *Modern Fiction Studies*, XIII, Summer 1966, 251–60.
Arnold, Matthew, *Selected Prose*, ed. and intro. P.J. Keating (Penguin: Harmondsworth, 1970).
______, 'The Study of Poetry', *Essays in Criticism*, intro. G.K. Chesterton (Everyman's Library, Dent: London; Dutton: New York, 1969).
Asals, Frederick, 'Flannery O'Connor's *The Lame Shall Enter First*', *Mississippi Quarterly*, 23, Spring 1970, 103–20.

Auden, W.H., *The Dyer's Hand and Other Essays* (Random House: New York, 1962).
Austen, Jane, *Mansfield Park*, ed. and intro. Tony Tanner (Penguin: Harmondsworth, 1966).
Baines, Jocelyn, *Joseph Conrad: A Critical Biography* (Weidenfeld & Nicolson: London, 1960).
Barber, Benjamin R., *Superman and Common Men: Freedom, Anarchy and the Revolution* (Penguin: Harmondsworth, 1972).
Baudelaire, Charles, *Poems*, ed. Francis Scarfe (Penguin: Harmondsworth, 1972).
Beardsley, Monroe, 'Dostoyevsky's Metaphor of the Underground', *Journal of the History of Ideas*, 3, 1942, 265–90.
Beaty, Frederick L., *The Ironic World of Evelyn Waugh* (Northern Illinois Press: De Kalb, 1992).
Beckett, Samuel, *Endgame* (Faber & Faber: London, 1972).
Bell, Millicent (ed.), *The Cambridge Companion to Edith Wharton* (Cambridge University Press, 1995).
Bellamy, W.J., 'Nathanael West', *Cambridge Quarterly*, Winter 1968, 95–106.
Bellow, Saul, *Herzog* (Penguin: Harmondsworth, 1965).
Bendixen, Alfred and Zilversmit, Annette (eds), *Edith Wharton: New Critical Essays* (Garland: New York, 1992).
Benstock, Shari, *No Gifts from Chance: A Biography of Edith Wharton* (Penguin: Harmondsworth, 1994).
Berdyaev, Nicholas, *Dostoyevsky*, trans. Donald Attwater (New American Library: New York, 1994).
Bergonzi, Bernard, 'Evelyn Waugh's Gentleman', *Critical Quarterly*, V, 1963, 23–36.
Bernanos, George, *The Diary of a Country Priest*, trans. Pamela Morris (Fontana: London, 1977).
Bernard, Kenneth, 'Imagery and Symbolism in *Ethan Frome*', *College English*, 22, December 1961, 178–84.
Bettelheim, Bruno, *The Uses of Enchantment: The Meaning and Importance of Fairy Tales* (Alfred A. Knopf: New York, 1976).
Blackall, Jean Frantz, 'The Sledding Accident in *Ethan Frome*', *Studies in Short Fiction*, Spring 1984, 145–6.
Bloom, Harold (ed.), *Nathanael West's 'Miss Lonelyhearts': Modern Critical Interpretations* (Chelsea House: New York, 1987).
______ (ed.), *Nathanael West: Modern Critical Views* (Chelsea House: New York, 1987).
______, 'Critical Views on the *Inferno*', in *Dante*, Bloom's Major Poets (Chelsea House: New York, 2001).
______, *Dante: Modern Critical Views* (Chelsea House: New York, 1986).
Bonhoeffer, Dietrich, *Ethics*, ed. Eberhard Bethge (SCM Press: London, 1955).
Boswell, James, *The Life of Johnson*, ed. Christopher Hibbert (Penguin: Harmondsworth, 1979).
Boyde, Patrick, *Perception and Passion in Dante's 'Comedy'* (Cambridge University Press, 1993).
Bradbury, Malcolm, *Evelyn Waugh* (Oliver & Boyd: Edinburgh and London, 1964).
______, *The Modern World: Ten Great Writers* (Penguin: Harmondsworth, 1989).
______ (ed.), *The Novel Today: Contemporary Writers on Modern Fiction* (Fontana, Collins: Glasgow, 1977).
Brée, Germaine, *Camus* (Rutger's University Press: New Brunswick, 1959), rev., Harbinger Edition, 1964.

Brod, Max, *Franz Kafka: A Biography* (Secker & Warburg: London, 1947).

Brown, Douglas, *Thomas Hardy* (Longmans Green: London, 1961).

Browning, Preston M., *Flannery O'Connor* (Southern Illinois University Press: Carbondale, IL, 1974).

Browning, Robert, 'Caliban on Setebos', *The Poems*, ed. John Pettigrew (Penguin: Harmondsworth, 1981).

Bunyan, John, *Grace Abounding and The Life and Death of Mr Badman*, intro. G.B. Harrison (Everyman's Library, Dent: London, 1956).

Burke, Edmund, *Reflections on the Revolution in France and Other Writings* (The World's Classics, Oxford University Press: London, 1958).

Butler, Bishop Joseph, *Fifteen Sermons* and *A dissertation upon the nature of virtue*, ed. W.R. Matthews (George Bell: London, 1953).

Butler, Samuel, *Erewhon*, ed. and intro. Peter Mudford (Penguin: Harmondsworth, 1970).

Butt, John (ed.), *The Poems of Alexander Pope* (Methuen: London, 1968).

Caesar, Michael (ed.), *Dante: The Critical Heritage 1314(?)–1870* (Routledge: London, 1989).

Camus, Albert, 'Hope and the Absurd in the Work of Franz Kafka', in *The Myth of Sisyphus*, trans. Justin O'Brien (Penguin: Harmondsworth, 1975), 112–24.

Canetti, Elias, 'Kafka's Other Trial', trans. Christopher Middleton, in *Letters to Felice*, ed. Erich Heller and Jürgen Born, trans. James Stern and Elizabeth Duckworth (Penguin: Harmondsworth, 1978), 7–94.

Carens, James F., *The Satiric Art of Evelyn Waugh* (University of Washington Press: Seattle and London, 1966).

______, *Critical Essays on Evelyn Waugh* (G.K. Hall: Boston, 1987).

Carpenter, Richard C., *Thomas Hardy* (Twayne: New York, 1964).

Carr, E.H., *Dostoyevsky* (George Allen & Unwin: London, 1962).

Carter, Daniel A., 'West's Revisions of *Miss Lonelyhearts*', *Studies in Bibliography*, XVI, 1963, 232–43.

Chaucer, Geoffrey, 'Troilus and Criseyde', *The Works of Geoffrey Chaucer*, ed. F.N. Robinson (Oxford University Press: London, 1957).

Chekhov, Anton, 'Three Sisters', in *Chekhov Plays*, trans. and intro. Elisaveta Fen (Penguin: Harmondsworth, 1951).

Chernyshevsky, Nikolai G., *What Is to Be Done?*, trans. Michael R. Katz, annot. William G. Wagner (Cornell University Press: Ithaca and London, 1984).

Cohen, Arthur, 'Nathanael West's Holy Fool', *Commonweal*, 64, June 15, 1956, 276–8.

Cohn, Norman, *Cosmos, Chaos and the World to Come* (Yale University Press: Baton Rouge and London, 1994).

Coleridge, Samuel Taylor, 'The Rime of the Ancient Mariner', *Poems*, ed. John Beer (Everyman, Dent: London; Charles E. Tuttle: Vermont, 1798).

Coles, Robert, *Flannery O'Connor's South* (Louisiana State University Press: Baton Rouge and London, 1980).

Comerchero, Victor, *Nathanael West: The Ironic Prophet* (Syracuse University Press: Syracuse, 1964).

Cook, William J. Jr, *Masks, Modes and Morals: The Art of Evelyn Waugh* (Dickinson University Press: Rutherford-Farleigh, 1971).

Cox, C.B., *Joseph Conrad: The Modern Imagination* (J.M. Dent: London; Rowman & Littlefield: Totowa, NJ, 1974).

Cox, Gary, *Tyrant and Victim in Dostoevsky* (Slavica Publishers: Columbus, OH, 1984).
Cox, R.G. (ed.), *Thomas Hardy: The Critical Heritage* (Routledge & Kegan Paul: London, 1970).
Cruickshank, John, *Albert Camus and the Literature of Revolt* (Oxford University Press: London; Galaxy: New York, 1960).
Curley, Edwin (ed. and trans.), *A Spinoza Reader: 'The Ethics' and Other Works* (Princeton University Press: Princeton, NJ, 1994).
Davidson, Donald, 'A Prophet Went Forth', *New York Times Book Review*, 28 February, 1960.
Davie, Michael (ed.), *The Diaries of Evelyn Waugh* (Weidenfeld & Nicolson: London, 1978).
Dennis, Nigel, 'Evelyn Waugh: The Pillar of Anchorage House', *Partisan Review*, New York, X, 1943, 350–61.
Devitis, A.A., *Roman Holiday: The Catholic Novels of Evelyn Waugh* (Bookman Associates: New York, 1956).
Dickens, Charles, *Hard Times*, ed. and intro. David Craig (Penguin: Harmondsworth, 1969).
Drake, Robert, *Flannery O'Connor: A Critical Essay* (W.B. Eerdmans: Grand Rapids, MI, 1966).
Draper, R.P., *Hardy: The Tragic Novels* (Macmillan: London and Basingstoke, 1975).
Dyson, A.E., 'Evelyn Waugh and the Mysteriously Disappearing Hero', *Critical Quarterly*, II, 1960, 16–22.
Eggenschwiler, David, *The Christian Humanism of Flannery O'Connor* (Wayne University Press: Detroit, 1972).
______, 'The Ordered Disorder of *Ethan Frome*', *Studies in the Novel*, 9, 1977, 237–46.
Ehrenfeld, Paul, *The Arrogance of Humanism* (Oxford University Press: New York, 1978).
Eliot, T.S., *After Strange Gods: A Primer of Modern Heresy* (Faber & Faber: London, 1934).
______, *Selected Prose*, ed. John Hayward (Penguin: Harmondsworth, 1953).
______, *The Complete Poems and Plays of T.S. Eliot* (Faber & Faber: London and Boston, 1969).
Fanger, Donald, *Dostoyevsky and Romantic Realism* (Harvard University Press: Cambridge, MA, 1967).
Feeley, Sister Kathleen, *Flannery O'Connor: The Voice of the Peacock* (Rutgers University Press: New Brunswick, 1972).
Feuerbach, Ludwig, *The Essence of Christianity*, trans. George Eliot (Harper & Row: New York; Hagerston: San Francisco and London, 1957).
Fielding, Henry, *Joseph Andrews*, ed. R.F. Brissenden (Penguin: Harmondsworth, 1977).
Fleishman, Avrom, *Conrad's Politics: Community and Anarchy in the Fiction of Joseph Conrad* (Johns Hopkins University Press: Baltimore and London, 1967).
Flores, Angel (ed.), *The Kafka Problem* (Octagon Books: New York, 1963).
______ (ed.), *The Kafka Debate: New Perspectives for Our Time* (Gordian Press: New York, 1977).
______ and Swander, Homer (eds), *Franz Kafka Today* (University of Wisconsin Press: Madison, 1958).
Ford, Jesse Hill, *Nashville Tennessean*, 4 September 1966.
Frank, Joseph D., *Dostoyevsky: The Miraculous Years* (Princeton University Press: Princeton, NJ, 1995).

______, 'Nihilism and *Notes from Underground*', *Sewanee Review*, LXIX, January–March 1961, 1–33.

Frank, Joseph D. and Goldstein, David I., *Selected Letters of Fyodor Dostoyevsky*, trans. Andrew R. MacAndrew (Rutgers University Press: New Brunswick and London, 1987).

Freccero, John, *Dante: A Collection of Critical Essays* (Prentice Hall: Englewood Cliffs, NJ, 1965).

Freud, Sigmund, 'Dostoyevsky and Parricide', *Collected Psychological Works*, ed. James Strachey (Hogarth Press: London, 1961), vol. XXI, 177–94.

Friedman, Milton J. and Lawson, Lewis A. (eds), *The Added Dimension: The Art and Mind of Flannery O'Connor* (Fordham University Press: New York, 1966).

Fukuyama, Francis, *The End of History and the Last Man* (Penguin: Harmondsworth, 1992).

Gallagher, Donat (ed.), *A Little Order: Evelyn Waugh, A Selection from his Journalism* (Little, Brown: Boston, 1977).

______, (ed.), *The Essays, Articles and Reviews of Evelyn Waugh* (Methuen: London, 1983).

Garnett, Edward (ed.), *Letters from Conrad 1895–1924* (Nonesuch: London, 1928).

Ghent, Dorothy van, *The English Novel: Form and Function* (Holt, Rinehart & Winston: New York, 1953).

Gide, André, *Dostoyevsky* (Gallimard: Paris, 1981).

Gilbert, Allan H., *Dante's Conception of Justice* (Duke University Press: Durham, NC, 1925). Reprinted New York, 1965.

Gilson, Etienne, *Dante and Philosophy*, trans. D. Moore (Sheed and Ward: London, 1948).

Gittings, Robert, *Young Thomas Hardy* (Heinemann: London, 1975).

Gordan, John Dozier, *Joseph Conrad: The Making of a Novelist* (Harvard University Press: Cambridge, MA, 1941). Reissued Russell & Russell: New York, 1963.

Gordon, Caroline, 'With a Glitter of Evil', *New York Times Book Review*, 12 June 1955.

Gossett, Louise Y., *Violence in Recent Southern Fiction* (Duke University Press: Durham, NC, 1965).

Gray, Ronald, *Franz Kafka* (Cambridge University Press: London and New York, 1973).

______, (ed.), *Kafka: A Collection of Critical Essays* (Prentice Hall: Englewood Cliffs, NJ, 1962).

Green, Peter, 'Du Côté de Chez Waugh', *Review of English Literature*, Leeds, II, 1961, 89–100.

Greenblatt, Stephen Jay, *Three Modern Satirists: Waugh, Orwell, and Huxley* (Yale University Press: New Haven, CT, 1965).

Gregor, Ian and Nicholas, Brian, *The Moral and the Story* (Faber & Faber: London, 1962).

Grossman, Leonid, *Dostoyevsky*, trans. Mary Mackler (Allen Lane: London, 1974).

Guerard, Albert J., *Thomas Hardy: The Novels and Stories* (Oxford University Press: London, 1949).

______, *Conrad the Novelist* (Harvard University Press: Cambridge, MA, 1958).

______, (ed.), *Hardy: A Collection of Critical Essays* (Prentice Hall: Englewood Cliffs, NJ, 1963).

Gurko, Leo, *Joseph Conrad: Giant in Exile* (Macmillan: New York, 1962).

Hafley, James, 'The Case against *Ethan Frome*', *Fresco* I, 1961, 194–201.

Hardy, Florence Emily, *The Life of Thomas Hardy 1840–1928* (Macmillan: London, 1962).

______, *The Later Years of Thomas Hardy, 1892–1928* (Macmillan: London, 1930).

Hassan, Ihab, *Radical Innocence* (Princeton University Press: Princeton, NJ, 1962).

Hastings, Selina, *Evelyn Waugh: A Biography* (Houghton Mifflin: Boston, 1994).

Hawkes, John, 'Flannery O'Connor's Devil', *Sewanee Review*, 70, Summer 1962.
______, 'An Interview', *Wisconsin Studies in Contemporary Literature*, Wisconsin, 1965.
Hawthorne, Nathanael, *Mosses from An Old Manse* (Fields, Osgood: Boston, 1870).
Hay, Eloise Knapp, *The Political Novels of Joseph Conrad: A Critical Study* (University of Chicago Press: Chicago and London, 1963).
Hayman, Ronald, *Kafka: A Biography of Kafka* (Weidenfeld & Nicolson: London, 1981).
Heath, Jeffrey, *The Picturesque Prison: Evelyn Waugh and His Writing* (Weidenfeld & Nicolson: London, 1982).
Heller, Erich, *The Disinherited Mind* (Penguin: Harmondsworth, 1961).
______, *Kafka* (Fontana, Collins: London, 1974).
Heller, Peter, 'On Not Understanding Kafka', in *The Kafka Debate: New Perspectives for our Time*, ed. Angel Flores (Gordian Press: New York, 1977), 24–41.
______, 'The Autonomy of Despair', *The Massachusetts Review*, Amherst, Winter 1960, 231–53.
Hemingway, Ernest, *A Farewell to Arms* (Penguin: Harmondsworth, 1958).
______, *The Essential Hemingway* (Penguin: Harmondsworth, 1967).
Hendin, Josephine, *The World of Flannery O'Connor* (Indiana University Press: Bloomington, 1970).
Herbst, Josephine, 'Nathanael West', *Kenyon Review*, XXIII, Autumn 1961.
Hewitt, Douglas, *Conrad: A Reassessment* (Bowers & Bowers: London, 1962).
Hingley, Ronald, *The Undiscovered Dostoyevsky* (Hamish Hamilton: London, 1962).
Hollis, Christopher, *Evelyn Waugh*, Writers and Their Work No. 46 (Longmans, Green and Co.: London, 1954). Reissued 1958.
Holquist, Michael, *Dostoyevsky and the Novel* (Northwestern University Press: Evanston, IL, 1977).
Hook, Andrew, *American Literature in Context 1865–1900* (Methuen: London and New York, 1983).
Howe, Irving, *Thomas Hardy* (Macmillan: Basingstoke and London, 1985).
______, *Politics and the Novel* (Columbia University Press: New York, 1992).
______ (ed.), *Edith Wharton: A Collection of Critical Essays* (Prentice Hall: Englewood Cliffs, NJ, 1962).
Howells, William Dean, *Selected Literary Criticism*, intro. Donald Pizer (Indiana University Press: Bloomington and Indianapolis, 1993).
Hume, David, *A Treatise of Human Nature*, ed. L.A. Selby-Bigge (Clarendon Press: Oxford, 1978).
Huxley, Aldous, 'Wordsworth in the Tropics', *Do What You Will* (Chatto & Windus: London, 1931).
Hyman, Stanley Edgar, *Nathanael West*, University of Minnesota Pamphlets on American Writing (University of Minnesota Press: Minneapolis, 1962).
______, *Flannery O'Connor 1925–64*, University of Minnesota Pamphlets on American Writing (University of Minnesota Press: Minneapolis, 1966).
Iyengoor, K.R. Srinivasa, 'A Note on *Ethan Frome*', *Literary Criterion* 5, Winter 1962, 168–78.
Jackson, Robert Louis, *Dostoyevsky's Quest for Form: A Study of His Philosophy of Art* (Yale University Press: New Haven, CT, 1966).
______, *Dostoyevsky's Underground Man in Russian Literature* (Mouton: The Hague, 1958).

______, *The Art of Dostoyevsky: Deliriums and Nocturnes* (Princeton University Press: Princeton, NJ, 1981).

Jackson, Thomas H. (ed.), *Twentieth Century Interpretations of 'Miss Lonelyhearts': A Collection of Critical Essays* (Prentice Hall: Englewood Cliffs, NJ, 1971).

Jacoff, Rachel (ed.), *The Cambridge Companion to Dante* (Cambridge University Press, 1993).

James, William, *The Varieties of Religious Experience* (Collins: Glasgow, 1977).

Johnson, Samuel, *The History of Rasselas, Prince of Abyssinia*, ed. and intro. D.J. Enright (Penguin: Harmondsworth, 1976).

Jonson, Ben, *Three Comedies*, ed. Michael Jamieson (Penguin: Harmondsworth, 1966).

Joyce, James, *Dubliners* (Penguin: Harmondsworth, 1956).

Karl, Frederick, *Joseph Conrad: The Three Lives* (Faber & Faber: London; Farrar, Straus & Giroux: New York, 1979).

Karl, Frederick and Davies, Laurence, *The Collected Letters of Joseph Conrad* (Cambridge University Press, 1996).

Katz, Michael (ed.), *Fyodor Dostoevsky: 'Notes from Underground'*, Norton Critical Edition (Norton: New York and London, 1989).

Keats, John, *The Letters of John Keats*, ed. Hyder Edward Rollins (Cambridge University Press, 1958).

______, *The Poems of John Keats*, ed. Miriam Allott (Longman Group Limited, W.W. Norton: New York, 1970).

Kermode, Frank, 'Mr Waugh's Cities', in *Puzzles and Epiphanies* (Routledge & Kegan Paul: London, 1962).

Kernan, A.B., 'The Wall and the Jungle: The Early Novels of Evelyn Waugh', *Yale Review*, LIII, Winter 1963, 199–220.

Kessler, Edward, *Flannery O'Connor and the Language of Apocalypse* (Princeton University Press: Princeton, NJ, 1986).

Kettle, Arnold, *An Introduction to the English Novel*, vol. 2 (Hutchinson Library: London, 1953).

King, Adèle, *Camus* (Oliver & Boyd: Edinburgh and London, 1964).

Kirkpatrick, Robin, *Dante: The Divine Comedy* (Cambridge University Press: Cambridge and New York, 1987).

______, *Dante's 'Inferno': Difficulty and Dead Poetry* (Cambridge University Press, Cambridge and New York, 1987).

Krzyanowski, Ludwik (ed.), *Joseph Conrad: Centennial Essays* (Polish Institute of Arts and Sciences in America: New York, 1960).

Kundera, Milan, *The Art of the Novel*, trans. Linda Asher (Faber & Faber, London and Boston, 1988).

Lamont, Corliss, *Humanism as a Philosophy* (Philosophical Library: New York, 1949).

Lane, Calvin, *Evelyn Waugh* (Twayne: Boston, 1981).

Leatherbarrow, William J., *Fyodor Dostoyevsky* (Twayne Publishers, G.K. Hall: Boston, 1981).

Lewis, R.W.B., *Edith Wharton: A Biography* (Harper & Row: New York, 1975).

______, *Trials of the Word: Essays in American Literature and the Humanistic Tradition* (Yale University Press: New Haven, CT, 1965).

Light, James F., *Nathanael West: An Interpretative Study* (Northwestern University Press: Evanston, IL, 1961).

______, '*Miss Lonelyhearts*: The Imagery of Nightmare', *American Quarterly*, VIII, Winter 1956, 316–27.

______, 'Violence, Dreams and Dostoyevsky: The Art of Nathanael West', *College English*, XIX, February 1958, 208–13.

Lorch, Thomas, 'West's *Miss Lonelyhearts*: Skepticism Mitigated?' *Renascence*, XVIII, Winter 1966, 90–109.

Lord, Robert, *Dostoyevsky: Essays and Perspectives* (University of California Press: Berkeley and Los Angeles, 1970).

Macaulay, Rose, 'Evelyn Waugh' in *Writers of Today*, 2nd series, ed. Denys Val Baker (Sidgwick and Jackson: London, 1946).

McMichael, George (ed.), *Anthology of American Literature*, 4th edn (Macmillan: New York, 1985).

Madden, David (ed.), *Nathanael West: The Cheaters and the Cheated*, A Collection of Critical Essays (Everett-Edwards: Deland, FL, 1973).

Malin, Irving, *Nathanael West's Novels* (Southern Illinois Press: Carbondale, IL, 1972).

Marcus, Steven, 'Evelyn Waugh and the Art of Entertainment', *Partisan Review*, XXIII, 1956, 348–57.

Marks III, W.S., 'Advertisements for Grace: Flannery O'Connor's *A Good Man Is Hard To Find*', *Studies in Short Fiction*, 4, Fall 1966, 19–27.

Marlowe, Christopher, *Doctor Faustus*, ed. Roma Gill (Ernest Benn: London; Norton: New York, 1965).

Martin, Carter W., *The True Country: Themes in the Fiction of Flannery O'Connor* (Vanderbilt University Press: Nashville, TN, 1968).

Martin, Jay, *Nathanael West: The Art of His Life* (Farrar, Straus & Giroux: New York, 1970).

______ (ed.), *Nathanael West: A Collection of Critical Essays* (Prentice Hall: Englewood Cliffs, NJ, 1971).

Marvell, Andrew, *The Complete Poems*, ed. Elizabeth Story Donno (Penguin: Harmondsworth, 1976).

May, John R., *The Pruning Word: The Parables of Flannery O'Connor* (University of Notre Dame Press: Notre Dame and London, 1976).

Melville, Herman, *Billy Budd, Sailor and Other Stories*, ed. and intro. Harold Beaver (Penguin: Harmondsworth, 1967).

______, *Moby Dick, or The White Whale* (Signet, Penguin: Harmondsworth, 1980).

Mendelson, Edward, *The English Auden: Essays and Dramatic Writings, 1927–1939* (Faber & Faber: London, 1977).

Meyer, Bernard, *Joseph Conrad: A Psychoanalytic Biography* (Princeton University Press: Princeton, NJ, 1967).

Mikhailovsky, Nikolai K., *A Cruel Talent*, trans. Spencer Cadmus (Ardis: Ann Arbor, 1978).

Mill, J.S., *On Liberty*, ed. and intro. Gertrude Himmelfarb (Penguin: Harmondsworth, 1974).

Miller, J. Hillis, *Poets of Reality: Six Twentieth-Century Writers* (Harvard University Press, Harvard, MA, 1966).

Millgate, Michael, *Thomas Hardy: His Career as a Novelist* (Random House: New York, 1971).

______, *Thomas Hardy: A Biography* (Oxford University Press: Oxford and Melbourne, 1982).

______ (ed.), *The Life and Work of Thomas Hardy by Thomas Hardy* (Macmillan: London and Basingstoke, 1984).

Milton, John, *Paradise Lost*, ed. Alastair Fowler (Longman Group Limited: London, 1971).
______, 'Comus', *Milton: Complete Shorter Poems*, ed. John Carey (Longman: London, 1981).
______, 'Areopagitica', *Prose Writings*, intro. K.M. Burton (Everyman's Library, Dent: London; Dutton: New York, 1965).
Mochulsky, K., *Dostoyevsky: His Life and Works*, trans. Michael Minihan (Princeton University Press: Princeton, NJ, 1967).
Modern Fiction Studies VIII, No. 1, 1962: Kafka Issue.
Montgomery, Marion, 'Miss Flannery's *Good Man*', *Denver Quarterly* 3, Autumn 1968.
______, 'Flannery O'Connor and the Jansenist Problem in Fiction', *Southern Review*, XIV, Summer 1978.
Morrell, Roy, *Thomas Hardy: The Will and the Way* (University of Malaya and Oxford University Press: Kuala Lumpur, 1965).
Moser, Thomas, *Joseph Conrad: Achievement and Decline* (Harvard University Press: Cambridge, MA, 1957).
Muller, G.H., *Nightmares and Visions: Flannery O'Connor and the Catholic Grotesque* (University of Georgia Press: Athens, GA, 1972).
Murfin, Ross C., *Conrad Revisited: Essays for the Eighties* (University of Alabama Press, 1985).
Murray, Rosalind, *The Good Pagan's Failure* (Fontana, Collins: London and Glasgow, 1962).
Nadjer, Zdzislaw, *Joseph Conrad: A Chronicle*, trans. Halina Carroll Nadjer (Cambridge University Press, 1983).
Neider, Charles, *Kafka: His Mind and Art* (Oxford University Press: London, 1949).
Neumeyer, Peter F., *Twentieth Century Interpretations of 'The Castle': A Collection of Critical Essays* (Prentice Hall: Englewood Cliffs, NJ, 1969).
Nevius, Blake, *Edith Wharton: A Study of Her Fiction* (University of California Press: Berkeley, 1953).
Newman, John Henry, *Apologia Pro Vita Sua* (Collins: Glasgow, 1977).
Nietzsche, Friedrich, *The Gay Science*, trans. Walter Kaufman (Vintage Books: New York, 1974).
O'Brien, Conor Cruise, *Maria Cross: Imaginative Patterns in a Group of Modern Catholic Writers* (Chatto & Windus: London, 1954).
______, *Camus* (Fontana, Collins: Glasgow, 1970).
O'Faolain, Sean, *The Vanishing Hero: Studies in the Novelists of The Twenties* (Eyre & Spottiswoode: London, 1956).
Orvell, Miles, *Invisible Parade: The Fiction of Flannery O'Connor* (Temple University Press: Philadelphia, 1972).
Orwell, George, *Nineteen Eighty-Four* (Penguin: Harmondsworth, 1954).
______, *Homage to Catalonia* (Penguin: Harmondsworth, 1962).
Orwell, Sonia and Angus, Ian, *Collected Essays, Journalism and Letters of George Orwell* (Penguin: Harmondsworth, 1970).
Osborne, Charles, *Kafka* (Oliver & Boyd: Edinburgh and London, 1967).
Ovid, *Metamorphoses*, trans. and intro. Mary M. Innes (Penguin: Harmondsworth, 1955).
Papini, Giovanni, 'The Cruelty of Dante', in *Dante Vivo*, trans. J Bertrand (Grasset: Paris, 1934).
Pascal, Blaise, *Pensées*, trans. and intro. A.J. Krailsheimer (Penguin: Harmondsworth, 1966).

Paton, Rodney J., *A Modern Reader's Guide to Dante's 'Inferno'* (Peter Lang: New York, 1992).

Peace, Richard, *Dostoyevsky: An Examination of the Major Novels* (Cambridge University Press, 1971).

______, *Dostoyevsky's 'Notes from Underground'* (Bristol Classical Press: London, 1993).

Pearce, Joseph, 'Waugh and Waste Land', in *Literary Converts: Spiritual Inspiration in an Age of Unbelief* (HarperCollins: London, 1998), 146–65.

Peter, John, *Vladimir's Carrot: Modern Drama and the Modern Imagination* (Methuen: London, 1988).

Plato, *The Republic*, trans. and intro. Desmond Lee (Penguin: Harmondsworth, 1977).

Podhoretz, Norman, 'A Particular Kind of Joking', *New Yorker*, 18 May 1957, 156–65.

Poggioli, R., 'Kafka and Dostoyevsky', in *The Kafka Problem*, ed. Angel Flores (Octagon Books: New York, 1963).

Politzer, Heinz, *Franz Kafka: Parable and Paradox* (Cornell University Press: Ithaca, NY, 1966).

Popper, Karl, *The Myth of the Framework: In Defence of Science and Rationality*, ed. M.A. Notturno (Routledge: London, 1994).

Pritchett, V.S., 'Miss Lonelyhearts', in *The Living Novel and Later Appreciations* (Random House: New York, 1964), 276–82.

Pryce-Jones, David (ed.), *Evelyn Waugh and His World* (Weidenfeld & Nicolson: London, 1973).

Rath, Sura P. and Shaw, Mary Neff (eds), *Flannery O'Connor: New Perspectives* (University of Georgia Press: Athens, GA, and London, 1996).

Ratner, Marc L., ' "Anywhere Out of This World": Baudelaire and Nathanael West', *American Literature*, XXXI, January 1960, 456–63.

Reade, M.H., *The Moral System of Dante's Inferno* (Clarendon Press: Oxford, 1909).

Reid, J.C., *Dickens: Little Dorrit*, Studies in English Literature (Edward Arnold: London, 1967).

Reid, Randall, *The Fiction of Nathanael West: No Redeemer, No Promised Land* (University of Chicago Press: Chicago and London, 1967).

Reilly, Patrick, *George Orwell: The Age's Adversary* (Macmillan: Basingstoke and London, 1986).

______, *Jonathan Swift: The Brave Desponder* (Manchester University Press, 1982).

Ricks, Christopher, *Tennyson* (Macmillan: New York, 1972).

Roper, Derek (ed.), *Wordsworth and Coleridge: Lyrical Ballads* (Collins: London and Glasgow, 1973).

Rosenfield, Claire, *Paradise of Snakes: An Archetypal Analysis of Conrad's Political Novels* (University of Chicago Press, 1967).

Rousseau, Jean-Jacques, 'Lettre à M. d'Alembert sur le Theâtre', *Oeuvres Complètes* (Gallimard: Paris, 1995), vol. V, 1–125.

Rusch, Frederik L., 'Reality and the Puritan Mind: Jonathan Edwards and *Ethan Frome*', *Journal of Evolutionary Psychology*, vol. 4 (August 1983), 238–47.

Russell, Bertrand, *Portraits from Memory and Other Essays* (George Allen & Unwin: London, 1956).

Said, Edward W., *Joseph Conrad and the Fiction of Autobiography* (Harvard University Press: Cambridge, MA, 1966).

Scanlan, James P., 'The Case against Rational Egoism in Dostoyevsky's *Notes from Underground*', *Journal of the History of Ideas*, 60, 1999, 549–67.
Schneider, Cyril, 'The Individuality of Nathanael West', *Western Review*, XX, Autumn 1955.
Schopenhauer, Arthur, *Essays and Aphorisms*, ed. R.J. Hollingdale (Penguin: Harmondsworth, 1970).
Scott, Nathan A., *Albert Camus* (Bowes & Bowes: London, 1962).
Scott, Sir Walter, *The Antiquary*, intro. W.M. Parker (Everyman's Library, Dent: London; Dutton: New York, 1969).
Shakespeare, William, *Othello*, ed. Kenneth Muir (Penguin: Harmondsworth, 1968).
Sherry, Norman, *Conrad's Western World* (Cambridge University Press, 1971).
______, *Conrad and his World* (Thames & Hudson: London, 1972).
______, (ed.), *Conrad: The Critical Heritage* (Routledge & Kegan Paul: London, 1973).
Shestov, Lev, *Dostoyevsky, Tolstoy and Nietzsche*, trans. Bernard Martin and Spencer Roberts (Ohio University Press, Swallow Press: Athens, OH, 1969).
Simmons, E.J., *Dostoevski: The Making of a Novelist* (Oxford University Press: New York, 1940).
Spender, Stephen, *The Creative Element: A Study of Vision, Orthodoxy and Despair Among Some Modern Writers* (Hamish Hamilton: London, 1953).
Spilka, Mark, *Dickens and Kafka* (Dobson: London, 1963).
______, 'Playing Crazy in the Underground', *Minnesota Review*, 6.3, 1966, 233–43.
Spivey, Ted Ray, 'Flannery O'Connor's Views of God and Man', *Studies in Short Fiction* 1, Spring 1964, 200–6.
Springer, Marlene, *'Ethan Frome': A Nightmare of Need* (Twayne Masterworks: New York, 1993).
St Augustine, *Confessions*, trans. and intro. R.S. Pine-Coffin (Penguin: Harmondsworth, 1961).
Stallman, Robert (ed.), *The Art of Joseph Conrad: A Critical Symposium* (Michigan State University Press: East Lansing, MI, 1960).
Stannard, Martin, *Evelyn Waugh: The Early Years, 1903–1939* (Paladin Books: London, 1988).
______ (ed.), *Evelyn Waugh: The Critical Heritage* (Routledge & Kegan Paul: London, 1984).
Steiner, George, *Tolstoy or Dostoyevsky* (Penguin: Harmondsworth, 1967).
______, *Real Presences: Is There Anything in What We Say?* (Faber & Faber: London and Boston, 1989).
Stephens, Martha, *The Question of Flannery O'Connor* (Louisiana State University: Baton Rouge and London, 1973).
Stern, J.P. (ed.), *The World of Franz Kafka* (Weidenfeld & Nicolson: London, 1980).
Stewart, J.I.M., *Thomas Hardy: A Critical Biography* (Longman: London, 1971).
Stopp, Frederick, *Evelyn Waugh: Portrait of an Artist* (Little, Brown: Boston, 1958).
Swift, Jonathan, *Gulliver's Travels*, ed. Peter Dixon and John Chalker (Penguin: Harmondsworth, 1967).
______, *The Prose Works of Jonathan Swift* (16 vols), ed. Herbert Davis *et al.* (Basil Blackwell: Oxford, 1939–68).
______, *The Poems of Jonathan Swift* (3 vols), ed. Harold Williams (Clarendon Press: Oxford, 1937 (rev. 1958)).

______, *The Correspondence of Jonathan Swift* (5 vols), ed. Harold Williams (Clarendon Press: Oxford, 1963–5).

Sykes, Christopher, *Evelyn Waugh: A Biography* (Collins: London and Glasgow, 1975).

Taber Cooper, Frederic, 'The Bigger Issues and Some Recent Books', *The Bookman*, XXXIV, no. 3 (November 1911).

Tambling, Jeremy (ed.), *Dante* (Longman: London and New York, 1999).

Tanner, Tony, 'Colour and Movement in Hardy's *Tess of the d'Urbervilles*', *Critical Quarterly*, X, 1968, 219–39.

Tertullian, *De Spectaculis*, trans. T.R. Glover (Harvard University Press: Cambridge, MA, 1931).

Thody, Philip, *Albert Camus 1913–1960* (Hamish Hamilton: London, 1957).

Thorburn, David, *Conrad's Romanticism* (Yale University Press: New Haven, CT, 1974).

Thorlby, Anthony, *Kafka: A Study* (Heinemann: London and Totowa, NJ, 1972).

Tibbetts, A.M., 'The Strange Half-World of Nathanael West', *Prairie Schooner*, XXXIV, Spring 1960.

Todd, Olivier, *Albert Camus: A Life*, trans. Benjamin Ivry (Chatto & Windus: London, 1997).

Trilling, Lionel, *Beyond Culture: Essays on Literature and Learning* (Penguin: Harmondsworth, 1967).

______, *Sincerity and Authenticity* (Oxford University Press: London, 1974).

Veitch, Jonathan, *American Superrealism: Nathanael West and the Politics of Representation in the 1930s* (University of Wisconsin Press: Madison, 1997).

Vigny, Alfred de, 'Le Mont des Oliviers', in *Oeuvres Complètes* (Gallimard: Paris, 1986), vol. 1, 149–52.

Volpe, Edmund L., 'The Waste Land of Nathanael West', *Renascence*, XIII, Winter 1961, 69–77.

Voorhees, Richard J., 'Evelyn Waugh Revisited', *South Atlantic Quarterly*, XLVIII, 1949, 270–80.

Walker, D.P., *The Decline of Hell: 17th Century Discussions of Eternal Torment* (University of Chicago Press, 1964).

Wall, Barbara, 'Critics and Evelyn Waugh', *America*, LXXVII, 1947.

Walters, Dorothy, *Flannery O'Connor* (Twayne: New York, 1973).

Warner, Oliver *et al.* (eds), 'Joseph Conrad: A Critical Symposium', *London Magazine* IV, November 1957, 21–49.

Warrack, Grace (ed.), *Revelations of Divine Love Recorded by Dame Julian of Norwich* (Methuen: London, 1901).

Wasiolek, Edward, *Dostoyevsky: The Major Fiction* (MIT Press: Cambridge, MA, 1964).

Wasson, Richard, '*A Handful of Dust*: Critique of Victorianism', *Modern Fiction Studies*, VII, 1961–2, 327–37.

Watt, Ian, *Conrad in the Nineteenth Century* (University of California Press: Berkeley and Los Angeles, 1979).

______ (ed.), *The Secret Agent: A Casebook* (Macmillan: London and Basingstoke, 1973).

Watts, Cedric, *A Preface to Conrad* (Longman: London, 1982).

Wellek, René (ed.), *Dostoyevsky: A Collection of Critical Essays* (Prentice Hall: Englewood Cliffs, NJ, 1962).

West, Rebecca, *The Court and the Castle* (Yale University Press: New Haven, CT, 1957).

Wicksteed, Philip, *Dante and Aquinas* (Dent: London and Toronto; Dutton: New York, 1913).

Widmer, Kingsley, *Nathanael West* (Twayne: Boston, 1982).

Wilson, Edmund, 'Never Apologize, Never Explain: The Art of Evelyn Waugh', 140–6; 'Splendors and Miseries of Evelyn Waugh', 298–305, in *Classics and Commercials: A Literary Chronicle of the Forties* (Farrar, Straus: New York, 1950, and London, 1951).

Wisker, Alistair, *The Writing of Nathanael West* (Macmillan: Basingstoke, 1990).

Wittgenstein, Ludwig, *Tractatus Logico-Philosophicus* (Routledge: London and New York, 1981).

Wolff, Cynthia Griffin, *A Feast of Words: The Triumph of Edith Wharton* (Oxford University Press: New York, 1977).

Woodcock, George, *Anarchism: A History of Libertarian Ideas and Movements* (Penguin: Harmondsworth, 1963).

______ (ed.), *The Anarchist Reader* (Fontana, Collins: Glasgow, 1977).

______, 'Evelyn Waugh: The Man and his Work', *World Review*, no. 1, 1949, 51–6.

Woolf, Virginia, *The Second Common Reader* (Harcourt, Brace: New York, 1932).

Wordsworth, William, 'Michael, a Pastoral Poem', in *Wordsworth and Coleridge, Lyrical Ballads*, ed. Derek Roper (Collins: London and Glasgow, 1973).

______, 'The Old Cumberland Beggar', *Selected Poetry and Prose*, ed. Philip Hobsbaum (Routledge: London and New York, 1989).

Wright, Austin (ed.), *Victorian Literature: Modern Essays in Criticism* (Oxford University Press: New York, 1961).

Yeats, W. B., 'On Those That Hated "The Playboy of the Western World" ', 1907, *Poems of W. B. Yeats*, with intro. and notes by A. Norman Jeffares (Macmillan: Basingstoke, 1988).

Index

Abraham 185
Absurd, The 23, 133, 134, 135, 142
Academy of Lagado 155, 157
Adorno, Theodor W. 99, 101
Aeschylus 4, 40, 150, 169
Agamemnon 83, 147
Age of Innocence, The 70
Alger, Horatio 125
Alonzo the Brave 47, 48
Alvarez, A. 46
Anarchism 34, 51
'Ancient Mariner, The' 5, 34
Animal Farm 128
Antiquary, The 163
Anouilh, Jean 136, 169
'Anywhere Out of This World' 124
Aquinas, St Thomas 123
Arnold, Matthew 9, 25, 54, 74, 95, 144
Atheism 38, 41, 42, 43, 44, 120, 121, 144, 178, 179, 180, 181, 182, 183
Auden, W.H. 99, 100, 115
Augustine, St 23, 41, 94, 155, 156
Austen, Jane 160

Bach, Johann Sebastian 126
Backward Glance, A 86
Bakunin, Mikhail Aleksandrovich 64
'Barbara of the House of Grebe' 46–50, 187
'Bartleby' 115–17, 121, 129, 186
Baudelaire, Charles Pierre 124, 126, 175, 176
Beatles, The 6
Beatrice 99, 115, 125
Beckett, Samuel 45, 46, 66, 106
Beethoven, Ludwig van 169
'Before the Law' 101, 105
Belinsky, Vissarion Grigorievich 25
Bellow, Saul 10, 85
'Benito Cereno' 98
Bentham, Jeremy 19
Bernanos, Georges 175
Billy Budd 23, 84, 147
Black Mischief 157–8
Blake, William 171
Bleak House 168
Bonhoeffer, Dietrich 4, 27, 49
Book of Job 114, 118, 174
Borden, Lizzie 66
Bradbury, Malcolm 101
Branco D'Oria 76
Brave New World 47
Brobdingnag 65
Brod, Max 109
Brothers Karamazov, The 15, 19, 23, 26, 114, 141, 174
Browning, Robert 9, 22, 31, 39, 41, 54, 83
Buber, Martin 101, 102
Büchner, Georg 82, 118
Buckle, Henry Thomas 21, 22
Bunyan, John 85, 104, 179
Burgess, Anthony 47
Burke, Edmund 13, 185
Butler, Bishop Joseph 111
Butler, Samuel 117

Cacciaguida 4, 61
Caligula 100, 134, 139, 150, 151, 174
Calvinist 5
Camus, Albert 5, 8, 10, 12, 13, 23, 26, 38, 46, 63, 93, 97, 99, 100, 103, 105, 133–51, 153, 174, 187, 188
Candide 146
Canetti, Elias 99
Canterbury Tales, The 180
Carlyle, Thomas 9
Castle, The 93, 98, 99, 106, 134
Catholic 65, 109, 155
Cervantes (Saavedra), Miguel de 130
Chaucer, Geoffrey 27, 170

Cheated, The 114, 131
see also The Day of the Locust
Chernyshevsky, H.G. 15, 18, 19, 20, 28
Chesterton, G.K. 155
'Childe Roland to the Dark Tower Came' 83
Christ, Christian 1, 6, 8, 10, 20, 22, 35, 36, 37, 38, 39, 41, 42, 43, 44, 59, 60, 64, 79, 91, 95, 96, 117, 119, 120, 126, 127, 133, 134, 135, 140, 141, 142, 144, 149, 151, 153, 154, 156, 158, 168, 171, 172, 173, 174, 175, 176, 177, 178, 179, 181, 182
Christie, Mr 159
Clockwork Orange, A 47
Cocytus 75, 76
Coleridge, Samuel Taylor 99, 169
'Comforts of Home, The' 172, 180
Communism 25, 34
'Comus' 74
Condorcet, Antoine Nicolas, Marquis de 20
Connolly, Cyril 164
Conrad, Joseph 7, 8, 10, 21, 51–67, 111, 153, 175, 188
Cool Million, A 114, 128
Copernicus, Nicolaus 133
'Counterparts' 27
Cowper, William 122
Crime and Punishment 18, 29, 42, 106
Cross Purpose 8, 46, 63, 134, 142–51
see also Le Malentendu
Culture and Anarchy 25

Dante Alighieri 1, 2, 3, 4, 5, 7, 8, 10, 11, 12, 24, 27, 53, 61, 64, 69, 72, 75, 76, 79, 81, 83, 86, 87, 95, 97, 98, 114, 115, 117, 122, 125, 126, 128, 136, 144, 148, 171, 175, 182
Darkness at Noon 46, 102
Darwin, Charles, Darwinian 10, 39, 43
'Day of Judgement, The' 54, 64
Day of the Locust, The 10, 46, 114, 115, 118, 128, 129–32
see also The Cheated
Decline and Fall 154–5, 157
Descartes, René 102, 111, 145
Devils, The 6, 30, 134
see also The Possessed
Diana of the Ephesians 141
Diana, Princess 163
Dickens, Charles 6, 8, 19, 91, 155, 159, 162, 168, 169, 186
'Digression concerning Madness' 37, 65, 66
Divine Comedy, The 176
Dobrolyubov, N.A. 15
Doctor Faustus 94
Dostoyevsky, Fyodor 5, 6, 10, 12, 13–32, 38, 91, 93, 114, 129, 131, 134, 147, 168, 173, 179, 186
'Dover Beach' 9
Dream Life of Balso Snell, The 114

'Earth's Holocaust' 115
Ecclesiastes 41, 86
Eichmann, Karl Adolf 102, 104
Elijah 38, 41
Eliot, George 6, 46
Eliot, T.S. 4, 9, 49, 66, 69, 83, 126, 156, 175, 176, 187
Elizabeth I, Queen 55, 56
Emerson, Ralph Waldo 161
'Encantadas, The or Enchanted Isles' 121, 122
Endgame 45
'Enduring Chill, The' 172, 180
Enlightenment, The 93
Epistle to the Philippians 155
Essays (T.H. Huxley) 36
Ethan Frome 7, 9, 10, 69–90, 143, 189
Euripides 150
'Everything That Rises Must Converge' 172, 180
Existentialism 18, 19, 24, 97, 141
Ezekiel 187

Fairfax, Beatrice 118
Fall, The 5, 10, 12, 13, 29, 30, 63, 100, 126, 147, 153, 187
Farewell to Arms, A 110, 136, 160, 162
Farinata degli Uberti 4
Fascism 113
Fetishism 46
Feuerbach, Ludwig Andreas von 43, 120, 125

Fielding, Henry 5, 169
Fitzgerald, Scott 130, 131, 176
Flaubert, Gustave 131
Forster, John 162
Francesca da Rimini 10, 114
Francis, St 60
French Revolution, The 13
Freud, Sigmund 10, 13, 36, 86
Friar Alberigo 75
Fukuyama, Francis 25

Galileo Galilei 45
Gambler, The 14
Genesis 64
Gnosticism 102, 126
Goethe, Johann Wolfgang von 169
Gogol, Nikolai Vasilyevich 118
Golding, William 8, 10
'Good Country People' 180–4
'Good Man Is Hard To Find, A' 173, 175, 189
Good Pagan's Failure, The 158
Goya, Francisco José de 130
Great Expectations 48
Great Gatsby, The 48, 130
'Great Wall of China, The' 105
Greene, Graham 147
'Greenleaf' 172, 180
Gulliver's Travels 7, 13, 29, 31, 32, 59, 72, 103, 118, 119, 121, 157

Handful of Dust, A 8, 154, 155, 157–70
Hard Times 19
Hardy, Thomas 5, 7, 9, 10, 23, 33–50, 105, 111, 144, 146, 153, 176, 188
Hawkes, John 187
Hawthorne, Nathanael 48, 115, 185
Hazlitt, William 10, 86
Heart of Darkness 44
Hegel, Georg Wilhel Friedrich 122
Heidegger, Martin 183
Helena 167
Heller, Erich 101
Hemingway, Ernest 40, 110, 136, 160, 175
Henry, Émile 12
History of the Royal Society, A 157
Hitler, Adolf 102, 141
Hollywood 129, 130
Homage to Catalonia 34
Horace, Quintus Horatius Flaccus 186
House of Mirth, The 69, 70 84, 86, 87
House of Usher 83
Housman, A.E. 35
Howells, William Dean 85
Hugo, Victor 6
Huit Clos 79
Humanism 8, 43, 140, 158, 159, 168, 170, 184
Hume, David 19
Huxley, Aldous 38, 47
Huxley, Thomas Henry 36, 38, 41, 46

Ibsen, Henrik 10
Iceman Cometh, The 10
'Immortality Ode, The' 36
Inferno 1, 10, 12, 30, 53, 69, 75, 81, 85, 91, 99, 114, 115, 144, 171, 172
Inquisition, The 45
Insulted and Injured, The 17, 18
'In the Cathedral' 109
'In the Penal Settlement' 53, 91, 92, 93–8, 109
'Investigations of a Dog' 104
Ionesco, Eugène 66
Iscariot, Judas 128, 175
Ivan the Terrible 15

Jacob 63, 156
James, Henry 84
James, William 116, 120, 121, 123, 124, 125
Jeremiah 94, 132
Jesus 145, 147, 149, 151, 172, 175, 176, 185, 187
Jewett, Sarah Orne 86, 86
John, St 20, 144, 145
Johnson, Samuel 114
Jonson, Ben 19
Joseph 63
'Journal of a Modern Lady, The' 155
Joyce James 27
Judaism, Jew 92, 102, 117, 126
Jude the Obscure 6

Kafka, Franz 8, 9, 40, 53, 66, 91–111, 113, 120, 133, 139, 153, 168,
Keats, John 1, 9, 20, 77, 83, 114, 130
Kenoma 126
Kierkegaard, Soren Abaye 93, 100, 104, 135, 175
King Lear 45, 46, 49, 75, 118, 130, 145, 146, 153, 162, 163, 165, 188
Koestler, Arthur 46
Kundera, Milan 106, 107

'La Belle Dame sans Merci' 8
Lamb, Charles 47
'Lame Shall Enter First, The' 8, 180, 181, 184–9
'Lamia' 8, 83
Landor, Walter Savage 12, 30
Lang, Andrew 45
Larkin, Philip 156
Lawrence, D.H. 20, 34
Lazarus 144, 151
Le Malentendu 8, 46, 63, 134, 142–51
see also Cross Purposes
'Le Mont des Oliviers' 151
Le Mythe Animal 169
Lennon, John 6
Leonidas 49
Les Miserables 187
'Letter to His Father' 94, 101, 103
Lilliput 65
Little Dorrit 162, 169
Lombroso, Cesare 59, 60, 64
Lord of the Flies 8
'Lotus Eaters, The' 54, 63
Lucan, Marcus Annaeus 1
Lucretius (Carus, Titus) 119
Luke, St 179
Luther, Martin 123

Macbeth 142, 173
Maistre, Joseph Marie, Comte de 153, 171
Malebranche, Nicolas 180, 181, 183
Malory, Sir Thomas 167
'Man Who Loved Dickens, The' 159
Manichaean 156
Mann, Thomas 52, 59, 94
Mansfield Park 165
Mariolatry 109
Marlowe, Christopher 75
Martin Chuzzlewit 168
Marvell, Andrew 88
Marx, Chico 106
Marx, Groucho 106, 126
Marx, Harpo 106
Marx, Karl 60, 64, 117, 121
Measure for Measure 9
Medea 21, 142
Medusa 75, 86
Melville, Hermann 23, 84, 115, 116, 117, 121, 122, 123, 125, 127, 147, 186
Mencken, H.L. 181
'Message from the Emperor, A' 101
'Metamorphosis' 94
'Michael' 8, 46, 50, 73, 74
Mikhailovsky, Nikolai K. 14, 15
Mill, J.S. 19, 46, 86
Milton, John 3, 21, 35, 61, 74, 82, 86, 101, 127, 162, 171, 187
Minos 2
Miss Lonelyhearts 8, 10, 46, 65, 114–28, 154, 168
Moby Dick 121, 122
'Modest Proposer' 121
Monroe, Marilyn 130
Montessori, Maria 157, 158
Montrefelto, Guido da 2
Moses 183
'Mycerinus' 144
Myth of Sisyphus, The 23, 97, 98, 99, 103, 109, 133–6, 145, 146, 148, 149
Murray, Gilbert 158
Murray, Rosalind 158, 159, 165

Nazism 102
Nekrasov, Nicholas A 28, 29
Nero 15
Newman, Cardinal John Henry 46, 187
Newton, Sir Isaac 101
'News from the Mediterranean' 84
'New Year's Eve' 33
Nietzsche, Friedrich Wilhelm 38, 42, 59, 60, 63, 92, 93, 105, 117, 141
Nineteen Eighty-Four 4, 8, 10, 17, 31, 43,

47, 48, 49, 69, 102, 109, 128, 159, 189
Notes from Underground 13–32, 53, 128, 147

O'Connor, Flannery 5, 8, 10, 12, 53, 66, 91, 153, 154, 171–89
'Ode to Joy' 6
Oedipus 48, 104, 118, 177
'Old Cumberland Beggar, The' 117
O'Neill, Eugene 10
Orwell, George 4, 6, 8, 10, 17, 34, 37, 38, 46, 47, 49, 56, 87, 108, 109, 128, 153, 162, 170
Othello 15, 49, 59, 83, 127, 149
Outsider, The 63, 93, 136–9
'Overcoat, The' 118
Ovid, Publius Ovidius Naso 21

Pall Mall Gazette 47
Paolo Malatesta 11
Paradise Lost 61
Paradise Regained 126
Paradiso 12
Pascal, Blaise 108, 120, 122, 133, 137, 139, 140, 146, 147, 156, 183
Paul, St, Pauline 21, 23, 63, 74, 101, 120, 135, 141, 160, 174, 177, 186
Pavlov, Ivan Petrovich 14, 46
Pelagian 174
Peter, St 187
Petrashevsky, Mikhail 13
Pharisaism, Pharisee 172, 173, 174, 179, 180, 184, 187
Pharsalia 1
Pindar 134
Plague, The 149
Poe, Edgar Allan 83, 88
Polyphemus 122
Poor Folk 13
Pope, Alexander 101, 154, 155
Popper, Sir Karl 5
Possessed, The 134
see also The Devils
Prague Zionists 92
'Prayer for my Daughter, A' 166
Protestant 65, 119
Purgatorio 12
Puritanism 85

Quiet American, The 147

Rahv, Philip 106
'Rape of the Lock, The' 154
Reflections on the Revolution in France 13
Religion of Healthy-Mindedness, The 121, 123, 125
Renan, Joseph Ernest 160
'Resolution and Independence' 46
Restoration Comedy 47, 161, 182
'Revelation' 91, 172, 180
'River, The' 173, 177–9, 189
Robespierre, Maximilien Francois Marie Isidore de 153
Romanticism 126, 185
Roth, Philip 106, 113
Rousseau, Jean Jacques 24, 122, 142, 185
Ruggieri degli Ubaldini, Archbishop 79
'Ruined Cottage, The' 8, 46

Sabbatian 126
Sade, Donatien Alphonse Francois, Comte de, Sadism 71, 89, 90, 91, 94, 97, 121, 129, 144, 151, 169, 187
Saint-Just, Louis Antoine de 153
Samson 166
Sartre, Jean-Paul 38, 79
Schiller, Friedrich von, Schillerism 6, 16, 17
Schopenhauer, Arthur 39, 93, 101, 102
Science 59
Scott, Sir Walter 163
Secret Agent, The 7, 11, 22, 51–67, 80, 143, 189
Shakespeare, William 4, 9, 26, 40, 45, 46, 49, 51, 106, 144, 149, 156, 177, 188
Shelley, Percy Bysshe 3, 171, 187
Shestov, Lev 15
Siberia 13, 14, 15, 17, 32
'Sick King in Bokhara, The' 95
Sick Soul, The 121, 123, 124, 125
Siéyès, Abbé Emmanuel Joseph 25
Smith, Stevie 70
Socialism 60, 117

Socrates 21
Song of Roland, The 138, 171
Sophocles 177
Soviets 14
Spender, Stephen 154
Spinoza, Benedict 22, 110
Sprat, Bishop Thomas 157
Stalin, Joseph 102
'Statue and the Bust, The' 31
Strafen (Punishments) 91
Struldbruggs 69
Suetonius, (Tranquillus), Gaius 141
Sun Also Rises, The 169
Swift, Jonathan 37, 54, 60, 62, 63, 64, 65, 66, 69, 72, 104, 106, 110, 113, 119, 154, 155, 157
Swinburne, Algernon Charles 41
Sybil 69
Sykes, Christopher 168

Talmudists 97
Tartuffe 181, 183
Tennyson, Alfred Tennyson 1st Baron 9, 41, 44, 63, 69
Tertullian 2, 184
Tess of the d'Urbervilles 6, 7, 8, 10, 33–46, 80
Thackeray, William Makepeace 32
Three Sisters 163
Thurber, James Grover 173
Tithonus 69
Tolstoy, Leo Nikolayevich, Count 6
Tom Jones 5, 98
Trial, The 8, 92, 93, 97, 98, 102–11
Trilling, Lionel 73, 85
Troilus and Criseyde 170
'Try-Works, The' 121, 122
Turn of the Screw, The 72

Ugolino della Gherardesca, Count 79, 115
Uncle's Dream 14
Utilitarianism 19

Vanni Fucci 1, 2, 3, 4, 5, 7, 8, 10, 11, 12, 14, 16, 23, 27, 28, 29, 30, 32, 40, 45, 53, 61, 64, 84, 87, 90, 91, 99, 111, 115, 126, 128, 131, 136, 144, 148, 171, 173, 174, 175, 189
Varieties of Religious Experience, The 121, 123
Veronica 91
Vespasian, Titus Flavius 183
Vigny, Alfred Victor, Comte de 148, 151
Vile Bodies 155–6
Violent Bear It Away, The 181, 187
Virgil, Publius Vergilius Maro 1, 2, 11, 12, 54, 64, 72, 86, 99, 115, 117, 122, 125, 153, 172, 182, 188
Volpone 19
Voltaire, Francois Marie Arouet 41, 137

Waiting for Godot 46, 100
Waste Land, The 83
Watson, J.B. 46
Waugh, Evelyn 8, 91, 153–70, 171
Weinstein, Nathaniel von Wallenstein Weinstein (*see* Nathanael West) 125
Welles, Orson 106
Wells, H.G. 17
Wesley, John 123
West, Nathanael 113–32, 168
Wharton, Edith 7, 69–90, 111, 188
What Is To Be Done? 28
Wild Duck, The 10
Wilkins, Mary 85, 86
Wilson, Edmund 85
Windsors, The 163
Winter Notes on Summer Impressions 25
Wise Blood 173, 176–77, 189
Wittgenstein, Ludwig Joseph Johann 98, 107
Woolf, Virginia 33
Wordsworth, William 7, 8 9, 36, 37, 38, 39, 41, 42, 43, 50, 73, 74, 82, 117, 118, 126, 185
Woyzeck 82, 118

Yeats, William Butler 114
Young, Edward 122

Zola, Emile 155